T0336483

PROJECT INTERFACE MANAGEMENT

Reducing Risk on Major Projects

Michael J. Bible and Susan S. Bivins

ISBN-13: 978-1-60427-130-0

Printed and bound in the U.S.A. Printed on acid-free paper.

10 9 8 7 6 5 4 3 2 1

Library of Congress Cataloging-in-Publication Data

Names: Bible, Michael J., 1966- author. | Bivins, Susan S., 1941- author.
Title: Project interface management : reducing risk on major projects / by Michael J. Bible and Susan S. Bivins.
Description: Plantation, FL : J. Ross Publishing, Inc., [2018] | Includes index.
Identifiers: LCCN 2018025761| ISBN 9781604271300 (hardcover : alk. paper) | ISBN 9781604278026 (e-book)
Subjects: LCSH: Portfolio management. | Risk management.
Classification: LCC HG4529.5 .B533 2018 | DDC 658.4/04—dc23 LC record available at https://lccn.loc.gov/2018025761

Direct all inquiries to J. Ross Publishing, Inc., 300 S. Pine Island Rd., Suite 305, Plantation, FL 33324.

Phone: (954) 727-9333
Fax: (561) 892-0700
Web: www.jrosspub.com

Contents

Preface

BACKGROUND

As an interesting and dynamic supersystem, the modern world continues to evolve and change to meet the demands, needs, and desires of its people while dealing with the ever-increasing challenges of sustaining our planet and minimizing our impact on the global environment. Technological advancements are permeating all facets of modern life, feeding an insatiable appetite for better, faster, cheaper. Safe and comfortable automobiles are no longer adequate. Rather, we need automobiles that are safe, comfortable, and drive themselves. Safe and fast air travel is no longer the standard. Rather, it is our ability to stay *connected* continuously while traveling. Coupled with increasing demands from an ever-growing and changing population, it is natural to expect this complexity to seep into projects.

Projects exist to create a result. Often, this *result* takes the form of a *system* to be used directly or indirectly to meet the needs, demands, or wants of the population. Whether the system is a new phone, automobile, airplane, space capsule, or online service, the projects undertaken to deliver these systems are becoming increasingly complex. The reasons are simple. First, systems created by these projects are becoming more complex as a result of technology and materials used to develop them; people want products that are lighter, more durable, and last longer. Often this requires the use of specialized equipment to develop the product. Second, requirements for what the system or product should deliver to the user are becoming more complicated. For example, we don't just want a phone, but a phone that takes photos and video, can connect to the internet anywhere in the world, function as a recording device, and even one that creates a virtual reality environment; in essence, a simple phone is no longer the standard; rather it must function more like a small personal computer with many times the power and capacity of yesteryear's supercomputers, yet with miniaturization unimaginable just a few decades ago. Such demands result in more complicated system architectures and project development approaches that require collaboration by myriad specialized entities; all of these factors contribute to geometrically increasing complexity in the project environment.

Many of the projects undertaken today are large-scale undertakings, and many are megaprojects, commonly defined as complex projects that cost $1 billion (U.S.) or more, take years to design and build, and involve multiple public and private stakeholders. They are deployed in the areas of infrastructure, oil and gas, mining, aerospace, defense, major events such as the Olympic Games, or massive information technology projects. It is not uncommon to hear the term *gigaproject* or even beyond, *the teraproject*, as we begin to comprehend giant projects costing $1 trillion (U.S.). According to Bent Flyvbjerg, a professor at the University of Oxford's Saïd Business School, megaprojects have grown explosively and now constitute eight percent of the global gross domestic product, and most are poorly executed. The "iron law of megaprojects," he wrote in a 2014 paper in the *Project Management Journal*, is that they are "over budget, over time, over and over again," (Flyvbjerg, 2014). Nine out of ten megaprojects experience cost overruns, and most take much longer to build than expected. What results, Flyvbjerg says, is the "survival of the un-fittest": the least deserving projects get built precisely because their cost-benefit estimates are so misleadingly optimistic (Flyvbjerg, 2014).

Edward Merrow states that in 2010, 65% of projects with budgets over one billion in U.S. dollars do not meet their business objectives, and most are unprofitable (Merrow, 2011).

Whether they are megaprojects or simply large-scale complex projects, their long planning horizons defy the common project management concepts of deterministic schedules, costs, risks, and assumptions. Cost overruns are large and benefit shortfalls are common. Virtually all major capital projects involve complex interfaces among diverse stakeholders and various contractors. The multiple stakeholders often have conflicting objectives; system interfaces are often complex and fall between or among stakeholder organizations without sufficient definition or management. In addition, many of these stakeholders have no direct contractual relationships, yet they share critical system interfaces that may mean the difference between great success and exceptional failure.

Interface management is an emerging discipline that aligns critical interactions among project management, systems engineering, and the organization's operations management to reduce risk and enhance the chances of successful system design and development, completion, and transition to the operation of major capital projects. As projects increase in scale and become more technically and contractually complex, there is a growing need to systematically identify, document, and manage technical, project, organizational, and industry interfaces to ensure effective system integration and adherence to project constraints (e.g., cost; schedule; scope; quality; and health, safety, environment, and security (HSES) requirements; etc.) while meeting stakeholder expectations and industry regulations.

The successful completion of complex projects requires synergy between technical and management personnel to complete the project scope of work and deliver a system that meets the need of the project sponsor. The multiple stakeholders often have conflicting objectives—system interfaces are often complex and fall between or among stakeholder organizations without sufficient definition or management. According to Merrow, the task of managing large complex projects "is a task centered around the effective management of the interfaces. The interfaces are opportunities for conflicts and misunderstandings to occur. They are the places where things tend to 'fall between the cracks,'" (Merrow, 2011).

Interface management performs a critical function by providing a systematic process for facilitating and managing information flow across shared boundaries by independent project and organizational entities without a contractual or functional relationship. Interface management is the mechanism by which these entities reach agreements associated with system interfaces and establish a common understanding along shared boundaries—preventing unexpected system integration problems late in project development.

ABOUT THIS BOOK

The purpose of this book is to assist organizations that are undertaking complex projects by helping project personnel and interface management professionals understand, implement, and effectively manage interfaces for large complex capital projects. It provides a holistic view of interface management that includes people, processes, tools, and techniques that work together to allow teams from multiple organizations to reduce project risk that is endemic to such large complex capital projects; much of this risk arises from the need to effectively manage and deliver numerous interfaces between and among multiple entities that may or may not have contractual obligations to one another. The book is offered as a practical reference guide to be used to:

- Familiarize project and organizational personnel with the scope of interface management to ensure a consistent and shared understanding of roles and responsibilities,

- Provide practical guidance for the implementation of a project interface management program that incorporates proven practices in a variety of domains, and
- Describe ways to effectively and efficiently manage interfaces during project execution that minimize the risk of rework during integration.

CONTENT AND ORGANIZATION

The book contains nine chapters and is structured sequentially with each chapter designed to build upon the previous one. Chapters 1 and 2 establish the foundation for understanding organizational strategy, the need for projects, and how complexity impacts project development. Chapters 3, 4, 5, and 6 describe the basics of interface management and the concepts underlying the interface management function. Chapters 7, 8, and 9 focus on the practical application of interface management during the project life cycle with an emphasis on sharing best practices.

Chapter 1 provides an introduction to organizational strategy and establishes the basis for why organizations undertake projects. Chapter 1 also prepares the context for interface management by providing a brief review of human history. This brief examination helps us to fully appreciate the incredible rate of change over recent history. The chapter also briefly describes portfolio management, project management, and systems engineering, including an overview of types of project development approaches. These project approaches often set the stage for the necessary interfaces because of the acquisition and contracting strategies employed. Understanding how projects are structured plays an important role in understanding how to apply interface management in a project environment. Chapter 2 presents a discussion of complexity and how complexity affects project development. Understanding the factors contributing to complexity can help in comprehending the need for interface management as an important means of reducing risk and enhancing the probability of project success.

Chapters 3 and 4 introduce interface management and the processes used to manage interfaces. Chapter 3 provides an introduction to interface management and describes key terms, definitions, and concepts. As expected in an emerging field, there are many alternative definitions, terminology, and meanings that sometimes conflict with one another. This chapter establishes a basis of common understanding of the concepts used throughout the book. Chapter 4 describes the interface management process and the interface life cycle. This description is not peculiar to a specific project environment, but rather is a generic process that can be tailored to any project environment.

Chapters 5 through 9 collectively address how to plan, implement, manage (execute), and close out interface management and the interfaces themselves. Chapter 5 discusses the interface analysis process and describes how to begin to decompose the necessary interfaces, forming the basis for interface planning. In Chapter 6, the authors discuss the interface planning process and describe how to develop a project interface management system (i.e., plans, procedures, personnel structure, tools, training, etc.). In essence, this chapter describes how to establish an interface management system appropriate to the project's interface complexity.

Chapter 7 builds upon Chapter 6 and focuses on how to implement the interface management system as actual project execution, or construction, commences. Implementing any management system in a large-scale complex project can be a challenge. Chapter 7 offers guidance and best practices suggested to implement interface management effectively and efficiently and to ensure a *fast start.*

Chapter 8 describes how to manage interfaces during project execution and discusses interface activity as project execution work gets under way and proceeds. This chapter takes a pragmatic approach to typical situations that might occur during project execution and describes how to address these situations. Finally, Chapter 9 describes how interface management supports technical compliance and interface integrity, including the interface verification process and interface close-out. This chapter completes the interface management cycle and illustrates how the intense interface activity during project execution concludes as various parts of the system are integrated and verified, and helps to ensure that the project result is delivered to expectations.

AUDIENCE

This book is not intended to replace existing project management processes or international systems engineering practices. Rather, it is aligned with and supports both the Project Management Institute (PMI) Project Management Body of Knowledge (PMBOK) and the International Council on Systems Engineering (INCOSE) Systems Engineering Handbook while focusing on the processes, roles and responsibilities, and activities associated with effective management of system interfaces during project development. More important, this book demonstrates how interface management not only simplifies system interface complexity between independent parties, but also aligns project management and systems engineering domains to break down barriers that might otherwise create delays, excessive cost overruns, and unnecessary integration risk.

This book provides a road map to effectively design, develop, implement, and manage a tailored project interface management process in a relatively short period of time. In addition to decomposing the process into easily understandable and logical steps, the book also identifies specific tools, techniques, and resources needed to support the process, together with examples throughout. With the guidance, engagement, and support of upper management, and reasonably effective project and program management infrastructure, any organization can implement its own interface management process, make better decisions, and increase its chances of achieving effective development and integration of complex interfaces. People whose organizations are already using interface management might think about how to use the concepts in this book to supplement or improve existing processes.

The book is also intended for use as a textbook in an interface management course within graduate and upper level undergraduate business and engineering degree programs. It provides a road map for students to understand interface management through the application of tools and techniques, using a defined process. By structuring the text to coincide with the logical progression of the interface management process and illustrating tools and techniques to use along the way, students will obtain a clear understanding of the emerging discipline of interface management.

SOFTWARE TOOLS

It is not the intent of the authors to endorse one software product over others. However, we do make it clear that effectively managing project interfaces is difficult or impossible without the right tools. On large-scale complex projects, the sheer volume of interface items and the depth and breadth of inter-entity relationships indicate the need for a specialized software solution for both management and reporting of progress on interfaces. In relevant chapters throughout the book, we use illustrations from Kongsberg's Seaflex Web Interface Register (WIR) (km.kongsberg.com) to illustrate the concepts presented. In Appendix B, we use Coreworx Interface Management (CIM) (coreworx.com) software to illustrate similar concepts. A number of other software products are available on the open market, including, but not limited to, Omega Pims Interface Management (omega.no) and Aconex Interface Management for Construction (aconex.com). Readers are encouraged to explore these and other relevant products to assess their capabilities with respect to specific interface management needs.

To enhance learning and provide you with hands-on experience in the processes described in the book, we feel that instructors and readers should be able to use a tool to practice the concepts provided in the book. As a result, the authors have entered into an agreement with Kongsberg to allow instructors who are using the book as a textbook along with their students who are also using the book, six-month temporary limited access to Kongsberg Seaflex WIR. In addition, the agreement allows individual readers who purchase new copies of this book from authorized distributors limited access to predefined projects.

Instructors and individual book purchasers may contact Kongsberg to sign up by navigating to https://www.interfaceregister.com/imbook.aspx. The terms of use are described and you will be asked to provide contact and login information and to verify that you are eligible to use the software. After registering, instructors will work with Kongsberg to arrange access for their students in accordance with the Instructor Guide that is provided as part of the WAV™ material of this book (found at www.jrosspub.com/wav).

Please note that the authors and the publisher have no other commercial arrangement with Kongsberg or any other software offer with respect to this book, do not receive payment for the use of, and provide no express or implied warranty for these software tools. Rather, this agreement was made solely for the purpose of allowing instructors and students the opportunity to use an interface management software tool and individual readers to access predefined projects in order to maximize the learning experience and reinforce the concepts presented in this book.

REFERENCES

Flyvbjerg, B. (2014). What You Should Know About Megaprojects and Why: An Overview. Project Management Journal, Vol. 45: pp. 6–19. doi:10.1002/pmj.21409, John Wiley & Sons, Ltd. Retrieved from http://dx.doi.org/10.1002/pmj.21409.

Merrow, E. W. (2011). *Industrial Megaprojects–Concepts, Strategies, and Practices for Success*. John Wiley & Sons, Hoboken, NJ, USA.

Acknowledgments

We wish to thank Kongsberg for allowing us to use the Seaflex Web Interface Register software tool to illustrate concepts in this book. The use of this tool enhances our ability to reinforce key principles and concepts. The authors would also like to thank Coreworx Inc. for providing illustrations and descriptions from the Coreworx Interface Management module in Appendix B of the book. These illustrations help to show the reader alternate ways of structuring and managing the interface register.

We also wish to express our sincere appreciation to Thomas Rivrud of Kongsberg and Kelly Maloney of Coreworx for reviewing early chapter drafts and providing feedback based on their experiences in numerous real-world projects representing multiple industries. Both Thomas and Kelly have extensive experience in supporting large-scale complex projects, and their input certainly enhanced the content of this book.

We are especially grateful to our families; Susan's husband, Jim Bivins, and Michael's wife and son, Hege and Ethan Bible. Throughout this project they provided unfaltering support for our efforts and made sacrifices to allow us time to focus on this project. Thank you, Jim, Hege, and Ethan! We could not have accomplished this without all of you.

About the Authors

Michael J. Bible, PMP, CSEP, MSPM, IPMA-A, ESEP, MSSE, has over 30 years of professional and leadership experience supporting major programs and projects in the United States Department of Defense and the Norwegian Oil and Gas industry. Mike is a project management and systems engineering professional with a successful history of applying project portfolio, project management, and systems engineering in large-scale complex project environments.

During his career, Mike has worked with several large corporations including URS (AECOM Corporation) and Scientific Application International Corporation (SAIC) on several large defense programs and projects including the Army's Mine Resistant Ambush Protected (MRAP) program and several Marine Corp Engineering Systems programs and projects. In addition, Mike served as a senior advisor to multiple, large-scale offshore oil and gas projects in the Norwegian Continental Shelf (NCS). Mike is a long-time member of the Project Management Institute (PMI) and the International Council on Systems Engineering (INCOSE) and has been honored to be a guest speaker at numerous PMI events including the Global Congress North America.

A retired United States Marine Corp officer, Mike earned a Master of Science in Project Management (MSPM) from George Washington University and a Master of Science in Systems Engineering (MSSE) from Johns Hopkins University. Mike currently lives with his wife and son in Trondheim, Norway, and can be reached at mb1775@gwu.edu.

Susan S. Bivins, PMP, MSPM, has more than thirty years of management and leadership experience dedicated to delivering successful information technology, organizational change management, and professional consulting services projects for major global corporations. She specializes in project and portfolio management; international, multicultural, and multi-company initiatives; and business strategy integration in the private and public sectors.

During her career with IBM, Sue managed multiple organizations and complex projects, including operations and support for the Olympics, and a strategic transformational change program. Since retiring from IBM, she has led multi-company joint initiatives with Hitachi, Microsoft, and Sun Microsystems (Oracle), and has served as Director of Project Management at Habitat for Humanity International.

She earned her MSPM from the Graduate School of Business at George Washington University, where she received the Dean's Award for Excellence and was admitted to the Beta Gamma Sigma business honorarium. A member of the Project Management Institute, she served on PMI standards teams, has authored several journal articles, and is a frequent webinar and conference speaker, including multiple presentations for the PMI Global Congress North America. Sue currently lives with her husband in St. Louis, Missouri, USA, and can be reached via e-mail at sbivins@gwu.edu.

This book has free material available for download from the Web Added Value™ resource center at *www.jrosspub.com*

At J. Ross Publishing we are committed to providing today's professional with practical, hands-on tools that enhance the learning experience and give readers an opportunity to apply what they have learned. That is why we offer free ancillary materials available for download on this book and all participating Web Added Value™ publications. These online resources may include interactive versions of material that appears in the book or supplemental templates, worksheets, models, plans, case studies, proposals, spreadsheets and assessment tools, among other things. Whenever you see the WAV™ symbol in any of our publications, it means bonus materials accompany the book and are available from the Web Added Value Download Resource Center at www.jrosspub.com.

Downloads for *Project Interface Management: Reducing Risk on Major Projects* consist of:

MATERIALS FOR ALL READERS

Figures and Tables

All figures and tables from each chapter are provided to be used in presentations or instructor teaching material with appropriate attribution.

Excel Workbook for Set-Up in Interface Management Software

This Excel workbook contains set-up sheets for the sample project that can be used to establish the sample Project Diamond interface management projects in the interface management tool for which temporary access has been granted to readers.

Project Document Templates

These documents established for the sample company ABC Corporation and sample Project Diamond can be used as templates for project and interface documents on real projects and include:

- ABC Management of Project Development
- Project Diamond Mandate
- Project Diamond Execution Plan
- Project Diamond Interface Control Document

INSTRUCTOR MATERIALS

In addition to the materials available for all readers, the following instructor-only materials are available.

PowerPoint Slide Deck for Each Chapter

A generic PowerPoint slide deck is provided covering the material in each chapter, including overview, content, and summary slides. The slides can be downloaded and tailored by the instructor or included with other lecture materials.

Instructor Guide

An Instructor Guide for a one-semester graduate course is provided. It contains example course objectives, course description, suggested subject/topic and student deliverables for each session, sample mid-term exam questions, sample final exam questions, suggested weekly discussion topics, description of class project, and information about contacting Kongsberg to obtain access to Seaflex WIR interface register tool for instructors and students. Of course, instructors may tailor the outline to reflect different course durations and add additional required or recommended readings, grading policies, meeting times, instructor information, logos, etc.

Other Benefits and Materials

As time permits, the authors and other interface management professionals are available to respond to occasional questions or discussion points from instructors using the book for their classes, for brief guest presentations, and for introductory interface management briefings.

From time to time, additional or updated materials may be provided for instructors, readers, or both. Updates will be identified in descriptions of the WAV materials, the Instructor Guide, and on the publisher's website. At present, we are considering developing a series of short videos to complement the textbook material with the authors' and other interface management professionals' real-world experiences. We anticipate making them available starting in late 2019.

1

Accelerating Change and the Context for Projects

"Life is really simple, but we insist on making it complicated."
—Confucius

"Project management is the science of project planning combined with the art of reacting to surprises during execution."
—Edward W. Merrow

While this book is about interface management, a short detour is taken to provide a historical perspective on the rise of human society, the accelerating pace of change, and the increasing magnitude of people-driven endeavors that will help us understand why the need for interface management in modern projects has evolved and why it will continue to occupy a place of importance in future projects. Modern life has changed rapidly during the information age mainly through technological breakthroughs, leading to advancement in virtually all facets of human life. Project interface management is driven by three main factors: complexity, communication, and people. These factors represent happenings in society. It is natural, then, to realize that projects and how they are developed, will change as society changes. Recognizing accelerating change and its inevitable impact on complexity helps explain the emerging need for new project management disciplines, such as interface management, to increase the likelihood of completing projects successfully.

An important aspect of understanding what interface management is and how to apply it on large complex capital projects is that of understanding the context for why and how these projects are undertaken in the first place—meaning we need to know why the project was selected and how it contributes to creating value for the entity undertaking or sponsoring such projects. So, in addition to the historical perspective, this chapter also provides a synopsis of the portfolio management, project management, and systems engineering (SE) milieu in which these projects are conceived and carried out. This chapter also provides an overview of why these projects are undertaken by organizations and the context in which they are performed, describes distinguishing factors of large-scale capital projects, discusses how the contract strategy influences project complexity (and certainly interface management), and provides insight into strategic decisions that will eventually mold the management system that will be used to manage the project.

It is often stated that "it is hard to see the forest when you're standing among the trees." This book is as much about the future of managing large-scale projects as it is about the present—but we need some historical background. How did we get here? To understand this basic question, we need to step away from the trees and take a brief look into our (mankind's) past. So, briefly, we go back to the beginning—a simpler time in human life—and reflect upon how we humans got to the point of requiring such systems and management processes. This brief look into human history provides a perspective on how slowly things changed in earlier times and how rapidly modern society is changing now, thus forming the basis for complexity in modern projects.

1.1 BRIEF HISTORY OF SOCIETAL EVOLUTION

While anthropologists are divided on when the genus *Homo* emerged, it is estimated that the first members of the human family (hominids) lived in Africa between six and seven million years ago, and spread to Europe and Asia about two million years ago. Early *modern* humans of the genus *Homo* species *sapiens* (*Homo sapiens*, or us) evolved in East Africa approximately and arguably 200,000 years ago, based on evidence from fossils found in Kenya and Ethiopia. Life for our early ancestors was nomadic, undoubtedly difficult, and focused on foraging, hunting, and surviving threats. Other earlier species of hominids such as Neanderthals (*Homo neanderthalensis*) lived alongside *Homo sapiens*, developing crude tools and harnessing fire, until becoming extinct. Of the six known species of humans (Harari, 2015), we *sapiens* are the only survivors.

1.1.1 Prehistory

Prehistory (the time before human language was developed sufficiently to capture it) is classified today into three discrete periods based on the types of artifacts and materials used—the Stone Age, the Bronze Age, and the Iron Age (Thomsen, 1836).

From about 2.5 million years ago to 14,000 years ago, the Stone Age was in full swing, a prehistoric period in which hominids used stone to make tools. The Stone Age is divided by some sources into the Paleolithic and Neolithic periods (Kulper, 2015) with the Paleolithic period humans leading nomadic lives as hunters and gatherers, and with the later Neolithic period humans discovering agriculture and domestication of animals, which allowed them to settle in one place (DifferenceBetween.net, 2011).

The Bronze Age ushered in the use of metals in tools and implements and is thought to have begun first with the creation of small precious objects from copper, and subsequently, with the creation of copper tools and weapons. Later in the Bronze Age, the true bronze alloy of tin and copper was used. The Bronze Age also fostered increased specialization of human skills and the invention of both the wheel and the ox-drawn plow (Kulper, 2015). Along with specialization, these inventions contributed to greater urbanization and the creation of social order (Metropolitan Museum of Art, 2017).

The Iron Age came later, beginning about 3,000 years ago when humans learned to heat and forge iron, which made way for more permanent settlements (Encyclopedia Britannica, 2015). Weapons forged of iron also armed large battle forces and enabled the migration of peoples that changed Europe and Asia over the next 2,000 years (Encyclopedia Britannica, 2015).

1.1.2 Beginning of History—the Cognitive, Agricultural, and Scientific Revolutions

Approximately 70,000 years ago, while *Homo sapiens* spread from Africa throughout Europe and East Asia, fictive language emerged (Gale, 1971) and history began. Harari identifies three revolutions that have shaped history—the Cognitive Revolution, which began about 70,000 years ago; the Agricultural Revolution, which began about 12,000 years ago; and the Scientific Revolution, which began only about 500 years ago (Harari, 2015).

During the Cognitive Revolution period, humans invented boats, oil lamps, needles for sewing, and bows and arrows (Harari, 2015). The same period shows evidence of art, religion, and social orders thought to be driven by dramatically increased cognitive function. It took a few thousand more years to develop kingdoms, early polytheistic religions, and money.

During the Agricultural Revolution, humans domesticated plants and animals, enabling the formation of permanent communities (Harari, 2015). About 5,000 years ago, the two early civilizations of Mesopotamia and Egypt were established (Gascoigne, 2001). Mesopotamia, on the land between the Tigris and Euphrates rivers, had rudimentary civil services and laws to protect people from one another, while ancient Egypt in northeastern Africa stretched along the fertile soils of the Nile river valley. Both civilizations used early forms of writing—cuneiform in Mesopotamia and hieroglyphs in Egypt. The Agricultural Revolution saw the rise of the first kingdoms, money, and religions. Over 2,000 years ago, the Han Empire in China, the Roman Empire around the Mediterranean, and Christianity all rose and flourished. Some other monotheistic religions arose earlier (Judaism) and later (Islam).

In just the last 500 years, humans have driven the Scientific Revolution by admitting our ignorance and striving to not just maintain the social order and status quo, but to "discover new medications, invent new weapons, and stimulate economic growth" (Harari, 2015). It also led to the development of weapons "not only to change the course of history, but to end it" with respect to nuclear weapons. Harari points out the astounding growth in human power (not to mention complexity) by pointing out that a peasant who fell asleep in the year 1000 AD could awaken in the year 1500 without missing a beat, but one who fell into a similar sleep in the year 1500 would have a rude awakening by "the ringtone of a twenty-first century iPhone" (Harari, 2015) and would find a world beyond comprehension. This statement by Harari is important as it illustrates an increasing rate of change over these two time periods.

1.1.3 The Growth in Human Power During the Scientific Revolution

According to Harari's research, in the last 500 years the human population has increased 14-fold (from 500 million to about 7 billion), production has increased 240-fold (as measured by the total value of goods and services produced by humankind, which has grown from $250 billion to $60 trillion in today's U.S. dollars), and energy consumption has increased 115-fold (as measured by calories of energy per day, from 13 trillion per day to 1,500 trillion per day) (Harari, 2015). In his book, Harari cites several examples of the acceleration of the rate of change. One of those examples is that, "Prior to the sixteenth century, no human had circumnavigated the earth. This changed in 1522, when Magellan's expedition returned to Spain after a journey of 44,000 miles. It took three years and cost the lives of almost all the crew members, Magellan included. In 1873, Jules Verne could imagine that Phileas Fogg . . . might just be able to make it around the world in eighty days" (Harari, 2015). By contrast, he points out, at present an individual can safely and easily travel around the world in 48 hours or less.

Of course, rather than having his own ships or balloons, the present-day traveler relies on the infrastructure of airlines and terminals, the technology of aircraft and air traffic control, the educated and highly skilled people who staff them, and the governments, markets, and societies that regulate and support them. In other words, the rate of human growth and societal change is accelerating at an ever-increasing pace, as is the complexity of living with these changes. The simple fact is that humanity has come a long way in a relatively short time, beginning with tens of thousands of years at a relatively languid pace, and continuing with fierce acceleration in more recent times. Progress begets change and it also begets complexity. In many ways, modern humans are struggling to adapt to the rapid rate of change.

1.2 IMPLICATIONS OF ACCELERATING SOCIETAL CHANGE

Human civilization has experienced a rate of change unimaginable by ancient humans. This rate of change is driven by advances in technology and science, along with the drivers of modern civilization. As Harari points out, although some may believe that science and technology hold the answers to all of our problems, science and technology must be ". . . shaped by economic, political, and religious interests" (Harari, 2015). It is governments, businesses, and other entities that have funded the scientific breakthroughs and innovations that have extended our life expectancy and perhaps, too, our quality of life.

1.2.1 Creating a Complicated Modern Civilization

These governments, businesses, religious, and other organizations, guided by their ideologies, determine what to fund and even what the future will contain; they allocate funds among the conflicting objectives and priorities of communities of life on earth. While continuous invention and innovation have given us modern conveniences and longer lives, they have also yielded massive population growth, ever-shifting demographics, peril for many cohabitant species of our planet, and explosive rates of change. They have also created a complicated or even complex modern civilization.

While we humans have, in general, progressed, the complication in modern society is evident in all parts of our lives—from the food we grow, to the way we travel, to how we communicate, etc. As societies, some of us have many choices (and complications) arising from the vast options we have about how to live our lives, even where we choose to live. Others in less developed nations and parts of the world are not as fortunate. It is reasonable to suggest that the world will continue to become even more complex with increasing populations, the development of new products with the advancement of technology, and the desire by governments and organizations to improve the quality of life for its citizens. Undoubtedly, projects will continue to be a part of the evolution of humans, but we need to recognize the rapid change that has occurred in the recent history of humanity and how this change has affected projects—more important, how it will continue to affect projects going forward into the future.

Modern society grapples with issues associated with the pace of change, as is evident in global opportunities to increase the application of robotics and artificial intelligence, while at the same time dealing with the basic need to dramatically increase global food production to keep pace with population growth facing environmental phenomena that threaten to reduce the capacity to do so. Projects, which are a major means of achieving positive change, also struggle with the forces of change. They too must adjust to the rapidity of change and how to properly handle complexity resulting from it. As evidenced by the almost universally high rate of large-scale project delays, overruns, and failure to fully achieve the operational results for which they were undertaken, we as project professionals in various industries have not been fully able to adapt to the rate of change and growth of complexity; meaning that often, project organizations are ill-equipped to effectively manage complex projects—often because of things we don't know that we need to know.

1.2.2 Evolving Layers of Complexity in the Systems We Create

The rapid advances in technology, especially over the past 30 years, have afforded humans incredible opportunities to share information through countless media, affecting the way we conduct communication. Face-to-face conversations have often been replaced by social media, and classroom learning by online self-paced and sometimes non-communal education—thereby making us alone in a crowded place. The ability to conduct real-time dialogue and video with anyone, virtually anywhere, also gives us the wherewithal to conduct business in real time across geospatial and cultural boundaries. In terms of technology, modern society has an insatiable appetite for more—more functionality, more capability, more everything. This affects the products people buy and use in everyday life and how we live.

Individuals and organizations create a perpetually escalating demand for new and improved products and services. Often, these products and services interact with other products and services, creating layers of complexity related to integrating new systems with existing or even other new systems. The challenges will be compounded by continued population growth, political conflicts, and environmental impacts—requiring even more advanced solutions. Given that the rate of change and evolution of societies will likely continue to accelerate, organizations will need ever-better management systems to address them and thus remain relevant and competitive. Thoughts of stand-alone systems operating independently are becoming the modern unicorn in an increasingly connected world where one system operates as part of an interconnected supersystem.

1.3 DEVELOPING THE STRATEGY

The modern global marketplace will continue to evolve to meet the needs, demands, and desires of a growing global population in search of a higher living standard and longer and higher quality of life. Companies and organizations providing those products and services are also subject to change and complexity. As a result, these companies and organizations continually innovate to improve the effectiveness and efficiency of existing products and services in order to remain competitive, and they also invent new products and services in order to meet a growing global demand. This is evident in everyday life products, such as our mobile phones, for example, where a single device is used for numerous functions: telephone, camera, voice and video recorder, texting, etc. (even tracking the steps we take in a day), that only 20 years ago required several devices in order to perform the same functionality and tasks, or that we couldn't perform at all. In recent decades, especially since the 1980s, we have experienced an increase in the global marketplace where companies and organizations can reach across countries and continents to identify suppliers, vendors, and manufacturers to aid in developing new products and services, creating product and system development possibilities that were not available only a few short decades ago.

Every organization exists for a purpose, which typically includes providing services and products to support customers and clients. Whether government agencies or multinational corporations, organizations undertake strategies to identify a long-term plan that hopefully leads to the achievement of organizational success factors: hiring more people, capturing a greater proportion of a particular market share, higher share price or earnings per share, providing more efficient services, etc. While a strategy does not guarantee a road map to organizational success, developing (and revising) a strategy demonstrates deliberate and careful decisions about what the organization should do in the future to remain successful. The process of establishing an organizational strategy is important in the rapidly changing global marketplace; poor strategic decisions certainly can lead to the demise of the organization, particularly when those decisions are based on faulty assumptions or fail to anticipate future changes in a complicated marketplace. These decisions ultimately and ideally result in the types of projects sanctioned, among other organizational activities.

In the book *Mastering Project Portfolio Management*, Bible and Bivins (2011) provide an appropriate analogy to explain the importance of strategic direction. In Lewis Carroll's *Alice's Adventures in Wonderland*, Alice comes to a crossroads in the *Pigs and Pepper* scene and is uncertain as to which direction she should go. In a nearby tree, she notices the Cheshire cat and asks the cat which way she should go. The cat responds, "That depends a good deal on where you want to get to." Alice replied that it really didn't matter. The cat replied, "Then it doesn't matter which way you go."

"Unlike Alice in Wonderland, an organization must have a destination in mind that leads to success and a proper road map to get there. In today's competitive environment, an organization must take the best road that leads to continued relevance, prosperity, and success. No easy task given the rapid rate of societal change. This is the purpose of strategic planning" (Bible and Bivins, 2011). An organization's strategy is driven by its mission, values, goals, and objectives. Its mission answers the questions "why are we here?" and "what is our purpose?" or "what do we do?" The vision is a fast-forward to some stated future time frame of how the world (or at least the portion of it affected by the organization's mission) will be if they succeed in the execution of the mission. An organization's values are shared beliefs that drive its people's behaviors; that is, they describe how employees or other stakeholders are to conduct themselves with respect to each other and other stakeholders. Values are often accompanied by a set of behaviors that describe each of the values. Goals and objectives state what is to be accomplished. When they are decomposed, they become more specific and time bound. The objectives are to be achieved within the mission, to be delivered in keeping with the organization's values, and to move the organization toward achieving its vision. With amazing rates of change all around us, of course, strategy must not remain static—it must be as agile as the environment in which it is developed.

A strategic plan allows an organization to (1) identify its aspirations and how it will attain them in order to stay relevant in the marketplace; (2) communicate, clarify, and align its commitments around the long- and short-term goals, and (3) provide consistent guidance for decision making, resource allocation, budget planning, and training (Urbanick, 2008). The essence of the strategic plan is to attain an organizational state in which everyone shares a common vision of what the organization wants to achieve in the future, understands what is required to achieve that vision, and is motivated to contribute to the organization's success.

In many large organizations, strategic planning is conducted at the corporate level and based on the corporate plan each group or division in the organization's hierarchy may perform its own strategic planning process, albeit at a more tactical level appropriate for the subset of corporate goals it supports. Ideally, these plans will roll up to form an integrated whole, and roll down so that the goals and objectives at the lower level and the initiatives undertaken all support the corporate strategy.

The organization's objectives are accomplished (or should be) by selecting and managing the optimal combination of projects that drive the organization's achievement of its strategy—that is the meaning of project portfolio management (PPM). We included this brief description of strategic planning to reinforce the importance of strategy to the PPM process and ultimately to the reasons why we perform projects. Projects, and more specifically, portfolios of projects and programs, are central to the achievement of organizational goals and objectives. The goals and objectives are the strategy, which, in turn, is key to the continued relevance and success of the organization.

1.4 INTRODUCTION TO PROJECT PORTFOLIO MANAGEMENT

PPM is an iterative process linking the strategic objectives of the organization to selecting and managing the right project portfolios. The less a project contributes to accomplishing an organization's goals and objectives, the less value it creates and the more resources are wasted or at least inefficiently utilized. To better utilize resources and achieve desired outcomes, organizations are becoming more concerned about which projects to undertake in the first place, which has led to a more formal process called PPM. Harvey Levine (2005) defines PPM as ". . . a set of business practices that brings the world of projects into tight integration with other business operations. It brings projects into harmony with the strategies, resources, and executive oversight of the enterprise and provides the structure and processes for project portfolio governance." The Project Management Institute (PMI) more broadly defines PPM as "... the coordinated management of portfolio components to achieve specific organizational objectives" (PMI, 2008). Bible and Bivins (2011) also suggest that PPM is a flexible, responsive, and iterative process to select and execute the right projects that maximize achievement of the organization's strategic goals and objectives subject to physical, political, financial, and other resource constraints.

The PPM process can be thought of as the actionable management process necessary to achieve the organization's strategic objectives through project portfolio selection, implementation, monitoring and control, and evaluation. PPM is not the same as enterprise project management or management of multiple related projects as the name might imply. A project portfolio is a group of projects selected and executed specifically because together they best help an organization to achieve its objectives. The objectives are the lowest level output of the strategic planning process, which produces the organization's mission, vision, goals, and the objectives that support each goal.

The fundamental task of PPM is selecting a portfolio of projects that maximizes the achievement of those objectives while achieving balance among, and coverage of, the objectives. Although effective PPM contributes to the achievement of organizational objectives, it is not the only source of achievement. The organization's ongoing business operations also contribute to the achievement of objectives as we will discuss later in this section. Every organization is resource constrained. An effective PPM process provides the structure to make reasoned trade-offs about how the resources should be allocated to maximize potential benefits. Thus, sound decision making through a disciplined and methodical process is a crucial attribute of an effective PPM process. Through such a process, the organization can make rational decisions as to how best to employ constrained resources across objectives to maximize the benefits of its project portfolios.

The foundation of the organization's PPM process is laid during the development of the strategic plan, which identifies the organization's destination and a road map to achieve desired future outcomes. The result of the PPM process is the selection and implementation of a group of projects, which are intended to achieve specific strategic objectives. Modern projects require management systems and processes to increase the likelihood of success; resulting in the rapid rise of project management and the adoption of formal project management tools, techniques, processes, and systems.

1.5 INTRODUCTION TO PROJECT MANAGEMENT

Project management is at least as old as the Great Pyramids so it predates the Scientific Revolution that began only 500 years ago. While the roots of project management extend to ancient times, only within the last half century has formal project management gained wide acceptance and traction in many organizations. Business and government agencies have become more aware of the need to manage projects using formal practices and processes to ensure greater project success, i.e., "doing the work right" (PMI, 2008). Meredith and Mantel provide three primary reasons to explain the emergence of project management "... (1) the exponential growth of human knowledge, (2) the growing demand for a broad range of complex, sophisticated, customized goods and services, and (3) the evolution of worldwide competitive markets for the production and consumption of goods and services" (Meredith and Mantel, 2006).

These reasons have not gone unnoticed. In 2016, U.S. President Barack Obama signed the Program Management Improvement and Accountability Act aimed at enhancing accountability and best practices in project and program management across the U.S. federal government. Throughout the United States' Department of Defense (DoD), there is an ever-growing emphasis on program and project management as acquisition personnel design, develop, and procure hundreds of billions of dollars of advanced military equipment. The DoD's Defense Acquisition University (DAU) is dedicated to formally training and educating personnel in defense acquisition program and project management and establishing standards for program management career field certification (DAU, 2010). Expanding beyond the DoD, the U.S. National Aeronautics and Space Administration established the Academy for Program/Project and Engineering Leadership and many leading corporations have established project management training programs and project, program, or portfolio management offices (PMOs) to develop project, program, and portfolio management methodologies tailored to organizational needs. Similar advances have occurred in other parts of the world, in, for example, the United Kingdom's Cabinet Office, which supports the British Prime Minister and Cabinet. The ever-growing emphasis on project management can also be illustrated through the expansion of project management professional certification from PMI.

Founded in 1969, PMI has grown to several hundred thousand members internationally with a "primary goal to advance the practice, science, and profession of project management throughout the world in a conscientious and proactive manner so that organizations everywhere will embrace, value, and utilize project management and then attribute their successes to it" (PMI, 2010). APMG International also provides certification training and examinations and accredits professionals in multiple disciplines, including project, program, and portfolio management. Not only do organizations want to complete projects successfully by *doing the work right*, they also want to successfully complete the *right* projects. Completing projects on time and within budget has little to no value if projects fail to contribute to the successful achievement of the organization's strategic objectives.

1.5.1 Defining Project Management

As defined by Harold Kerzner, "Successful project management can then be defined as achieving a continuous stream of project objectives within time, within cost, at the desired performance/technology level, while utilizing the assigned resources effectively and efficiently, and having the results accepted by the customer and/or stakeholders" (Kerzner, 2017). In essence, a project is a temporary endeavor to create a unique product, service, or result (a *system* for example) (PMI, 2008). The temporary nature of projects indicates that a project has a beginning and an end. Although considered *temporary*, project durations may equate to several years in some large-scale complex project developments, such as military weapon systems, enterprise information systems, offshore oil and gas processing facilities, etc.

The part that occurs between the beginning and the end of a project, in this book, is called the project development process. The project development process is defined by various project development *phases* such as: conceptual design, detailed engineering, procurement, fabrication and construction, transportation, installation, mechanical completion, and commissioning. In some organizations, procurement, fabrication, construction, transportation, installation, etc., may be grouped together and called execution. Different organizations and industries may call them by slightly different names, and different sets of contractors and ultimate end users may sometimes cause the names of the phases to be different, but the example should suffice to present the concept of development phases. As the project progresses through each development phase, various project management processes are used to initiate, plan, execute, monitor, and control, and close the related project work. Every industry, organization, and project is different, and the method used to develop the project will vary accordingly. Regardless, each project will follow a general development approach consisting of some form of engineering, procurement, and construction (EPC). In essence, we need engineering to design thoroughly the *result* of the project (engineering design), build or commercially procure (order and receive) material and equipment (procurement), and finally, assemble those items into the final system (construction). It is normal for this cycle to repeat itself through several project phases, or stages, until the final system is completed.

1.5.2 Balancing the Project Constraints

Managing projects requires constant focus on the scope of work and completing the work on time (i.e., as scheduled) and within budget while meeting quality and safety expectations. Ideally, the scope of a project is precisely defined early. By knowing the scope of work, the effort required (resources multiplied by time) can be accurately estimated, leading to an approximate cost to complete the project. In addition, knowing the scope of work allows for planners to optimize the work so that the activities are defined and resources are applied to complete the activities in the most efficient sequence, resulting in the schedule to perform the work. The foundation (but, of course, not the only factor) for an effective schedule is the amount of confidence in the scope of work—the greater the confidence in the scope of work, the better. Precise knowledge of the scope of work and what is required generally translates to less risk than a situation in which the scope of work is not well understood or defined. (Of course, in getting from concept through detailed design, such schedule and cost estimates become more definitive and less variable, or less stochastic and more deterministic. However, large-scale complex projects often overrun even those estimates. Reducing those costly overruns and under-delivery experiences are a major purpose of interface management.) This basic principle of scope certainty affects many aspects of managing projects and the system used to monitor and control project work. Ultimately, the goal of project management is to complete all defined project work with high quality according to the schedule, without overspending or getting anyone hurt (i.e., safety). The impact of risk and the ability to manage risk certainly affect the outcome of this goal.

This book is not intended to provide the reader a detailed examination of project management—there are many books on that subject. Here, we simply want to state that a central challenge in project management is to have a high degree of certainty about the scope as early as possible in the project. Knowing exactly what the project is to produce increases the chances of delivering the project successfully, assuming good management and safety practices during the project development process. Unfortunately, it is rare to have such certainty early in the project. In fact, *changes* (expected and unexpected) are common in all types of projects, large and small, which result in more work, extra cost, and increased time. The main point is that a *dependent relationship* exists among cost, schedule, and scope (also quality and safety). As scope increases, cost will increase and more time will be added to the schedule; requiring more quality and safety management. The simple question then is, why can't we always be certain about the work that needs to be completed by the project?

Several factors affect a project's success and management's ability to control scope, schedule, cost, quality, and safety. Naturally, as project complexity increases, the difficulty in managing the project increases. In Chapter 2, we will discuss the topic of complexity in more detail since complexity has a direct impact on project interface management. However, a project to build a single-family home is not the same in terms of complexity as a project to build a 150-story skyscraper. Building a single-family home, while still a project, is more like a *process* than a *project*, especially when using preconfigured blueprints—millions of homes have been built over the last decades and the technology has remained relatively stable. Comparatively, not many 150-story skyscraper buildings are being built. Such buildings incorporate technology and safety control systems exceedingly more advanced than those in single-family homes, and each one is unique. Thus, a 150-story skyscraper construction project is larger in scale and size, more unique, and more technologically complex than a project to build a traditional single-family home, making a skyscraper much more difficult to manage than a single-family home project. Add to that the fact that the forces of weather and other phenomena have an impact not only on construction schedule, but on the design as well. The uniqueness, scale, size, and complexity of such a project impacts the project team's ability to manage and control scope, cost, schedule, quality, and safety.

1.5.3 Rapid Change in Projects

While project management is a relatively new management discipline, it is greatly affected by the rapid rate of societal and global change. Here, project management is affected in two ways: (1) by the increasingly complicated project development approaches offered by a relatively new global marketplace and (2) by the complex systems resulting in rapidly changing technologies that projects must produce. The world has become a much more connected (technologically and physically) global society, allowing for greater flexibility for project developments and increased capability and functionality of the systems produced by projects.

The opening of the global marketplace through numerous trade agreements has resulted in opportunities for all participants, but while these new markets provide greater access, they have also resulted in complicated project development approaches. Organizations and companies are now able to select vendors, suppliers, fabricators, constructors, engineers, etc., from a global versus local marketplace, creating more opportunities for project sponsors to leverage global technologies, capabilities, and competencies. Essentially, the world is the global supermarket where the best products and services can be acquired for the cheapest price (albeit not always the most safe, the best quality, or morally acceptable). As expected, organizations that are sponsoring projects, especially large-scale projects, have the opportunity to subdivide a project's scope of work into several *parcels* and contract to global companies (vendors, suppliers, etc.), reaping the economic and business benefits of such a strategy.

In addition, the systems being created by the project continue to increase in complexity as a result of continued rapid technological advances, enabling constant opportunities to improve existing products and services and create new products and services with greater capabilities and functionality. The never-ending consumer requirement for *faster, better, cheaper* creates a competitive cycle to *one-up* business competitors in hopes of retaining or expanding market share in a particular market; this means organizations constantly search for a balance between the lowest price and the most product functionality and performance. Later in this chapter, we discuss this topic further; the main point here is to recognize that projects are changing rapidly as the world around us changes.

More precisely, projects are becoming more complicated because the systems developed by projects are increasingly more complex and so is the way we develop projects. In this book on project interface management, we provide a systems approach mentality to illustrate strategies for simplifying complexities and complication, such that it can be managed effectively. First, we focus on large-scale capital projects as they tend to fall in categories of higher complication and complexity. With this focus, we are not suggesting that interface management is only applicable to large-scale projects; on the contrary, interface management is applicable to any projects that have explicit or implicit interfaces. However, these large-scale capital projects do provide very good examples to illustrate the concepts in this book to those who may not be familiar with interface management. Clearly, these concepts can also be translated to less complicated and complex projects characterized with a high number of system interfaces and/or a complicated development approach.

1.5.4 Just a Few Words on Benefits Management

We mention benefits management here because, although it has always been necessary, it has only been recognized and practiced widely and explicitly during the past decade or two. Managing strategic benefit starts with opportunity identification and then the establishment of the business case. It is managed throughout the project life cycle and beyond. Surprisingly, many organizations stop measuring at just the time that real benefits begin to accrue. The actual benefits accrue to the sponsor or the end user, but the practice of benefits management has often been relegated to the project management level, where it can't possibly be managed. The likelihood that a project under development continues to promise the strategic benefit for which it was selected is a strategic issue and should be managed at that level. Once the project begins to deliver those actual benefits, assessing and tracking them against strategic expectations belongs to the sponsor or strategic portfolio or program management office, which will own and manage benefits long after the project ends.

Like interface management, benefits management is an emerging discipline. Steve Jenner in *Managing Benefits* defines a benefit as "The *measurable* improvement from change, which is perceived as positive by one or more stakeholders, and which contributes to organizational (including strategic) objectives." He defines benefits management as "the identification, quantification, analysis, planning, tracking, realization, and optimization of benefits" (Jenner, 2014). PMI defines a benefit as "an outcome of actions, behaviors, products, or services that provide utility to the sponsoring organization as well as to the program's intended beneficiaries (PMI, 2013). Levatec says that ". . . benefits are provided to a sponsoring organization *and* to intended beneficiaries; both are worthy of mention" (Levatec, 2014). For the first time, the PMI Pulse of the Profession survey in 2017 looked at levels of *benefits realization maturity* as one of the measures of project success, and stated that "the traditional measures of cost, scope, and time are no longer sufficient" and that it is time for projects to deliver the benefits for which they were selected (PMI, 2017).

As large complex projects sometimes overpromise and under deliver, it is worth noting that we need to be wary of obstacles we face in forecasting, particularly cognitive biases. Lovallo and Kahneman in *Harvard Business Review* argued that forecasters suffer from "delusional optimism: we overemphasize projects' potential and underestimate likely costs, spinning success scenarios while ignoring the possibility of success." Stephen Jenner wrote an excellent article on this subject in the *PM World Journal* (Jenner, 2012). In addition to cognitive bias, it may be wise to be wary of deliberate overstatement of benefits in order to achieve funding for major projects.

1.6 INTRODUCTION TO LARGE-SCALE CAPITAL PROJECTS

The term large-scale capital projects can be quite misleading and open to interpretation. In this book, the term *large-scale capital project* is characterized to mean a project requiring several hundred million, or billions, of U.S. dollars, requiring multiple years for project development and characterized by several organizations or entities contributing to project development. The authors' intention is not to precisely define *exactly* what does or does not constitute *large-scale*, but rather to provide a visual context and allow subjectivity to help categorization. Essentially, these projects tend to cost a considerable amount of money, require a small army of people and organizations to help with development (i.e., several hundred or thousands), and extend in duration over a long period of time (i.e., several years). Large-scale projects are highlighted because they tend to perform poorly as factors contributing to complexity are not well understood and/or not managed effectively.

Merrow identifies special challenges for megaproject teams that include geographic dispersion, integrating joint venture partners that "beg for no one to be in charge," and interface management (Merrow, 2011). In more than thirty years of studying megaprojects, Merrow says, "Most of the big mistakes that companies make in developing and executing these projects stem from a basic lack of being able to pursue a common goal with clarity and good behavior" (Merrow, 2011). Some of these mistakes come from greed, failure to understand who has the risk, failure to shape the opportunity and specify the governing principles of the contract or deal, and inappropriate actions to reduce cost—these projects fail at an "alarming and unsustainable rate." We would add failure to manage interfaces to Merrow's list. Virginia Greiman, who served on Boston's *Big Dig* project as deputy chief counsel and head of risk management, has identified 25 characteristics of megaprojects that go beyond simply long duration and scale, including projects that have a long, complex, and critical front end; complicated financing schemes; dynamic governance structures; and are subject to public scrutiny and/or policymaking, among other factors (Greiman, 2013).

On a brighter note, as reported by the PMI Pulse of the Profession (2017), project performance has improved, but much work remains. The PMI 9th Global Project Management Survey stated, "For the first time in five years, more projects are meeting original goals and business intent and being completed within budget. There has also been a significant decline in dollars lost. Organizations are wasting an average of $97 million for every $1 billion invested due to poor project performance—that's a 20% decline from one year ago" (PMI, 2017). Of the industries included in the study, healthcare reported the highest average waste on project spending. A more detailed breakout of several key industries included in the study, ranked from highest to lowest, demonstrates the range of project waste:

- Healthcare $112 million per $1 billion
- Telecom $106 million per $1 billion
- Energy $101 million per $1 billion
- Manufacturing $98 million per $1 billion
- Government $97 million per $1 billion
- Financial Services $97 million per $1 billion
- Construction $94 million per $1 billion
- IT $78 million per $1 billion

Of the geographic regions covered in the study, PMI noted specific markets stood out. India reported the lowest average monetary waste on projects ($73 million per $1 billion), followed by both China and the Middle East ($82 million per $1 billion). Conversely, Europe reported the highest average waste on project spending at $131 million per $1 billion (PMI, 2017). Many infrastructure projects fall into the *large-scale* project category so we provide some discussion of these in the next section.

1.7 INFRASTRUCTURE EXAMPLES OF LARGE-SCALE COMPLEX PROJECTS

Infrastructure development is an ongoing concern for cities, states, and nations around the world. From wastewater treatment facilities, transportation systems, and major road systems to national electricity grids and telecommunication systems, infrastructure supports and enables all of the comforts and capabilities of the modern lifestyle. Improving and adding to productive infrastructure represents an investment in the future—supporting economic growth and helping to raise living standards over time. Some examples of modern large-scale infrastructure projects are described in the following paragraphs.

1.7.1 California High-Speed Rail

There are numerous ongoing major (large-scale) projects underway around the world. In the United States, the state of California broke ground on the *California High Speed Rail* (CHSR) project in 2015 with an expected first stage development cost of $68 billion, which covers 520 miles between San Francisco and Los Angeles. Ultimately, the CHSR project will extend from Sacramento in the north to San Diego in the south. The system is designed for speeds up to 220 mph and a travel time of three hours from San Francisco to Los Angeles, which is less than half the driving time.

1.7.2 China-Pakistan Economic Corridor Project

The China-Pakistan Economic Corridor is a transportation and energy infrastructure project designed to link Kashgar in western China with Gwadar, a port city in Pakistan. Project plans include the construction of new roads and railways and the upgrade of existing transportation infrastructure. A substantial improvement of the Karakoram Highway, which travels over a 15,000-foot pass at the China-Pakistan border, is underway as of 2016, as are dozens of other transportation projects. China announced $46 billion in foreign direct investment and low-cost loans to bring the corridor to completion since it would provide faster access to markets in South Asia, the Middle East, and Africa.

1.7.3 Riyadh Metro (Rail & Bus) Project

The Riyadh Metro is an urban rail and bus transportation system under construction in Riyadh, Saudi Arabia. Construction began in 2013 and is expected to conclude by the end of 2018. Plans call for six rail lines traveling a combined 109 miles, in addition to a bus line network covering 715 miles. The project is designed to combat rising traffic congestion in a city expected to grow from 5.7 million people in 2014 to 8.2 million by 2030. The system will handle up to 3 million passengers per day. Construction includes 85 air-conditioned stations, 11 bridges, 16 miles of tunnels, and 21 park-and-ride facilities. Three international consortiums are handling the $22.5 billion project's design and construction. Major international firms participating in the project include the German engineering conglomerate, Siemens; the French rail transportation company, Alstom; and the Canadian transportation company, Bombardier. This does not include the complex network of sub-suppliers, vendors, and subcontractors.

1.7.4 Panama Canal Expansion Project

The Panama Canal, one of the most impressive modern infrastructure projects, is a shipping route connecting the Pacific Ocean with the Atlantic Ocean across the Isthmus of Panama. It utilizes a system of locks to raise ships about 85 feet above sea level to the shores of Gatun Lake in the middle of the isthmus. The Panama Canal Authority initiated construction on a $5.25 billion canal expansion project in 2007. The Panama Canal expansion project adds a third traffic lane to the canal and expands some existing canal channels. The new traffic lane and its locks will accommodate larger container ships equipped to carry nearly three times as many containers as the smaller ships, effectively doubling the canal's shipping capacity. The new traffic lane opened for business in 2017.

1.7.5 London *Crossrail* Project

The London *Crossrail* project is a capacity enhancement rail project centered on London. It involves the laying of a new 118 km rail track from Maidenhead and Heathrow in the west to Shenfield and Abbey Wood in the east. The project will allow an additional 1.5 million people to travel between London's key business districts in just 45 minutes. The world's first underground continues to grow, adding 26 miles of tunnel connecting 40 stations for quicker and more direct travel opportunities for travelers. The estimated cost of construction is $23 billion. The project is scheduled for completion in phases, with the first new track going into service in 2018 and all remaining tracks in service by 2020.

1.7.6 Large-Scale (Major) Infrastructure Project Summary

The aforementioned projects are only a small sampling of large-scale or major projects underway across the planet. Infrastructure projects are an example of how complexity affects large-scale projects in general. It's not just the sheer volume of equipment, people, materials, tools, regulations, and such, but the way these elements must interact over a long timeline to ensure various work activities are finished correctly and completely (and, of course, safely). The *Big Dig* project in Boston, formally named the Central Artery Tunnel project that rerouted a formerly elevated interstate highway through a 3.5-mile tunnel, built a bridge over the Charles River, and created a greenway in the space that was left by the former elevated highway, was one of the largest urban infrastructure projects ever undertaken in the United States. It also cost several contractors restitution fees. By its own reckoning, the *Big Dig* was "originally projected to cost $2.5 billion and was to be completed by 1998. Instead, the project cost $14.8 billion and was not completed until 2006" (Greiman, 2013). Nevertheless, it is not only a technical marvel, it has relieved transportation problems for millions in the Boston area, provided a series of parks and public spaces, and made Boston Logan International Airport much more accessible.

Modern railway and other infrastructure projects now incorporate highly advanced safety automation and control systems to ensure safety of operations—such as systems to signal, monitor, and control train operations as well as systems to provide comfort and safety to those using the rail system. These systems include everything from redundant emergency braking systems to efficient air (heat and cooling) systems.

Imagine life as a passenger on a train over 100 years ago that was rife with dangers—from the billowing smoke entering train cars from coal burning engines to trains that broke down constantly or failed to show up on time (or at all). Comfort was an option not afforded on early twentieth century trains, but is something taken for granted on modern rail systems. Modern train travel by comparison allows for a relatively inexpensive, safe, and comfortable method of modern travel. As seen from the infrastructure projects previously mentioned, transport projects continue to improve service, safety, and functionality for future passengers, but this example is recurring in all industries from defense to energy to telecommunications.

1.8 OVERVIEW OF PROJECT DEVELOPMENT STAGE-GATE PROCESS

Large-scale project developments are commonly guided by a deliberate decision-making process that examines the feasibility and progress of the project at specified points through a life cycle from idea to operation and ultimately through disposal. As mentioned, each project moves through a number of phases. For example, a feasibility phase, concept selection phase, evaluation/improve phase, execution phase, operation phase, and decommission and disposal phase. The aim of project development phases is to provide a structured road map to guide the project along its development. At the conclusion of each phase, a decision acts as the mechanism to enter the follow-on (or next) phase. In this way, the organization or project sponsor can evaluate progress, maturity, and continued relevance of a project. Project development processes, characterized by phases and decision points, provide a valuable mechanism to increase the likelihood of success and/or terminate project developments at the earliest point. Projects, especially large-scale developments, require extensive capital investments. Project development processes act as protection for capital investments by ensuring a process to make good decisions at predefined points in the project's development.

Early phases may focus on the feasibility of a particular project idea. During this phase, several concepts may be evaluated to ascertain if undertaking the project would result in value creation for the project sponsor. At the conclusion of the phase, a decision meeting is conducted to determine if the project should progress to the next phase. If successful, the project advances to the next phase, such as the concept selection phase where at the conclusion another decision meeting is performed. This process repeats itself until the project life cycle reaches an end, which may include termination during development or disposal after operation, for example. There are many different project development approaches, but all follow a similar process to the *stage-gate* process for new product development.

Dr. Scott J. Edgett and Dr. Robert G. Cooper developed the Stage-Gate® model to serve as a road map for effectively managing the process of new product development. The Stage-Gate® model is widely used to manage the idea-to-launch process (Cooper, 2011). Although originally devised for new product development, it has been adapted to project management and systems engineering projects across multiple industries, and is, in some circles, considered *de rigueure* for major capital projects. Figure 1.1 shows the Stage-Gate® model with sample phases and decision gates.

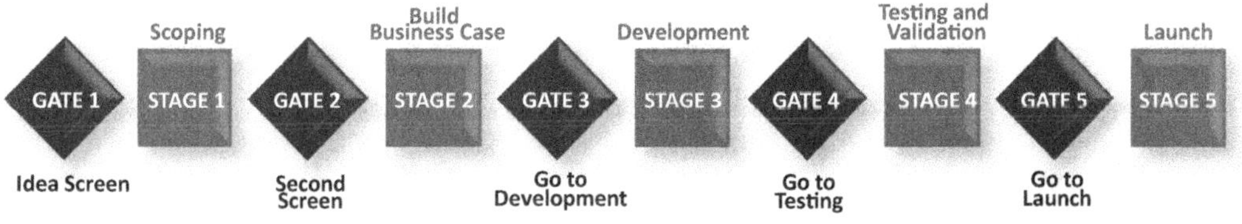

Figure 1.1 Stage-Gate Process. Stage-Gate® is a registered trademark of Stage-Gate Inc. (Used with permission from www.stage-gate.com.)

In the Stage-Gate® model, Dr. Edgett and Dr. Cooper describe a number of stages including: discovery (Stage 0), which is not shown; scoping (Stage 1); building the business case (Stage 2); development (Stage 3); test and validation (Stage 4); and launch (Stage 5). Between the stages, management decision points (gates) are established. Stages are where the action occurs and deliverables are developed. These deliverables then act as input to the decision-making process—at the decision gates—where the deliverables are measured against criteria; resulting in a decision output (i.e., go/no-go, hold, recycle, etc.).

The types of project development processes can vary between industries and between organizations within a specific industry. The choice of project development approach and the underlying project development process will affect a project's development in a good or not-so-good manner. Some development models may impose strict and expansive requirements that need to be met for each gate. Others may view such requirements as overly bureaucratic. Some project development processes may not provide sufficient structure, allowing for excessive free-form activity that could create problems with delayed manifestation later in the development process.

1.8.1 U.S. Department of Defense Project Development Example

Arguably, one of the most complex project development processes exists within the U.S. Department of Defense (DoD) to guide the department's system acquisition process. An overview of the process is illustrated in Figure 1.2, but a more comprehensive view of the process can be found at the DAU website (https://www.dau.mil/tools/t/Department-of-Defense-Acquisition-Life-Cycle-Chart). Granted, the DoD highly encourages tailoring the process for the specific nature of the project, but with such an expansive development framework, even the process of tailoring can be difficult. The

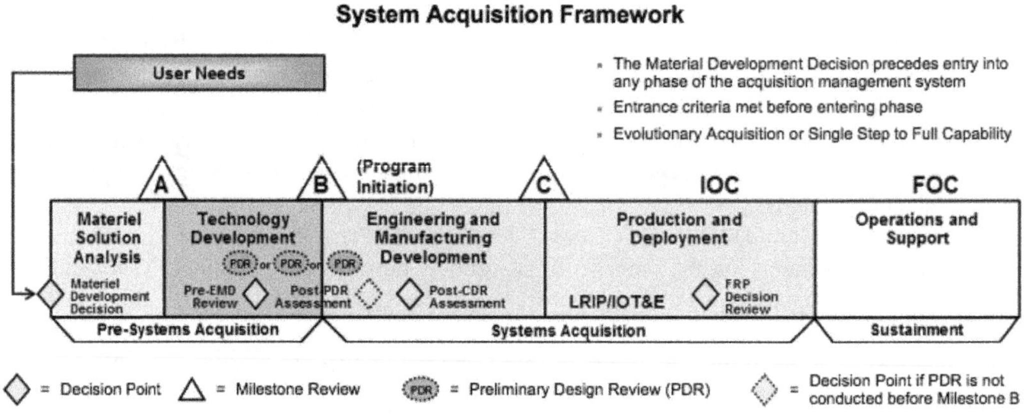

Figure 1.2 U.S. DoD *System Acquisition Framework*

DoD's *System Acquisition Framework* divides the acquisition process into *Pre-System Acquisition*, consisting of two phases (Material Solution Analysis and Technology Development), then System Acquisition (consisting of Engineering and Manufacture Development and Production System Deployment) and on to Sustainment (consisting of Operations and Support phases). *Milestones A, B, and C* act as *gates* between early phases with specific *decision points* embedded within the phases.

A deeper examination of the *System Acquisition Framework* reveals a network of stringent guidance requirements within each phase, including mandatory technical activities, major deliverables/products, inputs and outputs, etc. Many of the systems acquired by the DoD must integrate into an existing mission-oriented architecture, creating a maze of system interfaces between the system being acquired and the existing architecture with which the system is to be integrated.

1.8.2 Oil and Gas Industry Project Development Example

In comparison to the U.S. DoD System Acquisition Framework, a typical oil and gas project development process shown in Figure 1.3 seems quite basic and follows a less complicated project development approach. As is the case with the DoD's acquisition framework model, the oil and gas industry's project development process follows a prescribed path while providing management decision points before the start of each phase.

In a typical oil and gas project development, the *appraise* phase begins with a hydrocarbon discovery. This phase screens identified options for technical and commercial viability and establishes

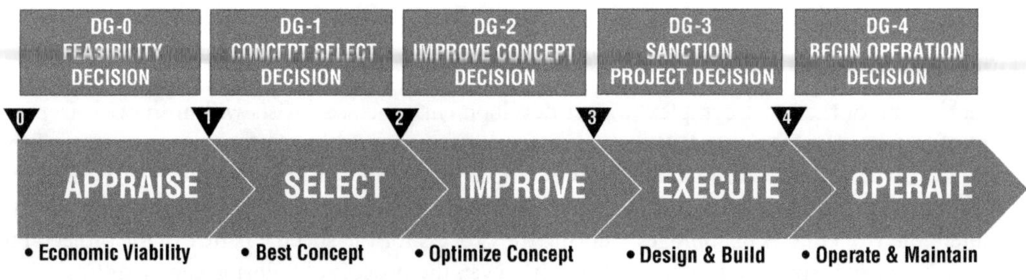

Figure 1.3 Oil and gas project development approach example

a short list of options to be advanced to the next stage. As the project continues to advance through the development process, the system concept matures. At decision gate DG3, the decision can be made to sanction the project and begin development. This phase can be the most time consuming and expensive, as it entails engineering, procurement, construction, transportation and installation, mechanical completion offshore, and commissioning (i.e., system verification and validation) in preparation for decision gate DG4 to put the system into production.

We show these project development phases and frameworks to indicate how the project progresses from an idea toward a stage at which it matures sufficiently that a decision can be made to develop the project (or, in the U.S. DoD's case, a program). When a project or program is sanctioned at DG3 for oil and gas (Milestone B for the U.S. DoD), this represents the stage at which the project as an *idea* begins the process of translating into an actual project result or *system*. After this decision gate, project execution or project development begins. Embedded within the project development process, systems engineering (SE) plays a vital role in structuring how the work will progress throughout the development process.

Also throughout the development process, projects require a systematic approach that focuses on how the work is being performed. The SE process is a key resource supporting project management and ensuring that modern systems are designed and developed correctly. By *correctly*, the authors mean in compliance with the governing regulations, codes, and standards while ensuring technical integrity of the system throughout development and integration of the system into the existing infrastructure, thus delivering a system that is safe to operate while meeting the needs of those who use it.

1.9 INTRODUCTION TO SYSTEMS ENGINEERING

Whereas project management is about *what* work needs to be completed, SE focuses on *how* to accomplish the technical work while maintaining a holistic perspective. SE is a key component of the work and activities that occur between the stage gates. As stated by the International Council on Systems Engineering (INCOSE): "Systems engineering is a discipline that concentrates on the design and application of the whole (system) as distinct from the parts. It involves looking at a problem in its entirety, taking into account all the facets and all the variables and relating the social to the technical aspect. Systems engineering is an iterative process of top-down synthesis, development, and operations of a real-world system that satisfies, in a near optimal manner, the full range of requirements... Systems engineering is an interdisciplinary approach and means to enable the realization of successful systems. It focuses on defining customer needs and required functionality early in the development cycle, documenting requirements, and then proceeding with design synthesis and system validation while considering the complete problem: operations, cost and schedule, performance, training and support, test, manufacturing, and disposal... Systems engineering considers both the business and the technical needs of all customers with the goal of providing a quality product that meets the user needs... Certain keywords emerge from this definition description including: interdisciplinary, iterative, socio-technical, and wholeness" (INCOSE, 2015). INCOSE describes SE as a process and a perspective as well as a profession.

The SE perspective is based on *systems thinking*, which "occurs through discovery, learning, and dialog; leading to sensing, modeling, and talking about the real-world in order to understand, define, and work with systems" (INCOSE, 2015). *Systems thinking* is a perspective and an awareness of the *whole system* and how parts within that system interrelate and the interrelationships between elements within the system as well as between the system and external systems. The SE process has an iterative nature that supports learning and continuous improvement. As the processes unfold, systems engineers uncover the real requirements and "the emergent properties of the system" (INCOSE,

2015). Complexity can lead to unexpected and unpredictable behavior of systems; hence, one of the objectives is to minimize undesirable consequences. This is accomplished by including and seeking contributions from experts across relevant disciplines coordinated by the systems engineer. Since SE has a horizontal orientation, the discipline (profession) includes both technical and management processes. Both processes depend upon good decision making. Decisions made early in the life cycle of a system, whose consequences are not clearly understood, can have enormous implications later in the life of a system. It is the task of the systems engineer to explore these issues and work to resolve these uncertainties as early as possible in project development.

1.9.1 Use of Systems Engineering

The SE discipline, working in unison with project management, has emerged as an effective way to manage project complexity and change. As both complexity and change continue to escalate in our products, services, and society, reducing the risk associated with new systems or modifications to complex systems continues to be a primary goal of SE. Every system life cycle consists of the business aspect (business case), the budget aspect (funding), and the technical aspect (product). SE creates technical solutions that are consistent with the business case and the funding constraints. Yet, system integrity requires that these three aspects be in balance and given equal emphasis at all decision gate reviews.

Whenever someone, whether an individual or an organization, desires to achieve a result, they must perform a series of actions and operations—not just randomly; these actions and operations must be performed in a mandatory order (considering their dependencies), who will be performing them, and what tools and techniques will be used. Because they want a specific result, individuals and organizations follow processes, whether predefined or ad hoc. Just as each project is unique from every other project to some degree, so too will the processes that are used to develop the project's *result*. Because these process components (activities, tools, sequence, etc.) and their interactions (information flow, artifact flow, communication, timing, and such) can vary, processes will differ even if being performed by organizations with the same goal.

In large-scale projects, mistakes made early in project development can ripple through later project phases (e.g., from engineering to procurement and construction) if not detected and corrected. SE, in unison with project management, provides the foundation for understanding what needs to be accomplished in order to deliver the project result and also how it should be accomplished to ensure minimal errors of commission and omission throughout the project development process. In SE, the technical processes enable systems engineers to coordinate the interactions between engineering specialists, project management functions, system stakeholders, operations, and other interested parties. These processes also address conformance with expectations and regulatory requirements of industries, governments, and others. Ultimately, SE technical processes lead to the creation of a full set of requirements (user and regulatory) that address the desired capabilities and functions for a specific system within the bounds of design constraints, performance, external interfaces, and the environment.

1.9.2 Project Management and Systems Engineering Combined

The combination of project management and SE provides powerful mechanisms to understand and effectively manage large-scale project developments. Even so, project development results in a web of highly complicated interactions among the parties who are contributing to the project result. As we've seen, modern projects rely on many geographically dispersed organizations with specialized knowledge, experience, competencies, technologies, and materials to contribute to highly complex system developments. These organizations are expected to contribute their respective deliveries at the right time to be integrated with other deliveries and assembled in a predefined sequence. Along the process, thousands or millions of details are coordinated through a variety of interactions across multiple communication channels, from formal to informal. The laws of probability suggest that something will go wrong, resulting in more work, extra time, and more cost than planned. However, project management and SE provide the foundation of structure and organization; they are emplaced together to lead, manage, control, and of course, produce the complex systems that are the purpose of major project development.

1.10 DESIGNING AND DEVELOPING COMPLEX SYSTEMS

Every project is undertaken to produce a result. The infrastructure projects presented earlier are examples of systems produced by large-scale projects. However, each of these systems created by the infrastructure projects consists of several different subsystems, components, logics (signals), etc. In essence, each of these systems has a hierarchy within the system. It is normal to think of a project as a stand-alone entity with no connection to the outside world. As evidenced by the previous infrastructure project examples, modern projects are typically integrated as part of an existing system architecture, or part of an urban landscape, or part of a transport network.

For example, a new offshore oil and gas processing facility off the coast of Norway will be integrated into existing subsea transportation lines or connected to surface transportation systems to move hydrocarbons from the point of recovery to global markets. Large wind farms need to be connected to existing power infrastructure architectures in order to deliver the power they create. New airplane development projects need to be integrated into existing air transportation networks and hubs. These *supersystems* also undergo routine upgrades and modifications, resulting in a trickle-down effect on the systems with which they interact or connect. Project development durations of several years increase the challenges of designing a system and integrating it with an existing architecture, especially one that may have undergone updates and changes during the development of the new project.

It is common in some industries to undertake multiple concurrent projects which are to be integrated with one another and need to finish at or near the same time. Parallel projects may or may not have the same sponsor; if they do not, the span of control over integration of the various project systems is more complicated. In the oil and gas industry, it is quite normal for one offshore field development project to integrate into the field development of another company. Naturally, the benefit is the reuse of the existing offshore subsea infrastructure to transport newly discovered hydrocarbons along an existing pipeline network. However, this requires the project team of one project to coordinate closely with the team of the other project to ensure smooth integration, thus increasing project management and SE complexity. Emerging problems within one project can quickly become the problem of the other project; potentially resulting in commercial and legal consequences. In an ever-connected and technologically advanced society with rapidly evolving conveniences, modern project design and development are difficult to manage (and are arguably impossible to control).

What then is the fate of future projects given the accelerating pace of change observed over the last fifty years? No one can predict the future, although some suggest otherwise, but it is possible to make reasonable inferences about the future based on trends over the last few decades. If the recent past is any indication, it is reasonable to suggest that, technologically, we will continue to advance in an effort to address existing and expected future challenges for a burgeoning global population. Growing and shifting populations will require more food, energy, infrastructure, health services, and protection. People are likely to further explore opportunities for efficiency, economy, capacity, and capabilities; the projects they spawn will continue the trend to capitalize on open markets and availability of global suppliers and vendors. Technology will continue to be a large part of increasing product capability and functionality; the need for sustainability will hopefully minimize the impact on natural resources and the environment. In essence, projects will continue the trend of producing increasingly complex systems through more complicated project developments. Project sponsors will continue to make selecting the most economical development approach a primary consideration. In essence, the intensity of change is likely to persist; continuing to make the delivery of systems created by projects more difficult. Our management processes must keep pace with—and harness—what is technologically possible.

1.11 COMMERCIAL CONTRACTING DECISIONS AND FACTORS INFLUENCING PROJECTS

At the heart of every sanctioned project are the capital investment costs (CAPEX) that are required in order to develop a project. Obviously, every project sponsor desires to minimize the CAPEX while achieving maximum return on investment (i.e., maximum value creation). Regardless of industry, this results in many creative commercial arrangements and strategies. When sanctioning a major capital project, the project sponsor (owner) must select a basic contracting strategy for developing the project. This strategy has two key components: (1) types of contracts and (2) how the project scope will be delivered.

Rarely does a single organization have sufficient resources to undertake a major project and deliver the entire scope itself. Various approaches exist—and for good reason: the choice of contracting approach can and will affect the outcome of the project. The commercial strategy must be selected with careful consideration not only for the potential upside of the approach (i.e., opportunities), but with consideration of the risk and appreciation of the demands that each strategy places on the owner's organization. Any contracting strategy, of course, can result in undesirable consequences if it is selected without the necessary resources in place and if the assumptions about the strategy are invalid. The appropriate approach to produce optimal results will be different depending on the structure and culture of the owner organization and the specific circumstances of a given project. The approach that produces favorable results for one owner could be problematic for another.

1.11.1 Types of Contracts

The type of contracts to be used for developing the project is largely dependent upon the degree of certainty of the scope of work; that is, how well the scope of work is understood, complete, and clear. When the client is certain of the scope of work, the client may shift more risk to the contractor, who may be willing to accept the risk because much of the scope uncertainty is removed. When the scope of work to be performed is more uncertain, the project sponsor is usually more willing to assume risk and the contractor will likely seek protection from that uncertainty. Obviously, this affects the type of contract the project sponsor can reasonably use.

1.11.1.1 Fixed Price Contract

A fixed price contract is used when the scope of work is well understood and clearly defined. In essence, prospective contractors submit bids as an all-inclusive *fixed* price to deliver the scope of work. By requesting and submitting a fixed price, both the client and contractor have high confidence in the work that needs to be completed and the scope is not expected to change. When a scope of work is clearly defined and well-understood, the risk to the contractor is (relatively) low. By submitting a fixed-price bid, the contractor is expressing its relative certainty of ability to deliver the scope of work on time and to quality expectations. Changes can be made to the scope of work, but this results in increased costs. However, in large-scale projects, precisely defining every aspect of the project scope can be a daunting task and other types of contracts may be used. Although we continue to derive deterministic schedule and cost estimates for large-scale complex projects, in reality, we'd be better served to use stochastic cost and schedule (ranges with probabilities) as many new product organizations do. An unusually naïve client may believe that he is shifting risk to the contractor by using a fixed price, but its use in the wrong circumstance has come back to bite many a client.

1.11.1.2 Cost Reimbursable

Cost reimbursable contracts are used when the scope of work is less understood or less precisely defined. In large-scale projects that require significant engineering activity, a cost reimbursable contract is often used. The engineering process by nature is an *iterative* process. That is, work is performed and checked, which results in input to improve the design. This then results in another engineering iteration until the design matures such that it is compliant with regulatory and user requirements. As expected, this is usually not a preferred contract method for the project sponsor since the sponsor assumes the cost risk. The lack of scope definition can easily result in a never-ending cycle of work, resulting in cost overruns, or at least larger costs than the sponsor had anticipated. In some situations this cannot be avoided, but in nearly all cases it is better to have a fully defined and well understood scope. From a practical matter, reimbursable contracts are more difficult to plan than fixed price contracts.

1.11.1.3 Cost Plus Incentive Fee

Since the scope of work may not be well-defined and understood, how can an organization plan and schedule activities when they are not certain what the end result is to be, what the activities will be, or how much effort they will require? Of course, the answer is that they cannot schedule with any certainty. In these cases, the result is often a dynamic schedule that changes routinely. It is normal for project sponsors to add financial *incentives* to these types of contracts to lessen this risk. These incentives are intended as motivation for the contractor to finish the work as quickly as possible. In principle, the contractor receives a financial incentive payment for completing certain amounts of work. In some cases, without a trusting relationship, the contractor may be more motivated to continue the reimbursable work than to collect the incentive and it is for this reason these types of contracts can be quite costly for the project sponsor if not managed carefully.

As we will discuss in upcoming sections, these contracts can also have a ripple effect on other contracts when the project sponsor elects to use a multiple contractor approach to deliver the project scope of work. This is the second aspect of the contract strategy, deciding how the scope of work will be delivered.

1.11.2 Multiple Contractors versus *Turnkey*

Combined with the types of contracts, the project sponsor also needs to decide whether the entire scope will be awarded to a single organization or if the scope will be subdivided and contracted to several parties. A multiple contract approach may divide the scope (i.e., *parcels*) into a few or many contracts. A client may choose this option when: (1) at least some parts of the project scope are well defined, (2) the client wants to take advantage of specialized capabilities, competencies, and skills, or (3) the client wants to obtain economic benefits afforded by the availability of many vendors and suppliers, or in other words, is looking for the lowest price among many qualified offerers.

As mentioned, the opening of the global marketplace has increased the availability of vendors, suppliers, and manufacturers, creating a virtual global supermarket for project sponsors. More contracts increase the owner's opportunity to save cost but also increases the owner's risk with respect to project integration. The multiple contractor approach allows the owner to leverage specialty firms with rare or critical competencies. It also allows the client to segment out the project scope so that it provides the least risk and best economic opportunities. However, segmenting the scope to many parties creates *interdependencies* between the scopes that need to be managed proactively to prevent late-stage development problems, which seem to be ever present in modern projects. When segmenting the scope to multiple contractors, the only contractual relationship is with the owner, and not between the contractors in most cases. That means that any implied interfaces usually are not explicitly specified in the scope of work for the contractors. Of course, how to manage that will be discussed in detail later in the book.

With a *turnkey* approach, the entire scope is provided by a single contractor on a *turnkey* basis and is seemingly straightforward. After award, the contractor develops a complete facility that requires the owner only to metaphorically *turn the key* and operate it. The contractor's scope is some form of EPC. In a turnkey approach, the project sponsor limits its options to the capabilities and competencies resident within the turnkey firm and any subcontractors it may obtain. A turnkey approach using a reimbursable contract, where the scope is not well defined, may be less beneficial as subdividing the scope into parcels and contracting some of the better-defined scope as fixed price; limiting the reimbursable to only those areas with uncertain scope. These are the types of trade-off the project sponsor will make in determining the optimal contract strategy.

1.11.3 Multiple Contractors, Multiple Contract Types

Regardless of approach, the contract strategy is an important element to project interface management. Certainly, the architecture of the system to be developed by the project is an important consideration (and will be discussed in more depth later in the book), but the parties responsible for the scope and the types of contracts are equally relevant. Arguably, one of the more popular contract strategies is to use multiple contractors and multiple contract types. From a client perspective, this can provide the optimal strategy in terms of minimizing capital investments and risk. As mentioned earlier, it is normal for parts of the project scope to be well understood and defined. It is natural to select a fixed price contract for this scope and advertise to the global marketplace. Typically, this results in a lower price for those segments of the work. For those parts of the scope that are less understood or for which the scope cannot be precisely defined, the client can use a reimbursable contract, but still has the option of opening the competition to global vendors and suppliers. In such cases, the client reaps the economic and risk benefits of both types of contracts.

Unfortunately, there is a key aspect of this strategy that is usually not well addressed. When undertaking an approach that uses multiple contractors with both fixed and reimbursable contracts, it is quite normal for the interdependencies among the different contractors to become challenging. On the one hand, the contractors with fixed price contracts understand their work quite well. This leads to a stable schedule and fixed price. On the other hand, the contractors with reimbursable contracts are less certain of the work they need to complete, which leads to a dynamic schedule that tends to change rapidly and to costs that are less well-known. As the work commences, if there are high levels of interdependency between fixed and reimbursable contracts, then it is challenging to align delivery of the interdependencies, resulting in problems for both parties. Even though the contractor with the fixed price understands the work that must be performed, this contractor can be dependent upon inputs from other parties, including those with reimbursable contracts. The contractor with the reimbursable contract may not be able to provide the material or information to other parties when needed. In fact, this contractor may not even be able to say when it can provide the material or information.

These types of situations are often, even typically, not considered as part of the contract strategy as the cost associated with the individual contracts tends to be the selection driver. But these challenges may be suboptimizing and will likely add to the complexity of the project and delivery of the scope of work necessary to complete the system or project result. From an interface management perspective, knowledge of the organization's strategy, its project development process, and the system to be developed by the project are key inputs to devising not only a contract strategy, but a project interface management system.

1.12 CONCLUSION

The accelerating pace of societal change has driven demand for increasingly complex products and services, which, in turn, have driven the rise of project-oriented organizations. Over the last 500 years (half a millennium!), mankind has experienced an explosion of change. Growing populations, technological advances, and opening of markets are only a few of the factors contributing to significant and rapid change that is affecting all parts of society. Regardless of individual views for or against the changes experienced in modern society, it has occurred, and there are no indications that this trend will subside. In fact, it is reasonable to expect the rate of change to continue to increase if the past 500 years or even the past 50 years are any indication.

Projects are becoming increasingly more difficult as development approaches become more complicated by the availability of globally dispersed vendors and suppliers and ever-increasing regulatory demands. In addition, systems created by projects are characterized by increasing complexity resulting from advancing technology to improve system efficiency, capabilities, and functionality. Whereas society is struggling with the rate of change, project environments are becoming increasingly complex and project professionals are struggling to adapt to how this change is affecting the systems developed by projects. As technology becomes geometrically more capable, we need to address how our management systems can keep pace. One of those critical emerging management systems to address complexity is interface management.

In Chapter 2, we set the stage for stakeholder and interface management by defining complexity and discussing how it affects project and technical management. This is one of the most important factors when considering project interface management. Since most large-scale projects involve multiple entities within and beyond the project scope early in project planning, the next chapter also addresses managing stakeholder complexity and using stakeholder analysis as a means of aligning the actors who are associated either directly or indirectly with the project, along with their needs and requirements. The result of this analysis will directly feed the interface management processes addressed in later chapters.

1.13 REFERENCES

Bible, M. J. and S. S. Bivins. (2011). *Mastering Project Portfolio Management.* J. Ross Publishing, Inc., Fort Lauderdale, FL.

Cooper, R. G. (2011). *Winning at New Products: Creating Value through Innovation,* Fourth Edition. Basic Books of Perseus Books Group, Philadelphia, PA.

Cooper, R. G., S. J. Edgett, and E. J. Kleinschmidt (2001). *Portfolio Management for New Products,* Second Edition. Basic Books of Perseus Books Group, Philadelphia, PA.

Defense Acquisition University (DAU) website. Retrieved 01/23/2010 from http://www.dau.mil/default.aspx.

DifferenceBetween.net. (2011). "Difference between Paleolithic and Neolithic." Retrieved from http://www.diffen.com/difference/Neolithic_vs_Paleolithic.

Editors of Encyclopedia Britannica. "Iron Age." *Encyclopedia Britannica.* (2015). Retrieved from https://www.britannica.com/event/Iron-Age.

Gale, R. M. (1971). 'The Fictive Use of Language.' *Philosophy,* 46(178), pp. 324–340. doi: 10.1017/S003181910001696X.

Gascoigne, Bamber. History World. From 2001, ongoing. http://www.historyworld.net.

Greiman, V. A. (2013). *Megaproject Management—Lessons on Risk and Project Management from the Big Dig.* John Wiley & Sons, Inc., Hoboken, NJ.

Harari, N. H. (2015). Sapiens, U.S. Edition. Harper Collins, New York, NY.

INCOSE. 2015. *Systems Engineering Handbook: A Guide for System Life Cycle Processes and Activities*, version 4.0. John Wiley & Sons, Inc., Hoboken, NJ.

Jenner, S. (2014). *Managing Benefits*, Second Edition. APMG International, High Wycombe, UK.

Jenner, S. (2012). "Benefits realization—building on (un)safe foundations or planning for success?" *PM World Journal*, Vol. 1, Issue 1, July, 2012.

Kerzner, H. (2017). *Project Management: A Systems Approach to Planning, Scheduling and Controlling*, Twelfth Edition. John Wiley & Sons, Inc., Hoboken, NJ.

Kulper, Kathleen. "Bronze Age." *Encyclopedia Britannica.* (2015). Retrieved from https://www.britannica.com/event/Bronze-Age.

Levatec, C. J. (2014). *Strategic Benefits Realization.* J. Ross Publishing, Inc., Plantation, FL.

Levine, Harvey A. (2005). *Project Portfolio Management: A Practical Guide to Selecting Projects, Managing Portfolios, and Maximizing Benefits.* Jossey-Bass Business and Management Series, San Francisco, CA.

Lovallo, D. and D. Kahneman. (2003). "Delusions of Success: How Optimism Undermines Executives' Decisions," *Harvard Business Review*, July, 2003.

Meredith, J. R. and S. J. Mantel. (2006). *Project Management—A Managerial Approach*, Sixth Edition. John Wiley & Sons, Inc., Hoboken, NJ.

Merrow, E. W. (2011). *Industrial Megaprojects—Concepts, Strategies, and Practices for Success.* John Wiley & Sons, Inc., Hoboken, NJ.

Metropolitan Museum of Art. (2017). Heilbrunn Timeline of Art History, New York, NY. Retrieved from http://www.metmuseum.org/toah/hd/shzh/hd_shzh.htm.

Project Management Institute (PMI). (2008). *The Standard for Portfolio Management*, Second Edition, ANSI / PMI 08-003-2008.

Project Management Institute (PMI). (2013). *The Standard for Program Management*, Third Edition, PMI, Inc., Newtown Square, PA.

Project Management Institute (PMI). (2017). Success Rates Rise. Transforming the High Cost of Low Performance. Pulse of the Profession. 9th Global Project Management Survey.

Thomsen, C. J. (1836). *Ledetraad til Nordisk Oldkundskab* (Guide to Northern Antiquity), published in English in 1848.

Urbanick, Janice. (2008). "Strategic Planning Essentials for Construction and Design Firms." Retrieved from http://www.nawic.org/images/nawic/stratplanningess.pdf.

This book has free material available for download from the Web Added Value™ resource center at *www.jrosspub.com*

2

Understanding Project Complexity

"The art of simplicity is a puzzle of complexity."
—Douglas Horton

The aim of interface management is to *simplify complicated interactions on complex capital projects.* Capital projects are becoming larger in size and scale with increasing involvement from external entities, making them more difficult to manage and control. It is then natural to ask, "What is project complexity? How do we define it, and ultimately, how do we simplify it?" In this chapter, we discuss project complexity and the factors driving this complexity. This is an important chapter in the book because it forms the basis for obtaining situational awareness of a respective project and applying the critical thinking necessary to perform the interface analysis and management processes described in later chapters. Project circumstances and characteristics provide the basis for determining the appropriate managerial actions required to complete a project successfully. Complexity is one such critical project dimension (Baccarini, 1996), but we need to understand what complexity is in order to simplify it.

"In some ways, complexity is rather like love: Everybody has experiences of it and knows what it is, but ask them to define precisely what they mean by it and you will end up with a broad range of definitions" (Cooke-Davies, 2011). Bennett (1991) observes that practitioners frequently describe their projects as simple or complex when they are discussing management issues, indicating a practical acceptance that complexity makes a difference in managing projects. It is not surprising then that complex projects demand an exceptional level of management. This is especially true when considering the application of conventional management systems developed for ordinary projects were found to be inappropriate for complex projects (Morris and Hough, 1986).

The International Council on Systems Engineering's (INCOSE) Complex Systems Working Group focuses on the challenges and opportunities presented by complex systems with large numbers of components with even greater numbers of interactions distributed in scope across multiple scales and/or across large areas. The working group notes that "complexity is a characteristic of more than just a technical system being developed. The socio-technical ecosystem in which a system under development will be employed exhibits these attributes, as does the environment that gave rise to the challenge or opportunity to which the system was developed in response. Further, the design and development of technical systems is a complex endeavor itself" (INCOSE Complex Systems Working Group, 2016). These statements begin to express the relationships among the system being developed, which is complex; the project management system emplaced to oversee the work of the project; and the project's external environment, which is certainly littered with stakeholders of varying power and influence with specific and often conflicting needs and requirements.

We start by defining complexity and then discuss factors contributing to project complexity in order to provide a context for the application of interface analysis and management, which is described later. The underlying rationale for applying interface management is to address complexity resulting from interfaces, interdependencies, and interactions among various entities and systems; it is necessary to discuss these factors and their contribution to project complexity in order to understand the desired outcome of performing interface analysis and management. It will be evident to the reader that project complexity is largely the result of an expansive web of interfaces and interdependencies between system elements (i.e., subsystems, components, etc.). One aspect of complexity is the interaction among various independent entities, including both the entities responsible for delivering parts of the project scope and those entities beyond the project's discrete scope boundary that can influence the project and the system being developed by the project. In addition to interaction, two other aspects of complexity are interfaces and interdependencies. It is important to differentiate among these three aspects of complexity, and understand how controlling each aspect helps to simplify project complexity, and thus reduces the chances of experiencing problems that can negatively affect project execution and delivery.

2.1 DEFINING COMPLEXITY

For many people, the term *complexity* can be difficult to visualize or explain and is open to wide and diverse interpretation. Merriam-Webster's Learner's dictionary definition of complexity is described as "the quality or state of not being simple: the quality or state of being complex. A part of something that is complicated or hard to understand." Evident in this definition is the subjective interpretation. What one person may find complex may be simple to another. Thus, this definition does not allow for a uniform understanding of when something is, or is not, complex. Baccarini (1996) provides two explanations of complexity and the first reinforces this contention.

In the first explanation, Baccarini (1996) describes complexity as "complicated, involved, and intricate." Again, this description of complexity is subjective, open to wide and diverse interpretation. It implies difficulty in understanding and dealing with an object at least in the eyes of some observers. Such a subjective measure of complexity has been found to be an unreliable basis for research analysis (Rowlinson, 1988)—in part because it doesn't enable a clear and common understanding of factors contributing to complexity. So, although this definition of complexity cannot be considered invalid, it does not provide a firm basis for the formulation of a concise and consistent standard.

In the second explanation, Baccarini identifies two types of complexity—organizational complexity and technological complexity—and describes project complexity as the association between the two types in terms of *differentiation* (the number of varied elements, such as tasks, specialists, or components) and *interdependency or connectivity* (the degree of interrelatedness between these elements). With this explanation, it becomes possible to classify the kind of complexity to be managed and to begin quantifying complexity in terms of the number of entities, their relationships, the amount of interaction needed between the parties, interfaces, or connection points between systems, subsystems, components, and elements, and so on. In this way, factors contributing to complexity can become measurable and manageable.

There is another practical way of thinking about complexity and determining whether a project or system is *complicated* or *complex*. One could describe a project or a system as complicated when it has large numbers of interconnections and interdependent parts, whereas complex means something more. Complexity implies that changes in one part of the project or system can impact other parts of the project or system. "A project or system is said to be complex if it contains many interdependent parts, each of which can change in ways that are not predictable, and which can then have unpredictable impacts on other elements that are themselves capable of change" (Cooke-Davies,

2011). So, this means we can evaluate the existence of complexity by assessing interdependencies within a project or system and the potential for unpredictable change.

For example, when comparing the development of a single simple component from a single entity using simple technology to the development of a system comprised of many subsystems that are comprised of thousands of different components from hundreds of entities and new cutting-edge technology, it is reasonable to assume higher complexity from the latter because we know that there are interfaces between various components, subsystems, and elements resulting in interdependencies among these elements, which require interactions among the various entities providing these elements.

In a *Harvard Business Review* article, Sargut and McGrath (2011) distinguish between complicated systems and complex systems by stating that "complicated systems have many moving parts, but they operate in patterned ways . . . It's possible to make accurate predictions about how a complicated system will behave." In the article, they distinguish the complicated from the complex by stating that "the main difference between complicated and complex systems is that with the former, one can usually predict outcomes by knowing the starting conditions," while with a complex system, "the same starting conditions can produce different outcomes, depending on interactions of the elements in the system." They go on to say "it's possible to understand . . . (simple and) complicated systems by identifying and modeling the relationships between the parts; the relationships can be reduced to clear, predictable interactions" (Sargut and McGrath, 2011). They use flying a commercial aircraft as an example of a complicated system because it involves "complicated, but predictable steps." What the pilot does with the controls usually has a predictable outcome.

On the other hand, Sargut and McGrath state, "complex systems . . . are imbued with features that may operate in patterned ways but whose interactions are continually changing." Sargut and McGrath further state that with complex systems, "all the elements are interacting continuously and unpredictably." Sargut and McGrath point to air traffic control as a complex system because it is always changing in reaction to weather, aircraft composition, traffic density, and other factors. What makes an air traffic control system's behavior predictable at all is that the system was designed to react and change as various conditions and components interact with one another (Sargut and McGrath, 2011).

According to John Kamensky of the IBM Center for The Business of Government, "Understanding the difference between a complicated problem and a complex one is important for today's leaders. They require different strategies and tools that are largely not interchangeable" (Kamensky, 2011). Using Sargut's and McGrath's differentiators, Kamensky provides an example of a complicated project: building a highway (predictable outcome when one knows the starting conditions); whereas managing urban traffic congestion is a complex project (different outcomes even with the same starting conditions due to interactions among the elements of the system). He recommends, as do Sargut and McGrath, several mechanisms to help teams and managers cope with the high ambiguity and uncertainty inherent in complex projects, including improved forecasting methods, better risk mitigation strategies, improved ability to weigh alternatives with imperfect information, and diversity of points of view when making decisions (Kamensky, 2011). A major element of all of these, especially better risk mitigation on complex projects is, of course, the effective management of interfaces.

Perhaps a very important factor in describing and managing complexity is the concept of emergence. "Emergence is . . . the opposite of reduction. The latter (reduction) tries to move from the whole to the parts. . . . The former (emergence) tries to generate the properties of the whole from an understanding of the parts" (Morowitz, 2002). It seems that reduction, or decomposition, has been a bastion of engineering and project management for a long time—think work breakdown structure: breaking the project down hierarchically and managing and measuring progress on the individual parts to make the whole of the project more manageable. Emergence, on the other hand, is currently a focus of studies of complexity. It is often impossible to predict the behavior of the whole by assessing the sum of its parts—think of the brilliantly beautiful but seemingly unpredictable murmuration of a flock of starlings. The behavior is much more than the sum of the individual birds in flight; likewise, how the human brain works is much more than the sum of the cells comprising it. Although a discussion of emergence is beyond the scope of this book, many complex projects have emergent properties. As project managers and systems engineers, we have much to learn in order to lead or design such complex projects to create productive outcomes.

From a management perspective, our perception of complexity and the factors driving complexity will affect our decisions and the management systems we choose to employ to control complexity factors. This is the challenge in large-scale complex projects where complexity drivers can take many forms and will vary from one project to another. If a project, or the system under development by the project, contains a substantial amount of complexity, then it is also likely to have aspects that need management in ways that extend beyond the traditional tools and techniques of project management. In such cases, it is necessary to begin identifying and understanding factors that are contributing to complexity and "designing complexity out of the project as far as possible" (Cooke-Davies, 2011). Remember, a project is a ". . . temporary endeavor undertaken to create a unique product, service, or result" (PMI, 2013)—and there are many dimensions and factors driving project complexity.

2.2 INFLUENCE OF COMPLEXITY ON PROJECT AND TECHNICAL MANAGEMENT

Understanding the factors contributing to complexity plays a vital role in project management and systems engineering (SE) (technical) management. Increased complexity and rapid changes make the governance of projects increasingly challenging. Complexity in this context includes external complexities such as stakeholder relationships, decision-making processes, and internal complexities such as technology and interfaces within and between systems (Williams et al., 2012). For every project, critical thinking and analysis needs to be applied to obtain situational awareness of the project and its context in order to fully understand complexity factors affecting the project and thence to determine appropriate processes, procedures, methods, and systems to manage and control the project.

There is widespread agreement among SE and project management practitioners that one factor that makes projects complex is the interaction of human beings who have their own roles, responsibilities, and objectives and are faced with making complex decisions. Thus, complexity occurs when people with different interests, loyalties, cultures, and interactions with one another are put together to deliver a particular project or program.

In simple terms, the larger the number of members on a team and the larger the number of teams involved in developing and delivering a project, the greater the likelihood of complexity affecting the project. In large projects that involve many teams, the behavior of individual teams can be hard to predict, especially if there are differences in national, organizational, or professional culture (Cooke-Davies, 2011). Thus, team size and the number of teams can contribute to complexity in a variety of ways that can inhibit project success.

In projects with a high degree of complexity, poor communication can be a significant source or cause of project failure. Although people have been practicing communication since the beginning of humanity (or at least of fictive language), we continue to experience communication challenges that affect everyday life. This may seem surprising since the need to communicate, relate, and interact is a basic human need. However, the processes of relating to one another can be complex because interaction among humans is always unpredictable to some extent (Cooke-Davies, 2011). Add to that the fact that stakeholders often have differing objectives and responsibilities and thus differing motivations, it is clear that genuine conflict may arise.

Project sponsors and other executives can affect multiple subprojects by delaying important decisions; such delays often result in additional work or rework and affect the project execution team or its resources. These issues are exacerbated in situations in which trust is lacking, resulting in workforce demotivation, poor morale, or exhaustion through the pressure to meet unrealistic schedule demands that may be due to such delayed decisions.

Project managers and project leaders can expect to be faced with human behavior and interaction complexity, but their responses can create additional complexity as noted by Cooke-Davies (2011). A common project management response to a schedule interruption might be to attempt recovery to the original planned schedule—for all kinds of reasons—and this can lead to unintended consequences and even failure. Failing to make or delaying a crucial decision can create complexity; for example, taking too long to decide whether to do activity A or B first can easily lead to having to perform activities A and B concurrently without sufficient resources and with concurrent ambiguities of each.

Delaying critical project decisions in the hopes of finding a more optimal solution later can result in continued uncertainty, which distracts the project team and results in additional work to prepare for eventual outcomes from likely decision alternatives. A fundamental principle in addressing complexity is to transition uncertainty into certainty as early as possible. Delaying important project decisions only serves to delay transitioning from uncertainty to certainty and increases factors contributing to project complexity.

Of course, the chemistry of project teams and between project teams and their management is a significant determinant of project success, even in a complex situation, However, even with perfect communication, by their very nature, large-scale, capital-intensive projects produce complexity.

2.3 PROJECT COMPLEXITY

Organizations sponsor large-scale capital projects to achieve strategic objectives, which if successful, result in value creation for the organization. Project value can translate to increased market share, higher profits for shareholders, and improved goods and services for consumers. However, value created by large-scale complex projects depends on the success achieved in designing, developing, and delivering the project result (i.e., the system created by the project) subject to project constraints, technical challenges of the system developed by the project, and external forces that can affect project delivery.

Combined, these factors create an ever more complex environment with increased difficulty in successfully completing large-scale projects and realizing the project's full value. Large-scale capital project success is becoming more difficult to achieve for many reasons. A recent study from IPA Inc. showed that "Large Capital Projects (those with capital expenditures larger than U.S. $1 billion) underperform in all industries" (Merrow, 2012). The fact that a project is *large-scale* does not mean the project is complex. However, adding the word *complex* to a large-scale project means that many factors and dimensions of the project contribute to complexity including:

- Strict regulatory oversight environment from external entities who can influence or intervene in project development or operation
- Complicated project development approaches that segment the project into smaller parts, creating multiple paths of interdependencies
- Intricate project contract strategies to procure products and services from global vendors and suppliers

- Concept of operation (for the system to be produced by the project) that requires integration with other projects and existing systems
- Use of new cutting-edge technology or manufacturing processes or materials

These factors and many others combine to influence and affect the project environment, the entities contributing to direct delivery of the project result, and those external entities outside the project scope boundary that can influence or intervene in the project. To obtain a correct picture of the environment, we must acknowledge and understand potential sources of complexity.

2.3.1 Project Environment

Projects are not conducted in a vacuum nor does the environment stop at the boundary of the project's scope. Rather, projects are executed by sponsoring organizations, governed and regulated by industry agencies, affected by external stakeholders such as regulators, and influenced by the project's concept of operations and the entities and facilities with which the project must engage, not only during project execution but also after transition into operation. Large-scale complex project environments tend to be dynamic. According to Collyer & Warren (2009), in project management the term *dynamic* means the extent to which a project is influenced by changes in the environment in which it is conducted, which are often initiated by various groups of stakeholder classes.

It is common to group stakeholders into internal and external categories (Aaltonen, 2011). Internal stakeholders are the entities that are formal members of the project and support the project (Morris and Pinto, 2004). These entities are often referred to as primary stakeholders (Cleland, 1998) or business actors (Cova and Salle, 2005) and reside within the discrete project scope boundary. Such stakeholders have a formal, official, or controlling relationship, such as contractual, with the sponsoring organization and are directly contributing to realization of the project result. External stakeholders are not formal members of the project coalition, but may be affected by the project or may intervene in or otherwise influence the project. Such groups are often referred to as nonbusiness stakeholders (Cova and Salle, 2005) or secondary stakeholders (Mitchell et al., 1997) and extend beyond the project's discrete scope boundary and into its sphere of influence.

The term *sphere of influence* in this book means an imaginary bounded area around the project environment at which entities inside the boundary can exert some level of influence on the design, development, and operations of the system of interest. That is, entities within the sphere of influence may extend beyond the discrete project scope boundary and into sponsoring organization(s), existing facilities, other projects and systems, government oversight agencies, and local or regional community interest agencies or organizations. All potentially relevant stakeholder entities outside the discrete project scope boundary but which are part of the sphere of influence must be identified in order to understand which entities can influence or affect SE activities related to design, development, and operation of the project's system of interest.

The project environment and the potential influences of external stakeholders can be difficult to predict. Every project is conducted within an industry, and most industries are guided by rules and regulations, standards, and government oversight. Industry oversight and governance are ripe sources of unexpected issues that are difficult to forecast precisely—such as changing regulations, stricter environmental laws, the state of economies, and the political landscape. Even recent major accidents within the industry can result in unexpected changes to the project's development. Thus, it is important to gain an understanding of and an appreciation for the project environment.

One way to think about the project environment is to classify each project's environment in three ways: (1) remote, (2) industry, and (3) competitive (Petit and Hobbs, 2010). While the specific terminology for these environments is not especially important, the concepts and what they describe are; thinking of project environment characterizations as described by Petit and Hobbs in this way can aid in understanding the influencers of complexity for, and obtaining situational awareness of, the project.

2.3.1.1 Remote Environment

A project's remote environment refers to the broad social, technical, and economic environment in which the project organization is developing the project. The remote environment is seen as changing slowly over time, but is characterized by cultural changes and population evolutions. While slow moving, some changes—such as political changes and political stability—can influence project organizations.

2.3.1.2 Industry Environment

The industry environment includes any factor affecting all competitors in a specific industry. This environment includes entry barriers, specific market regulations, common resources, and technologies to produce products or services. The industry environment can be a source for influencing project organizations through changes to industry standards and regulations and through concerns from environmental entities and populations affected by the project.

2.3.1.3 Competitive Environment

The competitive environment, while seen as directly impacting sponsoring organizations, has a trickle-down effect on project organizations. This environment includes relationships with direct or indirect competitors and collaborators (such as suppliers and partners), the channel of distribution, and the clients themselves. As will be described in more detail later in the book, in some industries systems developed by projects are often forced to integrate with other projects or the existing systems of competitors; interacting with competitors can create unpredictable behavior even when a cooperative agreement is established between the various competitive parties.

While the notion that organizations and their complex projects face changing environments is not new, it is generally acknowledged that project teams have difficulty grappling with sources of complexity beyond their jurisdictions (i.e., outside their discrete scope boundary or area of responsibility). Combined with the inherent complexity within the project's scope, dealing with influences and changes in the project environment only magnifies the intensity of complexity and unpredictability. Thus, understanding the project environment provides a foundation for creating the project's development and operations strategy or plan.

2.3.2 Complex Project Development Approaches

As a dynamic and complex system in itself, the global marketplace continues to evolve to meet the needs, demands, and desires of a growing and changing global population in search of a higher living standard and longer and better quality of life. As a result, global companies and organizations continually innovate to improve the effectiveness and efficiency of existing products and services to remain competitive and invent new products and services. As expected, companies and organizations develop strategies to anticipate and meet the ever-changing needs and desires of this dynamic and evolving global marketplace, which includes undertaking large capital projects that result in the design, development, and fielding of complex systems.

As markets continue to open and trade barriers fall, companies undertaking projects are now better able to take advantage of the global marketplace when developing their projects. In essence, the opening of new markets is providing sponsors of large-scale projects an increasing variety of products and services and competitive pricing from which to select contractors and suppliers for their projects. For example, "Global projects can use time zone differences to increase the number of productive work hours in a day, and secure scarce resources such as knowledge experts and other specialized resources no matter where they reside" (Nidiffer and Dolan, 2005).

For large-scale projects, the expanding global marketplace often translates to subdividing the project scope into various elements; resulting in more complicated contract structures and more complicated contract award timing as project sponsors segment the project to obtain the best value. While this approach certainly provides many economic benefits to project organizations, it also creates additional project risk by adding to complexity. "Complex procurements involve a large number of actors, they are often associated with a high degree of uncertainty and technological complexity, and will often last for several years" (Olsen et al., 2005).

Such a strategy of subdividing the project scope also means there are more entities, or *actors*, involved in bringing the project to delivery; creating more opportunities for miscommunication between entities within the project or those influencing the project, scope-of-work conflicts, and scope misalignment that result in costly delays. Further, large-scale capital projects typically require several years to complete (3–6 years or longer). Given a project's development strategy, the timing at which different entities come into and out of the project creates challenges especially when the project schedules of the respective project subparts are not aligned. In addition, complexity of the project environment can influence project success.

2.3.3 System Complexity

Every project is undertaken to develop a system, product, or service that will directly or indirectly contribute to meeting the needs of an ever-changing global marketplace and create value for the project sponsor. The desired result of the project influences and acts as a key driver in determining how the project is developed and managed. For example, the project may require specialized products that are only available through a few vendors or suppliers. Further, the system developed by the project may require the services of specialized organizations with critical competencies, such as technical engineering resources, to design the system.

From a project management perspective, the system and how the system will be realized during design and development will influence how the project is organized, the management system employed to monitor and control the work, and the processes and procedures to manage complexity and uncertainty. As this is an interface management book with the goal of simplifying complexity, we will describe some key terms here to ensure a consistent understanding of *project*, *system*, and some of the factors influencing system complexity.

2.3.3.1 What Is a Project?

A project is "a temporary endeavor undertaken to *create a unique product, service, or result*. The temporary nature of projects indicates that a project has a definite beginning and end. The end is reached when the project's objectives have been achieved or when the project is terminated because its objectives will not or cannot be met" (PMI, 2013). Key in this definition from the Project Management Institute (PMI) is that the project delivers a result. The project provides the infrastructure, in terms of people, tools, techniques, processes, structures, etc., in order to plan, execute, and deliver the desired result of the project. Every aspect of the project is concerned with delivering the *result* under specified conditions and constraints.

2.3.3.2 What Is a System?

While the definition of *system* is not precise or uniform, in project management terms it is the result of the project and is achieved by applying systems engineering to design, procure, and develop the system (i.e., the project result). Notable definitions of system are provided in this section to help the reader understand the basis of a system. Not surprisingly, the term system is subject to one's perception and interpretation. For example, the project manager will view the project's final result as a system while the sub-project manager of a major part of the project will also consider his scope of work a system.

Kossiakoff and Sweet (2003) define a system as "a set of interrelated components working together toward some common objective." While simple and concise, this definition implies a multiplicity of interacting parts that collectively perform a significant function and implies a *closed* system where all aspects of the system exist within its boundary. Further, this definition is oriented toward the integrated physical system to perform the common objective. As is evident, there is no mention of the infrastructure, such as people or processes, to translate the system from *idea to reality.*

Charles Wasson echoes Kossiakoff and Sweet's definition of a system by stating that a system is "an integrated set of interoperable elements, each with explicitly specified and bounded capabilities, working synergistically to perform value-added processing to enable a user to satisfy mission-oriented operational needs in a prescribed operating environment . . ." (Wasson, 2006). This definition expands Kossiakoff and Sweet's definition in that it acknowledges how the end user intends to operate the system.

Finally, the best definition in the view of the authors comes from Buede, who defines a system as a "collection of hardware, software, people, facilities, and procedures organized to accomplish some common objective" (Buede, 2011). The Buede definition takes a broader view of a system as compared to Wasson, Kossiakoff, and Sweet, where the definition is indicative of only the integrated physical system. Buede views a system as not just the physical outcome of the project, but the broader infrastructure necessary to deliver the system while recognizing that the system has an intended purpose. From an interface, interdependency, and interaction perspective described later in this chapter, this more holistic view of a system provides a better basis of understanding for performing interface analysis in Chapter 5 because it is precisely this holistic view of complexity that interface analysis seeks to simplify during project development.

The result of the project manifests in a variety of systems, such as:

- Military system to help defend a country's citizens
- Space shuttle to explore and research space
- Offshore oil and gas platform to recover increasingly hard-to-find hydrocarbons
- Nuclear power plant for providing electricity
- Telecommunications system to improve a developing country's aging or nonexistent communication services.

2.3.3.3 Factors Influencing System Complexity

Regardless of industry, a number of factors influence the degree of complexity of the system developed by large-scale projects. Some of the factors that often result in higher complexity include:

- Rapid technological advances
- Stricter performance standards
- Harsher operating environments
- Increasing environmental regulations and laws
- Specialized materials and manufacturing techniques needed to fabricate and construct the system
- Complicated procurement strategies, especially those needed to obtain specialized products and services
- Other approaches or strategies that create significant interdependencies between the sub-projects' scopes of work
- Complicated development strategies that create significant interdependencies with other independent or related projects

As Piciaccia, Faanes, and Lindland noted in 2004 while referring to the oil and gas sector, "At least equally challenging is the set of codes of practice, national and international regulations, and the license specific prescriptions that must be satisfied in order to receive the authorization to first develop the field and then operate it" (Piciaccia et al., 2004). The government approvals required of large-scale project developments are driving project organizations to maximize existing field architectures and existing systems in order to minimize a new project's physical *footprint*; this results in additional individual projects that must integrate into an ever-lengthening and sometimes convoluted string of existing project developments and existing system architectures. Increasingly advanced technical solutions of physical components, subsystems, and systems across these integrated architectures is needed to, for example, maximize hydrocarbon extraction, while ensuring complete human and environmental safety across multiple developments and existing system structures. In the information age, these demands are pervasive across many industries and are a reality of modern project environments and systems developed by these projects.

As we discuss complexity, we want to bring into focus the relationship and contrast between interfaces, interdependencies, and interactions. This relationship extends not only across independent entities and scopes contributing directly to the development and delivery of the project, but also out to the entities beyond the project's scope boundary to independent entities that can influence or intervene in the project, such as regulators and government oversight agencies; thus, it involves everyone within the project's sphere of influence.

2.4 INTERFACES, INTERDEPENDENCIES, AND INTERACTIONS

The factors discussed previously contribute to project complexity through an elaborate web of interdependencies, interfaces, and interactions to satisfy the informational requirements of each entity or actor (whether within the project scope or external to the project) that can influence the design and development of the system provided by the project. The various entities, and the interactions they need to undertake, can vary and change depending upon the role of each actor and the stage of development as the project moves through the project planning and execution phases. That is *who needs to talk to whom about what and when* needs to be well understood by the project team and include all actors working to deliver the project or able to influence its design, development, and delivery. This includes both internal and external actors, such as the sponsoring organization, contractors, industry oversight bodies, local civilian areas, and communities, etc.

"Wherever independent systems are combined into groups the interaction between the systems adds a further complexity; specifically, by constraining how the resulting system can be changed or controlled. This dimension of complexity affects the management and control aspects of the systems approach" (BKCASE, 2016). This statement begins to acknowledge the impact of relationships between interfacing systems and the entities responsible for delivering the respective system and their impact on complexity. The interface analysis process to be addressed in Chapter 5 is performed to unlock project and system complexity associated with interfaces, interdependencies, and interactions, which is simplified by decomposing complexity into smaller, more manageable and structured parts during the planning process.

2.4.1 Interfaces

An interface is a nonhuman thing related to the system under development by the project that is subject to agreement between parties, while interface management relates to the people responsible for planning, coordinating, and executing this agreement. Myriad definitions exist to describe an interface and some examples include:

- A surface forming a common boundary of two bodies, spaces, or phases (Merriam Webster, 2015)
- "The functional/logical relationships and physical characteristics required to exist as a system or entity boundary with its operating environment that enable the entity to provide a mission capability" (Wasson, 2006)
- The physical fit is accomplished at inter-component boundaries called interfaces (Kossiakoff and Sweet, 2003)
- Connection for hooking to another system (an external interface) or for hooking one system component to another (internal interface); the interface of a system contains both a logical element and a physical element (or link) that are responsible for carrying items (electromagnetic energy or information) from one component or system to another (Buede, 2011)
- Common boundaries between people, systems, equipment, or concepts (Nooteboom, 2004)

Interfaces can be thought of as interconnections between the systems, subsystems, components, and elements. These connections can be physical, functional, logical (signal or software), or mass (fluids, energy, etc.). At the lowest level, interfaces drive interdependencies between system elements, but also between human groups responsible for designing, developing, and delivering various parts of the system.

In this sense, interfaces form one pillar of the symbiotic relationship between interfaces, interdependencies, and interactions. In projects, these interfaces form the basis for interdependencies between objects (systems, subsystems, components, and elements) and the entities (organizations or people that must interact) responsible for delivering those objects.

2.4.2 Interdependencies

Interdependencies are dependencies between entities or people. Interdependencies exist when actions in one entity, engaged in its process, affect important outcomes in another unit or process; for example, when one entity affects the quality of deliverables, delivery time, costs, etc., in another entity. Interdependencies can take a number of forms including sequential, pooled, and reciprocal (Thompson, 2003).

Sequential interdependencies imply that one interface party is dependent on the completion of information or deliverables from another interface party in order to develop subsequent information or deliverables for its portion of the interface. Thus, each party in the sequence is dependent upon completion of activities or deliverables by a prior party.

Interdependencies can also be pooled where multiple entities are dependent upon data and information from other entities, but these entities may not be aware of the dependencies and the parties do not necessarily interact to produce their seemingly independent pieces of the whole.

Interdependencies can also be reciprocal, such as between engineering, procurement and construction. Procurement requires specific engineering data and information to progress procurement activities. Construction requires detailed drawings to fabricate and construct the system. Engineering is dependent upon procurement information from suppliers and vendors to finalize detailed design. The interdependent activities may be sequential, but they are iterative or cyclical (Thompson, 2003).

In general, interdependencies are thought to be static. However, dependencies between entities can be added, removed, or changed (strengthened and weakened) as the project progresses and the system transitions from idea to reality through the design and development process. Of course, the changing and evolving environment beyond the project's discrete scope boundary complicates interdependencies.

2.4.3 Interactions

While there are many types of interactions, the term *interaction* as defined in this book means communicative action between entities and their people necessary to achieve working interfaces in the project environment and relating to the project's social, technical, and managerial elements. Interactions are the necessary or desirable human communications among the parties to align their respective scopes, priorities, roles, and responsibilities (Whitty and Maylor, 2009). Interaction complexities are introduced by the dynamic effects of changing each of these elements (social, technical, and managerial) and then interacting as they change, causing further change in other parts of the system.

In project environments, especially those defined as large-scale complex project environments, the scale and scope of these relationships can vary in intensity and extend beyond the project's scope boundary. Interaction intensity (the intensity of the degree of interaction) varies among the specific project actors; interaction intensity describes the level of interaction required to achieve the interface. An intense interaction relationship indicates high frequency interaction between entities, whereas low intensity interaction implies infrequent interaction. Timing is another dimension affecting interaction intensity. The intensity between different entities ebbs and flows at different times in the project and depends upon when in the project the respective actors are needed to deliver or contribute their parts of the project.

However, the intensity of the interaction does not indicate the importance of the interaction. Actors within the project may have an interaction with an external actor related to the project that is low intensity, but the importance of that relationship may be very high, such as would be the case with the interaction between the project team and an industry oversight agency. Thus, when beginning to understand interaction relationships among various actors within the project scope and with external entities that can influence or intervene in the project outcome, then both interaction intensity and interaction importance must be factored in determining how to simplify and manage these interactions.

2.4.4 Relationship Among Interfaces, Interdependencies, and Interactions

In order to simplify complexity created by interfaces, interdependencies, and interactions, one must understand the relationship among these elements. In virtually all projects resulting in the development of a system, interfaces between system elements need to be aligned for the integrated whole to perform its intended function. These interfaces often result in project management interdependencies between entities where interfaces fall within their scope or area of responsibility. That is, one entity is dependent upon another entity for tangible information, material, equipment, etc., necessary to align interfaces completely. Interactions are the professional social interactions between people representing entities to ensure these interdependencies and interfaces within their areas of responsibility or scope are coordinated, managed, and ultimately aligned.

There tends to be a positive correlation between each two of these three elements. The more interfaces between entities, the higher the number of interdependencies, which increases interaction intensity. However, this relationship varies between entities. In some cases, there will be no interfaces between entities because their scopes of work or areas of responsibility do not share a common boundary; thus, there are no interfaces or interdependencies. Clearly, if there are no interfaces and interdependencies, then no interaction is required. On the other end of the spectrum, two or more of the entities may have a large number of interfaces, or a few significant interfaces, resulting in significant interdependencies and high interface intensity. In large-scale complex projects with many actors, with many different interfacing system elements, and with different scopes and areas of responsibility, stakeholder analysis processes are important in order to logically decompose complexity associated with stakeholders into smaller, more manageable parts. Decomposing and structuring this complexity is the central purpose of the interface analysis process, which will be introduced in a later chapter.

2.5 MANAGING STAKEHOLDER COMPLEXITY

Due to the variability of human behavior from those contributing to the development of the system (i.e., the project result) and the perceptions of people outside the system (i.e., the project sphere of influence), the human or *people* aspect of a system and project is often a contributor to complexity—and that may be a considerable understatement. The rational or irrational behavior of individuals in particular situations is a vital factor with respect to complexity (Kline, 1995). Checkland (1999) argues that a group of stakeholders will each have their own worldviews that lead them to form different but equally valid understandings of the system context and their respective contributions to developing the system within the project environment. Because they cannot be explained away or analyzed out, these differences in perspective must be understood and considered in formulating problems and creating potential solutions.

While sources of complexity are varied, it is people representing independent entities (organizations or groups) that are associated with the project and the system under development by the project who must interact to align their roles and responsibilities with people from other independent entities. "At the heart of any complex system is a set of interacting agents. If we track who interacts with whom, we can uncover a network of connections among the agents" (Miller, 2015). In the context of interface management, we begin by identifying entities contributing to the project and the system under development, including those extending beyond the project scope boundary that can affect system design and development. Then we can begin to group these entities by their relationships to define which independent entities need to interact with which other entities for the purpose of aligning interfaces, and the interdependencies related to these interfaces. Stakeholders, and the processes for identifying them, are described later on, along with their application during early project planning.

2.5.1 Stakeholder Classes

The spectrum of stakeholder classes ranges from those directly involved in delivering the project and the system of interest to those outside the discrete project scope boundary, but which can exert influence on, intervene in, or be affected by, the project and the design, development, and operation of the system of interest. While classes of stakeholders who are directly involved with the delivery of the project may be more obvious during the stakeholder identification process—such as contractors delivering various elements of the system of interest—those stakeholders extending beyond the discrete boundary can be more difficult to identify and more difficult to group into interface networks (also known as *interaction networks*). It may also be more difficult to determine their specific needs and requirements.

As noted by Aaltonen (2011), by conducting stakeholder analysis, project and technical managers attempt to build a *correct* picture of their stakeholder environment—a picture upon which appropriate organizational action concerning stakeholders can be determined. Building the correct picture of the stakeholder environment, however, is not as straightforward as current managerial methods and tools of stakeholder analysis would suggest (Aaltonen, 2011). Part of the challenge in building the correct picture is the need to understand those stakeholders that can influence or intrude upon project and SE management, assess their potential degree of intrusiveness, and determine when in the project development process these stakeholders are expected to exert their influence.

As stated, it is common to divide the stakeholders into internal and external stakeholder groups (Aaltonen, 2011). Internal stakeholders are entities that are formal members of the project and support the project (Morris and Pinto, 2004). These entities are often referred to as primary stakeholders (Cleland, 1998) or business actors (Cova and Salle, 2005); and they reside within the discrete project scope boundary as illustrated in Figure 2.1.

Internal stakeholders have a formal, official, or controlling relationship, such as contractual, with the sponsoring organization and are directly contributing to the realization of the project result. Internal stakeholder classes may include, for example, contractors, clients, vendors, subcontractors, and sponsoring organizations. External project stakeholders are not formal members of the project coalition, but may be affected by the project positively or negatively, or may intervene in the project through influence. Such groups are often referred to as non-business stakeholders (Cova and Salle, 2005) or secondary stakeholders (Mitchell et al., 1997), and extend beyond the project's discrete scope boundary and into its sphere of influence. External classes of stakeholders may include, for example, industry regulators, local communities, environmental groups, etc.

The impact of stakeholder entities whose interests and demands need to be considered to ensure the success of the project has been well documented (Cleland, 1986; Diallo and Thuillier, 2005; and Olander and Landin, 2005). It is a widely acknowledged assumption in both project management literature and in guidelines for infrastructure projects (IFC, 2007) that the project preparation phase is a stage during which stakeholders with differing opinions and objectives have the best opportunity to affect the project's objectives and outcomes (IFC, 2007; PMI, 2013). Lack of understanding of the various external stakeholder entities, the rationale behind their actions, and their potential to

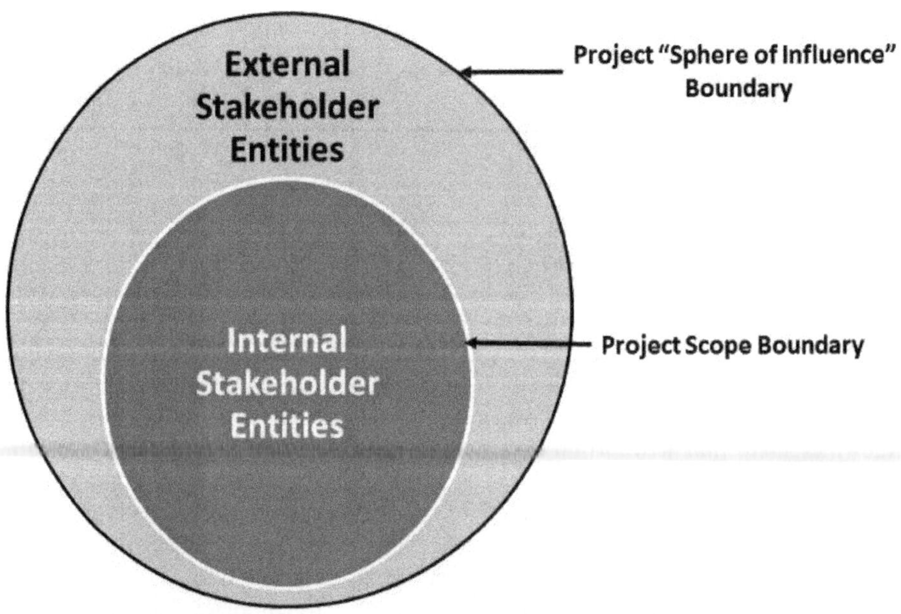

Figure 2.1 Project stakeholder entities

exert influence during the project life cycle have been identified as major challenges in international projects (IFC, 2007).

Both the systems engineering and project management domains prescribe processes related to stakeholder management in order to address both technical and nontechnical complexity from stakeholder sources in the project environment. Both domains' stakeholder management processes emphasize the importance of identifying stakeholders early during project planning and as part of initial SE activities. In the next section, we summarize the project management and SE management stakeholder management processes used early in the project as described in the *Project Management Body of Knowledge* (*PMBOK® Guide*) (PMI, 2017) and the Guide to the Systems Engineering Body of Knowledge (SEBoK) (BKCASE, 2016), as arguably two of the most popular and representative sources on the subject in use today.

2.5.2 Project Management Stakeholder Analysis Process

PMI in its *PMBOK® Guide* defines ten Knowledge Areas by which the processes are classified; one of those Knowledge Areas is Project Stakeholder Management. PMI states, "Project Stakeholder Management includes the processes required to identify the people, groups or organizations that could impact or be impacted by the project, to analyze stakeholder expectations and their impact on the project, and to develop appropriate management strategies for effectively engaging stakeholders in project decisions and execution" (PMI, 2017). The Project Stakeholder Management Knowledge Area consists of four processes: Identify Stakeholders, Plan Stakeholder Engagement, Manage Stakeholder Engagement, and Monitor Stakeholder Engagement. These are iterative and overlapping processes that "support the work of the project team to analyze stakeholder expectations, assess the degree to which they impact or are impacted by the project, and develop strategies to effectively engage stakeholders in support of project decisions" (and work) (PMI, 2017).

Stakeholders include customers, contractor companies, vendors, suppliers, and project sponsors or partners; other organizations which are contributing directly to the project; the public which are actively involved in or affected by the project and project partners; and government oversight entities, among others who are indirectly involved with the project's development process. As PMI notes, project stakeholders should be identified initially as the project charter is developed and then regularly at the start of each phase or when the project changes over time, and also documented to allow the project team to define how to engage each stakeholder or group of stakeholders appropriately (PMI, 2017). In several of its standards documents including the *PMBOK® Guide*, PMI describes each process using inputs, tools and techniques, and outputs. It does so for both the Identify Stakeholders and Plan Stakeholder Engagement processes, which in this book are together called stakeholder analysis.

PMI describes Identify Stakeholders as "the process of identifying project stakeholders regularly and analyzing and documenting relevant information regarding their interests, involvement, interdependencies, influence, and potential impact on project success" (PMI, 2017). PMI describes Plan Stakeholder Engagement as "the process of developing approaches to involve project stakeholders based on their needs, expectations, interests, and potential impact on the project. The key benefit is that it provides an actionable plan to interact effectively with stakeholders" (PMI, 2017). PMI goes on to suggest that the process be performed periodically as needed, for example, when stakeholders are added or their influence changes.

2.5.2.1 Stakeholder Analysis Inputs

Inputs are project-related documents that help to identify independent entities involved in the design and development of the system developed by the project, or entities that can influence or intervene in the projects. PMI's Identify Stakeholders process specifies several inputs: the project charter, business case and benefits management plan, relevant sections of the project management plan, agreements and contracts, and other related documents (PMI, 2017). In addition to organizational assets and enterprise environmental factors, these documents provide the inputs needed to perform the Identify Stakeholders process. The project charter provides basic information about the project and usually includes the common vision of the key stakeholders; it identifies the internal and external stakeholders affected by the result or the execution of the project. Procurement documents are important inputs as well as they are issued in accordance with the contract strategy to procure project products and services, and often, to segment the project into various elements. These documents can also address company-provided items, such as proprietary software, specialized equipment, black box equipment, etc. In addition to these inputs, the Stakeholder Register produced by the Identify Stakeholders process is an important input to the Plan Stakeholder Engagement process.

Enterprise environmental factor information can be useful in understanding the industry, governing regulations and standards, and the organizational culture and structure of the sponsoring organization. Finally, organizational process assets can provide stakeholder registers and templates from previous projects and lessons learned that are relevant to the new project (PMI, 2017).

The project management plan or plan for development and operations (or similarly named document) can provide a wealth of knowledge about the intended approach for developing the project—including key milestones, stage gates, entrance and exit criteria, major risks affecting the project, and tentative plans for transitioning the project into operations.

Currently, it is typical to undertake an environmental impact study for many major or large-scale projects. These studies can be quite useful in identifying major environmental issues impacted by the project and the various relevant interest groups. Concept of Employment (COE), often used by the U.S. Department of Defense to describe the background, purpose, and uses of a proposed system, provides a high-level description of major operations or missions to be performed by the system under development by the project. Architecture framework products can also be useful in understanding the project environment by helping to develop a clear understanding of other systems the project must integrate with to operate effectively.

However, the usefulness of these products depends on the quality and availability of documents and informational assets. In relatively new project organizations or those with little project management maturity, these assets may not provide the necessary information. Further, even if available, the applicability of these assets to the new project may be limited. Many assumptions are built into the stakeholder analysis process that may not reflect reality in a given circumstance and thus may limit its effectiveness. This is not to suggest the stakeholder analysis process is not useful, but users of this process should not limit their inputs only to those suggested in the *PMBOK® Guide* or any other specific source.

Other artifacts, such as architecture framework views or viewpoints, may be useful for identifying stakeholders. John Zachman, one of the recognized founders of architecture framework concepts, opines, "Seven thousand years of human history would establish that the key to complexity and change is Architecture. If it (whatever it is) gets so complex that you can't remember everything all at the same time, you have to write it down (Architecture). Then, if you want to change it (whatever it is), you start with what you wrote down (Architecture), the baseline for managing change" (Zachman, 2002). Now that the Information Age has succeeded the Industrial Age, it has become necessary to supplant what has been learned about architecture for increasingly complex products with architecture for the enterprise. Enterprises rely on information and that information must be delivered to the people who need it in an enterprise which is constantly changing and becoming more complex.

A key aspect of Zachman's position is the role architecture plays with respect to understanding and controlling complexity; that is, at some point, an enterprise (or anything else) reaches a degree of complexity requiring an architecture to enable it to survive and thrive. In certain industries—such as the defense industry—it is common for programs and projects to use architecture frameworks to aid in understanding the project's context within the larger enterprise organization. Context is communicated through a number of views and subsequent viewpoints, such as *operational views*. For interface management purposes, these views can be quite useful in visualizing the project environment as it will be during the operation of the system and in identifying entities with which the project must interact to align interfaces and interdependencies prior to transitioning to operation.

2.5.2.2 Stakeholder Analysis Tools and Techniques

According to PMI, the tools and techniques for identifying and planning engagement of stakeholders include expert judgment, data gathering (e.g., benchmarking), data analysis techniques (e.g., assumption and constraint analysis, root cause analysis, etc.), decision techniques (e.g., prioritization), data representation (e.g., mind mapping and stakeholder engagement assessment matrices), and, of course, meetings to discuss the input and develop first the stakeholder register and then the stakeholder engagement plan (PMI, 2017). Several classification models noted by PMI for stakeholder analysis include: (1) power/influence grid, (2) power/interest grid, (3) influence/impact grid, (4) salience model, and although not specifically named by PMI, (5) organization politics mapping tool (OPMT). The grids group stakeholders based on their power/influence and their active involvement (influence/interest) with respect to project outcomes. The salience model groups stakeholders based on their power, urgency, and legitimacy (Mitchell et al., 1997). The OPMT assesses the relationships among stakeholders, degree of organizational influence, and degree of applied influence at a particular point in time (DeLuca, 1999).

Several examples of such grids are widely used and tailored in various ways. A commonly used and simplified example of a power/influence grid is shown in Figure 2.2. Stakeholder influence and power can be plotted on this grid together with recommended actions for addressing each of the major stakeholders, particularly those in the upper right quadrant, but with due attention to those in other quadrants.

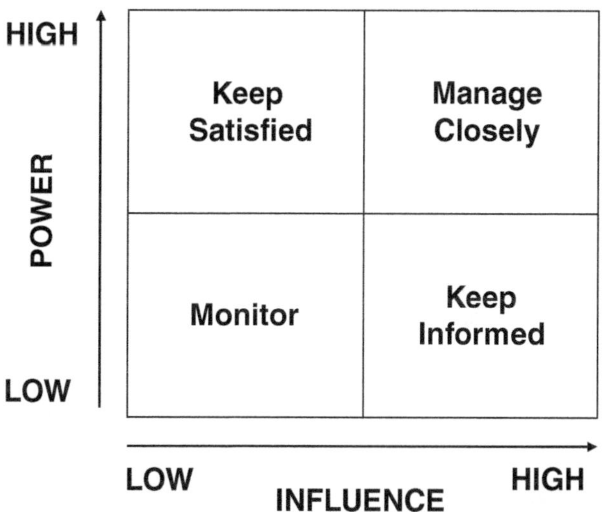

Figure 2.2 Power/Influence grid (PMI, 2013 and various similar models)

2.5.2.3 Identify Stakeholder and Plan Stakeholder Engagement Outputs

The main output of the Identify Stakeholders analysis process is the stakeholder register, which contains stakeholder identification information, assessment information, and classification. Identification information includes the name of the stakeholder, their organizational position, location, role in the project or with respect to the project, and contact information. Assessment information may also provide a stakeholder's significant requirements, expectations, influence level, phase in the project with the most interest, and classification if using the grid models described previously.

The main output of the Plan Stakeholder Engagement process is the stakeholder engagement plan, which becomes "a component of the project management plan that identifies the strategies and actions required to promote productive involvement of stakeholders in decision making and execution" (PMI, 2017). PMI goes on to say that this plan "may include but is not limited to specific strategies or approaches for engaging individuals or groups of stakeholders" (PMI, 2017). Of course, other project documents can be affected by the results of stakeholder analysis, such as change requests, project management plan updates, risk registers, issue logs, etc.

2.5.2.4 Identify Stakeholder and Plan Stakeholder Engagement Discussion

Initially, the stakeholder analysis processes are performed by the project's sponsoring organization during the early project planning phase. Remember, project development can take many forms and often involves the awarding of parts of the project's scope of work to many different parties, such as contractor companies, often at different times. In these cases, the project sponsor's organization normally maintains a management team to oversee and govern work by respective contractors and maintains project management systems that integrate the project as a whole. Thus, the project's sponsoring organization performs project processes and then, as contracts are awarded, contractors perform these processes for their respective scopes of work. Naturally, stakeholders identified from the perspective of the project's sponsoring organization will differ from those for a prime contractor responsible for a part of the project scope, and they will differ from those of the operator, etc. The outputs of these processes can be key inputs to interface analysis, described later in the book.

2.5.3 Systems Engineering Stakeholder Analysis Process

The SE domain has a corresponding technical process that also addresses stakeholders. These stakeholders are directly or indirectly associated with the design and development of the system (i.e., the project result). A project translates an idea or concept into a tangible result. This is accomplished through an SE process to architect, design, procure, and construct a system such that it can be transitioned into operation.

To identify stakeholder requirements that can provide the capabilities needed by users and other stakeholders in a defined environment, the SE domain prescribes the use of the *stakeholder's needs and requirements definition* technical process (INCOSE, 2015). From the SE viewpoint, a stakeholder is any entity (individual or organization) with a legitimate interest in the system, which can be "... users, operators, organizations, decision makers, parties to the agreement, regulatory bodies, developing agencies, supporting organizations, and society at large" (INCOSE, 2015).

"Stakeholder requirements play major roles in SE, as they:

- Form the basis of system requirements activities
- Form the basis of system validation and stakeholder acceptance
- Act as a reference for integration and verification activities

- Serve as a means of communication between the technical staff, management, project organization departments, and the stakeholder community" (INCOSE, 2015)

As noted by INCOSE, it is important for SE ". . . to pay close attention to interfaces where two or more systems or system elements work together, and establish an interaction network with stakeholders and other organizational units . . ." INCOSE therefore recognizes that while interfaces exist within and between the elements of the system being developed by the project, these interfaces create interdependencies between the systems and elements during operation that must be designed and aligned by appropriate entities during project development.

Thus, various classes of stakeholders, through proactive interaction, must align system interfaces. A full description of SE stakeholder processes can be found in the SEBoK (BKCASE, 2016). The current version of the SEBoK can be downloaded at no charge (at this writing) from http://sebokwiki.org/wiki/Download_SEBoK_PDF. The SEBoK specifies three processes related to stakeholders that are applicable for this book: (1) business or mission analysis, (2) stakeholder needs and analysis and (3) system requirements.

2.5.3.1 Business or Mission Analysis

Business or mission analysis (B/MA) focuses on the needs and requirements of the business or enterprise that:

- Defines the problem or opportunity that exists (in what is often called the problem space or problem situation)
- Understands the constraints on, and boundaries of, the selected system when it is fielded (in what is often called the solution space)

B/MA is used to define needed (or desired) operational actions, not hardware/software functions; that is, it is focused on defining the problem space, not the solution space. "During the concept definition stage of a life cycle, as the enterprise identifies new capabilities that are desired, the business or mission analysis develops a high level set of strategies and needs (which may be expressed as mission or business requirements) that reflect the problem space perspective" (INCOSE, 2015). For a military entity, this can mean a program to increase or enhance an existing military capability. For an industry entity, this can mean a project to create value in a new business area or to improve market position. "As the solution space is explored, and solution classes are characterized, stakeholder needs are developed and transformed into stakeholder requirements (from a user perspective)" (INCOSE, 2015).

"After the solution class has been determined and the specific solution is sought, during the system definition stage of a life cycle, the stakeholder requirements are transformed into system requirements (from a solution perspective). As the system definition recursively defines the lower level detail of the solution, requirements are defined with lower levels of abstraction. At the highest level, the ideal requirement is implementation-independent, and therefore not specific to a solution, allowing for a range of possible solutions. At their lowest level, requirements statements may become more specific to the selected solution" (INCOSE, 2015).

"The starting point of engineering any system-of-interest (SoI) (the project's result), is understanding the socioeconomic and technological context in which potential problems or opportunities reside. Then, the enterprise strategic goals and stakeholder needs, expectations, and requirements represent the problem or the opportunity from the viewpoint of business or enterprise decision makers while also taking into account the views of users, acquirers, and customers" (BKCASE, 2016). Here, we see involvement of SE early in the consideration of the project or program. This involvement takes the form of assessing the feasibility of the business concept and how the concept can be achieved to deliver the most value in terms of business need—at the lowest cost while delivering the highest quality.

2.5.3.2 Stakeholder Needs and Requirements

"The stakeholder needs and requirements (SNR) process explores and defines the operational aspects of a potential solution for the stakeholders from their point of view, independent of any specific solution. In these two concept definition activities, business or enterprise decision makers and other stakeholders describe *what* a solution should accomplish and *why* it is needed. Both *why* and *what* need to be answered before consideration is given to *how* the problem will be addressed (i.e., what type of solution will be implemented) and *how* the solution will be defined and developed" (BKCASE, 2016).

In describing the main purpose of the SNR activity during concept definition, the *Guide to the SEBoK* (BKCASE, 2016) states, "The stakeholder needs and requirements activity works with stakeholders across the life cycle to elicit and capture a set of needs, expectations, goals, or objectives for a desired solution to the problem or opportunity, referred to as "stakeholder needs." The stakeholder needs are used to produce a clear, concise, and verifiable set of stakeholder requirements. The SNR activities identify and define the needs and requirements of the stakeholders, in a manner that enables the characterization of the solution alternatives" (BKCASE, 2016).

New projects typically begin with an exploratory research phase, which generally includes the process of concept definition, which includes two main activities: analyzing the business or mission and understanding the SNR. These mature as the project goes from the exploratory stage to the concept stage to the development stage. "Mission analysis takes the business and stakeholders' needs and requirements and carries the analysis down from problem space to solution space, including concept, mission, and boundary or context so that a solution concept (at the black-box level) can be selected from the alternatives" (BKCASE, 2016).

2.5.3.2.1 Identifying Stakeholders

Since stakeholders of an SoI often vary throughout the life cycle, the *Guide to the SEBoK* suggests that ". . . in order to get a complete set of needs and subsequent requirements, it is important to consider all stages of the life-cycle model when identifying the stakeholders or classes of stakeholders." It goes on to say, "For each stage, a list of all stakeholders having an interest in the future system must be identified. The goal is to get every stakeholder's point of view for every stage of the system life in order to consolidate a complete set of stakeholder needs that can be prioritized and transformed into the set of stakeholder requirements as exhaustively as possible" (BKCASE, 2016).

2.5.3.2.2 Identifying Stakeholder Needs

After the *why* and *what* of the concept definition stage are established, definition of stakeholder needs can begin. "Once business management is satisfied their needs and requirements are reasonably complete, they pass them on to the business operations team. Here, the stakeholder needs and requirements (SNR) definition process uses the Concept of Operations (ConOps) or the strategic business plan (SBP) and life-cycle concepts as guidance. The requirements engineer (RE) or business analyst (BA) leads stakeholders from the business operations layer through a structured process to elicit stakeholder needs—in the form of a refined ConOps or similar document and other life-cycle concepts" and suggests that the requirements engineer or business analyst use "a structured process to elicit specific needs as documented in user stories, use cases, scenarios, system concepts, or operational concepts" (BKCASE, 2016).

2.5.3.2.3 Identifying Stakeholder Requirements

Continuing from the *Guide to the SEBoK*, "Stakeholder needs are transformed into a formal set of stakeholder requirements, which are captured as models or documented as textual requirements in an output typically called a stakeholder requirement specification, stakeholder requirement document, or something similar. That transformation should be guided by a well-defined, repeatable, rigorous, and documented process of requirements analysis. This requirements analysis may involve the use of functional flow diagrams, timeline analysis, N2 diagrams, design reference missions, modeling and simulations, organizational information assets (movies and pictures), states and modes analysis, fault tree analysis, failure modes and effects analysis, and trade studies" (BKCASE, 2016).

2.5.3.2.4 Collecting Stakeholder Needs and Requirements

Among the many ways to collect SNR, the *Guide to the SEBoK* recommends that several of the following techniques or approaches be considered while eliciting requirements to appropriately accommodate each of the diverse sets of sources:

- Structured brainstorming workshops
- Interviews and questionnaires
- Technical, operational, and/or strategy documentation review
- Simulations and visualizations
- Prototyping
- Modeling
- Feedback from verification and validation processes
- Review of the outcomes from the system analysis process (ISO/IEC 2015)
- Quality function deployment—can be used during the needs analysis and is a technique for deploying the *voice of the customer*. It provides a fast way to translate customer needs into requirements (Hauser and Clausing, 1988)
- Use case diagrams (OMG, 2010)
- Activity diagrams (OMG, 2010)
- Functional flow block diagrams (Oliver et al., 1997)

2.5.3.2.5 Classification of Stakeholder Requirements

The *Guide to the SEBoK* states that several classifications of stakeholder requirements are available. It references ISO/IEC 29148, section 9.4.2.3 (ISO 2011) as providing a useful set of elements for classification. "Examples of classification of stakeholder requirements include: service or functional, operational, interface, environmental, human factors, logistical, maintenance, design, production, verification requirements, validation, deployment, training, certification, retirement, regulatory, environmental, reliability, availability, maintainability, design, usability, quality, safety, and security requirements. Stakeholders will also be faced with a number of constraints, including: enterprise, business, project, design, realization, and process constraints" (BKCASE, 2016).

2.6 SETTING THE STAGE FOR STAKEHOLDER AND INTERFACE MANAGEMENT

What should become apparent is the challenge of aligning all the actors associated with the project, either directly or indirectly, and identifying their needs and requirements clearly and completely early in project planning. From the description of the project management and SE stakeholder analysis processes, one can appreciate the considerable effort and attention needed to achieve such elicitation and alignment.

During the stakeholder analysis process, we can fully appreciate that a number of different independent actors are associated with the project. Each of these stakeholders has its own motivations and self-interest with differing and often conflicting timelines and requirements. The resulting unpredictability of their actions and responses, occurring over a project life cycle that can span many years, is a great contributor to complexity. Although it may present a major challenge, applying an effective stakeholder analysis process can help to obtain the *correct picture*, and the frameworks provided by the *PMBOK® Guide* and SEBoK can be of great assistance. Perhaps more than any other element of large-scale complex projects, aligning these entities and their needs and requirements is the most important element to prevent or mitigate the impact of surprises rooted in not getting it right during planning; how well this is done will be felt throughout project development and delivery.

A close examination of the project management and SE stakeholder processes reveals an interesting dynamic. The project management stakeholder process tends to focus outward toward identifying stakeholders outside the project's discrete scope boundary, or at least outside the immediate project team. This includes organizational departments supporting the project, project partners, oversight and regulatory agencies, other independent projects, and existing facilities to name a few. Conversely, the SE stakeholder process tends to focus inward within the project's discrete scope boundary, perhaps because it is focused on engineering. Later in the book, the interface analysis process begins to align these two processes and domains to identify, organize, and simplify interfaces, interdependencies, and interactions, both between independent entities contributing directly to project development and with those independent entities that can influence and intervene in the project.

2.7 SUMMARY

In this chapter, we discussed complexity and the importance of understanding what complexity is in general and, more specifically, how it applies to the project context. Complexity is not easily understood nor simply defined; the foundation for managing complexity requires considerable thought during early project planning. Project management systems need to recognize elements or factors contributing to project complexity and implement appropriate management systems capable of monitoring and controlling these elements or factors. Of course, one cannot control the unpredictable outcomes or behaviors inherent in complexity; however, anticipating, assessing, and adjusting for them is mandatory.

One aspect of complexity relates to interfaces, interdependencies, and interactions among independent entities that are contributing to project development—and between the project and those entities that can influence or intervene in project development. Stakeholder analysis processes from the disciplines of project management and SE provide mechanisms to begin unraveling the complicated web of stakeholders intertwined in the project's development, but further effort is needed to structure these stakeholders such that the interfaces and interdependencies between them can be managed through a transparent and traceable project management system.

The outputs of the stakeholder analysis process provide valuable insight as to the entities within and those outside of the project, including their roles and responsibilities as the project progresses through its life cycle. This information helps to feed the interface management processes that will be described in later chapters. Whereas the stakeholder analysis process discussed in this chapter helps to answer *who* is involved and *what* their major needs and requirements are, the interface analysis process introduced in Chapter 5 further establishes the means to structure the project and interface management systems in order to manage these needs and requirements. It will build directly on the stakeholder analysis process outputs described in this chapter. In the next few chapters, we begin to structure the project's interface management system. First, however, in Chapter 3, we want to introduce interface management, then describe the interface management process in Chapter 4 to ensure a common understanding of interface management before taking a deeper dive into each stage in the practice of interface management.

2.8 REFERENCES

Aaltonen, Kirsi. (2011). "Project stakeholder analysis as an environmental interpretation process." *International Journal of Project Management* 29, no. 2: 165–183.

Baccarini, D. (1996). "The concept of project complexity—a review." *International Journal of Project Management*, Vp;/14. Mp/4/1996: 201–204.

Bennett, J. (1991). *International Construction Project Management: General Theory and Practice.* Butterworth-Heinemann, Oxford, UK.

BKCASE Editorial Board. (2016). *The Guide to the Systems Engineering Body of Knowledge (SEBoK)*, v. 1.6. R.D. Adcock (EIC). Hoboken, NJ: The Trustees of the Stevens Institute of Technology. Accessed August 07, 2016. www.sebokwiki.org. BKCASE is managed and maintained by the Stevens Institute of Technology Systems Engineering Research Center, the International Council on Systems Engineering, and the Institute of Electrical and Electronics Engineers Computer Society.

Buede, Dennis M. (2011). *The Engineering Design of Systems: Models and Methods.* Vol. 55. John Wiley & Sons, Inc., Hoboken, NJ.

Checkland, Page B. (1999). *Systems Thinking, Systems Practice.* John Wiley & Sons, Inc., Chichester, UK.

Cleland, David I. (1986). *Project Stakeholder Management.* John Wiley & Sons, Inc., Hoboken, NJ.

Cleland, David I. (1998). "Stakeholder management." *Project Management Handbook*: 55–72.

Collyer, Simon and Clive M. J. Warren. (2009). "Project management approaches for dynamic environments." *International Journal of Project Management* 27, no. 4: 355–364.

Cooke-Davies, T. and L. Crawford. (2011). *Aspects of Complexity: Managing Projects in a Complex World.* Project Management Institute.

Cova, Bernard and Robert Salle. (2005). "Six key points to merge project marketing into project management." *International Journal of Project Management* 23, no. 5: 354–359.

DeLuca, J. R. (1999). *Political Savvy.* EBG Publications, Berwyn, PA.

Diallo, A. and D. Thuillier. (2005). "The success of international development projects, trust and communication: an African perspective." *International Journal of Project Management* 23 (3): 237–252.

Hauser, J. and D. Clausing. (1988). "The House of Quality." *Harvard Business Review.* (May–June 1988).

IFC. (2007). Engagement, Stakeholder. "A good practice handbook for Companies Doing Business in Emerging Markets." *IFC, World Bank Group.*

INCOSE. (2015). *Systems Engineering Handbook: A Guide for System Life Cycle Processes and Activities*, version 4.0. John Wiley & Sons, Inc., Hoboken, NJ.

INCOSE. Complex Systems Working Group. (2016). Description of group purpose. Retrieved August 8, 2016 from http://www.incose.org/docs/default-source/default-document-library/complex-systems-wg-info-paper.pdf?sfvrsn=0.

INCOSE. (2016). "Complex Systems Working Group Mission and Objectives." Accessed 15 April 2016. http://www.incose.org/ChaptersGroups/WorkingGroups/knowledge/complex-systems.

ISO/IEC/IEEE. (2011). *Systems and Software Engineering—Requirements Engineering.* Geneva, Switzerland: International Organization for Standardization (ISO)/International Electrotechnical Commission/Institute of Electrical and Electronics Engineers (IEEE), (IEC), ISO/IEC/IEEE 29148.

Kamensky, John F. (2012). "Managing the Complicated vs. the Complex." IBM Center for The Business of Government. Retrieved July 16, 2016 from http://www.businessofgovernment.org/sites/default/files/JohnKamensky.pdf.

Kline, S. 1995. *Foundations of Multidisciplinary Thinking.* Stanford, CA, USA: Stanford University Press.

Kossiakoff, A. and William N. Sweet. (2003). *Systems Engineering Principles and Practice–First Edition.* John Wiley & Sons, Inc., Hoboken, NJ.

Merrow, Edward W. (2012). "Oil and gas industry megaprojects: Our recent track record." *Oil and Gas Facilities* 1, no. 2: 38–42.

Miller, John H. (2015). *A Crude Look at the Whole: The Science of Complex Systems in Business, Life, and Society.* Basic Books (Perseus Books Group), New York, NY.

Mitchell, Ronald K., Bradley R. Agle, and Donna J. Wood. (1997). "Toward a theory of stakeholder identification and salience: Defining the principle of who and what really counts." *Academy of Management Review* 22, no. 4: 853–886.

Morowitz, Harold J. (2002). *The Emergence of Everything: How the World Became Complex.* Oxford University Press, Oxford, UK.

Morris, Peter W. G., and George H. Hough. (1987). *The Anatomy of Major Projects: A Study of the Reality of Project Management.* John Wiley & Sons, Inc., Hoboken, NJ.

Morris, Peter W. G. and Jeffrey K. Pinto. (2004). *The Wiley Guide to Managing Projects.* John Wiley & Sons, Inc., Hoboken, NJ.

Nidiffer, Kenneth E. and Dana Dolan. (2005). "Evolving distributed project management." *Software, IEEE* 22, no. 5: 63–72.

Nooteboom, Uri. (2004). "Interface management improves on-time, on-budget delivery of megaprojects." *Journal of Petroleum Technology* 56, no. 08: 32–34.

Olander, Stefan and Anne Landin. (2005). "Evaluation of stakeholder influence in the implementation of construction projects." *International journal of project management* 23, no. 4: 321–328.

Oliver, D., T. Kelliher, and J. Keegan. (1997). *Engineering Complex Systems with Models and Objects.* McGraw-Hill, New York, NY.

Olsen, Bjørn Erik, Sven A. Haugland, Edgar Karlsen, and Geir Johan Husøy. (2005). "Governance of complex procurements in the oil and gas industry." *Journal of Purchasing and Supply Management* 11, no. 1: 1–13.

OMG. (2010). *OMG Systems Modeling Language Specification*, version 1.2. Needham, MA: Object Management Groupage, July 2010.

Petit, Yvan and Brian Hobbs. (2010). "Project portfolios in dynamic environments: Sources of uncertainty and sensing mechanisms." *Project Management Journal* 41, no. 4: 46–58.

Piciaccia, L. A., Tore Faanes, and Hans Jørgen Lindland. (2004). "2.2. 2 Complexity and change in the subsea oil production industry." In INCOSE International Symposium, vol. 14, no. 1: 257–272.

Project Management Institute (PMI). (2017). *A Guide to the Project Management Body of Knowledge (PMBOK® Guide)*, 6th Edition. Project Management Institute, Newtown Square, PA.

Rowlinson, Stephen M. (1988). "An analysis of factors affecting project performance in industrial buildings with particular reference to design build contracts." PhD diss., Brunel University School of Engineering and Design PhD Thesis.

Sargut, Gökce and Rita Gunther McGrath. (2011). "Learning to Live with Complexity." *Harvard Business Review* 89, no. 9: 68–76.

Thompson, J. D. (2003). *Organizations in Action: Social Science Bases of Administrative Theory* (Classics in Organization and Management Series). Transaction Publishers, New Brunswick, CT.

Wasson, Charles S. (2006). *System Analysis, Design, and Development Concepts, Principles, and Practices.* John Wiley & Sons, Inc, Hoboken, NJ.

Whitty, Stephen Jonathan and Harvey Maylor. (2009). "And then came complex project management (revised)." *International Journal of Project Management* 27, no. 3: 304–310.

Williams, Terry, Ole Jonny Klakegg, Derek H. T. Walker, Bjørn Andersen, and Ole Morten Magnussen. (2012) "Identifying and acting on early warning signs in complex projects." *Project Management Journal* 43, no. 2: 37–53.

Zachman, John. (2002). "The Zachman framework for enterprise architecture." *Zachman International* 79.

This book has free material available for download from the Web Added Value™ resource center at *www.jrosspub.com*

3

Interface Management Introduction

"The concept of randomness and coincidence will be obsolete when people can finally define a formulation of patterned interaction between all things within the universe."

—Toba Beta

Modern projects are increasingly difficult to execute as the systems they develop increase in complexity and project execution strategies become more complicated. Whether the project is delivering a new product, service, or supporting recovery of natural resources, system complexity and project complication continues to increase. As project execution strategies evolve to deliver ever more complicated or complex systems, management practices must evolve to reduce risk and ensure successful project completion to achieve business objectives.

Major industrial capital projects are inherently risky due to long planning and execution timelines and complex interfaces between the project and its context, and among different parts of the project (Flyvbjerg, 2007). As the number of independent entities contributing to the project increases, more interaction between the entities will be required. Interface management is a project management and systems engineering (SE) management discipline applied to address risk associated with project interfaces and the interactions they require—both internal to the project and between external entities that can influence the project.

To increase the chance of project success, complexities among the various systems being delivered by the project and among the stakeholders involved in the project must be managed and the accompanying risk reduced. This can be accomplished by establishing a simple, logical, and transparent management structure among the various independent entities contributing to large-scale complex projects. In this chapter, we introduce interface management, including key concepts, definitions, and terminology to be used throughout the remainder of the book.

3.1 THE BASICS OF INTERFACE MANAGEMENT

Interface management has become an essential management function as projects continue to increase in size and technical complexity, with stakeholders located across the globe, speaking multiple languages, and sharing significant cultural differences. Global competitiveness and the opening of new markets are providing organizations with opportunities to contract segments of their projects to various entities around the world. While this offers many economic benefits for organizations, it also introduces risk. Without effective and timely communication, and the exchange of vital information among the various parties as the project progresses across the various phases, the likelihood of errors and misalignment increases, resulting in costly problems during integration when combining various aspects of the technical solution. These problems are a major contributor to cost and schedule overruns that are common, even endemic, to complex projects. We propose that these errors and problems are controllable and preventable by employing the relatively new discipline of interface management.

On large complex projects with complicated contract strategies, the awarding of contracts is almost never exact and alignment among the disparate project schedules is rarely attained. Commonly on such projects, the interface stakeholders (delivery teams, contractors, subcontractors, vendors, and suppliers) have neither mutual contractual obligation with each other nor the means to control their implied but often unrecognized relationships. In such cases, the project owner and/or owner's representatives must facilitate communication and collaboration among these parties to ensure that critical information and material is exchanged and that the various segments of the project can integrate seamlessly later in project execution. Also, the project owner and each party to such relationships must ensure that appropriate information, material, and equipment are given to the other parties in a timely manner in order to prevent negative consequences.

The goals of interface management are to:

- Reduce or eliminate ambiguity with regard to responsibilities across the explicit and implicit boundaries
- Facilitate and encourage open communication among stakeholders
- Ensure agreements and common understanding are obtained between nonbinding parties
- Maintain transparency of critical project issues between independent entities
- Reduce risk by minimizing the possibility of miscommunication

Managing the complexity of stakeholder interactions is key to reducing a major risk associated with large-scale complex projects—ensuring alignment among the various parties contributing to design, development, and delivery of the project. The main goal of the project sponsor is to complete the project within project constraints of cost, schedule, and scope (including quality). By proactively and systematically managing these complicated interactions throughout the project life cycle, the project sponsor and relevant parties can better confirm that each party's scope of work and deliverables align with the scopes and deliverables of other relevant parties; and that when these deliverables are integrated with one another, they are integrated at the right time and connect together seamlessly—physically, logically, and functionally.

3.1.1 Recognizing Complexity

Uri Nooteboom, with nearly 40 years of experience in the design and implementation of offshore oil and gas subsea and floating production systems, has identified and stressed the importance of interface management, and calls it a *missing link* of project management. He further states that "Interface management has been a silent, hidden aspect of project management for a long time, but it was not specifically named or grasped until the rise of mega projects, many of which have suffered significant losses" (Nooteboom, 2004).

We argue that interface management is also a missing link *between* project management and SE. Project management functions and SE processes must work in unison to design and deliver the system produced by the project in accordance with the system requirements while subject to project constraints of cost, schedule, and scope. Often, in large-scale complex projects, project management and SE are conducted in silos with little or no synergy between them. When projects are decomposed into various parts, and contracted out to various entities around the globe, multiple levels of interaction complexity are created among organizations, projects, and technical disciplines. If not managed properly, these complexities manifest themselves as costly problems during the integration process.

We further argue that interface management is also the missing link between organizations and their projects. Management of the entity that is sponsoring the project often assumes that internal organizational procedures are adequate to cover interactions between the organization and the project or among multiple projects within the same sponsoring entity. Inevitably, interface issues arise between the organization and the project; these interface issues require a formal mechanism to reach alignment between the project and the organization or among cooperating projects within the same organization. These interactions must be viewed as *external influencers* on the project and should therefore be managed accordingly.

Modern large-scale projects typically require project parties to follow the organizational procedures and policies of the sponsoring entity. For example, the sponsoring organization may specify project control procedures, change processes, adherence to the protection of proprietary information or intellectual property, procedures for handling inquiries to industry oversight agencies and bodies, SE execution models, etc. Inevitably, these procedures and processes change over time and these changes may affect any projects that are being executed under previous procedures. Such changes represent potential disruptions, and thus, need to be fully communicated to the parties and agreed upon in order to prevent problems.

Further, the organization may provide *free issue* or *company provided items* (CPIs) in support of parts of the project. For example, a military organization can provide armor protection kits for a system produced by the contractor, or an oil and gas operator may provide drilling well services for offshore projects. The free issue or CPIs are vital to the project and are often delivered as items along the project's critical path, and by their very definition require interactions between the provider and the receiver. When these items are delayed or do not meet specifications or requirements, the project will be negatively affected.

3.1.2 Defining Interface Management

Given its relatively recent acceptance as a management practice, many definitions and descriptions of interface management exist and include:

- "The management of common boundaries between people, systems, equipment, or concepts" (Nooteboom, 2004)
- "The management of communication, coordination, and responsibility across a common boundary between two organizations, phases, or physical entities which are interdependent" (Wideman, 2002)

We define interface management in this book as: *the formal management process to identify, document, communicate, coordinate, monitor, control, and resolve issues occurring across common boundaries by independent projects, project phases, systems, contracts, scopes of work, or organizations.*

The definition implies alignment between project management and SE processes to ensure that consistent, transparent, and clear requirements are communicated among disparate parties contributing to a large-scale complex project, but without formal controlling relationships. This definition also accounts for entities extending beyond the project scope boundary but which have the ability to influence or intervene in the project. As with other project management and SE management practices, interface management must be viewed holistically and requires people, processes, procedures, tools, techniques, and training. In addition, interface management must be linked with existing project management and SE processes to align interfaces horizontally across all project entities and phases and vertically from within the project to the organization and external entities that influence the project.

3.2 INTERFACE CONCEPTS, DEFINITIONS, AND TERMINOLOGY

Interface management facilitates open and transparent communication and interaction between interface parties through an interface management program or system. This ensures that project issues between nonbinding parties are coordinated in a manner that minimizes risk and provides appropriate information to help address problems quickly when they do arise. Through oversight of these interactions, interface management affords visibility to the project sponsor as well as giving the sponsor the ability to intervene to defuse potential situations that will negatively affect the project.

Interface management cannot be discussed without a clear understanding of what an interface is and how it is distinguished from interface management.

An *interface* is characterized as:

- "A boundary where interdependency exists across that boundary and where responsibility for the interdependency changes across that boundary" (Healey, 1997)
- "The contact point between relatively autonomous organizations which are interdependent and interacting to achieve some larger system objectives" (Wren, 1967)
- "Common boundaries between people, systems, equipment, or concepts" (Nooteboom, 2004)

An interface is a non-human thing subject to agreement between parties, while interface management relates to the people responsible for planning, coordinating, and executing this agreement. The essence of interface management is the relationship between interfaces, interdependencies, and interactions. Interfaces exist between components, subsystems, systems, and a system of systems. In turn, these interfaces create interdependencies within the system and the environment in which the system will operate. They also create interdependencies during project development for the entities responsible for delivering various segments of the project. To ensure alignment, the related parties who are associated with each interface must interact to coordinate design and development interdependencies associated with the interface. Such interaction for the purposes of interface alignment increases the chances of smooth integration, verification, and validation later in project execution.

As previously noted, the boundary provides the basis for characterizing an interface, but interfaces do not resolve themselves. Rather, interfaces require people to proactively recognize and resolve them; more specifically, the people associated with each shared boundary must describe and define the interface between them, and agree upon how to resolve it. Too often in large-scale complex projects, the emphasis is on the interfaces, but not the entities involved in aligning those interfaces. Interface management focuses on both the interfaces themselves, and on the people (or entities) affected by these interfaces, including the way they must interact to resolve their interfaces.

3.2.1 Interface Defined

One of the most problematic aspects of interface management is a consistent understanding of what an interface is and is not within the project and SE community. In the real-world project community, views of what is and is not an interface vary widely. In large-scale complex projects, we must begin to think about interfaces more holistically across the project's internal and relevant external environment. From this holistic view, we can apply the management practices that allow us to manage the full scope of interactions within and external to the project.

For the purposes of this book, we define an interface as: *a common boundary between two or more independent projects, systems/subsystems, contract scopes of work, organizations, or project phases; thusly requiring an exchange of data or information to obtain agreement between entities.*

Establishing a common interface definition provides the foundation for preventing interface problems when elements of the project that fall along the common boundaries are developed and

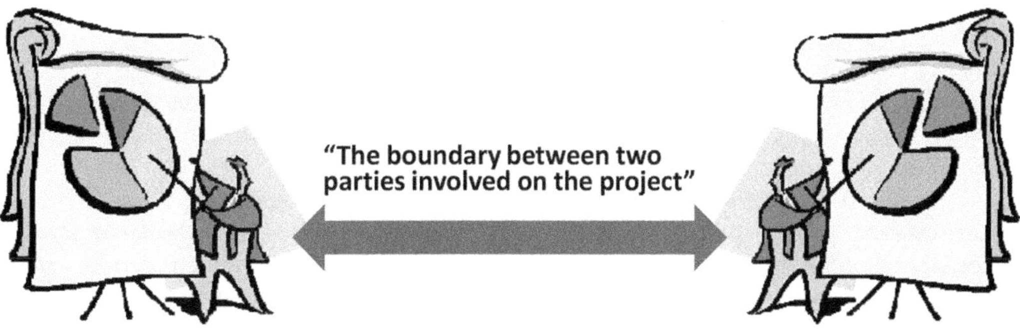

Figure 3.1 Interface between two parties

integrated. An interface recognizes an informational or material need between two (or more) independent parties as illustrated in Figure 3.1.

The reader will note two underlined terms in the aforementioned definition: (1) common boundary and (2) independent. These terms are underlined because they identify two aspects crucial to defining what is and is not considered an interface. Both aspects are discussed later in the book in more depth, but here, the *independent* aspect of an interface means the lack of a controlling relationship between the parties sharing the common boundary. The *common boundary* aspect of an interface means that deliverables or functions from the independent parties will meet or interact.

A controlling relationship is one in which the parties have some formal arrangement. For example, a client has a contract with a contractor. The contract forms the basis for a dependent (controlling) relationship. Specifically, the contractor agrees to provide the client with specific products and services in return for monetary payment. As expected, the contract describes the terms of the agreement between the two parties.

Another example can be provided within a client's project organization in the case of a project with multiple subprojects. Personnel within a given subproject must coordinate with each other because they have been assigned specific roles and responsibilities for the subproject's scope of work. In this sense, the established roles and responsibilities for the subproject form the basis for a control ling relationship between the various subproject personnel. However, one subproject team may be required to coordinate with a separate subproject team to align project changes in scope that affect multiple parts of the project. In this situation, neither subproject team is controlled by the other. Thus, they need some mechanism to formally communicate, coordinate, and document agreements for boundaries between their two subproject scopes.

The same analogy can be used for two different departments within the same organization. For example, the engineering department must coordinate and interact with the procurement department because their departments have been assigned specific roles and responsibilities within the organization relative to the project. However, in this case, neither department has a controlling relationship with the other, but each is dependent upon information and material to perform their related functions on the project. (We will describe the concept of a *controlling relationship* in more detail later in this chapter, but again this concept is key to understanding and defining an interface.) In some instances, existing processes and procedures may be adequate to govern interactions between the departments as might be the case in a mature organization with long-standing engineering, procurement, and construction processes. In many cases, though, the two example departments will require a formal interface management process. With the interface defined, the project team can assess and determine where in the project to apply interface management.

3.2.2 Interface Group

Two or more parties associated with a common boundary are referred to as an interface group (see Figure 3.2). For the purposes of this book, an interface group is defined as: *a group consisting of two (or more) independent parties who share a common boundary but have a relationship with limited or no direct control over one another's activities.*

As mentioned briefly previously, while these two parties share a common boundary, no formal control exists between the parties; this might be the case between two main contractors contracted to the same client on the same project. Each has a contract with the client, but no contract governs the relationship between the two main contractors; still, these entities must communicate and coordinate issues where their respective scopes of work collide to ensure successful integration with each other as they complete deliverables in their respective scopes of work. However, their need to communicate and coordinate is implicit rather than explicit. This can be problematic when neither party is under any obligation to the other party; that is, without a direct controlling relationship.

While each of the two contractors illustrated in Figure 3.2 has its own scope of work and deliverables, when these two scopes are performed together on the same project and the deliverables must integrate or align with each other, managing the interfaces becomes important. Therefore, in the best interest of the project, interface groups must be identified and established to ensure the alignment of issues associated with their respective boundaries. Such alignment early in the appropriate planning stages can prevent interface problems (and accompanying cost and schedule overruns) when the various components and subsystems are delivered and integrated later during project development.

Interface groups are identified by the project sponsor early in the project during project planning, preferably after the project management plan and contract strategy has been developed, but before project execution starts. To establish interface groups, common boundaries must first be identified and understood by all involved parties.

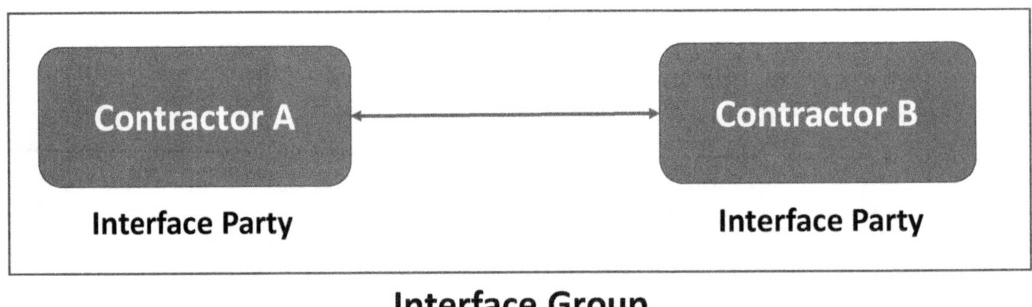

Figure 3.2 Interface group consisting of two parties

3.2.3 Common Boundary

As mentioned in Section 3.2.1, the *common boundary* (also known as a *battery limit*) is a key interface management concept. Figure 3.3 shows two parties that are independent of one another in terms of maintaining control or responsibility; that is, each party has its own area of responsibility and does not have a means to directly influence the other. Yet, both parties share areas of responsibilities that are dependent upon one another.

Let's use the previous contractor example to help make the point. Each of two independent main contractors has its own contract with the same client for the same project; each is responsible for

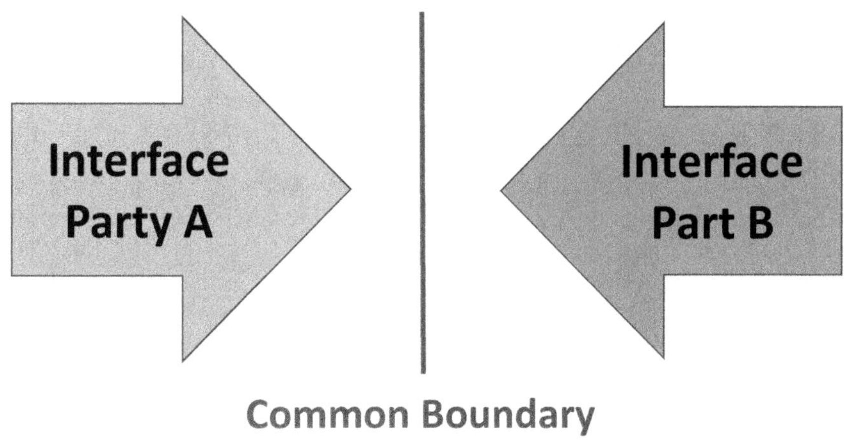

Figure 3.3 Common boundary

its own respective scope of work. The contract, i.e., the mechanism of control, is with the client and not with the other contractor. In this example, neither contractor maintains any contractual relationship with the other. Thus, they are under no direct obligation to deliver any goods and services to each other. The lack of such a mutual contractual relationship means that these two contactors have no direct controlling mechanism to ensure they cooperate in the best interest of the project. However, when the products or services these contractors are delivering connect to each other, either physically or functionally, it becomes necessary for these independent contractors to interface with each other to align their respective boundaries.

While the previous example involved one project with two independent contractors, in which the contracts defined the respective scopes and thus implicitly identified the common boundaries, other types of common boundaries can be established. For example:

- Between two independent projects that integrate with each other—it is common for two different projects to integrate together into a large system-of-systems or supersystem
- Between two different organizations (i.e., companies)—it is common for different companies to undertake projects that must integrate, or connect, to each other or into an existing system
- Between two different technical disciplines (e.g., electrical and structural)—whether automation, control, electrical, or piping and mechanical; it is routine for technical disciplines to interface during the design and development process
- Among functional departments such as risk management and safety—many issues require interface activities among an organization's functional departments, such as global safety issues, alignment and response to industry oversight agencies, alignment and response to formal management, or technical queries from a project's contractors, etc.

Identifying common boundaries between the parties is accomplished by undertaking interface analysis of the system being developed and defining how the project will be executed over its lifetime. For example, the client has contracted with an architect to design a modern office building and has separately contracted with a construction company to build the office building. The architectural and the construction parties must communicate and collaborate to ensure the final product—the building—meets the client's expectations and needs.

Analysis of the architecture of the system to be developed for the project will also help to identify boundaries between the parties. For example, in developing an aircraft, the parties designing and developing the aircraft wings must collaborate with the party developing the fuselage as they have physical, functional, and logical (signals and software) boundaries. These common boundaries are also useful for understanding the interface areas, issues, and items to address during interface activities.

3.2.4 Interface Areas, Issues, and Items

The interface groups described in Section 3.2.2 form the foundation for further defining the scope of interfaces between members of the groups; identifying the interface groups is prerequisite to defining interface areas, issues, and items. It should be noted that the intensity of interface interaction is dependent upon the scope of the interfaces between the respective parties. More interface scope will result in higher interface intensity between the groups.

After establishing which interface parties share a common boundary (i.e., once the interface groups are defined), interface areas, issues, and items are identified for each group. As illustrated in Figure 3.4, an *interface area* flows down to the *interface issues*, which are further decomposed into *interface items*. This construct helps to simplify interface complexity into manageable elements and is used as part of the interface analysis process described in Chapter 5.

An interface area is: *a defined area of interest on the common boundary between two or more interface parties*. An interface area (also known as interface point) is characterized by one or more interface issues, and requires interface parties to agree with the resolution of interface items associated with the issue. Interface areas represent discrete or specific segments along the common boundary that need to be aligned. For example, Interface Party A (aircraft fuselage) identifies hydraulic, electrical, and structural interface areas with Interface Party B (aircraft wing). These interface areas help to further define the scope of the interface with other parties and serve as a basis for identifying interface issues. For each interface area, there can be one or several interface issues.

An interface issue is: *a statement identifying specific aspects, such as physical or functional, of the interface area requiring interface activity with another interface party*. These further decompose or break down the interface area into specific issues that need detailed interface activity. For example, Interface Party A (aircraft fuselage) identifies an electrical interface area with Interface Party B (aircraft wing). From this point, Interface Party A identifies interface issues such as power management system, wing lighting, mechanical control, etc.

With interfaces issues identified, the interface parties can begin to derive specific interface items for each interface issue. For example, for two parties sharing an interface area such as the electrical

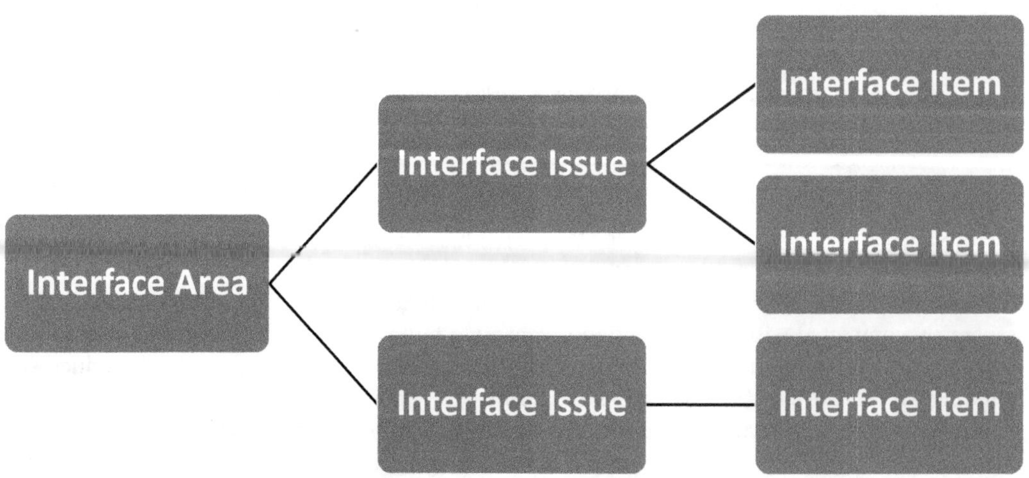

Figure 3.4 Interface areas, issues, and items

area, the power management system may be an *issue* that the two parties need to align since it crosses their respective boundaries. Other issues may include, for example, the alignment of power management system hardware compatibility to ensure that both parties have power management system physical components that can operate together.

Several factors influence the intensity of the interface activity between interface parties; these factors may include the project plan for development, system architecture, and external influences on the project, among others. Some interface groups will have very intense interface activity because they share several interface areas, while others may require very little interface activity. For each interface issue, there can be one or several interface items that need to be resolved to fully resolve the issue.

An interface item is: *a specific interface data or information request(s) resulting from an interface issue, which is generated from one interface party toward another interface party.* Interface items are typically coordinated using an interface management database tool and conducting interface management meetings with the respective interface groups. The items are coordinated and closed when an interface agreement has been reached by the parties.

As illustrated in Figure 3.5, two parties share an electrical interface. Two issues have been identified that relate to the electrical area, for which three interface items must be addressed to resolve the electrical interface across the common boundary shared by the two parties.

This construct can be used to analyze and decompose all categories and types of interfaces associated with the project and it helps to identify which parties need to interact to resolve interdependencies during project execution. More important, this construct provides a framework to ensure interface activity covers all relevant aspects across the project and between those entities that can influence or intervene in the project. A more detailed look at interface analysis is provided in Chapter 5.

3.2.5 Interface Agreement

When all interface items are resolved for an interface issue, the associated issue becomes resolved; when all interface issues are resolved for an interface area, the associated area becomes resolved. The objective of the interface group is to obtain agreement on all interface areas for the group. Caglar and Connolly state, "Interface agreements result in exchange of any project information generated by one party that is needed by another party in order that the other party can continue with its scheduled

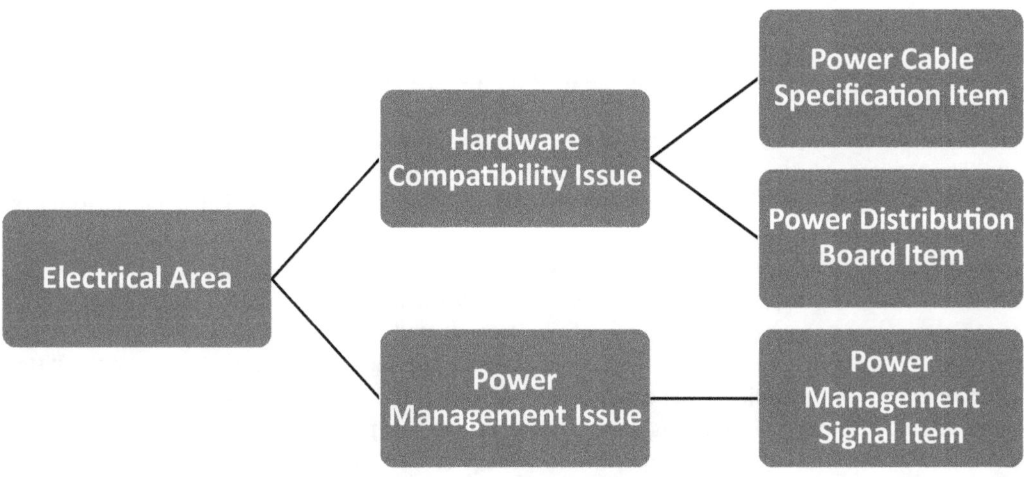

Figure 3.5 Electrical area example for interface area, issues, and items

project tasks. This can include but is not limited to the engineering drawings, specifications, design reports and calculations, equipment details and project schedule information, and delivery of free issue or CPIs. There is no limitation on the source of interface agreements. They can arise from several sources including members of the project team, contract requirements, responsibility matrices, customer requirements, third party vendors/suppliers, and other project contractors and project stakeholders" (Caglar, 2007).

An interface agreement is reached when the parties accept the proposed solution. The interface agreement mutually acknowledges a specific resolution by two or more interface parties for an interface item. Interface agreements form the foundation for effective interface management since they represent progress toward resolving interface issues and areas along the common boundary. For example, Interface Party A submits an interface item to Interface Party B to confirm the pipe sizing at a specific physical interface point. While this is a simple example, reaching interface agreements can require significant effort. Some challenges to be aware of are:

- Integrating the timing of the deliverables committed for the interface agreement into the schedules of both parties as well as into the overall integrated schedule
- Incorporating the elements of the agreement into the action tracking system in order to monitor progress towards implementation
- Monitoring to ensure the agreement is reflected in the respective parties' project, e.g., included in engineering designs, fabrication timelines, and such
- Assuring technical integrity of the systems, people, and processes associated with the interfaces—system integrity assurance

Obtaining the *agreemen*t between the interface parties for each interface item is essential to aligning the interfaces. An interface agreement is reached when both parties attain a suitable solution that addresses the concerns of both parties. When a suitable solution is reached, the item is said to be resolved. When all items for an interface issue are resolved, there is agreement at the issue level. When all issues for an interface area are resolved, there is agreement at the area level. When all interface areas are resolved, the interface group has achieved its objective. As can be expected, many factors impact the ease or difficulty in resolving interfaces. Remember, interface parties have no controlling relationship. Rather, they are dependent upon the willingness of each party to participate in good faith—which does not always happen. This topic will be discussed in more detail later in the book.

3.2.6 Interface Analysis

Interface analysis is a key component of interface management because the process provides the mechanism to begin understanding the breadth and depth of interfaces within and external to the project. Interface analysis answers questions about how to organize to ensure effective interface management and identifies the issues that need to be addressed among the relevant interface parties. The interface parties can be grouped during interface analysis to form interface networks; each interface network may include particular types of stakeholders or interfaces. Thus, interface analysis is defined as: *the process of examining the project environment and system architecture to determine the scope of interfaces, both within and external to the project, from which to identify and organize interface networks, interface groups, and interface areas, issues, and items.*

As a top-down approach, interface analysis is conducted as part of early project planning and begins by obtaining an understanding of the project environment and the architecture of the system to be developed by the project, including the industry, relevant regulations, and any oversight entities that can influence the project during the execution phase. This part of the analysis provides a view of the external environment and the key entities that require interaction with the project either directly or through the sponsoring organization (see Figure 3.6).

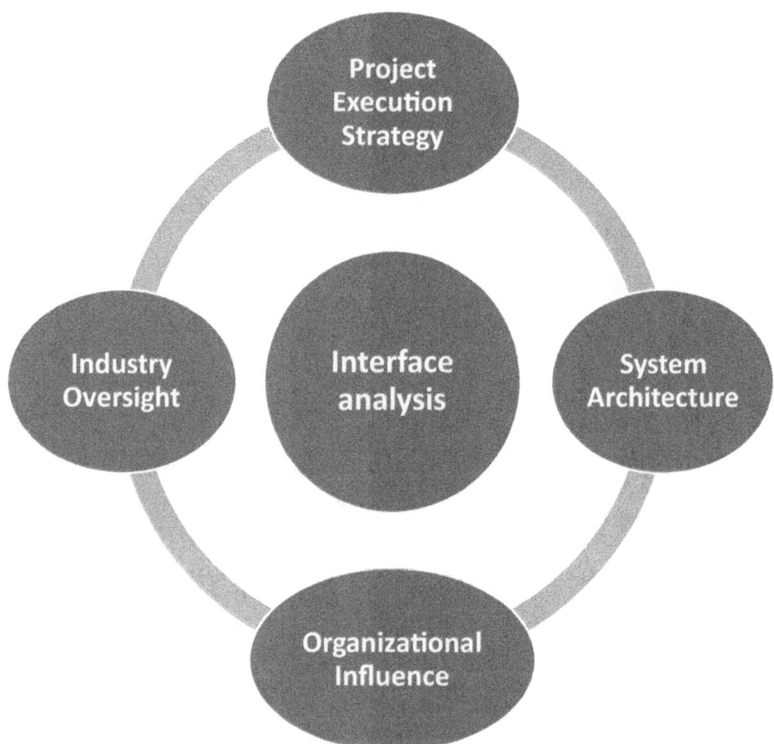

Figure 3.6 Interface analysis influences

In cases in which the project is required to interface with an existing system or another project, this part of the analysis is expanded to include these aspects of the environment because they will influence the project either directly or indirectly.

With the entities known, the interface analysis proceeds to identifying specific interface areas; for each interface area, specific interface issues and interface items are defined. In some instances, a contract or agreement may be established between projects that require integration with one another. If this is the case, the agreement or contract can include how the projects will cooperate to ensure successful integration, describing work processes and procedures as well as any requirements and specifications as shown in Figure 3.7.

In addition, the interface analysis process examines the project's planned development, including the strategy for contracting the project, the timing of milestones or key events, critical dependencies between entities, and project phases. It is important to obtain an understanding of how the project will be developed during the execution phase and what the key entrance criteria are for the respective milestones, stage gates, and key events along the project timeline. Equally important is gaining an understanding of other project processes and procedures, such as risk management, quality control and assurance (i.e., audits, verification, and validation), and change management. Interface analysis is discussed in more detail in Chapter 5.

3.2.6.1 Interface Management and Other Project Processes

Interface management is not a stand-alone management function. Rather, it must be aligned with, and will interact with, other project processes as conceptually illustrated in Figure 3.8. Thus, it is

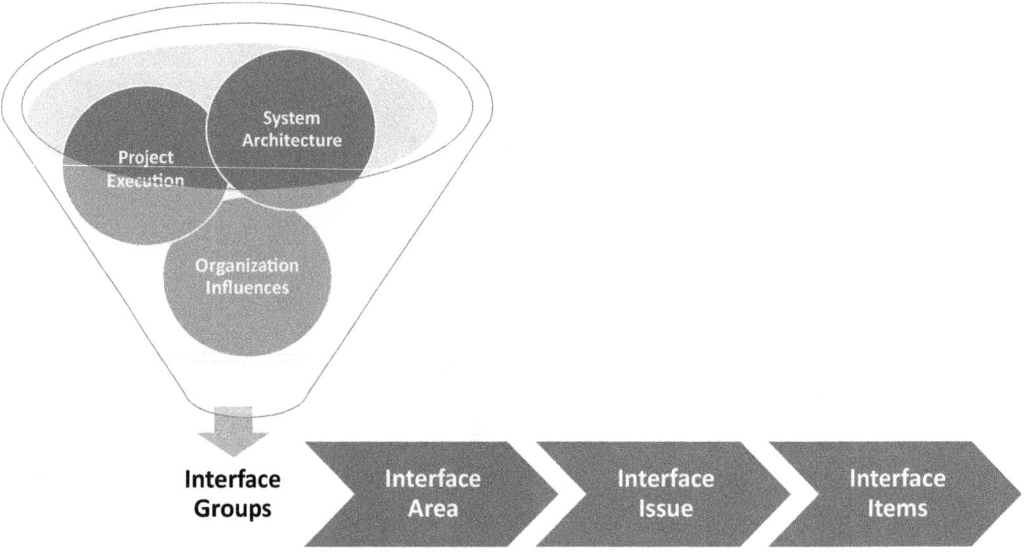

Figure 3.7 Influencers' impact on interface analysis process flow

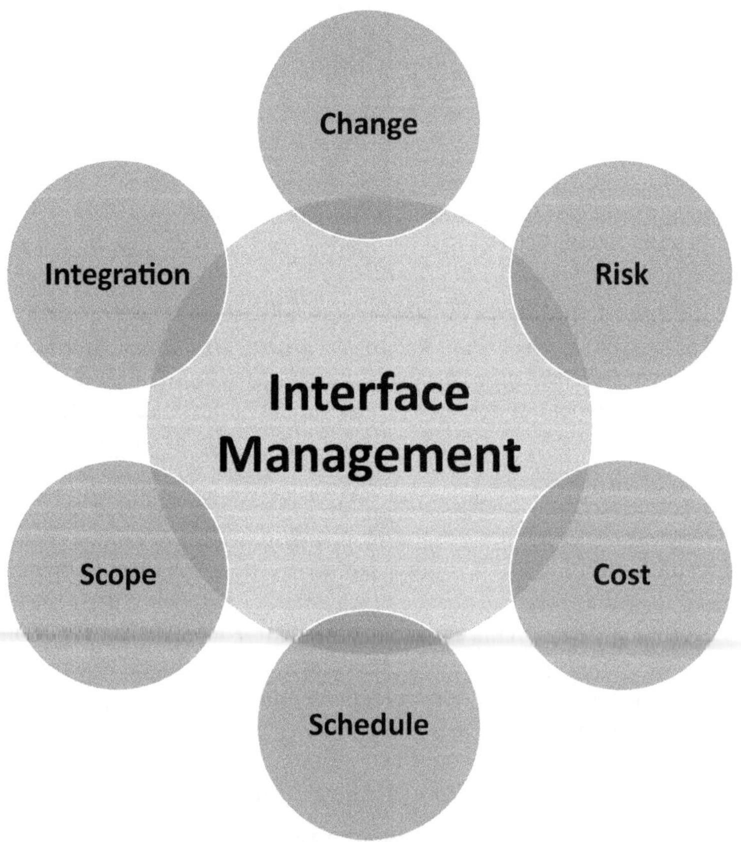

Figure 3.8 Interface management relationship to other project processes

important to ensure that these processes account for interface management and vice versa. For example, interfaces can represent risk and should be included as part of the risk management process. Similarly, project changes can cross common boundaries and affect more than a single entity. Thus, interfaces need to be included as part of the project's change management process. Interface management and its alignment to other project processes will be discussed in more detail later in the book.

3.2.6.2 Interface Networks

One critical output of the interface analysis process is the identification and organization of interface networks. Interfaces, and the interaction by various entities to resolve them, occur on several levels of a large-scale complex project. Interface networks are designed to identify and group relevant entities in an organized way that ensures efficient and effective interaction. An interface network is therefore defined as: *a group of interface parties established to coordinate interface issues associated with specific types of stakeholders of the project.*

For example, an interface network may be established for the client's main contractors to coordinate external interfaces and an internal interface network may be established within the client's organization to coordinate internal organizational interfaces associated with the project. Within the systems engineering domain, interface networks are referred to as *interaction networks* in the *Systems Engineering Body of Knowledge* (*SEBoK*). However, we have chosen to use the term *interface networks* for better alignment with the content of this book. In practice, what we call the networks matter little; it is more important to understand the networks' purpose and function within interface management (see Figure 3.9).

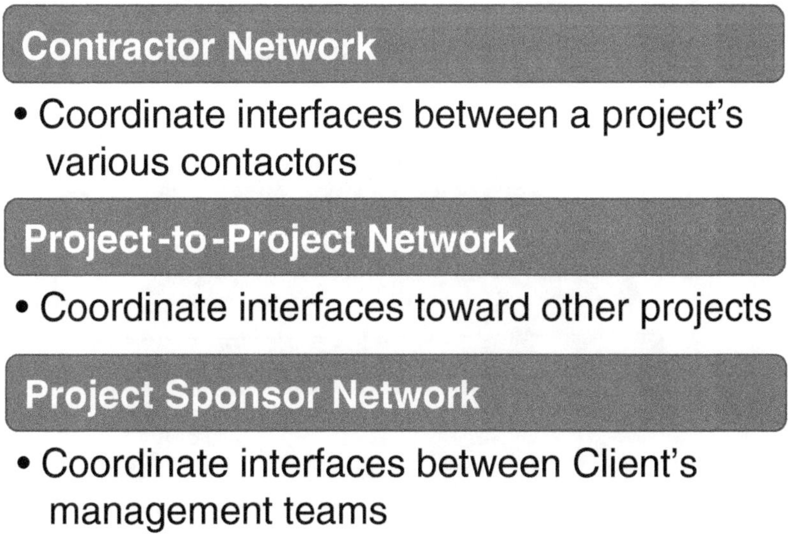

Contractor Network
• Coordinate interfaces between a project's various contactors
Project-to-Project Network
• Coordinate interfaces toward other projects
Project Sponsor Network
• Coordinate interfaces between Client's management teams

Figure 3.9 Interface network examples

3.3 INTERFACE CATEGORIES AND TYPES

As stated previously, one of the challenges in interface management is to understand what is and is not an interface. A common misconception about interfaces is that they are limited to the engineering department. Unfortunately, this misconception ignores the connection between engineering disciplines and the larger project, the project environment, the organization, and the specific industry environment. Modern large-scale projects are complex, with segmented areas of responsibility and scopes of work that are often complicated by elaborate contract strategies. Accordingly, interface management applies a holistic system view not only within the project, but also outside the project, to the external environment that can influence or affect the project or the system being developed by the project.

This section of the book provides a basis for the common understanding of potential interface categories and types. Ultimately, each organization will evaluate which types and categories of interfaces to manage and how they are managed. Understanding these types and categories assists in establishing interface networks and defining the scope of interface activity across the project, as part of the interface analysis process.

3.3.1 Interface Categories

This book recognizes four general categories of interfaces: technical, project, organizational, and industry. These interface categories are notionally illustrated in Figure 3.10, which conceptually shows layers of interfaces extending from technical to industry.

Technical (also known as *system*) interfaces represent interaction to deliver the product being developed by the project. These interfaces are directly associated with development of the system to be produced by the project; they reside mainly within the engineering departments. Thus, technical interfaces are shown in Figure 3.10 as existing within the project environment. Extending out from

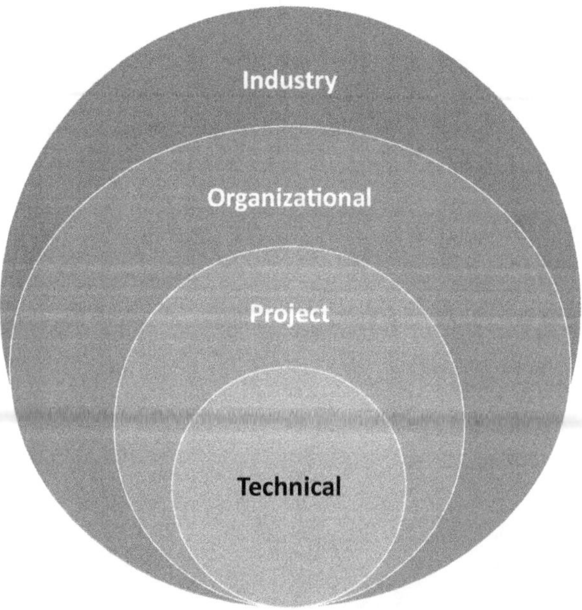

Figure 3.10 Interface categories

technical interfaces, project interfaces occur within the organizational environment, but also encompass technical interfaces. Project interfaces include technical interfaces, but also include interfaces related to project management activities among the various interface parties.

Extending out from the project layer, organizational interfaces are the next layer and encompass the project and technical interfaces. These interfaces typically are associated with free issue or CPIs. However, when integrating with another independent project, they can include organizational issues associated with agreements with other organizations. Organizational interfaces can flow both toward the project and toward the industry as the final layer, which is illustrated in Figure 3.10.

Industry interfaces typically are associated with regulations and requirements from industry oversight agencies and bodies, including audits of the project. Every project is conducted within an industry and is subject to industry safety, health, and environmental standards. Industry oversight agencies exist to ensure that project development is consistent with established safety and environmental regulations; to prevent accidental environmental impact and protect workers performing hazardous jobs, among other regulatory considerations.

While Figure 3.10 illustrates the various layers of interfaces, every layer may not be addressed within the interface management system. Each organization sponsoring a project will decide at what level to conduct the interface management system and how it relates to other organizational and project processes. However, categorizing interfaces in this way can help support interface analysis and assist in determining how to structure the interface management program for the project.

3.3.1.1 Technical Interfaces

Technical, or *system*, interfaces are normally associated with conceptual design and detailed engineering of the system being produced by the project. The International Council on Systems Engineering (INCOSE) Handbook v3.2.2 identifies technical interfaces as physical, logical, human-system, and energy (INCOSE, 2012)—and further describes them as follows:

- Physical—connection point between hardware systems, subsystems, and components
- Logical—data signals and signal exchange protocols, etc.
- Human-System—operator versus operator terminal
- Energy—electrical power (generating, distributing, transmitting, and consuming)

The SEBoK also defines technical interfaces as matter, energy, or information flows exchanged between the system-of-interest and its external components in the context of its use, including physical interfaces (BKCASE, 2015).

Technical interfaces occur across technical disciplines, often with different areas of responsibility, such as electrical, mechanical, piping, structural, safety, and process, among others. Typically, engineering processes address technical interfaces and interdiscipline coordination within a single entity's scope of work. However, technical interfaces can also result when two different contractors provide interconnected systems for the same project. In the latter case, the technical interface has two or more interface parties.

3.3.1.2 Project Interfaces

Project management related interfaces occur across the 10 Project Management Institute (PMI) project management Knowledge Areas (PMI, 2015) and the project's life cycle or phases, called Process Groups by PMI (2015). A brief description of each PMI Knowledge Area is provided below:

- Project Integration Management—coordinates the other project areas to work together, especially to manage the interdependencies among the Knowledge Areas. These interfaces include issues related to free issue items provided to contractors from other contractors, company/client provided items to contractors, deliverables to support milestones, or the stage-gate process, etc.

- Project Scope Management—used to ensure that the project includes all of the work required and that no new work is added outside the defined scope. Interfaces include resolving overlap, conflicts, or gaps in scopes of work between interface parties. In large-scale complex projects utilizing complicated contract strategies, scope misalignments are common and even likely.
- Project Schedule Management—includes the processes to manage the schedule and timely completion of the project. Typical interfaces associated with this management area are related to aligning project schedules among various interface parties.
- Project Cost Management—includes the processes to plan, manage, and control costs in order to complete the project within the approved budget.
- Project Quality Management—works to ensure that the project meets its requirements or, in other words, does what it is expected to do. It is common for interface parties to request results from acceptance tests and other verification and validation events for products being delivered to them from other contractors. These interfaces can also include documentation of procedures for receiving the item and verifying their condition upon receipt.
- Project Resource Management—includes the processes used to develop, acquire, manage, and lead the project team.
- Project Communications Management—includes the processes to effectively communicate the right project information among the right stakeholders (both internal and external) at the right time. This includes how interface progress is reported through respective project management chains.
- Project Risk Management—includes identifying, managing, and controlling project risk (both positive and negative). It is typical for the project plan to change as a result of re-baselining or unexpected events. Interfaces related to risk are normally associated with time-critical events that require rapid resolution to prevent negative consequences. On the other hand, from the point of view of informed risk management, interfaces represent risks that can be addressed through effective project interface management.
- Project Procurement Management—includes the processes necessary to acquire the materials and services needed to complete the project, including contract development and administration. Interfaces related to procurement typically include managing the delivery of specified products, services, or information from interface parties' sub-suppliers and vendors to avoid negative impact on deliveries for another interface party.
- Project Stakeholder Management—includes the processes used to identify and manage the people and entities impacted by the project and engaging them in project activities and decisions.

Effective interface management reduces the risk inherent in common boundaries with explicit or implicit dependencies; thus, it is directly related to project risk management. During all phases or process groups, addressing these risks involves considerations for all the Knowledge Areas identified by PMI. The project material or information needs between interface parties can extend to all facets of project management: shared risks, alignment of project schedules, quality control methods, inspection routines, use of preferred vendors lists, coordination of critical skills/personnel, etc.

Interfaces across these management areas can be related to procurement activities, contract clarifications, safety procedures during installation and commissioning, critical material deliveries between contractors and subcontractors, and risk mitigation strategies across different contractors that have no formal controlling relationship. Effective interface management is unequivocally crucial to effective project scope, schedule, and cost management on large-scale complex projects. We submit that failure to manage interfaces can have a devastating impact on scope, and especially schedule and cost on such projects.

3.3.1.3 Organizational Interfaces

Managing a complex project often requires the integration of plans and resources from multiple organizations that may not have a direct contractual relationship. Each such organization likely has its own approach to what INCOSE calls the Organizational Project-Enabling Processes (INCOSE, 2012), which includes:

- Life-cycle model management process—this includes the approach to the entire project process
- Infrastructure management process for a project—this may include such items as facilities and computer networks and other information technology infrastructure
- Project portfolio management process—this includes how project selection decisions are made and resources allocated between the organization's projects
- Human resource management process—this includes how people are managed and how skills are developed
- Quality management process—this can include quality control, quality assurance, and verification and validation issues for the various parties on a complex project

Organizational interfaces extend from the project and into the client or contractors base organization and functional areas. This means that when entities need to cooperate to address interfaces, their personnel must recognize and understand the differences in organizational processes and may need to consider them in developing the interface solution. As an example, during project execution, it is common to have CPIs provided by the client or contractor. These CPIs need to be delivered by the organization to the project at a specified time and to detailed specifications. Coordination at the organizational level is necessary to align the CPI with the project design and development. Misalignment can create unwanted delays, rework, and added cost.

Organizational interfaces also include operations; i.e., the organizational entity that will take control of the project after completion. Operator input during the design and development of the project is critical; ultimately, they are the end users of the system being realized by the project. For projects delivering elements that integrate with an existing system or another project, organizational interfaces may involve obtaining agreement on integration requirements and specification, timelines, allocations, etc.

To manage an organizational interface, it is necessary to address what each party will do to collaborate in terms of internal business processes at their respective organizational boundaries. For example, for projects integrating with other projects with different clients, the organizational interfaces might be addressed by a cooperative agreement between the two parties (projects) that establish guidance and integration requirements, administrative policies, and management practices.

3.3.1.4 Industry Interfaces

The final category of interfaces is industry interfaces. Nearly every project is developed within a specific industry, which is guided by industry standards and regulations and under the oversight of government agencies. In large-scale complex projects, involvement with industry regulators is expected to ensure the project is adhering to regulatory requirements. For example, in the oil and gas industry, a plan for development and operations must be submitted to authorities for review and approval prior to project execution. During project execution, it is not uncommon to seek clarification of industry standards and regulations. Large-scale projects integrating with existing government facilities, such as rail network or oil process facilities, must interface effectively with government counterparts.

These categories of interfaces help illustrate how interface management applies in a project from lower levels in technical disciplines, such as engineering, up through higher oversight levels, such as senior executives or industry oversight agencies. Interface management identifies the layers of interfaces, devises a structure to organize the interactions, and reduces the complexity of interactions among independent entities on a project. This helps to ensure that clear interface requirements are transmitted from the party that has the requirement to the party that needs to fulfill it. In addition to the categories, interfaces can be described by type, as discussed in the next section.

3.3.2 Interface Types—Internal and External

We recognize two types of interfaces—internal and external. An internal interface is defined in this book as: *an interface occurring within an interface party's scope of work or area of responsibility, within the same project for the same client contract, including any derived subcontracts.* An external interface is defined to be: *an interface requiring coordination along common boundaries between two independent entities (interface parties) with no controlling, contractual, or organizational relationship.*

3.3.2.1 Internal Interfaces

Whether an interface is identified as internal or external depends upon what is used to discriminate between these two types, in other words, how the client or the higher-level contractor defines what is *internal* and what is *external.*

Contracts are a common method of defining the boundary between internal and external interfaces. In the example in Figure 3.11, Contractor A is the main contractor. Contractor A's scope of work establishes which interfaces are under the contractor's control (internal interfaces), and which are outside its control (external interfaces). As shown, the main contractor is using two subcontractors to execute the contract. From the main contractor's (Contractor A's) perspective, any and all interfaces occurring within Contractor A's contract will be managed as internal interfaces. This includes any interfaces that may exist between the two subcontractors shown in Figure 3.11.

In some cases, contractual or cooperative agreements are reached between subcontractors as is indicated by the arrow between the two subcontractors. This is often the case when subcontractors

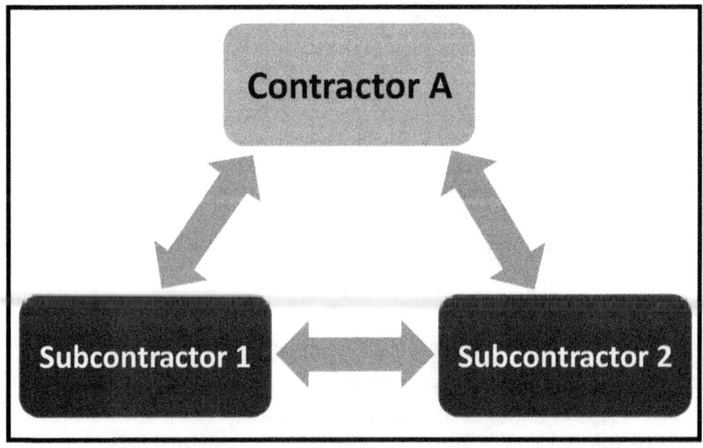

Figure 3.11 Contractor internal interfaces

have a history of working together and whose specialized products are reliant upon the other. Thus they have an interest in working closely together to ensure their two products align as they have done on previous projects.

While the previous example used the main contractor's contract to differentiate internal from external interfaces, there are many other ways to establish the boundary between the two interface types. For example, the client may establish internal interfaces among its management teams who are managing various subprojects or between various functional departments in its organization that are supporting the project, such as safety and environment. In this case, the client has designated its organization or entity as the boundary establishing which are internal and which are external interfaces. So, in such a case, interfaces between the organization's functional departments are defined as internal.

3.3.2.2 External Interfaces

External interfaces occur between two (or more) parties that do not have a controlling relationship. Because there is no controlling relationship, these interfaces typically represent the highest risk to a project. This is illustrated through the relationships shown in Figure 3.12.

In Figure 3.12, the client has contracted with two separate contractors (A and B). The contractors have established their own organizations to complete their respective work. These two main contractors (A and B) do not have a contractual relationship with one another, but they must nonetheless cooperate and communicate in order to deliver their respective portions of the project. The interfaces between Contractor A and Contractor B are defined as external interfaces. Also shown in Figure 3.12, each main contractor (A and B) has control over their internal interfaces through a contractual relationship with their subcontractors. This contractual relationship makes it easier to dictate the processes, procedures, and tools to be used to manage interfaces, which of course is more difficult when managing external interfaces.

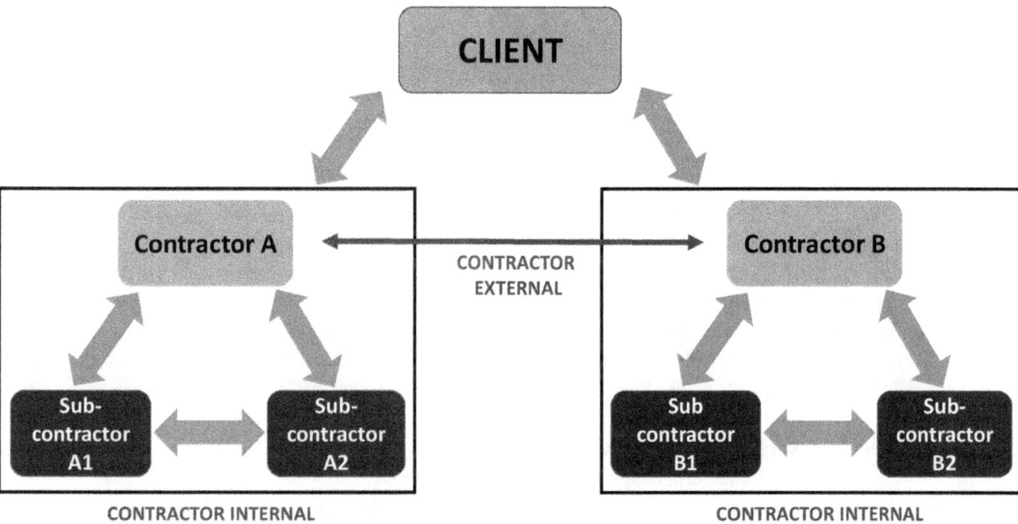

Figure 3.12 Contractor external interfaces

3.4 SUMMARY

In this chapter, basic interface definitions, terminology, and concepts have been presented to provide a consistent foundation for the remainder of the book. As a relatively new management function, interface management acts to align project management with SE, and with the project's external influencers, to reduce risk. It provides a structured, transparent, and logical process to identify and organize interfaces within complex projects, including external entities that influence the project. Complex interactions can be identified, organized, and resolved methodically to prevent unwanted or unintended negative consequences to scope (including quality), schedule, and cost during project integration.

Obtaining a consistent understanding of interface management enables diverse organizations and teams to identify and manage all of the interfaces across the project internally and externally. Although all interfaces must be properly identified and managed, the majority are generated during project planning and early execution. This is an ideal opportunity to recognize the interfaces to be managed, and to define their scope and resolution plans. Interfaces that are not properly managed can introduce safety, cost, and schedule risk. Failure to do so can and does create negative outcomes for the project later during the life cycle. It is significantly easier to influence the project's outcome when interface issues are identified early in the project.

With this chapter providing an introduction to the concepts and terminology of interface management, the next chapter focuses on the basic interface management process. An inherent challenge for major capital projects is determining the scope of interfaces and how to best manage them in order to provide positive outcomes and prevent negative consequences. Chapter 4 describes the process for identifying, organizing, and resolving interfaces both within the project and with external entities that influence the project.

3.5 REFERENCES

BKCASE Editorial Board (2015). *The Guide to the Systems Engineering Body of Knowledge (SEBoK)*, v. 1.4. R.D. Adcock (EIC). Hoboken, NJ: The Trustees of the Stevens Institute of Technology. Retrieved August 8, 2014 from www.sebokwiki.org.

Caglar, J. and M. Connolly. (2007). *Interface Management—Effective information exchange through improved communication*. ABB, Inc. Value Paper Series, Houston, TX.

Flyvbjerg, B. (2007). "Truth and Lies About Megaprojects." Inaugural Speech, Faculty of Technology, Policy, and Management, Delft University of Technology, September 2007.

Healey, P. (1997). *Project Management: Getting the Job Done on Time and in Budget*, ISBN: 0750689439, Butterworth-Heinemann, Woburn, MA. 01801-2041.

INCOSE (2012). *Systems Engineering Handbook: A Guide for System Life Cycle Processes and Activities*, version 3.2.2. San Diego, CA: International Council on Systems Engineering (INCOSE), INCOSE-TP-2003-002-03.2.2.

Nooteboom, U. (2004). "Interface management improves on-time, on-budget delivery of megaprojects," JPT Online, The Society of Petroleum Engineers, August, 2004. p. 32–34. Retrieved June 7, 2014 from http://www.intecsea.com/publications/technical-publications/267-interface-management-improves-on-time-on-budget-delivery-of-megaprojects.

Project Management Institute. (2017). *A Guide to the Project Management Body of Knowledge (PMBOK® Guide)*. 6th Edition. Project Management Institute, Newtown Square, PA.

Wideman, R. M. (2002). *Wideman Comparative Glossary of Project Management Terms*, v3.1. Retrieved June 2, 2014 from http://maxwideman.com/pmglossary/PMG_I03.htm.

Wren, Daniel A. (1967). "Interface and interorganizational coordination." Academy of Management, Journal 10, no. 1: 69–81.

4

Basic Interface Management Process

"The unlike is joined together, and from differences results the most beautiful harmony."
—Heraclitus

Management is the *planning, organizing, leading, and controlling of human and other resources to achieve organizational goals efficiently and effectively* (Jones and George, 2014); these are often identified as some of the *functions* of management. Applying management functions to projects helps to structure and simplify complexity. By establishing management processes in the project, the organization is setting the foundation to drive the actions of people, communicate expectations of desired outcomes, build a framework to monitor and control activities, and provide order and structure. Similar to other management functions, project management processes are an important aspect of planning, organizing, monitoring, controlling performance, and ensuring completeness during project execution.

Project interface management is one of many project and systems engineering (SE) management functions within large-scale projects. Interface management focuses on simplifying complex interface interactions resulting from complicated project development strategies and complexity in designing and developing the system resulting from the project. Like other management functions, interface management provides a holistic framework to include people, processes, procedures, tools, and techniques. Equally important, interface management considers the project environment and how project development occurs over time. Against this backdrop, the project team can begin to understand the breadth and depth of interfaces needed to deliver the project, and can begin to plan and emplace the appropriate management system to ensure effective and efficient interface activity and interaction. As expected, interface management shares many similarities with other management functions and includes a heavy reliance on a basic process, which consists of a number of steps and activities to help guide the actions of those within, or associated with, the project interfaces.

In this chapter, we focus on the basic interface management process model and the actions essential to completing the steps and activities in the process. The basic interface management process is presented conceptually in Figure 4.1. Rather than prescribing strict adherence to this model, we use the model to describe the process as a general guideline. As with any other management process models, the process illustrated in Figure 4.1 can and should be tailored and applied by the project team to the unique circumstances and environment of each project. Further, the application of each step and activity in the process, or the need for additional steps, is at the discretion of each project team.

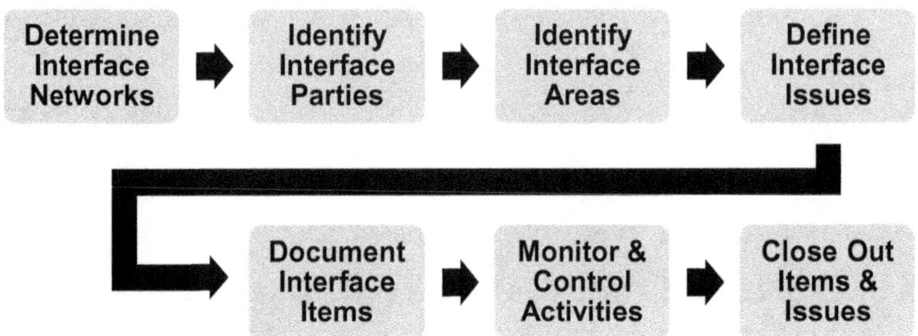

Figure 4.1 Basic Interface Management Process Model

The seven basic steps in the process model in Figure 4.1 include:

- Determine Interface Networks
- Identify Interface Parties
- Identify Interface Areas
- Define Interface Issues
- Identify, Plan, and Document
- Monitor and Control Activities
- Resolve and Close Out Interface Items and Issues

One may view this process as strictly linear—where one step follows the other. However, this is not the case. There is considerable overlap and iteration between the steps and within the process. Further, given the many different interface networks, interface groups, and intensity of interface activity within a large-scale complex project, the process is nearly always at different stages for different actors (i.e., entities affected by the process). The process is presented in a simple linear manner in this chapter to illustrate the flow of activities associated with managing interfaces. This helps those unfamiliar with interface management to gain a better understanding of the flow of activities across the spectrum of the process.

As with any management process, the interface management process is part of a larger interface management system or program, including the people, tools, techniques, and procedures needed to perform the process. In essence, the interface management process acts as the nerve center for the project's interface management system and provides the structure to guide the project's interface personnel and others involved in managing interfaces in the performance of their roles and responsibilities. As stated, the process is not a series of isolated *stovepipe* activities, but is aligned to and integrated with the use of an interface management tool to help manage the volumes of data and information that flow within—into and out of the process.

Inherent in the process is the use of analysis and management techniques that support identification of project interfaces, and ensure that interfaces are logically structured and are managed in alignment with the other parts of the interface management system. Thus, the process is essential in order to align the various pieces of the project and to help maintain interface management effectiveness and efficiency. That is, the process drives the simplification and control of complex interactions between entities such that each entity receives the right information or material at the right rime to prevent unwanted schedule delays or costly scope misalignments. In addition, this process is not stand-alone; it is connected to other project management processes, which will be discussed later in the book.

Subprocesses established within each step help to better define how activities are performed to complete the step. For example, the *Monitor and Control Activities* process step is usually specified in the project's interface management procedure or philosophy, which is distributed via contracts to contractors and to the sponsoring organization's project team. In this book, we provide an overview of the process with examples. However, as with any process, there are myriad possibilities when implementing a management process and the project team for each individual project must consider the best way given their existing project management system, organizational culture, and the specific circumstances of the project under development.

4.1 INTERFACE PROCESS—PROJECT PHASES

The timing for completing the activities within the interface management process is graphically depicted in Figure 4.2 along the project phases. This illustration is not intended to be exact, but rather activity completion is approximated and subject to the circumstances of each project.

The step *Determining Interface Networks* generally occurs during project initiation or very early in the planning phase. At this point, sufficient information should exist to begin crafting the various interface networks. Depending on the project approach, iteration may be required during the project life cycle to update interface networks, especially if the project management plan or approach changes significantly. This step is typically performed by the client's project team, but is also applicable to the main contractors' teams after contract award if it is determined that the scope of work requires the management of multiple interface networks. Performing this step is also necessary when integrating with another project or into an existing system.

The steps *Identify Interface Parties*, *Identify Interface Areas*, and *Determine Interface Issues* are shown from the project's initiation phase and well into the planning phase. Again, the client's project team performs this step initially to help gather information to set up the project's interface management system and begin to form the basis for *what information* needs sharing between the respective interface groups within each interface network. Once the client begins to award contracts for the various scopes of work or establishes cooperation agreements with other projects and existing systems, interface groups are initiated and begin collaborating to identify and plan their respective interface

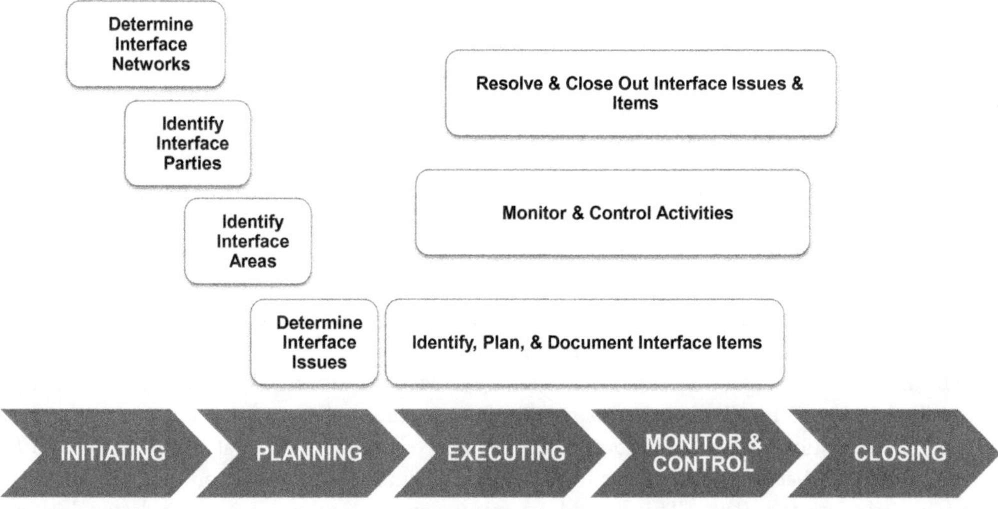

Figure 4.2 Basic Interface Management Process—Project Phases

items. It may be necessary to iterate back to the *Identify Interface Parties*, *Identify Interface Areas*, and *Determine Interface Issues* if the scope of work has changed prior to contract award. Regardless, it is good practice to allow each interface group to iterate through these steps after initiating the group to make sure no interfaces were accidentally omitted during initial completion of these steps.

After initiating the interface group, each group will work to identify specific interface items associated with each interface issue that needs to be resolved to ensure their scopes of work and their areas of responsibility and deliverables align. Each interface item is planned in accordance with the project schedules of each interface party. If this step in the process is performed correctly, and the project schedules are accurate and reliable, then this is the time where interface *clashes* are identified. A clash means that one party requires resolution of an interface, but the other party is unable to meet the required timeline. As an example, out-of-sequence engineering can result in numerous technical interface clashes.

The *Monitor and Control Activities* step is an activity performed by all parties in the interface management system; although the client, as the benefactor, is the main party of concern. Clearly, it is in the client's best interest, and the project's, to ensure interface management activity is progressing as planned between all parties. This step requires the establishment of interface management key performance indicators (KPIs), which are measures of performance (Bible and Bivins, 2011), and collection of data and information to evaluate how the interface management system is performing during project execution. As with nearly every management function, reporting progress is a standard part of the project reporting process. Information and results from this step of interface management will flow into the project's reporting process. This step also includes interface verifications and audits to ensure management procedures are implemented as required and interface agreements are implemented as agreed by the interface parties. We will discuss this step in much more detail later in the book.

Finally, the *Resolve and Close Out Interface Issues and Items* steps are performed throughout most of the project execution phase and into the project's closing phase. During project execution, regular interface activity normally results in reaching agreement on how to resolve individual interface items, which are then implemented by the responsible interface parties, and then the interface item is closed. Ultimately, resolution of all interface items will result in corresponding interface issues being closed, which eventually leads to all interface areas being closed. This step interacts with the Monitor and Control Activities interface process step in that as interface issues and areas are closed, it may be necessary to conduct interface verification, audits, or design reviews to confirm that all interface agreements have been implemented by the respective parties.

4.1.1 Top-Down Analysis—Bottom-Up Synthesis

It should be clear from Figure 4.2 that the interface management process requires *analysis* during the project planning phase and *synthesis* during the project execution phase. Analysis is the means of separating any material or abstract entity into its composite elements, which is the opposite of synthesis, which involves putting together or combining parts into a whole (Forman and Selly, 2001). Analysis serves a crucial role during planning because it simplifies complexity by using a structured and logical approach. Similarly, synthesis provides the framework to ensure traceability of interface activity and full resolution of interfaces between parties.

The interface management process is *top-down* decomposition requiring interface analysis (described in detail in Chapter 6) during the project planning phase and *bottom-up* synthesis during the execution phase. More specifically, the analysis process starts at a high level from *Determine Interface Networks* and works toward a more detailed view as the process progresses toward *Identify Interface Items*. This provides a framework to segment complex relationships and required interactions into manageable pieces so that they can be logically analyzed while reducing the chances of omitting interfaces. As all interface items are identified, we begin to move up the process model (i.e., bottom-up) to synthesize the results starting at the interface items level and working toward final resolution and closeout of all interface areas.

4.2 DETERMINE INTERFACE NETWORKS

Recall from Chapter 3, an interface network is a group of interface parties established to coordinate interface issues associated with specific stakeholders of the project. These interface networks are logical groupings of related project entities that need to interact with each other in order to resolve interface issues relevant to their group. According to the International Council on Systems Engineering (INCOSE, 2011), system architecture is a selection of the types of system elements, their characteristics, and their arrangement; also sometimes expressed as system components and their relationships. Interface networks are derived from the system architecture developed for the project and the development environment of the project. Both the architecture and the environment influence the composition of interface networks, which can include external elements that can influence the project, such as oversight agencies, other projects, and existing systems with which the project must integrate.

4.2.1 Interface Network Overview

Interface networks are analogous to communication interaction networks (CINs) (Wang et al., 2012). A CIN is essentially a graphical representation of *who talks to whom* among a group of individuals. In the case of interface networks, the who or whom are entities or groups rather than individual people. However, just as important as who talks to whom is what information these parties need to convey to one another and when. In everyday terminology, one can think of our individual social and professional networks as an example of interface networks; however, interface networks represent entities or groups and not individual people. For example, an individual may use a social network site to communicate and interact with family and friends, and a professional networking internet site (such as LinkedIn) to communicate and interact with professional colleagues. These networks provide a way for people to structure networks so that they can control, either intentionally or subconsciously, the types of information shared with the parties within each network. In addition, the means to communicate may vary. For instance, the family network may choose to use a phone system while interaction with professional colleagues may use an internet site such as LinkedIn.

Our family members are generally organized into one interface network, friends into a second interface network, and our colleagues at work as a third. Each of these networks serves to organize the type of interaction we have with its constituent members (i.e., interface parties) within each network. Within the family interface network, private or sensitive family matters are communicated among individuals as part of personal interactions. Different relevant information is communicated within networks associated with friends and within networks associated with work. Specifically, the interactions focus on information that is appropriate within the network.

If we examine our family and work interface networks (a.k.a. *interaction networks*) closely, we find it is not usually necessary for those in our work network to interact with those in our family network, except in unusual circumstances, such as a medical emergency or annual social gathering. Rather, these networks are normally separated and logically organized by the types of interface activity occurring within these groups and the type of information that needs to be shared among its members. The point is that we naturally organize our interactions with others into groupings because it helps to establish boundaries for the types of interactions we have with the individuals within those networks.

The same is true for the various entities involved in large-scale complex projects. The difference is that members of project interface networks are entities (e.g., companies or other projects) rather than individuals. In project interface networks, individuals communicate and interact on behalf of entities.

Interface networks on large-scale capital projects typically include the client's prime contractor network (for interactions between the client and prime contractors) and the client's internal interface network (for interactions within the client's internal structure). However, the project may include many more interface networks depending upon the system architecture, the project's development environment, and operational conditions after transitioning the system to its owner. Projects that require integration into a national infrastructure, such as rail or oil and gas transfer, may include civilian and government interface networks.

The central role these interface networks play is to organize different independent parties or entities into logical groupings for interaction purposes. That is, interface networks are related to specific aspects of the project under development and/or the system produced by the project. It is reasonable to say these interface networks are simply groups of related stakeholders.

4.2.2 Interface Network Examples

The number and type of interface networks utilized is dependent upon a number of factors including the project development strategy, the system produced by the project, the environment in which the project is developed, and the operating environment in which the system is fielded, installed, or transitioned. Later in the book, we discuss analysis techniques and tools to identify and organize interface networks. Some examples of interface networks include:

- Client's prime contractor (CPC)
- Client internal project (CIP)
- Project-to-project (P2P)
- Project-to-existing system (P2ES)
- Project sponsor-to-industry (PSI)
- Organization-to-organization (O2O)
- Contractor Internal (CI) or Prime Contractor Internal (PCI)

4.2.2.1 Client's Prime Contractor Interface Network

The CPC interface network provides a communication interaction network for the client and one or more main contractors contributing to the same project that have no contractual relationships. Main contractors have a contract directly with the client and thus the controlling relationship is toward the client and not toward other main contractors or their teams. This type of network allows the various contractors to interact on interface issues related to their respective scopes of work. More precisely, it allows these contractors to interact on issues that cross their common boundaries, which are established by their scopes of work. This network can also include any client entity, which is supplying *free issue items* or *company provided items* (CPIs) to interface parties within the network. These items typically require interface alignment on technical specifications and management requirements, such as related project constraints of time, cost, and scope.

4.2.2.2 Client Internal Project Interface Network

A routine practice on large-scale complex capital projects is to subdivide the project into different parts or subprojects, which reduces organizational and communication complexity, and, for many entities, can leverage a greater variety of products and services across a global marketplace. In practice, this approach often results in several main contractors or contractor teams contributing to the project, such as described in the CPC interface network previously mentioned. In doing so, the client establishes *subproject teams*, each of which represents the client for a main contractor or main contractor team. It is normal for these teams within the client entity to interact with each other in order to implement changes that extend across scope boundaries for their contractors, provide input to technical queries from main contractors or government oversight agencies, and establish common interface risk responses to uncertainties extending across scope boundaries.

In addition, the sponsoring organization may be providing substantial CPIs to the various subproject teams. In these situations, the client's internal organization can establish an internal interface network to identify entities within the organization and project that need to interact to coordinate and agree on interface issues across the sponsoring organization's subproject teams, such as technical queries, approved changes, etc.

4.2.2.3 Project-to-Project Interface Network

In a P2P network, one project under development is integrated to or with another project under development. These projects can be part of the same organization or belong to a completely different organization or even to a competitor. This type of network provides a direct P2P communication channel to formally interact and coordinate related interface issues between independent projects that are required to integrate with each other. This is fairly common in the American defense industry where several military system projects are under development at the same time, but are required to operate as a *family of systems* when fielded. This form of interface network is also common in the oil and gas industry where offshore project *tie-ins* are standard practice to minimize the offshore footprint and maximize the effectiveness of existing field architectures.

4.2.2.4 Project-to-Existing System Interface Network

Many large-scale capital projects are required to integrate into existing systems, such as a new oil or gas pipeline into an existing processing facility, a new rail line into an existing railway infrastructure, or a new airplane model into the existing aerospace infrastructure. In these cases, it may be necessary to establish a P2ES interface network for interface parties between the existing system and the project. The basis of this network is the activity necessary to integrate the project into the existing system or infrastructure.

4.2.2.5 Project Sponsor-to-Industry Interface Network

In some situations, the project's sponsoring organization may need to establish an interface network with industry agencies, such as safety and environmental bodies. Either the client or members from the project team on behalf of the client can fill the role of *project sponsor*. Such an interface network may be needed where large-scale projects are conducted close to sensitive wildlife areas and require environmental monitoring, or involve adherence to strict safety protocols during development. Such networks can be useful where projects extend across significant distances and involve many local communities and state governments and interest groups.

4.2.2.6 Organization-to-Organization Interface Network

In some cases, competing organizations or businesses sponsor separate projects, but these projects require collaboration, cross-contribution, or other joint cooperation between the projects. Such arrangements are typically governed by an *agreement* between the two organizations and result in various specifications and requirements, in addition to commercial terms, to be met by the respective project organizations when the systems are fielded to operations. Such an arrangement also requires the two organizations to establish common processes, procedures, tools, etc., for the development of their respective projects. If these projects are operated in unison or together to create value for the respective companies, then this interface management network is useful to coordinate common operating procedures and joint response procedures for emergency situations.

4.2.2.7 Prime Contractor Internal Interface Network

In some situations, the prime contractor's scope of work or teaming arrangement may force the establishment of a Prime Contractor Internal (PCI) interface network. It is common for major companies to agree to a teaming arrangement by which a number of companies divide the scope of work for their related specializations. For example, one company may be responsible for engineering, another company in the team for procurement, and still a third company for fabrication and construction. In such an arrangement, especially when there is no prior teaming experience between the contractors, an internal interface network can help to synchronize interfaces among the various entities. This is especially true when the contractors' management systems are different.

This type of network is also useful when the scope of work is expansive or exceedingly complex, which requires the dispersion of work to be carried out by different divisions of the same company at different geographic locations. For example, a main contractor awarded a contract for engineering decides to subcontract part of the work to an engineering company, which then decides to disperse the engineering scope to several locations and departments within their company. A similar case could be true for construction activities where the scope is being conducted at several locations and then assembled, i.e., integrated, at another site.

4.2.3 Output of Interface Network Analysis

The output of this process activity is the identification of the total number and types of interface networks. As stated previously, each project environment and each sponsoring organization is different. Therefore, after identifying project interface networks, the project team needs to ascertain the appropriate process to manage each network. For example, an organization may elect to manage an O2O interface network through the company's legal department or the P2P interface network through the project management office (PMO), while the remainder of the networks are managed through the project's interface management system. Regardless, all interface networks affecting the project need to be accounted for within a management system, either the sponsoring organization's (such as a project or portfolio management office) or the project's interface management system.

Later in the book, we will discuss how the interface networks, managed under the project's interface management processes, are used as the basis for setting up the project's interface management system and preparing for the implementation of that system prior to the start of the project execution phase. Identifying and managing interface networks in the interface management system rather than as part of other organizational processes or management systems forms the foundation for the scope of interface management for the project. This distinction means that the interface networks assigned for management in the project's interface management system are the basis of responsibility for the client's project interface manager. Placing interface networks under other organizational processes means that responsibility for these networks is outside the scope of the project's interface manager unless otherwise specified by the project manager or project director. As is the case in all roles, it is important to be clear about what is and is not within the responsibility of the project's interface management system in order to prevent confusion, overlap, or duplication of effort.

4.2.4 Common Pitfalls

A common mistake is putting all interface parties into one interface network. On the surface, it may appear to be easier and simpler to establish one network with all interface parties, but in reality, this approach often creates a number of problems including: increased difficulty in verification and auditing, confusion in monitoring and control, uncertainty over roles and responsibilities, and failure to reduce complexity.

4.2.4.1 Difficulty in Verification and Auditing

It is much more difficult to audit and conduct verifications. Each network represents an aspect of the project and the system developed by the project. When placing all interface parties into a single interface network, it is much more difficult to identify which aspects of the interface management system are performing poorly. It is much easier to audit the network and conduct verifications on the areas between the respective interface groups when separate interface networks are specified.

4.2.4.2 Monitoring and Controlling Confusion

In large-scale complex capital projects, the number of interface groups can be extensive (often up to 50 interface parties). When these groups are located within the same network, it can create confusion as to which parties should be assigned to interface groups, missing interface issues, and difficulty in identifying specific sources of interface breakdowns. By defining the interface network as the first activity during interface planning, the aspect of the interface network span of interaction can be better defined, monitored, and controlled.

4.2.4.3 Failure to Reduce Complexity

Finally, one of the primary objectives of interface management is to simplify interaction complexity by logically organizing complicated interactions into management segments. Interface networks are a key tool in meeting this objective because they segment interface parties by related area. Mixing unrelated groups increases the chances of miscommunication or interaction interference and detracts from the effectiveness of interface analysis during the planning phase at least in part because it delays the *down-plan* decisions on interface parties until after sorting out which entities should be involved, one of the main purposes of interface network analysis.

4.3 IDENTIFY INTERFACE PARTIES

The purpose of identifying interface parties is to ascertain which parties within an interface network need to interface and establish important interface roles between the relevant interface groups. This activity also includes the steps to designating interface groups and establishing the lead interface party (LIP) and interface party relationships for each interface group.

4.3.1 Analyze Interface Networks

Each interface network must have at least two interface parties and normally contains several (20 or more). The reason for the minimum is obvious since there would be no need to establish a network for a single entity. Once the interface network is determined, interface analysis aids in identifying all parties within the network that potentially need to interface. At this point, the purpose is to understand the role each party in each interface network plays. This activity is normally performed by the project sponsor's organization during the early part of the planning phase. More specifically, the project's interface manager or someone on the project team performs this responsibility during early project planning. With a total list of network parties, each party is reviewed to ascertain whether they share any common boundary or boundaries with another party or parties in the network.

In cases where the number of parties is high, approximately 20 or more, the initial intention is to eliminate parties that clearly do not need to interface in order to reduce the total amount to a more manageable number. In many cases, it will be very easy to ascertain which entities share a boundary. For example, two parties sharing a physical connection point, or physical interfaces, are normally easy to identify. In other cases, the shared boundary will be more difficult to determine and will require more in-depth analysis, such as those with logical (i.e., signals or software) interfaces. The output of this activity is a preliminary list of interface parties based on interface boundaries determined by scopes of work or responsibility.

4.3.2 Designate Interface Groups

With a complete list of interface parties within each interface network, the needs of each interface party are evaluated against all other parties to determine which interface parties need to interface with other parties within each interface network. To be assigned as an interface party in an interface group, it is only necessary to share a boundary with another party, however trivial and minor. In fact, the intensity of interfaces will vary from interface group to interface group and align directly to the scope of work and the system developed or products or services provided by the respective parties. A preliminary interface party matrix (i.e., high-level responsibility matrix) is developed to identify all the interface parties that must interface with each other. This analysis also forms the basis for identifying which parties do not need to interface and confirming there are no shared boundaries or interface points.

An important aspect of this analysis is that consideration needs to be given throughout the life of the project, not just a specific time period, such as during the engineering phase. Interface management applies from early project planning and conceptual design through the transition of the project to the project sponsor (i.e., operator, sponsoring organization, etc.). In practical terms, this means that some interface groups will activate early in the project life while others may lie dormant until later in the project life. Regardless, it is important to identify all interface groups early in the project and update as needed. For example, updates may be necessary when the contract strategy changes, the project enters or exits a stage gate, or after a formal systems engineering design review where it may be discovered that new interface parties are needed. As will be discussed later, the timing for initiating each group needs to be considered during interface management planning.

4.3.2.1 Interface Group Analysis

When establishing interface groups, it is necessary to understand how important one party is to the other. The project execution plan, often called the project management plan, will provide an overview of how the project is executed by describing the project phases and execution model to be followed, including decision gates. This plan is an important source for helping to establish LIPs within interface groups. The decision gates in the plan are important for establishing project phase boundaries and identifying which entities will be involved at which stages of the project. This helps to understand how roles and responsibilities migrate over the life of the project. In turn, these roles and responsibilities translate to increased or changing importance of certain areas of the project at different points in the project life. This analysis helps to determine if and when to transition an interface party to the lead interface role of the LIP.

In addition, the architecture of the system delivered as a result of the project is another source to help establish interface parties. The system is the realization of the project such as a new aircraft, power plant, offshore oil facility, etc. The system architecture identifies the major subsystems and components and indicates how the system is to be designed, developed, and integrated. By studying the system's technical architecture, which elements represent more critical aspects of the design can be inferred.

A third important source for identifying the interface parties is the project's contract strategy. There are many approaches for contracting on a project; for example, using a single main contractor to perform all the work or using multiple main (prime) contractors with numerous subcontractors, suppliers, and vendors. The contract strategy will also include planned time frames for awarding and executing contracts. Often, contracts are awarded at different times during project execution to maximize efficiency and coincide with availability of resources. Once contracts are awarded to specific main contractors, interface parties can be named and interface groups formed and initiated, which will be discussed later in the book.

Depending upon the project's operational concept, when the project under development is integrated with another project or into an existing system or facility, it may be necessary to review cooperation agreements with the other projects and requirements documents from existing systems. These agreements, or contracts between projects, are a means to establish tie-in specifications, management arrangements, commercial terms, and organizational responsibilities relative to the cooperation.

4.3.2.2 Define Shared Boundaries

Defining shared boundaries is a step that both the client and contractors perform. While it is common for the client to list the general boundaries as part of a *responsibilities matrix* or similar document as part of the contract, the common boundaries (or battery limits) are often at a high level. After a contract is awarded and interface parties are identified, the respective interface groups will perform further analysis of their respective scopes of work to refine the common boundaries. The common boundaries serve as a starting point for further top-down decomposition to interface areas, issues, and items.

4.3.3 Establish Lead Interface Party and Interface Party Relationships

The final step in identifying interface parties is to establish which party will be designated as the LIP, and which party will be the interface party. The LIP is the interface party that is assigned as the one responsible for an interface group by the owner of the project's interface management system. The LIP is responsible for managing interface activity with an interface group. Each interface group is assigned an LIP. A standard practice is for the client or owner of the project's interface management function to assign the LIP to the interface party with the most critical need in the group or the party with system integrity responsibility. Thus the LIP typically represents the interface party who has the most urgent or important requirements in the relationship or represents the most important package, component, subsystem, or system contributing to the project. The output of this process activity is an interface group matrix identifying each interface group. The LIP and interface party relationship is illustrated in Figure 4.3.

Figure 4.3 illustrates a generic offshore oil and gas project. The figure shows that the project is subdivided into several sections, which are later contracted to different companies. At this point, the respective contractors for each segment of work is not known, or at least they should not be known

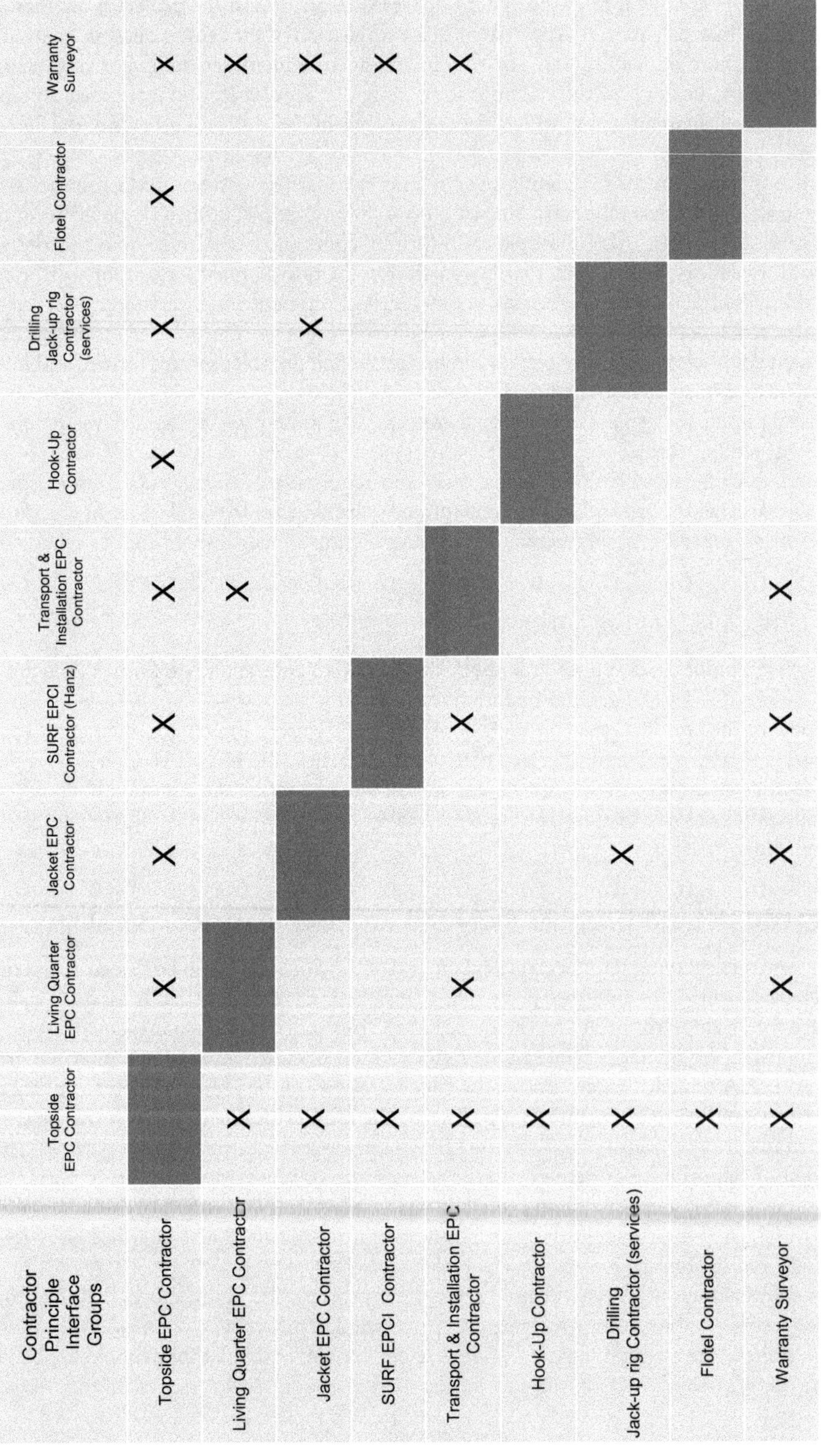

Contractor Principle Interface Groups	Topside EPC Contractor	Living Quarter EPC Contractor	Jacket EPC Contractor	SURF EPCI Contractor (Hanz)	Transport & Installation EPC Contractor	Hook-Up Contractor	Drilling Jack-up rig Contractor (services)	Flotel Contractor	Warranty Surveyor
Topside EPC Contractor		X	X	X	X	X	X	X	X
Living Quarter EPC Contractor	X				X				X
Jacket EPC Contractor	X						X		X
SURF EPCI Contractor	X								X
Transport & Installation EPC Contractor	X	X		X					X
Hook-Up Contractor	X								
Drilling Jack-up rig Contractor (services)	X		X						
Flotel Contractor	X								
Warranty Surveyor	X	X	X	X	X				

Figure 4.3 Interface group matrix (oil and gas project example)

when this activity is being performed. If the project has already awarded contracts for the various scopes of work, then the project is well behind in planning for interface management. Developing this interface group matrix should be completed before the first contract is awarded. Remember, the analysis thus far only correlates to the project environment and system architecture, but identification of this structure helps to set up the interface management system in preparation for the initial contracts and the start of the project execution phase. In the illustration, we observe several interface parties. A brief description of each party is provided for readers who are unfamiliar with the oil and gas industry. This is meant only as an example and is applicable to any industry.

- Topside EPC—This interface party's scope of work requires the contractor to engineer, procure, and construct (EPC) the topside facility. A *topside* facility is the part of the offshore platform where hydrocarbons are produced and processed.
- Living quarters (LQ) EPC—The scope of work for the LQ requires the contractor to EPC the facility's living quarters. The *living quarters* can be thought of as an offshore hotel on the platform. It accommodates offshore personnel and provides a platform monitor and control functional facility.
- Jacket EPC—The scope of work for the jacket requires the contractor to EPC the jacket structure to support the offshore platform. The *jacket* is the steel structure supporting the offshore platform.
- SURF EPCI—The scope of work for subsurface umbilical (electrical, signal, and fluid cable bundles) risers and flowlines (SURF) requires the contractor to engineer, procure, construct, transport and install (EPCI) all subsurface components that allow the offshore platform to transport hydrocarbons from the facility to a transport carrier or pipeline.
- Transportation and Installation (T&I) EPC—The scope of work for T&I requires the contractor to EPC the systems necessary to T&I topside and living quarters from their construction site to the offshore field.
- Hook-up—The scope of work for the hook-up contractor is to engineer, procure, and fabricate all hook-up items necessary to physically connect the topside, jacket, and LQ after installation. Hook-up activities result in *mechanical completion* in most cases, which acts as an entry to start the commissioning process.
- Drilling and wells (D&W) jack-up rig (JUR)—The D&W JUR scope of work requires the contractor to drill and complete a specific number of offshore wells.
- Flotel—The scope of work for the flotel is to provide temporary accommodation for personnel offshore during mechanical completion (i.e., physical connection of the facility) and commissioning (i.e. the validation that the system is ready to be transitioned to operations). The flotel is analogous to a floating hotel that provides accommodations for offshore personnel.

As shown in Figure 4.3, all interface parties are assigned within at least one interface group. Further, one of the interface parties within the interface group has been designated as the LIP, as shown by the *gray* top row where several interface parties have been designated as the LIP. Most important, the interface group matrix shows every group with an LIP and an interface party.

In this example, contractors shown in the top row are LIPs against any party in which they have an *X* in the corresponding column. For example, Topside EPC is LIP against seven interface parties, as shown in the *Topside EPC* row. In essence, the project sponsor, or owner of the interface management process has designated *Topside EPC* to be the most important interface party within this interface network. Priority is given to the LIP role by working from left to right in the top row. This means that *Topside EPC* is the main priority, then for any group in which topside EPC is not a member, this LIP designation has then been assigned to *Living Quarters*.

This process is repeated for every interface network, which results in an interface group matrix for each interface network. As will be demonstrated later, the interface group matrix serves as the basis for setting up the interface management software tool, which the interface groups will use to conduct interface activity.

4.3.3.1 General LIP Role and Responsibility

The operative word in the LIP title is *lead.* This word does not imply a master/servant relationship. Rather, it denotes additional responsibility given to one party over the other by the owner of the interface management process to ensure interface activity is initiated and sustained, and that progress is made in resolving interface areas between the groups. Some of the responsibilities entrusted to the LIP are:

- Prepare a schedule for interface group kickoff meetings with interface contractors
- Plan and schedule regular interface working group meetings with other interface contractors to include preparing meeting agendas, recording meeting minutes, hosting meetings, etc.
- Develop and maintain the interface management database (i.e., interface register) in cooperation with respective interfacing parties
- Ensure that all interfaces are satisfactorily planned and closed out within a time scale that will not jeopardize the project schedule
- Develop action plans consisting of required activities, decisions, timelines, and personnel required to resolve complex interface issues
- Deliver status reports

4.4 IDENTIFY INTERFACE AREAS

Managers use project plans, timelines, and budgets to reduce *execution risk*, the risk that designated activities will not be carried out properly. However, they inevitably neglect two other critical risks, the *white space risk*—that some required activities won't be identified in advance, leaving gaps in the project plan; and the *integration risk*—that the disparate activities won't come together at the end (Matta and Ashkenas, 2003). Identifying interface areas during early project planning helps to prevent these problematic issues later in project execution.

With the common boundaries established among the various interface groups, it is now possible to begin identifying and documenting the relevant interface areas that need to be resolved within the interface group. As defined in Chapter 3, an interface area is . . . *a defined area of interest on the common boundary between two or more interface parties.* An interface area is characterized by one or more interface issues that the interface parties must agree upon and resolve. It should be noted that each interface group has different interface areas, issues, and items, which are dependent upon the common boundary they share.

It is preferable that both the client and contractors perform this step. The client should perform this activity early in the project planning phase to help develop the responsibility matrix for the respective prime contracts. The responsibility matrix illustrates the broad division of responsibility among the various contracts as the project proceeds through its life cycle. Prime contractors should also perform this activity immediately after contract award as part of project and interface planning. This helps to prevent misalignments in their scope of work and establishes a foundation for common understanding for future interface activity with other interface partners.

A common understanding of the interface areas between the interface parties is important to ensure that both the scope of work or responsibility and their respective plans for delivering their services and products align with one another. In addition, a common understanding of the interface areas serves as the base for further decomposition into specific interface issues and items, which will be discussed later in this chapter. Examples of interface areas are piping, electrical, telecommunications, safety, control, automation, pipelines, structural, schedule, signal exchange, process, procurement, free issue items, transportation, installation, etc. The aim is to first identify the main areas between the two (or more) parties, which serves as a basis for further decomposition.

A common method for identifying and confirming interface areas is conducting an interface kickoff meeting between interface groups, often with client personnel present. Each interface party reviews the relevant portion of their scope of work with the other interface party and provides each party an opportunity to query the other. This results in an understanding of which technical (electrical, structural, process, etc.) and management (project management, procurement, etc.) personnel are required to support future interface activity (see Figure 4.4). Identifying these interface areas is critical to more detailed activity by the interface groups during interface meetings that result in further defining interface issues and specific interface items related to each issue.

Establishing and agreeing to the interface areas ensures that each party can identify respective personnel within their organization to handle these areas. For example, an interface group with an electrical interface area will likely identify their respective project electrical leads as the owners of this interface area. Thus, these personnel become key to follow-on activities of determining interface issues and items within the interface management process. What should become evident in the description of the interface process thus far is that while the process may start with activities by the project sponsor's project organization, such as identifying interface networks and groups, the process quickly begins to involve interface parties more as it moves into identifying interface areas. As the reader will notice going forward, this is especially true during the next steps in the process.

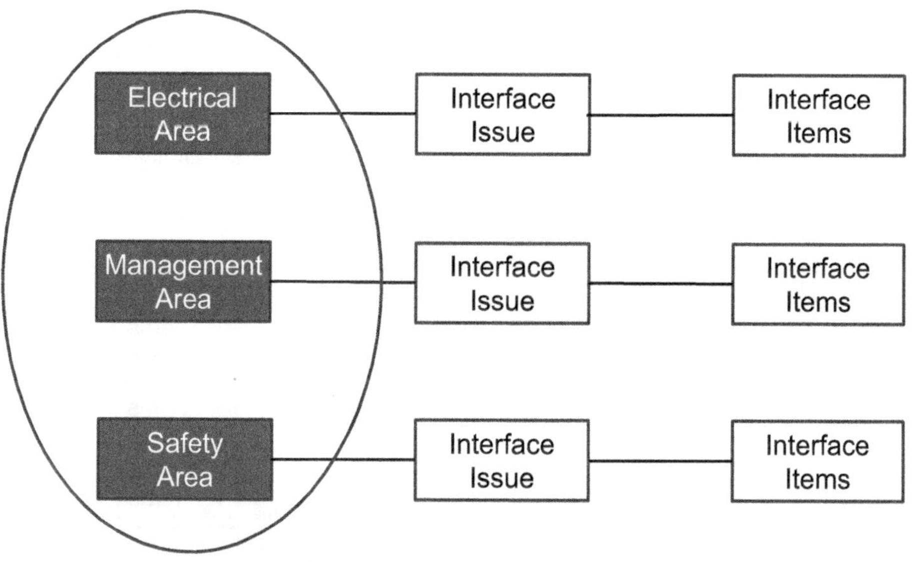

Figure 4.4 Identifying interface areas

4.5 DETERMINE INTERFACE ISSUES

To this point in the interface process, interface networks are established, interface groups determined, and the interface areas within each interface group established. It is now possible to begin a more thorough analysis of each interface area for each interface group to describe the scope of interface issues as illustrated in Figure 4.5. As defined in Chapter 3, an interface issue is a statement identifying specific aspects of the interface area, such as physical compatibility or functional conformance, requiring interface activity within an interface group.

The interface parties within each interface group commonly determine interface issues after the interface group is initiated. However, it is possible for the project sponsor's organization to generate a preliminary list of interface issues from organizational informational archive assets if similar projects have been completed previously. While it is not always necessary to perform this step, it is helpful in complex system architectures where interfaces extend across many technical and managerial areas. This process also provides a mechanism to further organize interface items and to prevent identification and coordination of redundant items. This is especially true for multidiscipline interfaces. In essence, this step aids in further decomposition of interface areas into individual interface items.

As illustrated in Figure 4.5, three interface areas are identified for an interface group: electrical, management, and safety. Further analysis during the *Identify Interface Issues* step reveals there are five issues across the three areas that need coordinating through interface activity and interaction.

In the electrical area, the interface group, and/or client, has determined *power protection* and *power management* for alignment between their areas of responsibility. In this situation, *power* crosses the systems being designed, developed, and delivered by the interface group. In this context, the interface group with technical representatives from the electrical discipline can begin to identify specific

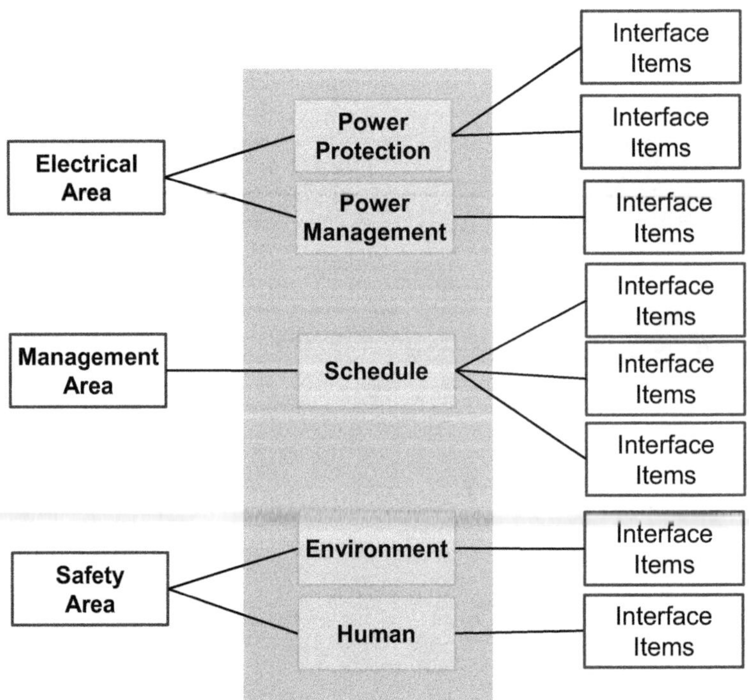

Figure 4.5 Identifying interface issues

interface items associated with each issue. The aim of these issues is to ensure that power is protected across the systems being developed by the interface group and that power flow can be managed effectively and safely. Thus, both system designs must align to prevent integration problems.

4.6 IDENTIFY AND PLAN INTERFACE ITEMS

An interface item is a specific data or information request(s) resulting from an interface issue from one interface party to the other interface party. Arguably, interface items are the most important aspect of interface activity as they produce the documented agreements between the parties in an interface group. Interface items are identified by each of the interface parties in the interface group to the other party or parties, and are typically coordinated through an interface management database tool. Figure 4.6 shows eight interface items resulting from the five interface issues identified previously.

When an interface item is identified, it is important that all parties agree on the delivery due date for the information, data, or item. It is common for interfacing parties to establish a regular meeting schedule (i.e., weekly or bi-weekly, or as otherwise appropriate) to review and discuss each interface item.

The output resulting from interface meetings typically includes the following:

1. A number of action items related to the interface items for the respective parties to make progress on existing interface items
2. Identification of new interface items
3. Realization of an agreement on some of the existing interfaces that can now be closed
4. Identification of critical interface items that can create negative consequences to the project if not resolved

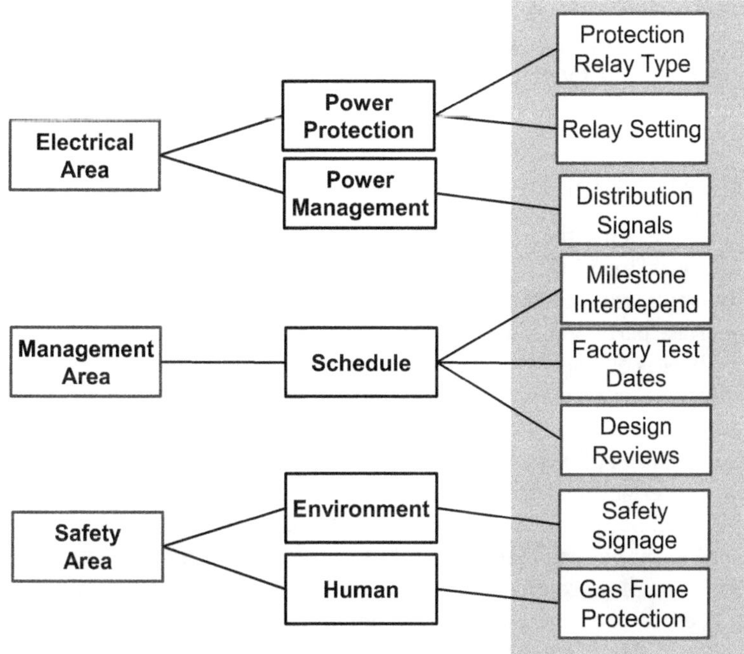

Figure 4.6 Identifying interface items

When an interface agreement is obtained, interface items are closed. However, to reach agreement on an interface item requires the interface parties to maintain close communication and work collaboratively. Interface items are the focus of daily interface activities between the groups and the daily interface activities are focused on obtaining agreement.

While Figure 4.6 only shows an abbreviated title for the interface item, in actuality, when entering the interface into the interface management tool much more data is included. At a minimum, the interface item includes the following information:

- Brief title
- Applicable system or component
- Discipline (electrical, process, mechanical, multidiscipline, etc.)
- Description of the interface and what is required
- Planning dates
- Attachments (if necessary)

A number of interface software tools are available in the market, including proprietary tools developed by large companies. Depending on the interface software tool, the amount and types of information to be included can vary greatly. Regardless, each item should contain sufficient information to ensure a clear understanding by the other party.

4.6.1 Responsible and Receiving Parties

By now, it may appear obvious that a dependency relationship develops between two interface parties as they undertake interface activity. Both interface parties can identify and raise an interface item in the interface management system. When one party does so, it is dependent upon the other party to provide the information. Different interface management systems will describe this relationship differently, but we use the terms *receiving party* and *responsible party*. While this concept is discussed later in the book, the basic premise is that the initiator of the interface is termed the receiving party because they will receive the information. The party providing the interface to the receiving party is termed the responsible party because this party is responsible for providing the information necessary to resolve and close the interface. Both parties must be satisfied with the exchange of information to resolve an item. If not, the process is repeated back and forth until sufficiently addressed.

4.6.2 Planning Interface Items

In identifying interface items, the first hurdle to overcome is determining whether or not the item is a valid interface. A valid interface is one in which both parties agree is related to their scope or area of responsibility. Interfaces are sometimes raised erroneously; for example, an interface may be directed to the wrong interface party or it might be a duplicate of a previously identified interface. Ensuring sound interface analysis during the interface planning process can prevent costly errors with interface activity during the project execution phase. Assuming an identified interface is deemed valid, the interface group can begin to plan for its resolution and assign target dates for completion.

Planning the resolution of interface items must be based on accurate and reliable project schedules versus arbitrarily established dates or those based on "hope" and "wish". During this process, any interface "clashes" will become clear. An interface clash arises when the "need" date of the receiving party cannot be met by the other (responsible) party. In fact, these situations almost certainly arise in large-scale complex projects because it is extremely difficult to maintain total alignment of project schedules, especially if there are many different interface parties involved in the project. Any clashes that cannot be resolved are brought to the attention of the client, or owner of the interface management system, for arbitration. It may be necessary for the client to clarify priorities or to assist with mitigating action to prevent serious negative consequences.

4.7 MONITOR AND CONTROL INTERFACE ACTIVITIES

Monitoring and controlling consists of those processes that are required in order to track, review, and orchestrate the progress and performance of the project (PMI, 2017). In any interface management system, it is necessary to ensure that the respective parties are working in good faith. This includes meeting regularly, documenting the results of these interface meetings (including action items), meeting interface planning dates, and working together to respond to changing situations which inevitably happen in large-scale projects. The Monitoring & Controlling step in the interface management process provides the framework for measuring, monitoring, and controlling interface performance during project execution. Interface performance is monitored using two basic methods: objective and subjective.

Objective methods rely on quantitative metrics to measure performance against numerical performance targets. Subjective methods rely on qualitative factors to provide context for objective metrics. In its simplest form, objective methods rely on numbers while subjective methods are based on judgment. To make the distinction, a simple example of a patient being admitted to a hospital is provided. It is common for patients to have their vital signs and blood samples tested at regular intervals. These objective measures use specific equipment and the results are compared against specific criteria to ascertain whether a measurement is too high, too low, or within expected performance levels. In addition to these standard objective measures, the medical staff personnel perform subjective assessments, such as observing the color of the patient's skin, shining a light into the eyes to evaluate responses, etc., and then use them to make judgments about the condition of the patient. These objective and subjective assessments combine to help the hospital staff gain a better understanding of the patient's health.

4.7.1 Subjective Monitoring Methods

Subjective methods include observation of interface activity through participation in interface activity events, inquiry and interaction with interface management personnel, and review of interface meeting results. The aim of subjective monitoring is not to replace objective methods, but to supplement them and provide context and help to explain the underlying cause when performance deviates from expectations. Subjective methods rely on human senses and judgment formed through sensory inputs, which is then compared to expectations. For example, objective methods describe performance, but the performance metric itself is not very useful in explaining why performance deviates from expectations. Subjective methods allow us as humans to observe the environment in which the performance is occurring and better understand the factors contributing to the performance result—good or bad.

4.7.1.1 Participation in Interface Activity Events

Participation in interface activity meetings and reviews with interface groups is a useful way to gain insight into how a group is performing. Such participation helps the client or owner of the interface management system to assess the professional relationship between the interface parties. Individuals from either interface party who are less than cooperative can disrupt progress. By observing events within these meetings, it is possible to ascertain whether the interface group is working in *good faith* or whether members are presenting obstacles or challenges that impede the resolution of key issues.

By participating in interface meetings and reviews, the client or owner of the project's interface management system can maintain visibility of developing issues within various interface groups and networks. In this way, the client can ensure regular interface interaction is occurring, adequate resources are provided by each party to coordinate the relevant issues, and human interaction remains professional and conducive to working toward the resolution of issues. In this regard, there is a human element and dynamic that serves to help move progress forward or prevent problems.

4.7.1.2 Inquiry and Interaction with Interface Management Personnel

It is also possible to gather performance information through regular interaction with the project's interface personnel or those assigned with interface responsibility. It is nearly impossible to understand the concerns of people within the interface system by reviewing quantitative results. Rather, it is through personal interaction with members within the system that valuable information can be obtained. Short conversations, email inquiries, and impromptu meetings at the coffee machine can yield valuable insight into the thoughts and feelings of interface personnel, such as early manifestation of frustration, which can foretell problems that are more serious if not dealt with early.

4.7.1.3 Review of Interface Meeting Results

Every interaction between interface parties in the form of a meeting results in minutes that outline who was present, what topics were discussed, highlights of each topic, status of actions from previous meetings, and identification of new actions. By reviewing these minutes and other information generated during these meetings, it is possible to form an opinion of how well the group appears to be operating. Build up of actions, week after week, with little progress, poor attendance, and continued cancellation of meetings can all be signs of group problems; these subjective opinions can be compared against objective performance measures to form a more thorough judgment.

4.7.2 Objective Monitoring Methods

Objective measurements are quantitative and require the collection of measurable data, such as number, volume, weight, height, flow, pressure, etc. Most often, these methods appear in the form of important metrics that are meant to indicate the level of performance of a management function. As mentioned previously, objective methods are similar to someone being admitted to a hospital where one's vital signs and blood samples are taken regularly to provide insight into how the body is functioning. Objective metrics are an important element of the management function and often take the form of basic statistics and KPIs.

4.7.2.1 Basic Performance Statistics

A number of basic statistics are used to monitor interface performance; these are based on the four main status conditions for an interface at any given time: identified, open, overdue, and closed. Most available interface software tools provide basic statistics on the number of interfaces in identified, closed, open, or overdue status at any given time.

An identified interface is an interface that has been identified by one or more of the interface parties and has been recorded in the interface system but has not yet been validated by the interface group as suitable to *open*. An open interface means that the interface parties agree that the item is a valid interface, have agreed to open the item, and have planned response and resolution dates. An overdue interface item is an interface that is still open, but is past its planned resolution date. A closed interface item means that the interface parties have agreed to the completion of the information exchange and have therefore closed the item. An interface item cannot be closed unless all parties within the interface group have reached agreement.

4.7.2.2 Other Potential Performance Statistics

However, other statistics may be valuable to track—such as the number of meetings conducted by an interface group, the number of canceled meetings, technology disruptions, etc., that focus not just on the progress of interfaces, but the humans and the tools driving the process. Such statistics might help ensure that the environment is conducive for effective interface activity.

4.7.3 Establishing KPIs

KPIs are items that, if monitored properly, provide measurable assessment of project performance. KPIs are used for monitoring changes from one reporting period to another and should a change occur, for understanding the significance of the performance change (Salapatas, 1985). The key to establishing KPIs as an objective performance measuring method is determining which metrics matter for each specific project and which performance level is expected. Some general metrics are provided below for guidance, but this list is not meant to be all-inclusive. Rather, it is intended to stimulate thought about which aspects of the interface management system are important for measuring its performance. This will vary from project to project and it is the responsibility of each project team to decide the best metrics for their respective situations.

4.7.3.1 Excessive "Identified" Interfaces

As stated earlier, an *identified* interface item means the interface item is recorded in the interface management software tool by one of the interface parties and is waiting for acceptance or confirmation, but is not yet open. Typically, one party or the other will input what they believe are interfaces into the interface management system for discussion at the next interface meeting. At the meeting, the interface group will determine whether the item is a valid interface and if so, will open it and plan dates. If not, it will be deleted from the system. While this is an acceptable practice, occasionally a large volume of interfaces will remain in *identified* status for long periods.

From an interface management performance perspective, when these items are in *identified* status, they tend to be overlooked by the interface groups and therefore the number of interface items in this status should be monitored and managed to ensure the number is as low as possible. Ultimately, the goal is to monitor and manage interface activity to ensure items are resolved, which leads to the resolution of interface issues and the closeout of interface areas between the interface parties.

Excessive interface items in an *identified* status can indicate problems within the group. While some interfaces items can be in this status for temporary periods, it is expected that the interface group will work to open and resolve the interface items as quickly as possible. One KPI could be *number of identified interfaces*. To establish a performance target, the client can mandate the project remain below a certain number or percentage, such as 5 or 10%. Meaning, the number of identified interface items should remain below 5 or 10% of open interfaces. Remember, KPIs are indicators. It could be that the project exceeds the performance target for valid reasons. The performance target exists to notify management that something is happening in the system and requires further investigation.

4.7.3.2 Excessive "Overdue" Interfaces

Open interfaces that are past their planned resolution dates is termed an *overdue* interface. Presuming that the interface dates are connected in some way to the project schedules and other project plans, overdue interfaces represent project risks. Excessive overdue interfaces can indicate poor planning and interface group dysfunction. Thus, it is important to monitor these interfaces carefully. In some cases, these interfaces can give indications of a more serious problem on the horizon, such as schedule delays. There are a number of reasons why an *open* interface item can become overdue (i.e., is not resolved by the planned resolution date). These may include:

- Lack of agreement between the parties on how to resolve the interface
- Establishing resolution dates incorrectly (i.e., not linked to the project plans)
- Unexpected delay in work from one of the parties
- Relationship breakdown between the parties
- Change in work priority
- Unforeseen absence of key personnel
- Scheduling resolution dates without considering holidays, vacations, and other resource issues

Nevertheless, the challenge is to correct the situation by performing some form of controlling action to either resolve these interfaces or establish a new resolution date that is suitable to all parties.

4.7.3.3 High-Priority Interfaces

Some interface management programs develop a process to identify specific interface items as high priority or critical. These interface items can cause negative consequences to either the interface parties or to the project if not resolved as planned. Most interface management software has functionality to allow interface groups to identify high priority or critical interface items and highlight those items for management.

This designation is set by the receiving party (that is, the party that initiated the interface) and indicates that negative consequences will result if the item is not resolved within the planned dates. Some clients prefer to monitor the total number of high-priority interfaces because they represent near-term risk that requires action. This is a metric to signify the importance of taking corrective action immediately, which helps to focus the attention of key management on the issue.

An example KPI using this designation is *number of high-priority* or *percent of high-priority* interfaces. The client may accept a certain number and set the KPI to less than "*n*" (where "*n*" represents some value). If the project is managing a few thousand interfaces, then it may be acceptable to have a few situations (low percentage) that results in changes to the interface planned dates. A large percentage of high-priority interfaces relative to the total number of open interfaces could indicate planning problems, schedule changes, or lack of adequate interface activity.

4.7.3.4 Overdue High-Priority Interfaces

As the description implies, these high-priority interfaces are past their expected resolution or planned dates. This situation no longer represents risk; the risk has now become an issue. This metric signifies to the client that some negative consequence has occurred and is likely to manifest in the form of a change request or variation order request.

From a monitoring perspective, an overdue interface item means that the interface parties have not been able to resolve the interface items by the planned resolution date they established in earlier interface meetings. Assuming the planned resolution dates are connected to the respective project plan, then these overdue high-priority interface items represent interface issues and require some controlling action.

4.7.4 Interface Performance Reporting

Performance reporting plays an important part in the Monitoring & Control step because it represents the mechanism to communicate interface performance to key project members. Whether as part of a subproject weekly or monthly status report, project status report, or as part of the project portfolio status report, interface performance reporting serves to focus attention on parts of the interface process, or specific interface issues, which require increased attention. An example of interface information reporting is discussed later in the book, but the inclusion of KPI information and standard statistics in the report are recommended as part of the weekly and monthly trend information. It is important, however, to ensure the performance metrics are put in context when reporting to prevent misunderstanding by those in the reporting chain.

4.8 RESOLVE INTERFACE ISSUES AND ITEMS

The final step is to resolve each interface item and the parent issues, which will lead to the close out of interface areas. This step in the interface process is a direct result of interface activity; it occurs primarily during project execution and extends into the project closeout phase. As discussed previously, this part of the process is bottom-up, requiring synthesis, and is not completed until all items and issues are resolved and verified as implemented. Once verified as implemented, interface areas are closed out. It is important to note that interface item resolution often only indicates an agreement on an interface issue.

However, that does not always mean the agreements have been properly implemented, for example, in the respective detailed engineering designs; they must be verified. Verification of interface activities can occur immediately after the agreement is made between the parties or significant time may pass before the agreement is implemented. Regardless, verification of interface agreements must be included in the project plan; verification can include analysis, demonstration, inspection, test, analogy, simulation, and sampling (INCOSE, 2015).

The owner of the project's interface management system normally prescribes this part of the interface management process in more detail through an interface management procedure or policy for the verification step to ensure that all parties are operating consistently across the project. For example, it is common for the client's project team to establish a procedure that governs interface management during the project's execution phase, which serves as a reference document in the respective contracts with contractors that are contributing to the project. This procedure also specifies applicability of the procedure to other interface networks; for example, in some cases, one project may have to adapt to the interface management system of another project. In addition, each contractor establishes its own interface management system based on the requirements from the client. This topic will be discussed in more detail later in the book.

To resolve an interface issue and, subsequently, an interface area, the interface parties must reach consensus or agreement on each item. While this sounds fairly straightforward and simple to accomplish, many factors influence how well the parties achieve agreement. First, each party may have its own interests, typically contractual or functional responsibility, as its first priority. However, alignment with strategic objectives of the project tends to align parties with the same priorities. When a proposed solution is presented that does not conflict with their priority or interest, then agreement is typically not difficult to obtain.

However, when a proposed solution to interface items conflicts with the other party's interests or functional responsibilities, it can be very difficult to obtain agreement on an interface item. For example, a proposed solution that would transfer more work to the other party is typically met with resistance. Thus, it is important for both parties to work in a constructive way and maintain a good relationship to achieve agreement and resolution of interface items.

Unfortunately, there are times when the two parties are not able to reach agreement and the issue needs to be escalated to higher management for facilitation. The inability to reach agreement imposes some level of risk as one party or both parties are not obtaining what they need to fulfill their respective scopes of work or responsibility. As it is not possible to leave interfaces unresolved, some intervention by the contractor's management team or the client may be required to ensure a reasonable agreement is reached.

When an interface is agreed upon by both parties, it can be closed. This process transfers the interface item from an open status to a closed status and archives any information related to the interface item. Interface information includes the interface *sheet* that details the final agreement between the interface parties, which includes any documentation, such as drawings or schedules, and any attached documentation exchanged between the parties to reach the agreement.

After an item is resolved and closed, each party must take action to ensure the agreement is implemented and adhered to within the scope of work or responsibility. Occasionally, the agreement is reflected as part of the closeout, such as on a final and approved technical drawing. In other cases, it must be incorporated at a later date, such as an agreement by one party to deliver material to the other party by a future date. In cases where the agreement must be enforced after the interface is closed, some verification activity needs to be performed to confirm adherence to the agreement.

4.9 SUMMARY

As with any management function, a process is required to guide the actions of those within and affected by the process. The interface management process presented in this chapter illustrates the general flow of activities from identifying interface networks to close out of individual interface items and ultimately all interface areas. Since each project produces a unique result and is conducted under different circumstances and environments, the project team should view the process presented in this chapter as a guide. The main purpose of this discussion is to show that establishing an interface management process can assist in structuring, organizing, and segmenting complex interface interaction into manageable parts. This minimizes the opportunity for gaps in scopes of work or areas of responsibility and helps prevent integration problems later in the project's life cycle.

An effective process, including the interface management process, relies on tools and analytical techniques to support the people assigned, in this case, with interface responsibilities. This is especially true during project planning when the interface management system architecture needs to be established. In Chapter 5, we begin to explore analytical techniques from the project management and SE disciplines to support the interface management process. Then, in Chapter 6, we address interface management tools and their use to increase effectiveness and efficiency of the process. The aim of this chapter and the next two are to provide the reader with the skill, knowledge, and ability to plan and prepare a project's interface management system for the execution phase.

4.10 REFERENCES

Bible, Michael J. and Susan S. Bivins. (2011). *Mastering Project Portfolio Management: A Systems Approach to Achieving Strategic Objectives.* ISBN 10: 1604270667. J. Ross Publishing, Inc., Plantation, FL.

Forman, E. H. and M. A. Selly. (2001). *Decision by Objectives.* World Scientific, River Edge, NJ.

INCOSE (2015). *Systems Engineering Handbook: A Guide for System Life Cycle Processes and Activities,* Fourth Edition. San Diego, CA: International Council on Systems Engineering (INCOSE). ISBN: 978-1-118-99940-0.

Jones, G. R. and J. M. George. (2014). *Contemporary Management,* 8th Edition, McGraw-Hill, New York, NY.

Matta, N. F. and R. N. Ashkenas. (2003). "Why Good Projects Fail Anyway." *Harvard Business Review,* September 2003 Issue.

Project Management Institute (PMI). (2017). *A Guide to the Project Management Body of Knowledge (PMBOK® Guide),* 6th Edition. Project Management Institution, Newtown Square, PA.

Salapatas, J. N. (1985). *Performance Measurements for Projects and Project Management.* Price Waterhouse. August 1965. Pittsburgh, PA.

Yi Wang, Marios Iliofotou, Michalis Faloutsos, and Bin Wu. (2012). *Analyzing Interaction Communication Networks in Enterprises and Identifying Hierarchies,* Department of Computer Science and Engineering, University of California–Riverside, Riverside, CA.

5

Interface Analysis

"Analysis is the art of creation through destruction."
—P.S. Baber, *Cassie Draws the Universe*

This chapter on interface analysis is important to this book because it forms the basis for applying the critical thinking that is necessary to decompose the factors contributing to interface complexity into simpler and more manageable elements—by understanding, structuring, and organizing them. By methodically and logically analyzing the project environment, the system to be developed, and the relationships (or lack thereof) among stakeholders, the project team can better understand the factors driving interface and interdependency complexity and define how best to manage this complexity during project execution. In essence, the interface analysis process forms the foundation for the project's interface management system and directly affects the management of interfaces and interdependencies during project execution.

Performing the interface analysis process thoroughly during early project planning can pay dividends throughout the remainder of the project by increasing the likelihood of establishing a management system to monitor and control interactions between various entities contributing to the project or affected by the project. This is especially the case for the project sponsor, for whom the project delivers the most benefit. Conversely, getting this process wrong, or not performing it at all, will likely have the opposite affect and create significant problems and challenges for the project, the project sponsor, and those contributing to, or affected by, the project. So, how does one *get it right*? That is, how can the project proceed to devise a management system that will effectively manage and control the complexity inherent in interfaces, interdependencies, and interactions as the project progresses through its life cycle? In short, it starts by breaking the complexity problem down into smaller and more manageable elements.

Since every project is unique, the factors contributing to its complexity will vary from project to project. The intent of this chapter is to provide a road map, presented as sequential steps, to methodically break down the complexity problem and manage the factors driving interface complexity. The outcome of the interface analysis process is a clear understanding of interfaces and interdependencies existing within the project and those influenced by external sources such that reasonable decisions can be taken to structure an interface management system to manage complexity during project execution.

While a road map is provided in this chapter, analysis always requires critical thinking by those undertaking the process. Thus, the process presented here is meant to guide the actions of those who are assigned responsibility for establishing the project's interface management system, but it is not intended as a recipe to be followed blindly. Specifically, the process provides a starting point to help responsible persons make the best possible decisions about the management system that most effectively and efficiently addresses interface-driven complexity for their respective projects. Also, the process is intended to help these responsible persons to implement a system to manage interfaces and interdependencies—a system that will reduce risk associated with interface complexity and prevent unwanted negative consequences.

The basic interface management process was presented briefly in Chapter 4 where the discussion focused primarily on defining *what* the process is in relation to the project life cycle. In this chapter, we focus more closely on *how to perform* the initial steps in the process; we address how to apply project management and systems engineering (SE) tools and techniques to analyze, that is decompose or break down, complexity into more manageable elements. The understanding of interface analysis in this chapter enables building the interface management system that will be discussed in Chapter 6.

The interface analysis steps are shown in Figure 5.1 along the left side of the process with shaded boxes. Steps in the process are performed during the initiating and planning stages of the project, normally by the project sponsor's organization, and, as stated, serve as the basis for the project interface management system to be implemented throughout the project during the execution phase.

Interface analysis uses a *top-down* approach. That is, we start by exploring the broader project context and logically work to reduce complexity by breaking it into manageable segments—first determining which interface networks are applicable for the project, next identifying the interface parties within those networks, and then defining the main interface areas and issues between the relevant interface parties. Combined, these steps provide the mechanism to deconstruct the project environment so that reasonable decisions can be made about where interface complexity and risk reside and how to manage interfaces during the execution phase.

In Figure 5.1, the steps in the analysis process are shown as linear and occurring across the project initiating and planning phases for the sake of simplicity in illustrating how to perform interface analysis. In reality, these steps overlap, and require iteration, especially if the project has a complicated development approach with multiple phases, such as engineering, procurement, and construction phases. As mentioned, this process is performed by *the client or project sponsor organization*, which is ultimately responsible for implementing project and SE management systems to ensure that the

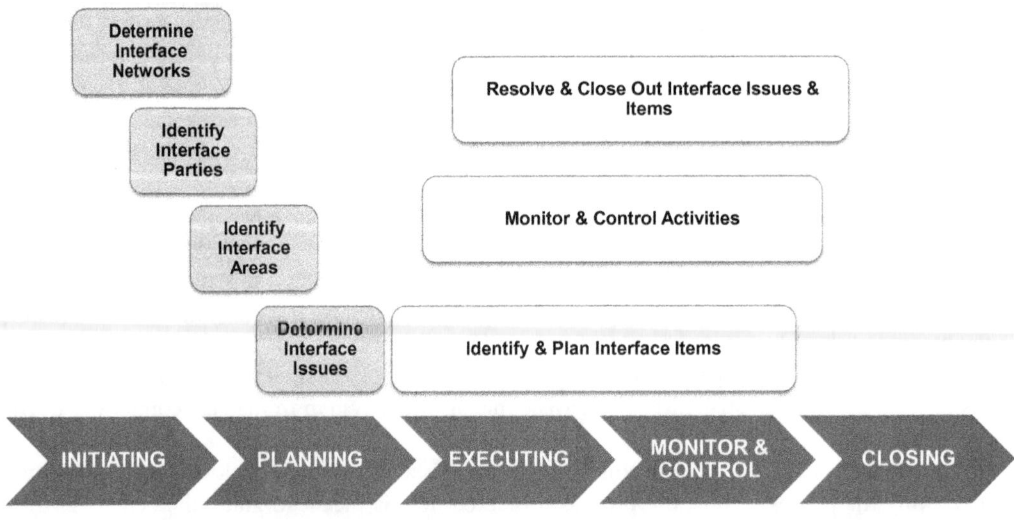

Figure 5.1 Application of interface analysis in the interface management process

project is managed to a successful conclusion. However, it is natural for the project's governing system to flow down these systems to scopes of work and areas of responsibilities by those contributing to the project's development, and thus this analysis may be performed or at least validated at every level.

In some cases, it may be necessary for parties within the project, such as main contractors, to perform this process to implement interface management within their respective scopes of work to enable them to manage internal interfaces and interdependencies. The same interface analysis process provides a useful road map for these situations. Regardless, the client's management team will dictate the interface management system for the project and the terms and conditions under which it is expected to operate. All subordinate interface management systems within the project must align with the client's expectations and guidance.

The output, or outcome, of the interface analysis process is the information necessary to establish the basis for an interface management system that is appropriate to the circumstances of the project. That is, the output provides sufficient information to enable decisions for establishing an interface management system—one that provides the most effective means of mitigating interface and interdependency risk as the project progresses through its life cycle, which can often last many years. The results of interface management analysis are then used in Chapter 6 to produce an interface management system that describes, prior to contract awards and prior to actual contractor performance of work, how the project sponsor expects interfaces to be managed. The interface analysis process identifies what groups may need to communicate, about what interface areas and issues, and provides a foundation for:

- Aiding the sponsor's project organization to develop a procedure or plan that explains how interfaces will be managed across the project
- Determining how interface management will link to other project processes, such as risk, document control, and quality management processes
- Setting up an automated software interface register tool to manage high volumes of expected interface activity
- Establishing the basis for interface training to ensure that project personnel who are entrusted with interface responsibilities are well prepared to execute those responsibilities

This chapter addresses how to apply interface analysis and the tools and techniques that are available to perform it. We introduce a notional project example in the next section to help reinforce the concepts presented in this chapter.

5.1 NOTIONAL PROJECT EXAMPLE

To reinforce the tools and techniques described in this chapter, along with how they support the interface analysis process, we have elected to introduce a notional project example from the oil and gas industry. This example project provides context and a sense of realism to better illustrate how to apply tools and techniques to the analysis process. It is used throughout the remainder of this book. The reader is not expected to be an expert in the oil and gas industry or have knowledge of oil and gas projects or system architectures. Instead, high-level information about the notional project, called Project Diamond (to be performed by the fictitious ABC Corporation), is provided in the appendices described in Section 5.2.

While a notional project example from the oil and gas industry is used, the approach, tools, and techniques are equally applicable to other industries such as defense, information technology, telecommunications, aerospace, etc., where complicated project development approaches are employed to deliver large-scale projects. All companies and organizations in the notional project are fictitious.

5.2 PROJECT DIAMOND OVERVIEW

ABC Incorporated is a global oil and gas company operating in many energy markets around the world, including Europe, Asia, and North America. ABC's Global Energy Division remains focused on continued value creation in its oil and gas business segment, especially in the European market where new hydrocarbon exploration opportunities have arisen in the Barents Sea area.

In terms of hydrocarbon exploration, the area is divided into the Russian side on the East and the Norwegian side on the West, with the two areas showing different petroleum geology. The Russian side contains a number of very large gas fields contained in upper Jurassic sandstone reservoirs, whereas the Norwegian side contains much smaller middle-lower Jurassic sandstone reservoirs bounded by fault blocks, which are large areas of rock created by stresses in the Earth's crust. Some of the largest discoveries were made in the 1980s, but have still not been brought into production because of a combination of the extreme climate conditions, political instability, and the historically low price of gas. However, given current global oil and gas market conditions, and the realization of a substantial reduction in the costs of goods and services, ABC Inc.'s Project Diamond field has been deemed economically viable based on future energy price projections.

Project Diamond encompasses a 20 km area on the Norwegian side of the Barents Sea within the development licenses DL 0072 and DL 0046. ABC Corporation (65%) is the operator for Project Diamond, while TDN, Inc. (25%) and Waverly Exploration (10%) are partners and are contributing capital funding equal to their filed percent of ownership. The project has previously received favorable 1 and 2 gate decisions in 2013 and 2014. However, the project has been on hold since the downturn in the global oil and gas market. Recently, ABC and its Project Diamond partners have submitted the plan for development and operation (PDO) to the Norwegian authorities and received approval this year. As a result, a gate 3 decision has been issued to move forward with project development.

Project Diamond has been found to be economically viable with proven reserves of 250 million barrels of oil equivalents (MMBOE), probable reserves of 300 MMBOE, and possible reserves of 350 MMBOE. Project Diamond is envisioned with a fixed offshore platform partial processing, drilling, and living quarters (pdQ) and with a subsea development to transfer the Project Diamond well's combined oil and gas stream to another project's platform, the Sapphire platform (located 10 kms to the east on the Russian side of the Barents Sea). Once separated at Sapphire, the hydrocarbons are transferred to onshore processing facilities via separate oil and gas pipelines.

Project Sapphire is operated by XYZ, Inc. and is envisioned as a fixed offshore processing platform pdQ with subsea oil and gas pipelines to shore-based terminal facilities. In addition, Project Sapphire will provide power to operate Project Diamond, which will be delivered through a subsea power and fiber cable from Sapphire to Diamond. The Oil Pipeline Project has been awarded by POL Industries and the Gas Pipeline Project is being performed by PGP Industries. All four projects are under development at the same time. Project Sapphire is expected to deliver first oil about 3 years from now, while Project Diamond is expected to deliver first oil about 4 years from now. Oil and gas pipelines are expected to be ready to connect to Project Sapphire 2 years from now.

Additional information about Project Diamond is provided in Appendices C, D, and E, which respectively include the documents briefly described here:

- *Appendix C—ABC Management of Project Development*: This document states ABC Corporation's requirements for evaluating, planning, maturing, and executing field development projects from the decision to initiate a commercialization project of petroleum resources up to the handover to the operating organization. The key objective is to ensure orderly planning and execution of all development projects and to ensure a consistent evaluation and decision process within ABC and with contractors and other stakeholders. ABC Corporation uses a decision gate (DG) process with specific requirements for achieving a decision at each gate. Each of the project development DGs are described in this document.

- *Appendix D—Project Diamond Mandate*: Project Diamond has successfully achieved DG3 and is now preparing for the project execution phase, which at ABC is the phase performed after DG3 and up to DG4. This document serves as ABC's guidance for further development of the Project Diamond project execution plan (PEP).
- *Appendix E—Project Diamond PEP for DG3 to DG4*: The purpose of this document is to outline how Project Diamond is planned to be executed from DG3 to DG4. This document describes project targets, strategies, and the management and control systems that are established to meet the project objectives. It outlines the most important elements in the project execution phase, and how the project intends to handle these in order to achieve the timely, cost effective, and safe development of Project Diamond.

It is highly recommended that the reader review this material and become familiar with its content and the sample project, Project Diamond. The material will give the reader greater context for the project used to illustrate the interface management concepts and processes discussed throughout this and subsequent chapters.

5.3 INTERFACE ANALYSIS PREPARATION

One of the more difficult aspects of devising a management system for a large complex project is that of knowing where to begin, which can be overwhelming, especially if the person responsible for establishing the management system is new to the project organization and has little or no knowledge of the project or its environment. In fact, it can be quite an advantage if the person responsible for establishing the management system is a permanent employee of the sponsoring organization and has some understanding of the project's history and other personnel to be involved in the project. As a member of the sponsoring organization, an individual will be familiar with existing policies and procedures, organizational culture, and possibly will be involved in or have knowledge of early project activities, such as those occurring during earlier DGs. However, it is common for sponsoring organizations to acquire competency or expertise from industry professionals to help establish project management systems, such as interface management.

Arguably, one of the worst-case scenarios for a person responsible for devising a management system is to join the project organization as an employee or as a consultant after a gate 3 decision. As a project receives a favorable gate 3 decision, it is common for the sponsoring organization to rapidly acquire project personnel and start the process of devising and planning for implementation of the project's management systems. A gate 3 decision, or similar decision, initiates activity to begin developing the project. In essence, the project begins its execution phase to realize the *project result*. Typically, the pace of activity after DG3 can be described as *hectic*; and joining a project organization *cold* can be quite overwhelming. One strategy to counter this situation and ensure time is used efficiently and effectively is to have a plan to guide one's actions and activities from the moment of joining the sponsoring organization. This section provides suggestions for such a new member of the project team who is brought on board to address or assist with interface management.

While it may be argued that these initial activities to establish oneself as part of the project organization are self-explanatory and need not be described in this book, they are included since they are important for ensuring thoroughness, robustness, and quality during interface analysis and devising a management system that is appropriate for the project's circumstances. It is simply not reasonable to suggest that anyone can join a large, evolving project organization and immediately start devising a management system without being properly oriented, familiarized, and prepared. Williams (2003) noted that on average, the time for new external hires to achieve full productivity ranged from eight weeks for clerical jobs to 20 weeks for professionals to more than 26 weeks for executives. Although the acclimation process may be shorter for consultants with specific expertise, the period of rapid acceleration after DG3 can be a challenge for newer people in large complex projects who are attempting to *get off to a fast start.*

5.3.1 Orientation and Onboarding Phase

The orientation phase begins once an individual has been selected and has agreed to join the project organization; it includes the initial days after joining the project organization. This phase is characterized by getting established in human resource systems, completing the administrative check-in process, obtaining access to sponsoring organization systems (such as security systems), and getting settled in the project office environment. Orientation is an introductory period aimed at obtaining an awareness of new surroundings, including people, environment, and routines. While this phase can last a number of weeks as the project organization establishes itself, it is normal to complete the main activities within the first week of joining the organization.

The efficiency and effectiveness of the project organization's orientation and onboarding process can vary. One should not expect the organization to provide the optimal plan. Rather, each joining individual should have an expectation of what needs to be accomplished in order to become comfortable in the new work environment. Orientation and onboarding can relieve a great deal of stress and improve the effectiveness of the interface analysis process because it ensures that the individuals performing the process have the right tools and familiarity with the project organization and environment to facilitate the steps in the process.

5.3.2 Familiarization Phase

The familiarization phase leverages the orientation phase. In this phase, the individual becomes familiar with the project organization and how it intends to operate. The familiarization phase answers the questions who, what, when, where, and why about the project environment. A key aspect of this phase involves becoming familiar with project personnel, their roles and responsibilities, and their relationship to the interface management function. It is equally important to understand what project organization roles have not been filled—as this may influence completeness or require assumptions when performing interface analysis. In addition, it is important to understand how the project organization will operate—such as:

- Determining which software tools have been chosen and obtaining access to relevant programs, including training
- Understanding how project information is organized and where it will be stored
- Identifying which governing documents one is responsible for or will contribute to developing or updating
- Confirming regular meeting schedules and plans
- Learning project organizational administrative processes such as scheduling meeting rooms, obtaining organizational charts, contact and location information, etc.

Interface analysis is not performed in a vacuum. Rather it is reliant upon access to and contributions from other project organization members. Establishing a plan to become familiar with the project organization and how it will operate will serve to initiate the interface management process efficiently and quickly.

5.3.3 Preparation Phase

Upon completing the orientation and familiarization phases, a new project member has sufficient understanding about the new project organization to begin preparing for interface analysis and starting the interface management process. The preparation phase is focused on the preparatory activities that are necessary to perform interface analysis, such as obtaining information and data about the project—including historical information. As the reader now understands, we assume the reader is entering a large-scale complex project immediately after a successful DG3 and the project is now entering the project execution phase.

During the preparation phase, relevant data and information needs to be identified, gathered, and reviewed in preparation for starting the analysis process. Specifically, key project documents are collected such as the sponsoring organization's approach to managing development projects, the PEP (or similarly named document), the project mandate, relevant organizational procedures, and other project governing documents. These documents contain information that can help to establish assumptions, constraints, and unknowns prior to starting the interface analysis process. For example, the project organization can mandate that the project's interface management system must comply with and use specific interface management register tools (constraint). These documents may not provide the necessary detail related to establishing an interface management system for the project; these missing details must be clarified with document owners, such as how interface management is envisioned to interact with other project management processes, such as risk management to manage interface risks, and document control to understand how interface documentation will be exchanged.

This phase is also about collecting information from activities that provide inputs to the DG process. Typically, project organizations use some version of a stage-gate project development model to guide their projects. Each DG, or stage gate, requires specific information to support the decision process. These inputs provide valuable information about the project and help to explain why it received a decision to proceed. These input artifacts are useful during the interface analysis process because they help to provide context for the project and further identify any assumptions, constraints, and unknowns. More important, these documents can shed light on the factors driving or contributing to interface and interdependency complexity, which will need to be addressed by the interface management system.

5.4 INTERFACE ANALYSIS PROCESS

Analysis is defined as a careful study of something to learn about its parts, what they do, and how they are related to each other (http://www.merriam-webster.com/dictionary/analysis). An important aspect of the analysis definition is *careful study*, which implies a logical and structured approach to ensure complete and thorough understanding of what is being studied. Following a methodical approach when performing analysis can increase thoroughness and completeness, ideally leading to a better outcome.

From a high-level perspective, analysis requires steps to be performed in a logical or structured sequence. Each step in the process requires the collection of relevant data and information, which is used as inputs to applying appropriate tools and techniques. Processing data and information inputs using appropriate tools and techniques results in outputs designed to provide incrementally better understanding of what is being studied. Depending on the result of the outputs, additional repetition through the analytical steps may be needed. When combined (or synthesized), the results from the analysis process provide a better understanding of what is being studied as well as information to assist in making decisions.

This general description of analysis is applied to interface analysis. For each of the interface analysis steps, we identify the relevant data and information inputs, the tools and techniques useful in processing the data and information, and the outcome to be achieved by performing the step. Back in Chapter 2, we described complexity, the elements needed to address it, and stakeholder analysis and its outputs as important inputs to interface analysis, which is, of course, the subject of this chapter.

Then, in Chapter 6, we show how interface analysis outputs serve the decision-making process and how they serve as inputs to creating the project's interface management system.

Figure 5.2 shows the interface analysis steps; these steps help to form the basis for establishing an interface management system. The outputs of the steps provide the foundation for formulating an implementation plan to be addressed in Chapter 6; the implementation plan describes how the project's interface management system will be implemented across the project and throughout the project life cycle. Finally, once the interface management system has been implemented by the project sponsor organizations, the outputs of interface analysis—(1) interface networks, (2) interface parties, (3) interface areas, and (4) interface issues—serve as inputs to the relevant interface parties to further decompose and address interfaces and reduce interface complexity.

The client (or project sponsor organization) is responsible for the project's interface management system and is thus responsible for performing the interface analysis process described in the coming sections. It is important that this process be conducted as thoroughly and completely as possible since the main objective is to establish the best possible interface management system for the circumstances of the project.

5.4.1 Interface Network Analysis

As briefly discussed earlier in this book, we can look to social networking as an analogy to describing interface networks. In social networking, as individuals we establish (join) multiple networks (personal and professional) to segment dimensions of our lives. By segmenting or compartmentalizing other individuals into various network groupings, we are decomposing and handling complexity in our lives. As a result, many people belong to multiple personal and professional networks such as a *Facebook* network where relevant personal information is shared with selected friends and family, a professional *LinkedIn* network to interact with like-minded professionals, and perhaps many other *special interest* networks such as carpentry, sports, outdoor activities, etc. This same segmenting of our respective personal networks is very similar to that which is being accomplished using project interface networks.

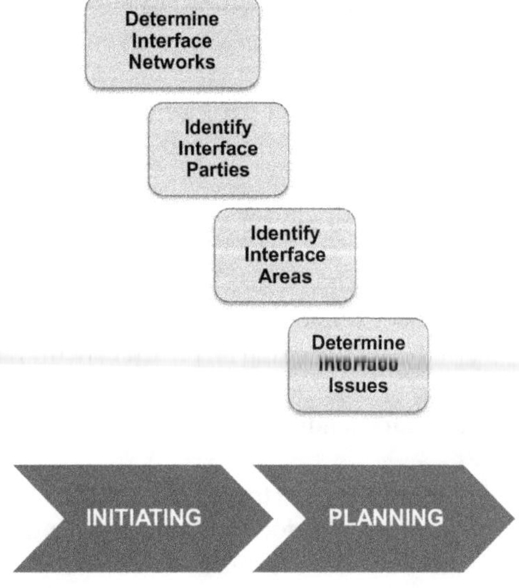

Figure 5.2 Interface analysis steps

Interface network analysis is necessary to understand how to group interface parties by their respective interface purviews. In large-scale complex projects, there are many different parties, with many different scopes, areas of responsibility, and degrees of influence at various organizational and project layers, or levels. The aim of interface network analysis is to segment related interface parties into networks of like entities, such that they share a common interface perspective. Interface network analysis takes a high-level view of the project environment with project entities both inside and outside the project scope and attempts to understand the different potential interface dimensions of the project. By *interface dimensions*, we are referring to potential interface activity from various interface perspectives. A dimension could be the scope of work, industry regulations, tie-in to other projects, etc. Once again, this is similar to social networking where we segment our social networks by family, friends, work colleagues, and personal and professional interests. These dimensions of our lives help to establish relevant social networks as the interface dimensions help to identify the interface networks for a project.

As shown in Figure 5.3, the process used to perform the *interface network analysis* step is to gather relevant project information to identify potential interface networks and compare them against typical interface networks in order to specify the interface networks applicable for the project.

Relevant project information can include the PEP, the project mandate, and the contract strategy, among other documents. When reviewing project information, it is possible to ascertain how the project is to be developed using the sponsoring organization's project development process and how the system being developed by the project will function when in operation. In these project information documents, the desired information may take the form of a textual description, may be illustrated in architectural renderings, or contain reference to animated model simulations—or some combination of these. This information will describe or illustrate other entities outside the project, such as those that will operate with the system developed by the project; that is, how the project fits within the environment within which it is expected to operate. In addition, the PEP may provide varying degrees of detail about project development and is dependent upon the organization's preferences.

The project's contract strategy and company provided items (CPIs) can help to define interface entities within the project environment. The contract strategy will lay out an approach for how the project is segmented to deliver the project result. Remember, it is uncommon for a single contractor to have sufficient expertise and competency to deliver all elements of a large-scale project. Instead, the project sponsor organization will look to maximize value while acquiring the best products and services throughout the marketplace by sourcing from multiple firms.

More important, review of these project documents leads to the identification of additional documents that may need to be gathered and reviewed. For instance, if we find in reviewing the PEP that the system to be developed by the project integrates into an existing facility or another project, then

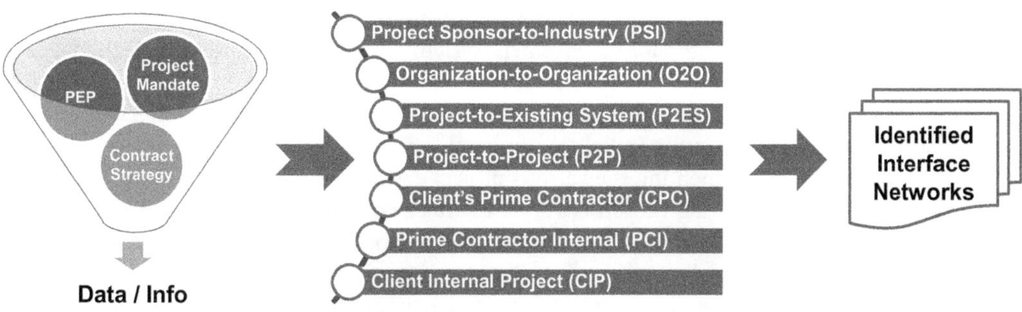

Figure 5.3 Interface network analysis

additional research is needed to identify relevant information about these systems and their relationships during the project's development. A cooperation agreement may exist between firms that are developing parallel projects that must integrate during operation. In such a case, access to the cooperation agreement is needed to understand the extent of the integration. As expected, this part of the process can be a journey of discovery until sufficient information has been obtained to provide a clear picture of the project development and its environment.

When adequate data and information has been collected and reviewed, the analysis team begins comparing collected project information against a list of most common interface networks, which were included in Chapter 4. For ease of reference, these networks include:

- Client's prime contractor (CPC)
- Client internal project (CIP)
- Project-to-project (P2P)
- Project-to-existing system (P2ES)
- Project sponsor-to-industry (PSI)
- Organization-to-organization (O2O)
- Contractor Internal (CI) or Prime Contractor Internal (PCI)

This network list is not intended to be all-inclusive, but it serves as a starting point. It may be necessary to include other possible interface networks depending on the unique aspects of the project. It is important to understand that modern, large-scale complex projects are typically not independent endeavors. Rather, systems being developed by projects are often required to integrate with other projects and existing systems. This is an important aspect of the project environment, which certainly impacts effective management of the project's interfaces.

In some cases, it may be necessary for one project to be a participant in the interface management system of other projects, either within the same organization or toward projects undertaken by other organizations. Earlier in the book, we discussed the interface group concept and the roles of the *lead interface party (LIP)* and the *interface party*. The central notion is that in an interface group, each of the two (or more) parties has specific roles and responsibilities. One party is identified as the *lead*, or LIP, while the other is known as the *interface party*. This relationship denotes one party being more reliant upon the other. The *interface group* and LIP concept is not only applicable within a project; it may also apply at the project level where one project must interface with another project or existing system.

One cannot assume that interface activity toward an external entity will be conducted using its project interface management system. Rather, there are many factors to be considered and agreement must be obtained with other projects and existing facilities. In cases in which it is agreed to use another project's interface management system, specifically how this will be accomplished needs to be addressed within the relevant interface management plan or procedure and accounted for in the project interface implementation plan to be described in Chapter 6.

The interface network analysis step ends with determining (1) which interface networks will be managed within the project's interface management system, (2) which networks will be managed as part of another project's processes, and (3) which networks are covered by other projects or existing facility interface management programs in which your project will be a participating member.

Interface network analysis is the initial step in breaking down a project's interface and interdependency complexity. By segmenting the various project entities into networks and understanding who is responsible for managing those networks, interface complexity is compartmentalized into manageable elements, which can be further decomposed during follow-on analysis steps.

It may be questioned why all parties cannot be placed in a single network. Grouping all interface parties into a single network creates practical challenges in devising the interface management system and managing interfaces, which is counter to the purpose of establishing an interface management system in the first place. For most major projects, the reasons for organizing multiple interface networks as opposed to a single network include:

- *Creates confusion*: Establishing an interface register with a high number of interface parties within a single network can be confusing, not only affecting the visual appearance and setup of the register, but also locating the group you are looking for and the specific interfaces. Grouping interface parties into related networks makes it much easier to locate and understand interface dimensions. Individuals can be members of many groups; from a management perspective, it can be difficult to maintain control of who is to have access to what groups, especially in large-scale projects where hundreds of people have access to the interface management system.
- *Different rules*: There are times when specific interface parties may establish the rules of the interface group, such as when interfacing to an industry party or another project. It is common to establish special interface rules to govern how certain interface groups will interact. Using an interface network makes it easy to segment out these groups and handle them according to the unique rules that govern their interaction. For example, a cooperation agreement between two companies whose projects must integrate may establish principles that need to be accounted for within their interaction, but these principles may not be applicable to other unrelated interface parties. The different rules may also apply to interface groups working on a classified project where certain information may need to be handled according to specific security procedures.
- *Controlling access*: It can be quite a challenge to segment information even within one interface group to the people that need access. An individual, such as a manager, may belong to many different interface groups and be involved in many different aspects of interface management. Information being discussed in one group may not be applicable for people involved in other groups. When all interface groups belong to a single interface network, controlling which interface dimensions relate to which entities can be difficult. For example, when one company is interfaced with a separate company about technical integration issues, it can become problematic when commercial (e.g., procurement, sales, etc.) issues are raised, because these may be addressed in another interface group, which may have different members, rules, and access permissions.
- *Reporting challenges*: From an interface management reporting perspective, when interface parties are bunched into a single network, it can be difficult to assess how certain groups or types of participants are performing. By establishing interface networks, it is easy to determine which aspects of the project are performing well, or not well, through a simple review of basic statistics. For example, contractors performing work to deliver the project may account for 40% of the total interface groups within a single network. It can be problematic to extract just these groups to determine how they are performing. While some software tools have the functionality to aid in this process, obtaining the right information may still require unnecessary time and data manipulation, when it could instead be easily reported through basic statistics provided for each network.

5.4.1.1 Project Diamond Example

In reviewing the Project Diamond information provided in Appendices C, D, and E of this book, several project characteristics emerge that are appropriate for identifying potential interface networks, including:

- Significant oversight by government safety and industry agencies
- Requires integration with other project(s) and as such, is governed by a *Project Development Cooperation Agreement*

- The project development approach segments Project Diamond into many subprojects
- Employs a complicated contract approach to support project development (numerous engineer, procure, and construct (EPC) and engineer, procure, construct, and install (EPCI) contracts)
- Sponsoring organization employs internal subproject teams to manage each contract
- Topside EPC (process, drilling, and utilities) is central to system functionality
- Extensive *CPIs* and *free issue* provided by sponsoring organization to the project

Given these project characteristics, the following interface networks are recommended.

5.4.1.1.1 Project Organization-to-Organization Interface Network

This network is proposed for Project Diamond to conduct interface coordination between *companies* whose projects are involved in the combined *field development and operation*—Project Diamond (ABC, Inc.), Project Sapphire (XYZ Corporation), Project Oil Pipeline (POL), and Project Gas Pipeline (PGP). This group is established for the purpose of coordinating and agreeing to interfaces related to the *field development cooperation agreement* established among the four companies including commercial issues, production license, hydrocarbon allocation, cooperation agreement conditions, legal, etc. It has been agreed by the respective companies that this interface network will be established and managed by ABC, Inc. However, personnel access to this interface network will be strictly controlled due to concerns over sensitive commercial information.

5.4.1.1.2 Project-to-Project Interface Network

This network is proposed to conduct interface coordination among the four *projects* involved in the *combined field development*:

- Project Diamond (ABC, Inc.),
- Project Sapphire (XYZ Corporation),
- Project Oil Pipeline (POL), and
- Project Gas Pipeline (PGP).

The operational concept of the area specifies Project Diamond to recover its hydrocarbons, partially process them by removing water content, and transfer the hydrocarbons along subsea pipelines to Project Sapphire. At Sapphire, Diamond's hydrocarbons will be received and combined with Sapphire's hydrocarbons. Sapphire will separate the oil and gas and transfer each along separate oil (POL) and gas pipelines (PGP) to onshore facilities. Sapphire will also provide power to Diamond. The purpose of this interface network is to manage technical, management, and industry interfaces related to hydrocarbon production and transfer; including power transfer from Sapphire to Diamond. It has been agreed by the respective projects to establish this interface network and that Project Diamond will manage this interface network within its interface management system.

5.4.1.1.3 Project Sponsor-to-Industry Interface Network

This network is proposed to be established toward the industry safety agency, and other associated projects in the field development (Diamond, Sapphire, POL, and PGP), to ensure alignment between the projects' designs and compliance with industry health, safety, and environmental (HSE) regulations. This network is intended to manage interfaces related to HSE aspects of the overall field design and development to support safety audits and verifications, the safety application process, etc. The Safety agency and each project have agreed to provide representation and this interface network will be managed within the Project Diamond interface management system.

5.4.1.1.4 Client's Prime Contractor Interface Network

Project Diamond's development approach requires a complicated contract strategy composed of several EPC and EPCI contracts to segment the project (Topside, Living Quarters, Jacket, Subsea). This network will be established to manage technical, management, and other interfaces between Project Diamond's contractors and issues along their shared scope of work boundaries. This network includes contractors providing *CPI* on behalf of ABC, Inc. and is the main focus of Project Diamond's interface management system since it is directly focused on the work to deliver the project result.

5.4.1.1.5 Project Diamond (Client) Internal Project Interface Network

ABC, Inc. utilizes subproject management teams to oversee the project's complicated contracts in order to deliver the project result. As a result, a subproject team for each EPC and EPCI contract oversees the contract on behalf of the client (ABC, Inc.). This network is established for the client's (ABC, Inc.) internal subproject teams to formally communicate interface issues affecting their subproject areas of responsibility and their contractors' scopes of work. This network is intended for the client's management teams to align interface risk mitigation strategies, scope changes, and other issues affecting multiple parts of the project. This ensures alignment of respective company personnel prior to the client teams issuing formal correspondence to their respective subproject contractors.

5.4.1.1.6 Prime Contractor Internal Interface Network

Closer examination of the project's contract strategy confirms the importance of the Topside EPC contract as central to key functionality to be delivered in the final system. This scope includes engineering, procurement, and construction as well as implementing the safety automation system (SAS) throughout the facility. Also, this scope assigns *system integrity* responsibility to the Topside EPC contractor who must ensure standardization, commonality, and integration of the entire offshore facility. In this context, *system integrity* means the Topside EPC contractor is charged with the responsibility for ensuring commonality, standardization, alignment of equipment and processes, etc., across the project so that the system developed by the project can integrate seamlessly. This network manages internal interfaces within the Topside EPC scope of work and is comprised of only those companies representing the Topside EPC/SAS team.

5.4.1.1.7 Project Diamond Interface Network Summary

In defining the relevant interface networks, the first step in simplifying interface complexity is achieved; and it is these networks that form the basis for structuring the project's interface management process during implementation. In Chapter 6, the interface management procedures are developed. It is important to understand that each network is unique and how these networks will operate and be guided mostly by the same rules; however, the process should be flexible enough to allow for special circumstances, such as cases in which a network includes other companies or projects.

With the interface networks established, we can continue to analyze each network to understand the parties that need to belong to each network and their relationship to other entities within the network. Figure 5.4 provides a summary of Project Diamond's proposed interface networks and the preliminary list of interface entities within each group.

In Figure 5.4 it can be observed that *interface entities* comprise different types of organizations including projects, contractor companies, project sponsoring companies, industry agencies, organizational departments (operations and drilling & wells), and subproject management teams. This illustrates one of the advantages of interface management; it provides a means to account for disparate entities associated with the project—both those inside the scope boundary and those who can

DIAMOND PROJECT INTERFACE NETWORKS						
	Client's Prime Contractor (CPC)	Client Internal Project (CIP)	Prime Contractor Internal (PCI)	Project-to-Project (P2P)	Organization-to-Organization (O2O)	Project Sponsor-to-Industry (PSI)
INTERFACE PARTIES	Topside EPC	Topside EPC	Topside Engineering	Project Diamond (ABC)	ABC Corporation	Industry Safety (PSA)
	Jacket EPC	Jacket EPC	Topside Procurement	Project Sapphire (XYZ)	XYZ Corporation	Project Diamond (ABC)
	Transport & Install	Transport & Install	Topside Construction	Project Oil Pipe (POL)	POL Industries	Project Sapphire (XYZ)
	Living Quarters	Living Quarters	Topside SAS	Project Gas Pipe (PGP)	PGP Incorporated	Project Oil Pipe (POL)
	Hook-Up	Hook-Up				Project Gas Pipe (PGP)
	Drilling & Wells	Drilling & Wells				
	SURF	SURF				
		Operations				

Figure 5.4 Project Diamond interface networks and parties

influence the project from outside the project boundary, so that they can be grouped into networks by shared interface interest.

5.4.2 Interface Parties (Interface Group) Analysis

Within each network, the entity population set needs to be defined to understand the scope of participation within each network and the relationships shared between the various entities. This analysis process identifies the relevant actors to participate in the network and their relationship (or non-relationship) to all other actors in the network. The relationship state between actors in a network is binary (1 or 0); either there is a relationship or there is not. That is, in a given interface network the entities within that network may or may not have a relationship with each of the other actors in the network.

As illustrated in Figure 5.5, interface party analysis requires inputs including the interface networks identified previously, project information, and organizational information assets. As they are the output of interface network analysis, the interface networks serve as a starting point to determine the entities in each of the networks. Project information and organizational information assets serve to describe and establish the relationships between the entities. Tools and techniques are then applied to these inputs to derive an interface group matrix for each network. These tools and techniques include interviews, interface entity relationship models, and a template for interface group matrices.

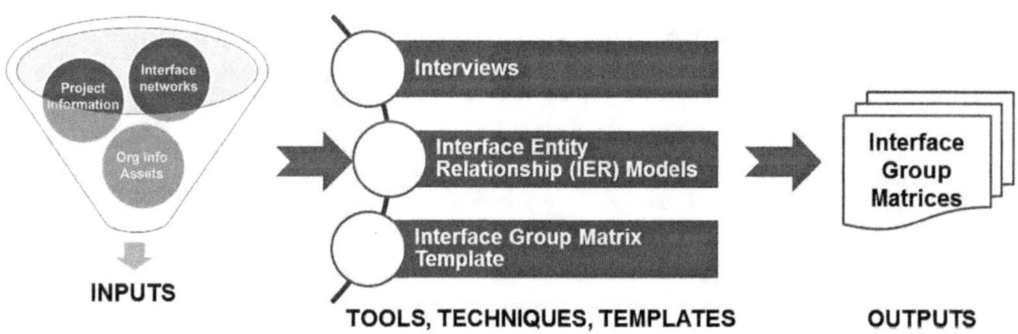

Figure 5.5 Interface party analysis

The number of participants within an interface network can vary from just two entities to many (up to 50 or more in special cases). The number of entities within a network influences the difficulty in determining the interface groups. In networks with only a few entities (3 or 4), this process can be straightforward and may only require interviews with relevant project personnel. In networks with a large number of entities, more advanced techniques to establish relationships may be needed—such as the development of an interface entity relationship (IER) model. After determining that a relationship exists, the interface group matrix template provides a format to establish the *LIP* and structure the interface groups. The output is an interface group matrix for each interface network that identifies the interface parties and their relationships to other parties in the network.

5.4.2.1 Interface Entity Relationship Models

In interface networks comprised of many entities, an IER model can aid in visualizing relationships between different entities within a network. IER models are based on concepts used in entity-relationship modeling techniques, which aid in understanding the relationships among various system and software objects. Peter Chen, then a faculty member at M.I.T. Sloan and later at Carnegie-Mellon University, published a seminal 1976 paper on entity relationship modeling, which has been widely adopted for database design, business process engineering, and information systems. In his paper, Chen proposed an entity-relationship model to supplant and enhance three earlier data modeling approaches. The entity-relationship model views the world as consisting of entities (persons, things, events, or organizations) and relationships (the association between entities or members of entities); such as mother-daughter, the relationship between two person-type entities (Chen, 1976). An entity relationship model describes interrelated things of interest in a specific domain of knowledge and how they are related.

For the purposes of interface management, a *domain of knowledge* is analogous to *interface networks*. An entity relationship model is composed of entity types (nouns which classify the things of interest) and specifies relationships (verbs) that can exist between instances of those entity types. In reference to interface networks, entities are organizations (companies, departments, projects, existing systems, oversight agencies, local interest groups, etc.). The concepts of entity relationship modeling are useful in identifying and visualizing relationships between interface entities within a network of several parties.

It is worth noting that IER models are subject to defined symbols and construct rules. While appropriate for systems and software engineering purposes and also database development, strict rules and symbols are not necessary in developing IER models. Rather, simple construct methods are preferred. The intention of the IER model is to gain an appreciable understanding of the relationships that exist between various entities within an interface network. As such, the reader is encouraged to utilize creativity and simplicity in developing IER models and be less concerned with strict adherence to entity relationship construct rules.

Using the information provided in Figure 5.4, an IER model has been constructed in Figure 5.6 that represents the CPC interface network. This IER example model provides an abstract visualization

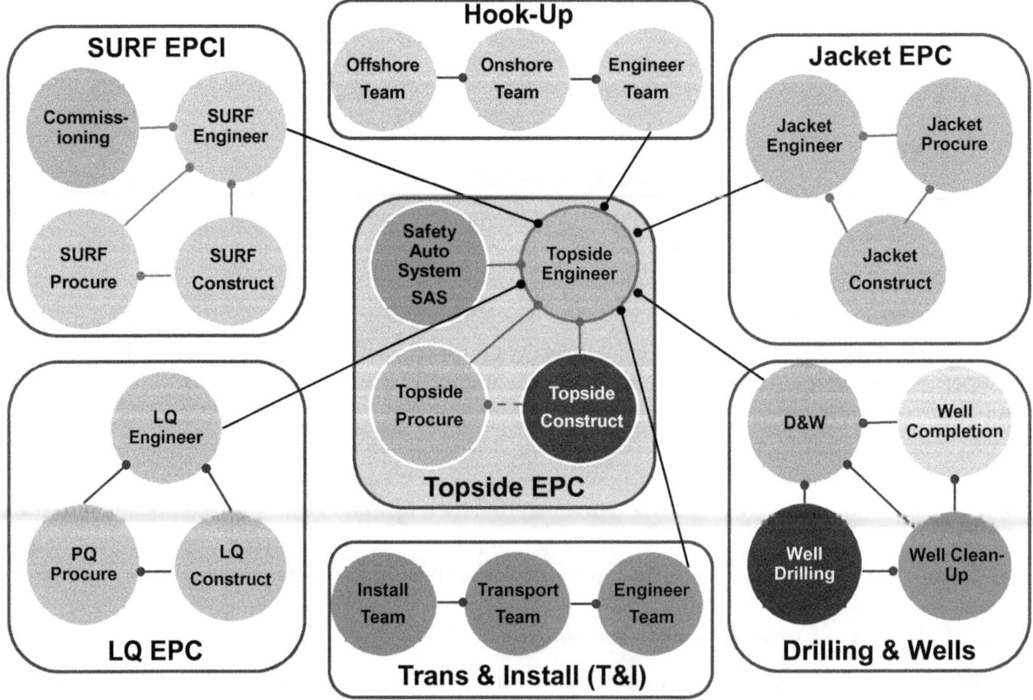

Figure 5.6 Project Diamond—Topside EPC IER model (CPC interface network)

of the *relationships* between *Topside EPC* (the *light gray* box in the center) and all other entities within the CPC interface network. Specifically, the model explores from the perspective of Topside EPC whether or not a relationship exists with other entities within the network and which entity should be designated as the *LIP*. While the Topside EPC perspective for the CPC interface network is displayed in this model, additional IER models can be developed to show the perspectives of other entities existing within the interface network or any other interface network.

In constructing the model, boxes are used to represent *entities*. In this case, entities represent contractors within the CPC network where each contractor is depicted by an *entity box*. Within each entity box, major sub-entities are displayed using circles. The sub-entities represent sub-organizations contributing to delivering the scope of work in this case, whether the sub-organizations in a contract belong to one organization or multiple organizations. Sub-entities shown with the same shade of gray within an entity box belong to the same organization, such as all the sub-entities with the *Trans & Install (T&I)* entity box. Sub-entities belonging to different organizations are depicted in different shades of gray within the entity box, as shown in the *Drilling & Wells* entity box, which depicts four different organizations representing the entity in four different shades of gray. In all cases, the entity box is defined using the various scopes of work and areas of responsibility described in project documents.

Solid lines are used to depict which entities within the Project Diamond CPC interface network have a relationship to the *Topside EPC* entity box. In Figure 5.6, lines have been connected to *Topside Engineer* to indicate that Topside Engineering will be managing interfaces on behalf of the Topside EPC entity. However, this may or may not be known at the time the relationship diagram is first drawn and connecting to the Topside EPC entity box is initially sufficient; the diagram can be refined later, after contract award, if it is not readily apparent which sub-entity will be responsible for managing interfaces.

In any case, where a solid black line connects two parties within a network, an interface group will be established. In Figure 5.6, interface groups will be established against six interface entities (Hook-Up, SURF EPCI, Drilling & Wells, Trans & Install, Jacket EPC, and LQ EPC). However, it is necessary to identify which of the interface parties should be established as the *LIP*.

While the solid black line simply denotes an interface relationship, each solid black line has a termination point with a *black ball* at one end of the line. The location of the *black ball* at the end of the line identifies the party to be designated as the *LIP* when establishing the interface groups. In some cases, this designation may be obvious and included in the terms and conditions of a contract or department area of responsibility description. In other cases, this designation may not be clear and may require additional analysis or research. Regardless, the *LIP* responsibilities are included in the interface management procedure, which will be discussed in Chapter 6, and are an important aspect of ensuring that the project's interface management system operates effectively and efficiently.

An interesting by-product of this process is a clearer picture of interface, interdependency, and interaction complexity existing within this network. A quick scan of the Figure 5.6 diagram shows a complicated web of intertwined entity relationships with significant dependencies. For example, it is clear in viewing this IER that *Topside Engineering* is a critical sub-entity, not only within the Topside EPC organization, but to all other interface entities within the CPC interface network. It is reasonable to expect that other interface entities would be negatively affected by delayed Topside engineering activities or poor quality of interface material and information. As a result, it is this type of insight to be gained from interface analysis and from which appropriate management processes can be emplaced to monitor and control interface activities between interface entities. This information can be captured in an interface group matrix.

5.4.2.2 *Interface Group Matrix Template*

The interface group matrix template is a formatted matrix to aid in structuring interface parties that have an interface relationship into interface groups. The group matrix template helps to easily identify which interface parties are assigned interface lead roles. As shown in the sample interface group matrix in Figure 5.7, the matrix is structured with lead interface parties across the top row and corresponding interface parties along the first column on the left (shown as Entity #1–5). The *LIP* is assigned based on each entity's *criticality* to the project and its role and responsibility. Several entities are listed in the *lead interface parties* row from left to right.

INTERFACE NETWORK - INTERFACE GROUPS					
Lead Interface Party → Interface Party ↓	LIP #1	LIP #2	LIP #3	LIP #4	LIP #5
Entity #1					
Entity #2	X				
Entity #3	X	X			
Entity #4	X		X		
Entity #5	X	X		X	

Figure 5.7 Interface group matrix example

A relationship between parties is denoted by an *X* in the cells that align between the LIP and the corresponding interface party. The *X* indicates a member of an interface group (an interface party), while the entity in the Lead Interface Party row indicates the LIP for that interface group. As indicated in Figure 5.7, eight interface groups are proposed within this interface network. In this example, the project sponsor has assigned LIP #1 as the main LIP given its importance to the project and relationship to all other parties. In interface groups not involving LIP #1, the priority has been assigned to LIP #2, then LIP #3, etc. For example, in the interface group containing LIP #2 and Entity #3, LIP #2 is the LIP, while in the interface group containing LIP #4 and Entity #5, LIP #4 is assigned as the LIP.

It is reasonable to question how the determination is made to define one party as a *LIP*. Typically, for project contractors, this determination is made after concept development when the project's system architecture is decided. This responsibility is then assigned as a formal contract requirement to the contractor delivering critical elements of the system's functionality. For P2P and O2O networks, this designation is normally included in the cooperation or commercial agreement between the two projects or organizations.

The technique of identifying interface parties, and using the matrix template to assign interface groups, provides the means to determine which parties need to interface with other parties. More important, it helps to establish which of the parties is more dependent upon the other party and to determine lead interface responsibility. It is also important to note that in projects spanning many years or those with considerable scope changes, this process may need to be reviewed periodically, or as appropriate, and adjustments made to parties and interface groups within a network.

5.4.2.3 *Project Diamond Interface Group Matrices*

Continuing with our CPC interface network from Project Diamond, Figure 5.8 illustrates the interface group matrix for the CPC interface analysis. Here we see the results of our analysis using the

PROJECT DIAMOND PRIME CONTRACTOR (CPC) INTERFACE NETWORK - INTERFACE GROUPS						
Lead Interface Party / **Interface Party ↓**	**Topside EPC**	**Jacket EPCI**	**SURF EPCI**	**Living Quarters EPC**	**T&I**	**Hook-Up**
Jacket EPCI	X					
SURF EPCI	X	X				
Living Quarters EPC	X					
Trans & Install (T&I)	X		X	X		
Hook-Up	X	X	X	X	X	
Drilling & Wells	X	X				X

Figure 5.8 Project Diamond CPC interface network matrix

IER model (Figure 5.6) and after completing similar IER models with the other interface entities, perhaps one from the point of view of each entity. Figure 5.8 shows how the CPC interface network is structured, including which entities comprise the network, what the interface groups are, and which entities have been assigned *lead interface responsibility*. In addition, it is now possible to observe that 15 interface groups have been established for the network. Looking at the first column of Xs, we see that it contains six interface groups, one for each interface party paired with Topside EPC as the LIP for each of the six groups. In the case of Project Diamond, Topside EPC is central to all the main system functions, and as such, it is designated the main LIP except in the interface groups in this network for which it has no direct role except oversight. As another example, we can see that one interface group comprises the Hook-up and Drilling & Wells *entities* with Hook-up assigned as the LIP for the interface group. Later in the book, as we discuss setting up the interface management system, implementation, and managing interfaces during the project's execution phase, it will become much easier to understand the central role these groups play in managing interface and interdependency complexity throughout the project.

5.4.3 Interface Area Analysis

Using project management based artifacts (e.g., PEP, contract strategy, scopes of work, etc.), interface parties have now been organized into networks of entities with related interface interest and paired into interface groups. As is now realized, this only requires a high level of understanding of interfaces between entities. Analysis of interface areas marks a transition point from identifying who the interfacing parties are to what they need to interface about at a high level.

The aim of interface area analysis is to determine the interaction domains relevant for an interface network that are needed to establish the interface management register, which will be covered in Chapter 7. Interaction domains are the basis for interactions between the parties and are based on relevant information and material needed by a party from other interface parties in the network in order to deliver the respective scope of work or area of responsibility within the interface network. In essence, interface areas bind interface parties within a network to relevant interface domains for their network. In some ways, these interface areas act as restrictions to support interaction in relevant domains while preventing interaction on topics that are not relevant for some interface parties within a network. For example, it may be appropriate for interface parties in one interface network to interact over commercial (i.e., nontechnical business disciplines such as contracts, supply chain, procurement, revenue/expenses) interfaces and issues, but inappropriate for them to do so in another interface network.

In Section 5.4.1.1, six interface networks were established for Project Diamond. A closer examination of these networks reveals that each network consists of different types of interface entities, each with different purposes. In interface area analysis, the aim is to obtain a better understanding of the breadth of interface domains between interface parties within a network. Thus, this aspect of interface analysis relies heavily upon technical artifacts developed during early SE activities to understand the connections between entities within a network.

Interface areas are typically established by *discipline* or *system*, although other categories may be relevant, such as *subsystem* and *procurement packages* for internal networks and *nodes* for software-, control-, and automation-related networks.

5.4.3.1 Interface Area Disciplines

Interface area disciplines include both technical and management disciplines. By *discipline*, we are referring to the occupational field within an entity, which has responsibility for interacting with other interface parties related to interfaces within their occupational field.

Technical disciplines reside primarily within engineering, research, and technology departments and include: electrical; process; automation; instrumentation and metering; hydraulic; structural; piping; heating, ventilating, and air conditioning; avionics, etc., among many others. These disciplines serve as the interaction point for solving technical interfaces within a project and to entities extending beyond the project's scope boundary. As previously defined in Chapter 3, technical interfaces are normally associated with conceptual design and detailed engineering of the system under development by the project. The *Systems Engineering Body of Knowledge* (BKCASE, 2015) also defines technical interfaces as matter, energy, or information flows exchanged between the system-of-interest and its external components in the context of its use, including physical interfaces.

Management disciplines reside primarily within project management, but can also extend to the sponsoring organization. In this book, we refer to these types of interfaces as *project* and *organizational* interfaces. Project management related interfaces occur across the 10 Project Management Institute (PMI) project management Knowledge Areas (PMI, 2017) and the project's life cycle or phases—called *Process Groups* by PMI (see Chapter 3, Section 3.3.1.2 *Project Interfaces*). Management disciplines across the project interface areas include project control, schedule, operations, commercial, legal, change management, risk, etc.—among several others that may be specific to an organization or project. Project material or information needs between interface parties can extend to all facets of project management—such as shared risks, alignment of project schedules, quality control methods, inspection routines, use of preferred vendor lists, coordination of critical skills/personnel, and others. Interface interaction across these management areas can relate to a wide spectrum of topics—including procurement activities, contract clarifications, safety procedures during installation and commissioning, critical material deliveries between contractors and subcontractors, and risk mitigation strategies.

5.4.3.2 Interface Area Systems

Arguably, one of the most overused and least understood words in the English language is *system*. This word is used to convey many different intentions and meanings, as noted in Chapter 2 (Section 2.3.3.2 *What Is a System?*). In the context of defining interface areas, we are referring inwardly to the system developed by the project and its physical elements. Kossiakoff and Sweet (2003) define *system* as a set of interrelated components working together toward some common objective. While simple and concise, this definition implies a multiplicity of interacting parts that collectively perform a significant function and also implies a *closed* system where all aspects of the system exist within its boundary. Further, this definition is oriented toward the integrated *physical system* to perform the common objective. At least on the surface, there is no mention of the infrastructure, such as people or processes, to translate the system from *idea to reality*.

System-related interface areas comprise the main (physical) systems needed to perform the functionality of the project's outcome. For example, an airplane requires airframe, fuselage, wing, landing, guidance, and other systems to perform its main system function of air transportation. An offshore oil and gas platform requires the well, separation, treatment, transfer, and safety systems that when combined into a unified system (i.e., a *supersystem* comprised of many individual systems) can perform its main functions to recover, process, and transport hydrocarbons. Understanding the true meaning of *system* often relies on the perspective under which the word is used and is the reason we incessantly focus on defining its context to ensure the right perspective.

In establishing interface areas by system, it is common to identify each system by a number followed by a title, such as System 13 Flowlines, System 22 Guidance, System 43 Avionics, etc. System identifiers are not random; they are usually identified during early SE activity during concept development and are contained in the project's SE management plan or similarly titled document. Figure 5.9 provides an example of interface areas by discipline, system, and nodes.

5.4.3.3 Interface Area Approaches

In general, there are two approaches to establishing interface areas; predetermined (preset) and specified. Both approaches require the use of some method to categorize interface areas (i.e., disciplines, systems, nodes, etc.). In simple terms, a predefined approach relies on a predetermined template of interface areas that is applied automatically to an interface network while a specified approach requires interface areas to be tailored to the specifics of the interface network. In establishing predetermined or specified approaches, any combination of interface area categories can be used to best describe the interface area. This can, and will vary, based on the unique aspects of each project and preferences of project personnel.

5.4.3.3.1 Predetermined Interface Areas

In a predetermined approach, interface areas are established using a predetermined set of project disciplines or systems. Predetermined interface areas are a way of leveraging commonalities for similar projects within a specific industry. While the system being developed by the project may be unique, it likely shares significant similarities with other projects within the same industry. For example, new airplane development projects share common technical traits with previous airplane models, which allows for interface areas to be predetermined. The same is true for oil and gas projects where similar management and technical disciplines are utilized to develop offshore oil and gas platforms (facilities). In both examples, projects within these industries use similar technical and management disciplines to deliver the project result. The predetermined approach is quite useful when undertaking a project similar to a previous project where the system developed by the project is similar and will involve similar interfaces.

5.4.3.3.2 Specified Interface Areas

In a specified approach, interface areas are determined based on the specific circumstances of the project and the interface network. There are many occasions in which projects are unique and thus have no similar project precedent. Thus, the project organization and interface personnel must analyze the precise nature of the interface activity within a network to determine the areas that apply. Specified approaches also occur when technological advances within an industry change the way system functions are performed, which introduces new technical or management domains. For example, in the defense industry, significant progress has been made on remotely operated military systems, which introduces new and unique technical and management interface domains for project development. The oil and gas industry has continued to introduce and advance techniques for enhanced or improved oil recovery, which introduce new methods, procedures, and processes

Discipline Code	Discipline	System Code	System Title	Node Code	Node Title
A	Administration	10	Drilling	C31	Process Control - Wells
B	Procurement	27	Gas Transfer	C32	Process Control - Injection
C	Civil/architect	21	Crude Oil Transfer	C33	Process Control - Utilities
D	Drilling	29	Water Injection	C34	Process Control- HVAC
E	Electrical	30	Oil Pipeline	F21	Fire & Gas Control - Platform
F	Project control/cost/economy	32	Gas Pipeline	F22	Fire & Gas Control- Living Quarters
G	Geology	35	Chemical Injection	P41	Planned Shutdown - Wellhead
H	HVAC	89	Power	P42	Planned Shutdown - Utilities
I	Instrumentation/metering	14	Control and Monitor	E11	Emergency Shutdown- Platorm
J	Marine operation	20	Hydrocarbon Separation	E12	Emergency Shutdown- Onshore Control
K	Inspection	70	Fire and Gas Detection	L01	Power Distr. & Control
L	Piping/layout	86	Telecommunication	V51	Process Control - Fuel & Water Pumps
M	Material technology	87	Automation	001	General

Figure 5.9 Interface area—discipline, system, and node example

domains. Technology advancements change and extend the boundaries of interface activities to new domains, which then need to be accounted for more precisely in some interface networks.

5.4.3.4 Project Diamond Interface Areas

In the Project Diamond example, six interface networks are proposed. To illustrate how interface areas are applied to an interface network, we will use just three of the six networks; CPC and P2P between Projects Diamond and Sapphire, and the Topside EPC PCI interface networks.

5.4.3.4.1 Project Diamond Client's Prime Contractor Interface Network

This network is established to manage technical, management, and other interfaces between Project Diamond's contractors and issues along their shared scope of work boundaries. This network includes contractors providing CPIs on behalf of ABC, Inc. and is the main focus of Project Diamond's interface management system since it is directly focused on the work to deliver the project result. Figure 5.10 shows a wide range of technical and management discipline areas among the client's prime contractors. This is because Topside retains central control of main systems and has been contracted to provide system integrity. The main emphasis of interface activity is to ensure integrity across all systems. Thus, only disciplines are used as interface areas for the CPC network. That said, it is not wrong if *system* were to be included as an interface area. In this example, it was determined not to be necessary.

5.4.3.4.2 Project-to-Project Interface Network

This network is proposed to conduct interface coordination between *projects* involved in the *combined field development*—Project Diamond (ABC, Inc.), Project Sapphire (XYZ Corporation), Project Oil Pipeline (POL), and Project Gas Pipeline (PGP). The operational concept of the area specifies Project Diamond to recover its own hydrocarbons, to partially process them by removing water content, and to transfer the hydrocarbons along subsea pipelines to Project Sapphire. As shown in Figure 5.10, in the P2P network, interface areas have been established both by discipline and by system. Although Project Diamond has many more systems resident within the Topside module, only those systems listed in Figure 5.10 are appropriate for interface interaction within this P2P network because they are directly associated with transferring hydrocarbons between the projects in the network.

5.4.3.4.3 Topside EPC Prime Contractor Internal Interface Network

Closer examination of the project's contract strategy confirms the importance of the Topside EPC contract as central to key functionality to be delivered in the final system, as illustrated earlier in the IER diagram in Figure 5.6. The scope of the Topside EPC contract includes engineering, procurement, and construction as well as implementing the SAS throughout the facility. The SAS is critical to safe operation of the offshore facility and involves intense interaction among elements of the Topside EPC contract team. As a result, interface areas have been established by *node* as shown in the Topside Engineering PCI interface network interface areas in Figure 5.10. The *node* areas relate to major SAS elements and serve to focus interface interaction and interdependencies on these areas during execution of the contract.

5.4.4 Interface Issue Analysis

This purpose of this step in the interface analysis process is to identify interface issues. In Chapter 3, interface issues were defined as: *a statement identifying specific aspects, such as physical or functional,*

Project Diamond Client's Prime Contractor (CPC) Interface Network		Project Diamond & Sapphire Project-to-Project (P2P) Interface Network				Project Diamond Topside Engineering Prime Contractor Internal (PCI) Interface Network	
Discipline Code	**Discipline Title**	**System Code**	**System Title**	**Discipline Code**	**Discipline Title**	**Node Code**	**Node Title**
A	Administration	10	Drilling	A	Administration	C31	Process Control - Wells
B	Procurement	27	Gas Transfer	B	Procurement	C32	Process Control - Injection
C	Civil/architect	21	Crude Oil Transfer	C	Civil/architect	C33	Process Control - Utilities
D	Drilling	29	Water Injection	D	Drilling	C34	Process Control - HVAC
E	Electrical	30	Oil Pipeline	E	Electrical	F21	Fire & Gas Control - Platform
F	Project control/cost/economy	32	Gas Pipeline	F	Project control/cost/economy	F22	Fire & Gas Control - Living Quarters
G	Geology	35	Chemical Injection	G	Geology	P41	Planned Shutdown - Wellhead
H	HVAC	89	Power	H	HVAC	P42	Planned Shutdown - Utilities
I	Instrumentation/metering	14	Control and Monitor	I	Instrumentation/metering	E11	Emergency Shutdown - Platorm
J	Marine operation	20	Hydrocarbon Separation	J	Marine operation	E12	Emergency Shutdown - Onshore Control
K	Inspection	70	Fire and Gas Detection	K	Inspection	L01	Power Distr. & Control
L	Piping/layout	86	Telecommunication	L	Piping/layout	V51	Process Control - Fuel & Water Pumps
M	Material technology	87	Automation	M	Material technology	001	General
N	Structural	76	Emergency Shutdown	N	Structural		
O	Operation			O	Operation		
P	Process			P	Process		
Q	Quality management			Q	Quality management		
R	Mechanical			R	Mechanical		
S	Health, safety and environ (HSE)			S	Health, safety and environ (HSE)		
T	Telecommunication			T	Telecommunication		
U	Subsea			U	Subsea		
W	Weight control			W	Weight control		
X	Reservoir			X	Reservoir		
Y	Pipeline			Y	Pipeline		
Z	Multidiscipline			Z	Multidiscipline		

Figure 5.10 Project Diamond—interface areas example

of the interface area requiring interface activity with another interface party. Interface issues are specific questions or statements and serve as a foundation from which to later verify interface activity. In projects with extremely high interface complexity, there may be many interface dimensions for a single interface area, requiring further decomposition. In these cases, interface issues provide the means to further decompose and categorize high-level interface areas into more discrete segments.

Admittedly, this step is not widely utilized currently nor is it included as part of the example project illustrated in this book, and thus will not be mentioned beyond this chapter. However, as systems developed through projects become increasingly more complex over time, the importance and applicability of this step will increase. Thus, the main reason for including it in this chapter is to make the reader aware of this technique and its benefits, as well as ways to perform it—should that be required.

In most large-scale projects, it is often sufficient to simply identify the interface areas, bypass interface issues, and move directly to identifying related interface items associated with each interface area. Where interface areas have minimal dimensions or aspects, it is quite reasonable to manage without interface issues, but this is not always recommended, especially in complex areas of the project. In situations in which the interface area is expansive, involving many dimensions or aspects, and for which the criticality of the interface area is high, further analysis should be applied to decompose, segment, and structure the interface area into manageable elements. In this way, interface groups can initiate interface items for each issue; ensuring complete coverage across the entire interface area.

In situations in which a single interface area requires interface interaction across several dimensions of the interface area, then further decomposition, segmenting, and organizing into interface issues will aid in reducing complexity by dividing it into more manageable elements. This is the benefit of decomposition and hierarchical analysis; it provides a logical and methodical way to further deconstruct interface areas into relevant interface issues. There are a number of techniques to identify interface issues for a single interface area, but this book will focus on two: hierarchical decomposition and design structure matrix (DSM).

5.4.4.1 Hierarchical Decomposition Diagram

A hierarchical decomposition diagram (HDD) shows a high-level function, process, organization, data subject area, or other type of object broken down into lower level, more detailed components. For example, decomposition diagrams may represent organizational structure or functional decomposition into processes. For purposes of decomposing interface areas to identify related issues, decomposition diagrams provide a logical process to visualize issues as interface area sub-elements for complex or complicated interface areas, especially if these areas involve different sub-groups, entities, or parts of the organizations. The HDD allows for increasing decomposition appropriate to the level of complexity for relevant interface areas.

Figure 5.11 shows different interface issues related to an electrical (power) interface area shared between two interface parties. Here we observe a single interface area involving numerous interface dimensions or aspects including: power equipment, management signals, protection equipment and settings, and emergency shutdown, among others. In situations such as this interface area, each issue could require the attention of different entities or sub-entities or teams within each interface party, each of which has responsibility for different aspects of the interface area. Further, in highly complex interface areas, it may be necessary to subdivide into sub-interface issues as illustrated in Figure 5.12.

Further, decomposing interface issues into sub-issues is directly related to one's perception of the level of complexity of the issue in the context of other factors, such as when multiple teams or sub-entities within the interface party must contribute to resolving interface items (e.g., reaching interface agreements). Also, when multiple interface items are related, or when there is a need for specialized resources to contribute to specific sub-issues. Sub-issues might also be needed when elements of the issue are proprietary or on a *need to know* basis. Again, one must apply critical thinking

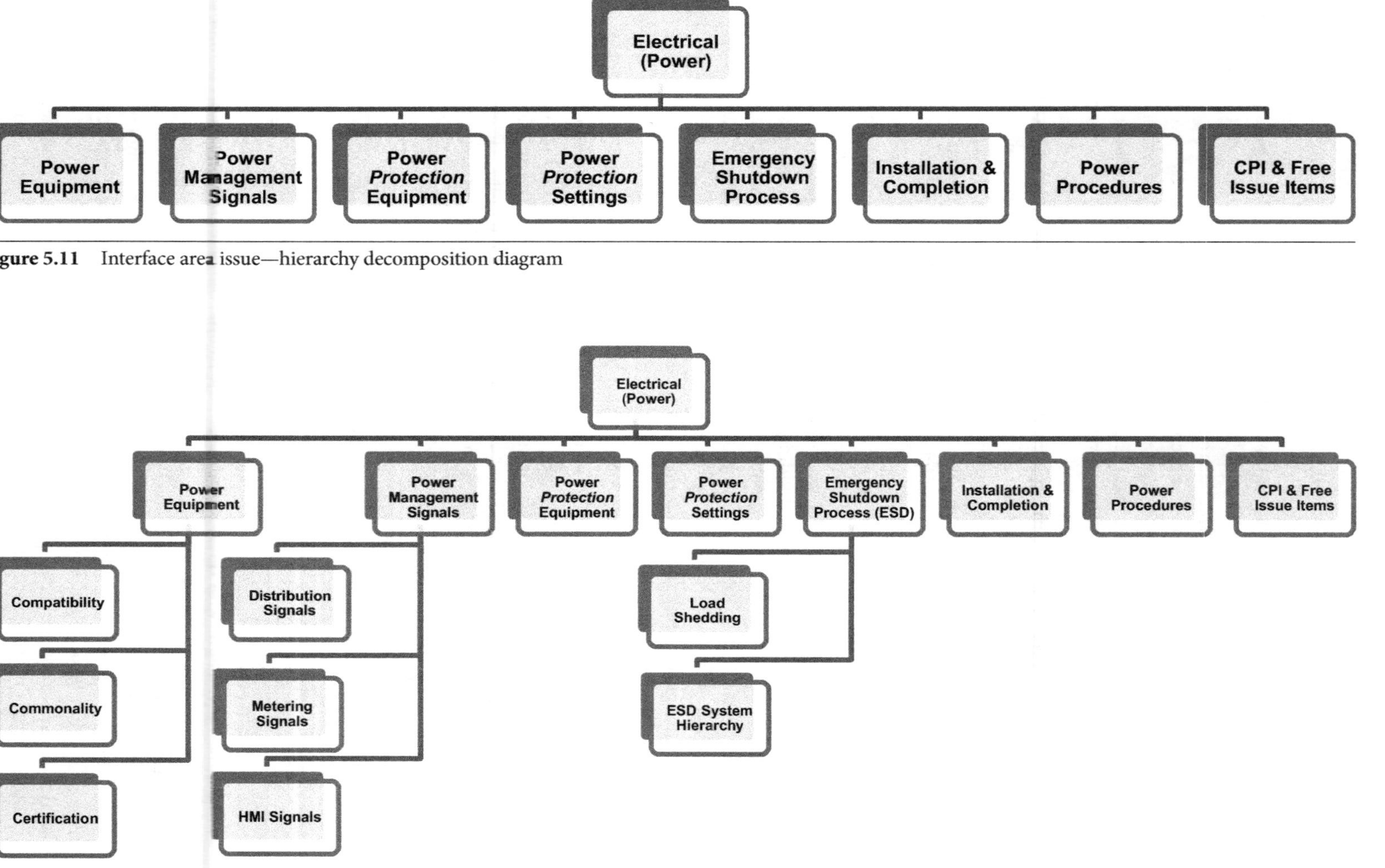

Figure 5.11 Interface area issue—hierarchy decomposition diagram

Figure 5.12 Interface area issues and sub-issues—hierarchy decomposition diagram

to understand the appropriate level at which to decompose an interface area, but it is important to realize that when an interface area may be less straightforward than it initially appears, techniques such as creating interface issues and sub-issues are useful and available.

The purpose of decomposing interface areas is to simplify complexity associated with expansive, complicated, or multifaceted interface areas. As demonstrated throughout this chapter, managing interface complexity is about breaking down the problem into manageable elements through decomposition, and then structuring and organizing those elements in a way to increase clarity and minimize confusion. Another technique to aid in understanding interface issues is the use of a DSM.

5.4.4.2 Design Structure Matrix

A DSM provides a simple, compact, and visual representation of a complex system that supports innovative solutions to decomposition and integration problems (Browning, 2001). This is accomplished by displaying the relationships between components of a system in a compact, visual, and analytically advantageous format. A DSM is a square matrix with identical row and column labels. Elements are represented by the shaded elements along the diagonal. An off-diagonal mark signifies the dependency of one element on another. "Reading across a row reveals what other elements the element (in that row) provides to; scanning down a column reveals what other elements the element (in that column) depends on. That is, reading down a column reveals input sources, while reading across a row indicates output sinks" (Browning, 2001). This technique allows for a visual presentation of and logical progression through dependencies that exist among the elements in a complex system.

Browning notes two main categories of DSMs: static and time-based. "Static DSMs represent system elements existing simultaneously, such as components of a product architecture or groups in an organization. Static DSMs are usually analyzed with clustering algorithms. In time-based DSMs, the ordering of the rows and columns indicates a flow through time: upstream activities in a process precede downstream activities" (Browning, 2001).

Static DSMs are essentially variations of the square matrix called an N^2 diagram and have been used by systems engineers to represent architectural components and interfaces (Becker et al., 2000). Yet, DSMs provide the flexibility to model components, teams, activities, and parameters, which align well for the purposes of understanding relationships within interface areas, including disciplines, systems, and nodes. Browning's paper reviews four applications of a DSM that are useful to project management and SE professionals:

- Component-based or architecture DSM
- Team-based or organization DSM
- Activity-based or schedule DSM
- Parameter-based (or low-level schedule) DSM (Browning, 2001)

The first two are static DSMs, while the third and fourth are considered time-based. Decomposing interface areas into issues may require one or more of the following DSMs to fully explore the breadth and depth of the complex interface areas to understand the spectrum of disciplines, systems (subsystems), and nodes involved in the area.

5.4.4.2.1 Component-Based or Architecture DSM

This DSM can be used to model system architectures based on components and/or subsystems and their relationships. This type of DSM is beneficial for understanding interface issues associated with system-based interface areas. "A DSM can represent a system architecture in terms of the relationships between its constituent components. Such a model informs system decomposition into subsystems. Intelligent decomposition, or partitioning, is important to managing system complexity" (Browning, 2001).

5.4.4.2.2 Team-Based or Organization DSM

This DSM can be used to model organizational structures based on teams, individuals, or groups and their interactions. The team-based DSM is useful for decomposing discipline-based interface areas. As discussed in the stakeholder analysis topic in Chapter 2, developing complex systems requires various groups and teams to effectively exchange information, often through interfaces. "Building and analyzing a team-based DSM highlights inter-team interfaces, which provide the greatest leverage for improving the organization" (Browning, 2001).

5.4.4.2.3 Activity-Based or Schedule DSM

This type of DSM is used to model processes and activity networks based on their activities, information flow, and other dependencies. As shown in Figure 5.10 in Topside Engineering Prime Contractor Internal Interface Network interface areas, those interface areas can be established based on nodes. In essence, an activity-based DSM represents process input and output relationships, such as in software *nodes* for a fire and gas function. In systems exposed to dangerous or flammable chemicals, a fire and gas system is useful to detect and notify the appearance of such chemicals to allow for operations to cease and thus prevent a dangerous or deadly situation from occurring. Activity-based DSMs are useful in understanding the process flow from detection, alarm, and notification through the fire and gas network. Equally important is understanding how this process transitions across various parts of the system operation. Within the project environment, different entities may be responsible for different parts of the fire and gas system, which can be provided by different entities during project development. An activity-based DSM is useful in understanding product design, which "is characterized by highly coupled, interdependent activities—solving engineering *chicken and egg* problems—which must converge iteratively to an acceptable design solution. When activities begin work without the necessary information, the arrival or change of that information causes rework. Thus, rework results from information arriving at the wrong time, perhaps because of poor activity sequencing, changes, delays, mistakes, etc. Knowing which activities produce and depend on what information can help planners better understand and mitigate unintentional iteration or rework as a source of schedule risk" (Browning, 2001).

5.4.4.2.4 Parameter-Based (or Low-Level Schedule) DSM

This type of DSM is used to model "low-level relationships between design decisions and parameters, systems of equations, subroutine, parameter exchanges, etc." (Browning, 2001). "Thus, a difference between activity- and parameter-based DSMs is the level of analysis. Activity- and parameter-based DSMs also differ in the scope of their representations. While an activity-based DSM models a design process, a parameter-based DSM merely documents the physical relationships between the parameters that determine a design. Thus, an activity-based DSM may include reviews, tests, and coordination links that would not typically appear in a parameter-based DSM" (Browning, 2001).

5.4.4.2.5 DSM Resources

Given DSMs' application across the spectrum of project management and SE, resources are available at DSMWeb.org (http://www.dsmweb.org/en/dsm.html). DSMWeb.org is a not-for-profit organization that provides free tutorials, use cases, and publications with resources and tools for developing various types of DSMs. In addition, an example DSM is illustrated in Figure 5.13. An Excel DSM macro, including user guide, is also available for download from http://www.dsmweb.org/en/dsm-tools/research-tools/excel-macros-for-partitioning.html.

Element Name		1	2	3	4	5	6	7	8	9	10	11	12	13	14	15	16	17	18	19	20
Element 1	1	1																			
Element 2	2		2																		
Element 3	3			3																	
Element 4	4				4																
Element 5	5					5															
Element 6	6						6														
Element 7	7	1	1	1	1	1		7	1	1	1	1	1	1		1					1
Element 8	8	1				1	1		8	1				1		1	1			1	1
Element 9	9	1					1			9						1	1	1	1	1	1
Element 10	10	1					1				10					1		1	1		1
Element 11	11	1					1					11				1					1
Element 12	12	1					1						12			1					1
Element 13	13	1				1	1		1				1	13		1					1
Element 14	14	1	1	1	1	1			1	1	1	1	1	1	14	1					1
Element 15	15															15					
Element 16	16																16				
Element 17	17																	17			
Element 18	18																		18		
Element 19	19																			19	
Element 20	20																				20

Figure 5.13 DSM Excel macro template

5.5 SUMMARY

By performing the interface analysis process, the client or sponsoring organization has established the basic structure of the project's interface management system by identifying the relevant interface networks, interface parties existing within those networks (who needs to talk to whom), the interface groups, and at a high level, the interface areas and issues that exist between the parties (what they need to interact about). This structure is captured in the interface group matrix for each interface network. Using this process, we have structured entities into related interface domains using interface networks and identified which parties belong to each interface network and their relationships.

As we move into Chapter 6, we use this information as the basis for formalizing the project's interface management system and preparing for implementation. This includes preparing the interface management procedure, setting-up the interface register tool in preparation for start of interface activities, establishing the interface organization and preparing roles and responsibilities, planning for interface training, and preparing for interface kick-off meetings with interface organizations and contractors. The output of the analysis in this chapter is crucial for establishing the foundation for the interface management plan discussed in Chapter 6 that defines how the project will manage interfaces throughout the project's life cycle in order to minimize and control the complexity of interfaces and interdependencies.

5.6 REFERENCES

Analysis (n.d.). In Merriam-Webster.com. Retrieved from http://www.merriam-webster.com/dictionary/analysis.

Becker, O., J. Ben-Asher, and I. Ackerman. (2000). "A method for system interface reduction using N charts," *Systems Engineering*, vol. 3, pp. 27–37.

BKCASE Editorial Board. (2015). *The Guide to the Systems Engineering Body of Knowledge (SEBoK)*, v. 1.4. R.D. Adcock (EIC). Hoboken, NJ: The Trustees of the Stevens Institute of Technology. Accessed August 8, 2014. www.sebokwiki.org.

Browning, Tyson R. (2001). "Applying the design structure matrix to system decomposition and integration problems: a review and new directions." *IEEE Transactions on Engineering Management* 48, no. 3: 292–306.

Chen, Peter. (March 1976). "The Entity-Relationship Model—Toward a Unified View of Data". ACM Transactions on Database Systems 1 (1): 9–36. doi:10.1145/320434.320440.

Kossiakoff, A. and William N. Sweet. (2003). *Systems Engineering Principles and Practice–First Edition*. John Wiley & Sons, Inc., Hoboken, NJ.

Pimmler, T. U. and S. D. Eppinger. (1994). "Integration Analysis of Product Decompositions," in *Proc. ASME 6th Int. Conf. on Design Theory and Methodology*, Minneapolis, MN.

Project Management Institute (PMI). (2017). *A Guide to the Project Management Body of Knowledge (PMBOK® Guide)*, 6th Edition. Project Management Institute, Newtown Square, PA.

Williams, R. (2003). *Mellon Learning Curve Research Study*. Mellon Corp, New York, NY.

6

Interface Management Planning

"Reduce your plan to writing. The moment you complete this, you will have definitely given concrete form to the intangible desire."
—Napoleon Hill

The foundation for interface planning was established during the interface analysis process in Chapter 5. Awareness of the factors influencing interface and interdependency complexity in the project and its environment is obtained from the result, or output, of the interface analysis process. This awareness provides a basis for informed, reasoned, and rational decisions about how best to manage these complexity factors with available resources and devise the project's interface management program to handle interfaces and interdependencies effectively during project execution.

However, these decisions about how to best manage interfaces affect a diverse project audience and thus, need to be communicated and conveyed in a way that is easily and clearly understood by disparate entities that contribute to—and are affected by—the project. More important, these decisions need to be interpreted consistently by all personnel with interface roles and responsibilities and by any entities actively involved in the interface management process. This includes those personnel within the project, parties external to the project (such as other projects or existing facilities), and entities that can influence or intervene in the project, such as safety or regulatory agencies.

As implied by Napoleon Hill in the opening quote, decisions and intentions that are firmly locked away in the brain of an individual serve little purpose to the greater project audience. Instead, these intentions and decisions need to be crafted into a holistic message and communicated by the client or the project's sponsoring organization team in the form of a project interface management strategy, procedure, and/or plan that is aligned with the project's development approach and the sponsoring organization's mandate. As will be discussed later in this chapter and also in Chapter 7, communicating the interface management approach (which is alternatively called the interface management policy, strategy, plan, or procedure) is accomplished through a variety of means with the interface management guiding document from the project sponsor (client) as the central element. In this book, we call the guiding interface management document the *interface management plan (IMP)*.

Just as important as preparing and providing the IMP document is ensuring proper planning and preparation prior to implementing the project's interface management program. This planning helps to ensure smooth, effective, and efficient initiation of the interface management function during the initial phase of project execution. Building upon the interface analysis work described in Chapter 5, in this chapter we devise and establish the project's IMP and prepare for its implementation.

As illustrated in Figure 6.1, an interface management program implies a holistic approach comprising several elements, including:

- Determining the interface management strategy and defining it in an IMP or procedure document
- Establishing lean interface work processes and routines to maximize efficiency and reduce interface action responses and agreement resolutions
- Documenting the client's interface guidance in a procedure to ensure consistent management throughout the project and over the life of the project
- Identifying organizational and project resources and structure
- Defining roles and responsibilities for personnel assigned to interface management
- Identifying and implementing a standardized automated interface tool to manage the interface register
- Planning and implementing techniques that ensure smooth interaction between interface parties and maintain alignment as the project progresses through the execution phase
- Preparing for initial and follow-on training to ensure personnel with interface responsibility are properly informed as to how the interface program will operate and their roles and responsibilities in the management system

In essence, the purpose of this chapter is to address planning, preparing, and developing the elements needed to build the necessary infrastructure to initiate an effective and efficient project interface management program.

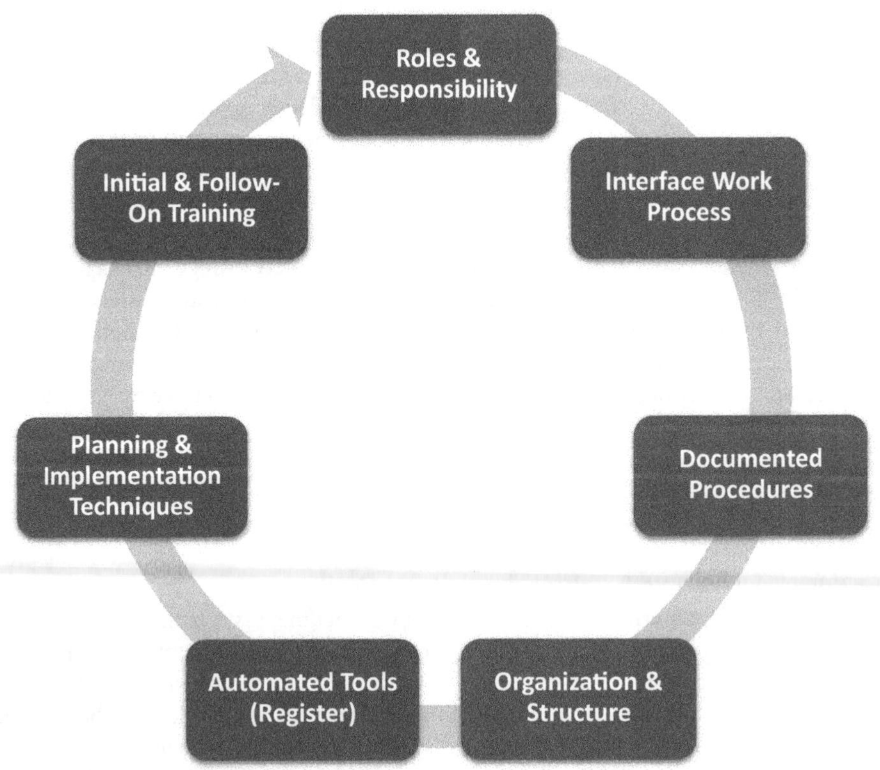

Figure 6.1 Project interface management elements

6.1 THE PROJECT MANAGEMENT PLAN GOVERNS THE INTERFACE MANAGEMENT PLAN

During early project planning, the sponsoring organization's (client's) project management team determines the principles and philosophy that support the development of subsequent project management systems. These project management systems address the many project and technical management functions needed to effectively manage the entire project—such as risk, project cost control, quality, changes, and interfaces among other management functions. Establishing these overarching project principles and philosophies is typically accomplished after the project manager receives the project mandate and has formed the core management team. This high-level guidance is documented in the project management plan or similarly titled document. In Chapter 5, the *project execution plan (PEP)* for Project Diamond, similar to a project management plan, was used to govern the interface analysis process. While the title, structure, and content of the document varies from project to project and organization to organization, the project management plan generally characterizes the main governing management principles, philosophies, and values necessary to executing the projects.

This project management plan document provides information to subordinate project managers, functional managers, and others about aspects of managing the project and key information they need to consider when developing their subordinate plans and procedures. For example, the project management plan can include a high-level description of the project scope and development strategy, key milestone dates that are important for meeting final delivery of the project, how the sponsoring organization views risk, references to the sponsoring organization's policies, etc.

In many ways, the project management plan acts as a steering document for the project manager's subordinate managers to aid in developing management systems for their respective management functions (risk, interface, quality, change, life-cycle information, description of main project tools, engineering management, and so on). In this way, this document serves a very useful function to ensure subordinate management systems used on the project comply with the sponsoring organization's overarching policies, principles, and philosophies, while also remaining consistent with the project's development approach.

Much like the project management plan provides guidance about the project's overall management approach, scope, high-level milestones, and the system to be developed, subordinate management plans and procedures rely upon and extend the project management plan into the guiding documents for their respective project and technical management domains. In essence, subordinate project managers and other managers of various project and technical management domain functions (risk, interface, quality, engineering, etc.) flow down guidance they receive from the project management plan into their respective plans, procedures, and processes.

As expected, these subordinate plans and procedures delve into more detail about how the specific management function will be performed and provide the basis for how the project will operate for all entities contributing to or affected by the project during its development. In terms of the subordinate plan for interface management, the IMP described in the following section acts as the guiding document for the project's interface management domain.

6.2 INTERFACE MANAGEMENT PLAN

The IMP described in this book can also be called an interface management strategy or interface management procedure. Whatever we call it, the content of the document is most important. In this book, we use the term interface management plan to define the overarching, or governing, interface management document, which contains the description of the project's interface management approach and its guiding principles and philosophies so that all parties involved in the management of the project's interfaces understand how interfaces are to be managed over the life of the project. Ownership of this document is typically assigned to the interface manager for the project's sponsoring organization (client) and approved by the project manager.

The input for the content within the IMP stems from the work completed during the interface analysis process that was discussed in Chapter 5. The IMP is the primary tool to communicate interface management guidance within the project and to entities beyond the project scope boundaries (i.e., to other projects, existing facilities, etc.). Communicating the content of this document is accomplished in many ways. It is common for the project sponsor to include this document as a governing document in commercial contracts to prime contractors or companies providing products and services during project development. It is also referenced in cooperation agreements where one project needs to integrate into another project or an existing facility.

This document is also used to communicate with other departments or business units within the project sponsor's organization, which helps these groups understand how they will participate in the project's interface management. Remember, it is common for sponsoring organizations to provide *free issue* or *company provided items (CPIs)* to the organization's projects. These free issue or CPIs can be proprietary (such as software) or unique product hardware (such as standard instrumentation packages, metering equipment, and specialty safety devices among others). As a document, the IMP can serve as an excellent communication tool, but of course, the usefulness of the communicated content is most important.

The IMP contains the project sponsoring organization's expectations of all parties regarding interface management during project execution. Large-scale complex projects require involvement by myriad internal and external organizations and entities with varying levels of interaction intensity. The IMP is the thread that binds all parties to ensure that management of interfaces is consistent and at a performance level that is expected by the client (project sponsor organization) to reduce the risk of interface problems manifesting as schedule delays, cost overruns, quality rework, and other issues that are harmful to the achievement of the project's objectives.

6.2.1 Interface Management Plan Content Overview

The question of what information to include in an IMP is a source of near constant debate. In this book, we provide suggestions based on experience from projects across different industries. Since each project is unique, the content of the procedure will vary. Sometimes it may need more specific details because aspects of managing the interfaces require it, such as when projects are using proprietary technology or when projects contain areas under development that are classified in terms of information security. In other situations, the IMP may be quite general because the organization is using a well-established interface management procedure that was adapted from previous projects. In this book, we offer a practical approach that can be used as a starting point. From this starting point, those responsible for the development of the plans and procedures can adjust the content to the peculiar needs of their respective projects. An example of main content areas includes:

- Overview of the project and its development
- Reference to organizational policies on interface management
- Key definitions and terms
- Description of interface networks
- Interface register
- Planned organization and structure of interface personnel

- Roles and responsibilities of key interface positions
- Description of the interface management process

It is important to understand that the IMP is not about detailing specific interfaces—that is the purview of the interface register and related documents; rather, the IMP document focuses on how interfaces will be managed and on the project infrastructure that is necessary to facilitate efficient and effective collaboration among the relevant interface entities. More detail on each of the IMP content areas is provided in the following pages.

6.2.2 Overview of the Project and Its Development

It cannot be assumed that all personnel assigned with interface responsibilities have a firm grasp of the system to be delivered by the project and how the project is to be developed. Rather, the level of understanding will vary from person to person. Typically, individuals tend to focus solely on the scope for which their interface responsibilities apply. If a section is included at the beginning of the IMP that describes the project's result (the final result), it will help to expand the perspective of the individual beyond the scope of that individual's interface responsibilities. If possible, including a high-level conceptual rendering or illustration of what the project will look like when completed may also help the individual visualize the extent of the project boundaries—especially when integrating with other projects or existing systems. In essence, it helps to provide context for where their individual interface responsibilities fit within the larger project architecture. This information is typically reused from other sources, such as the project management plan, project mandate, or other approved project document. Reusing information from previously approved sources ensures accuracy of the content. When duplicating content from other sources, it is important to represent the details exactly as those in the approved sources.

6.2.3 References to Governing Documents

It is important to reference sponsoring organization policies and practices where applicable. Very often, corporations undertaking large-scale projects have established project development organizations with mature policies and practices. Where applicable, the IMP should reference these documents to reflect that the content of the plan aligns with organizational policies and practices. As described in Chapter 5, applicable governing documents are assembled and reviewed during the interface analysis process. More important, these references provide material for those with interface management responsibilities to obtain deeper insight into why certain principles or practices are being applied to their project's interface management program.

6.2.4 Key Definitions and Terms

Within the interface management community, terms and definitions are still being standardized—this is one of the main reasons for this book. In fact, one's understanding of a term or definition related to interface management can differ substantially from project to project, organization to organization, and industry to industry. Using specific terminology and defining exactly what it means helps to ensure consistent understanding of important aspects of the project's interface management program. This book includes terms and their definitions to explain what we are trying to communicate. It is likely that some readers will be familiar with some of these terms, but the definitions may be different, and others may be familiar with the concepts while the terminology may be different. This is exactly why it is important to include terms and their definitions in the IMP to prevent any misunderstanding and confusion. Each term used in the IMP should be defined such that each diverse entity will clearly and consistently understand the term's meaning.

Commencing a new project, especially a large-scale project with high complexity, often means assembling many entities and literally thousands of people from diverse experiences, knowledge, backgrounds, cultures, etc. Their knowledge and experience concerning the application of interface management (if any) will also vary. Those with little or no experience in performing interface management will have minimal understanding of interface terms. This is not to suggest that the IMP be so detailed as to act as a *training guide*; but rather, that key philosophies and concepts must be included and clearly described. Training, discussed later in this chapter, will provide the much-needed detail to familiarize and orient project personnel to the finer points of these concepts.

6.2.5 Description of Interface Networks

The IMP should identify and describe each interface network, including any unique aspect of managing the specific network. In many projects, the same person may be required to participate in more than one network based on their role and responsibility. Providing a description makes it easier to identify these people, and helps them to understand what aspect of the project interfaces the network is intended to address. These networks form the basis of interface management coverage across the project, including interfaces with external entities (i.e., other projects, existing facilities, or oversight and regulatory agencies, and the like). This part of the IMP describes the relationship among the parties in the interface network and the basics of how each interface network will operate. Descriptions of these networks, combined with the earlier overview of the project development and illustration of the project's end result, help the reader better understand how to access and function as part of the other interface entities.

6.2.6 Interface Register and Use of Automated Tools

One of the most important aspects of managing interfaces is cataloging them within an automated interface register database. Large-scale complex projects generate large numbers of interfaces, which require thousands of agreements; each interface and subsequent agreement can involve significant associated data and information.

The number of interfaces, the volume of data associated with each interface, and the timing for agreement on each interface can result in a complicated web of thousands of individual interfaces. Such a massive amount of interrelated information requires a database. Attempting to manage a large number of individual interfaces without a database will create interface problems, diminish the effectiveness of the interface program (which exists to reduce a common source of risk on complex projects), and thus will likely create other issues—such as negative cost and schedule impact.

As in all fields in the modern information age, effectiveness of the management system is dependent upon the project team's ability to manage information. Interface management is no different. The IMP should describe the automated tools that will be used to house the interface register. It is typical for the project's sponsor to specify the automated tool that will house the interface register, which can range from an off-the-shelf commercial software tool to custom automated tools that were developed by the sponsoring organization. Along with the brief description of this tool, a statement about how access will be provided should be included in the IMP. Later in this chapter, we will cover the preparations needed to set up and establish the interface register prior to implementation.

6.2.7 Planned Organizational Structure

The IMP should also include the organization and structure of key interface positions and entities that will be involved in managing project interfaces. This helps readers to understand the reporting structure and how the client's interface personnel are aligned with contractors, other projects, and existing facilities, and with other entities and stakeholders. The authors discourage the use of individual names in the procedure. For obvious reasons, personnel can change in large-scale projects with execution phases extending for several years. It may also be necessary to include specific interface groups to be organized within an interface network. For example, when integrating with another project, it can be useful to identify specific technical (electrical, telecommunication, etc.) and management (commercial, procurement, etc.) interface groups that will be established between the two projects.

6.2.8 Roles and Responsibilities of Key Interface Positions

A number of key positions within the project's interface management program require position descriptions, including but not limited to interface manager, interface leads, interface coordinators, and the relationship between the lead interface party (LIP) and the interface party. Depending on the involvement of the interface register software vendor, it may be worthwhile to explain their roles and responsibilities, which can include providing introductory and sustainment training on the software tool used to house the interface register and other administrative duties related to maintaining the interface register. The point is to highlight for the reader the main roles and responsibilities; in most cases it is not necessary to explain each and every duty that each position must perform. Individuals performing interface work should know whom to contact when they encounter situations or challenges; this can be documented in this section.

6.2.9 Overview of the Interface Process

It can be helpful to include a high-level process diagram to illustrate the basic interface process established for the respective project. Every project will employ some differences based on preferences, experiences from previous projects, uniqueness of organizational procedures, etc., that will naturally flow into the project interface management process. By process, we mean the steps necessary to matriculate one interface from inception through resolution. The process description and the accompanying process diagram provide those who are new to interface management and the project with an understanding of how the process operates within the project setting.

6.2.10 Other Information

As mentioned previously, there is a delicate balance between providing too much detailed information and not enough information, which leaves the reader with more questions than answers. On projects where information security is a priority, especially if some project information is subject to classification (Top Secret, Secret, Confidential, etc.), then certainly including this as part of the IMP is important. It could also be necessary to describe how interface management will evolve if the project has a unique development process or the respective project is part of another project's interface management system.

6.2.11 Interface Management Plan Summary

The project's IMP forms the basis for how interfaces, and interdependencies, will be managed within the project, and towards external entities. Based on output from the interface analysis process, the plan describes important information about the principles, philosophies, and constraints that govern the project's interface management. This document is developed by the project's sponsoring organization and is likely led by the project's interface manager and approved by the project manager. As a key management document, it is normal for the project sponsor to include the procedures as a contractual reference document as well as a governing document within the sponsoring organization and subordinate departments. While it is desired to obtain a document that remains stable throughout project development, it is highly likely that changes will be needed for a variety of reasons. Any changes to this document should be formally communicated to the affected parties using formal communication channels such as letters or document change notices.

6.3 ESTABLISHING THE INTERFACE REGISTER

To maintain client visibility and traceability, monitor progress of interface activity, and maximize efficiency and timeliness in resolving large volumes of interfaces, an automated interface management tool is necessary to house the interface register. The *register* is a database where each interface item and its associated information are stored. This includes a history of the interaction between interface parties to reach agreement and all information exchanged between the parties leading to the agreement. In essence, it is the client's *evidence* reservoir in the event of disputes between the interface parties at a later stage, or when one party fails to comply with agreements made earlier in the process. This register is crucial to documenting the formalities between independent parties. More important, the register is a chief source of status in developing interfaces and achieving agreements.

As mentioned previously, interfaces are resolved through agreements between *parties*, not individuals. Interface personnel act on behalf of an entity, or interface party, and when an agreement is reached, it is expected that both parties will honor the agreement. As discussed later, verification and validation of these agreements are performed using a variety of techniques both by the respective parties and by the client.

As a reference and archive tool, the interface register is critical to verifying compliance with interface agreements; failure to comply with agreements can result in problems for the project including delayed work, integration challenges, unexpected costs, technical integrity gaps, and the like. When this occurs—and the laws of probability suggest that it will on large-scale projects—the client has a basis for assessing the agreement from early interface activity to the current situation. As stated, a software tool is key to automating the interface register so that information about a specific interface item (a.k.a. an *agreement*) is retrievable quickly. Such tools allow for information searches based on a variety of criteria, which are simply not possible using manual methods, or at least not possible without significant effort and time.

While some large, well-established companies have developed their own proprietary software tools to manage interfaces, several products are readily available in the marketplace. Among available products, this book uses Kongsberg's Web Interface Register (WIR) to illustrate relevant concepts throughout specific chapters. Software and services company Coreworx has assisted us in replicating the concepts using the Coreworx Interface Management (CIM) software tool in Appendix B. Other options are also available and can be quickly located through an internet search. Selection of an appropriate tool, if one is not provided by the project organization, is outside the scope of this book.

Regardless of the software tool used, it is important that interface personnel coordinate with the software tool representative (either the sponsoring organization's representative if using a proprietary tool, or the vendor representative if using a software tool from the marketplace). Preferably, contact is made as soon as possible after project initiation to allow time to complete any administrative processing. Brief descriptions of both Kongsberg's WIR and Coreworx's CIM are provided below. More information can be found through an internet search or on their websites—www.kongsberg.com and www.coreworx.com.

6.3.1 Kongsberg WIR

The Kongsberg WIR is a specialized interface management tool to structure, manage, monitor, and document the interface information exchange among different parties in a project. The initial version of the WIR software solution was created in 2003 as part of the development of a natural gas field on the Norwegian continental shelf called *Ormen Lange*. The intention of Kongsberg's WIR interface tool was to create a web-based solution where all unnecessary manual administration could be eliminated to make interface communication and follow-up as efficient and effective as possible.

As a web-based solution, WIR requires no software installation or download; enabling simultaneous users from all over the world to access and communicate directly using the application. This ensures that particular information and queries reach the right people at the right time during the entire project lifetime. The WIR solution gathers all interface information in one place and the information is managed centrally. This helps users easily obtain full control of interface items or project status. Access rights (write, read) are tailored based on the role and responsibility of the individual. The tool is equipped with a number of features that can be tailored by the interface network to correspond to the rules governing the interface network. It also contains general features, such as the *minutes of meeting* function, which helps to facilitate interaction between interface parties.

6.3.2 Coreworx CIM

The CIM software tool is provided as part of Coreworx's Project Information Control (PIC) Suite of software built for the execution of large complex capital projects in the energy and civil infrastructure industries. Owners, operators, and contractors involved in the engineering, building, operation, and maintenance of industrial and infrastructure facilities use the Coreworx PIC Suite as an information management system to provide increased project execution certainty through good governance and information control for on-time and on-budget project delivery. The Coreworx PIC Suite provides functionality to enable document tracking and reporting, along with workflow practices indicating clear roles and responsibilities. It embeds the integration of project execution groups to a single, well-structured project information and project execution tool.

CIM software is web-based and can be provided as a site-deployed solution or hosted through a software-as-a-service delivery model. CIM provides a simple, easy-to-use user interface tool, which has been developed in partnership with some leading oil and gas companies. Perspectives from owner operators and engineering, procurement, and construction (EPC) companies have resulted in a system for managing both internal and external project interfaces. Preconfigured work processes are delivered *out-of-the-box* as part of the standard solution and are estimated to provide a high-percentage fit. Alerts, notifications, and task-based actions are embedded in each work process to ensure that users are aware of task assignments and of any modifications or additions that were made to the interface register.

The creation of interface documents is provided with prepopulated forms. All interested parties can be kept informed via automated notifications routed using the Coreworx Distribution Matrix. A roles-based security model ensures appropriate visibility levels and confidentiality requirements of interface activity.

6.3.3 Interface Register Setup

The interface register serves as the repository for interface information for the project, including detailed information about each interface area and issue, which parties are responsible for what, relevant documentation and diagrams, information flow between parties, and detailed interface status as the project progresses.

Referring back to Chapter 5 and Figure 5.4, an early output of the interface analysis process was the identification and description of interface networks and subsequent interface groups. The analysis process also identified relationships between *LIPs* and *interface parties*. This information serves as the basis for how the sponsoring organization will set up the register, which directly impacts how interfaces will be managed during project execution. Remember, these networks represent dividing various interface parties into logical groupings and each network must be managed within the project's interface management system. Figure 6.2 shows the basic steps for establishing the interface register.

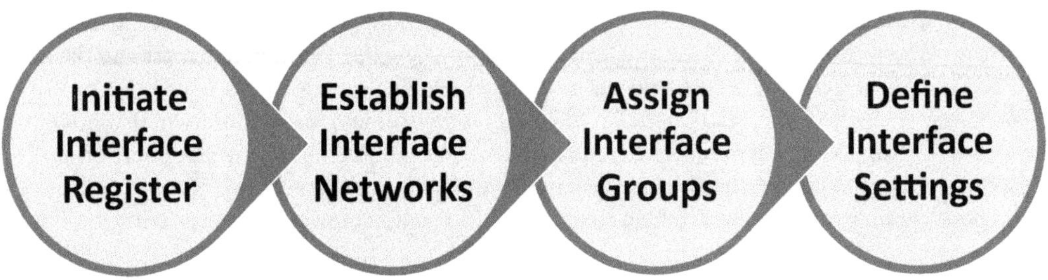

Figure 6.2 Establishing the interface register

6.3.3.1 Initiating the Interface Register

The first step in setting up the register is to contact the interface register software tool representative to initiate the interface register (either the company representative for proprietary tools or the commercial vendor representative when using market-based products). Initiating the interface register means the representative for the tool will perform administrative activities to establish an area of the interface tool for the respective project.

During initiation of the register, the project organizers and the register tool representative discuss which settings to implement and which to exclude. Each software tool typically contains a number of features, which may or may not be applicable for the respective project. For example, some register tools allow for *preliminary information* settings to be established, which can be useful during the detailed engineering phase since most engineering activities are iterative and require multiple iterations to become finalized. In some cases, project sponsors allow an interface to be *closed* based on agreements from *preliminary information* versus *final information*. For example, detailed engineering is iterative because technical details about the system's design mature with each iteration; several preliminary iterations of engineering documentation are generated before obtaining a final *as-built* state after construction. This results in numerous revisions of engineering documentation—such as process and instrument drawings (P&ID) depicting the flow of a process with relevant instrumentation equipment, general layout drawings showing where specific equipment will be located in a particular area, telecommunication topology illustrating an overview of a system's communications architecture, etc. In some cases, the interface party requiring this information may not need the final information to reach agreement on a particular interface. This topic is discussed and illustrated more thoroughly in upcoming chapters, but it is important to recognize this aspect of interface management and how it affects the establishment of the interface register and the governing of the project's interface management.

These settings may also include features such as *priority*, which allows interface parties to designate specific interface items as *high priority*; indicating potential negative consequences to the project or subproject if not resolved. These settings can be global and applicable to all interface networks or tailored specifically for the conditions of each network. For example, when one project is integrating into another project, a formal agreement is normally established between the two projects that contains information about how the projects will *interface*. This may require some unique settings or features in the project-to-project (*P2P*) interface register (in the Project Diamond example) that is different from the settings or features for other interface networks being managed.

Setting up the register also includes assigning various *administrative* rights to designated client (company) personnel and assessing the level of support needed to manage the interface register during implementation—such as estimates for the number of people who will have access to the interface register and planning to provide that access. During implementation of the system, it can be expected that a high number (perhaps hundreds) of personnel will need access (either *read only* or *write*) to the interface register.

It should be noted that in this process, the roles and responsibilities between the owner of the interface register tool and the project should be explained. Whether using a proprietary tool or a commercial product, interface register setup nearly always requires assistance from the register tool representative. This is natural since they are the experts with the software register tool and how it operates. Thus, access to these setup functions is typically restricted. Once the tool is established, then the designated *client* personnel, such as the project's interface manager, are given *administrative* rights to the project's interface networks to perform some functions—such as deletions, access control, etc.

6.3.3.2 Establish Interface Networks

Once the interface register is initiated, the structure of the project interface management system can now be implemented by establishing interface networks in the interface register. In Chapter 5, interface network analysis resulted in a matrix identifying the networks and their constituent parties to be managed within the project's interface management system—shown in Figure 5.4 and repeated here as Figure 6.3. The interface network matrix shown is a summary of Project Diamond's proposed interface networks and the preliminary list of interface entities within each network. This matrix is essential for establishing the foundation and structure for the project's interface register.

The next task in structuring the interface register is to establish the interface networks to be managed in the WIR software tool as shown in Figure 6.4. In the column titled "Project", each network name is listed, which is followed to the right by the name of the company *owning* the network. In the case of our Project Diamond example, *ABC Corporation* owns all networks and is responsible for managing these networks. To the right of the *company* column, the status of the interface network is provided to illustrate whether a network is still open and active, or closed and thus inactive. Regardless of open or closed, the final column illustrates the number of interfaces—0/0/0/0—(identified, open, closed, overdue), indicating how many interfaces are in each of the four statuses. The terms *identified*, *open*, *closed*, and *overdue* will be explained in more depth later in the chapter. However, these terms refer to the summary status of all interfaces generated in the network and provide a quick indication of each interface group's progress in resolving their existing interfaces. Since these networks have only been established, they are active, but have not yet undertaken any activity; thus, the reason for no interfaces statistics shown in the *interface status* column.

As discussed earlier in the book, these networks correspond to the segments of the final system architecture (see Figure 6.5), and the relevant players, or actors, involved in these various segments of the system architecture. As noted by Shuman and Twombly (2010) when discussing collaborative networks for organizations, "Organizing in collaborative networks is a dynamic process, requiring great agility and resourcefulness. In light of the global reach of today's organizations, it is entirely realistic to expect that any organization may seek to satisfy different sets of customers' needs, regardless of whether the organization is large or small. As such, it may require a different collaborative

DIAMOND PROJECT INTERFACE NETWORKS						
	Client Prime Contractor (CPC)	Client Internal Project (CIP)	Prime Contractor Internal (PCI)	Project to Project (P2P)	Organization to Organization (O2O)	Project Sponsor to Industry (SPI)
INTERFACE PARTIES	Topside EPC	Topside EPC	Topside Engineering	Project Diamond (ABC)	ABC Corporation	Industry Safety (PSA)
	Jacket EPC	Jacket EPC	Topside Procurement	Project Sapphire (XYZ)	XYZ Corporation	Project Diamond (ABC)
	Transport & Install	Transport & Install	Topside Construction	Project Oil Pipe (POL)	POL Industries	Project Sapphire (XYZ)
	Living Quarters	Living Quarters	Topside SAS	Project Gas Pipe (PGP)	PGP Incorporated	Project Oil Pipe (POL)
	Hook-Up	Hook-Up				Project Gas Pipe (PGP)
	Drilling & Wells	Drilling & Wells				
	SURF	SURF				
		Operations				

Figure 6.3 Project Diamond interface networks and parties

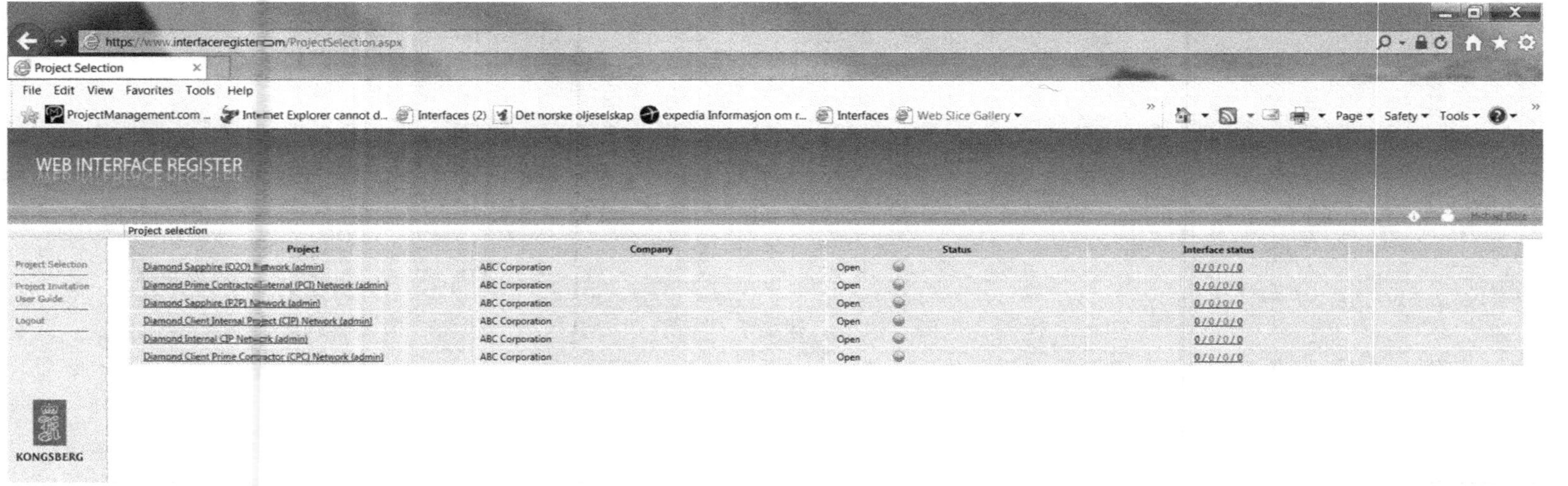

Figure 6.4 Interface networks established in Seaflex WIR interface register

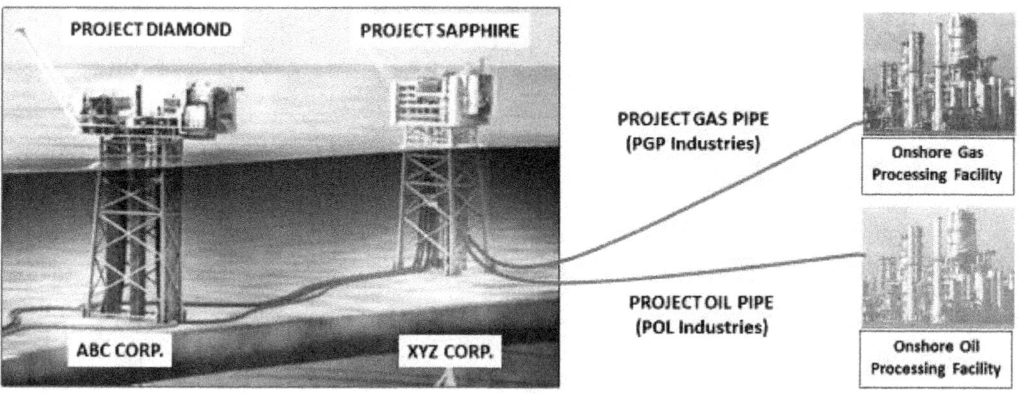

Figure 6.5 Project Diamond operational concept

network to address each set of needs. Thus, it is likely that an organization will participate in multiple collaborative networks concurrently. It will be the network organizer or choreographer as we refer to the role, in certain networks and a member firm in others. These networks may have competing purposes or be comprised of competitive firms." In the case of Project Diamond, ABC Corporation is acting as the network choreographer.

In essence, the collaborative networks to which Shuman and Twombly refer are analogous to a project's interface networks. Without knowing specifically which entities are contributing to the architecture in Figure 6.5, it is reasonable to assume a vast array of independent companies and organizations acting as project owners, contractors and subcontractors, vendors and suppliers, oversight and regulators, and stakeholders seeking to obtain some benefit from the collaboration. It is typical to think of monetary benefit as the key unifying factor in motivating independent entities to collaborate, but other nonmonetary benefit factors include health, safety, and environmental protection. Yet, to realize the architecture (shown in Figure 6.5) through projects and to realize value or benefits from these projects, these individual entities need to collaborate (i.e., work together in the best interest of creating value for all involved). Regardless, the key principle in motivating entities to participate in these collaborative networks is that each participating entity will achieve a greater value than the effort and time allocated to actually participating in the network. The same can be said for the interface networks that may be established for any given project. Once the interface networks are established, the next step in setting up the interface register is to add the interface parties within each network and assign interface groups.

6.3.3.3 Assign Interface Groups (Within Each Interface Network)

Interface groups are established by identifying all the interface parties within a network and then determining which parties need to interface with which other parties based on identified interfaces. For each interface group, the *relationship* between the parties must be established; that is, we need to determine which party is the *LIP* as we described in Section 5.4.2. Identifying the LIP for each group allows us to produce an interface group matrix for each network (see Figure 5.7). The groups represented in the interface group matrix are then transferred to the interface register. Transferring the group matrix to the interface register is shown in Figure 6.6 for the Project Diamond *Client's Prime Contractor (CPC) network*. Remember, this is the network to collaborate on interfaces across their respective scopes-of-work boundaries.

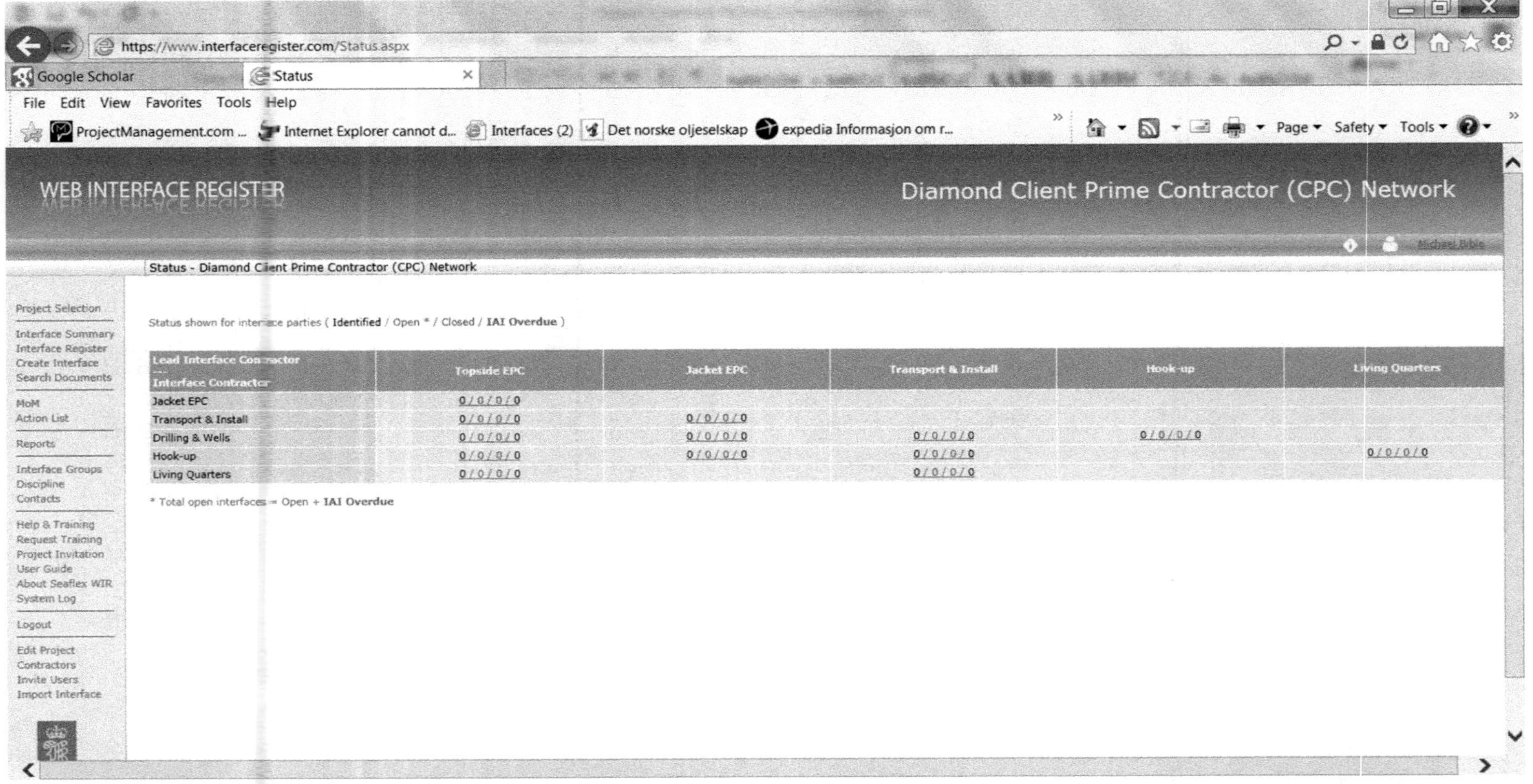

Figure 6.6 Interface register (Project Diamond, CPC network)

As shown in Figure 6.6, the *LIP* is listed across the top row in the matrix, and is titled *Lead Interface Contractor.* Since all parties within this network are *contractor* companies responsible for providing goods and services to the project client, it is quite normal to list the LIP as lead interface contractor (LIC instead of LIP), and the interface party (non-lead) as the interface contractor (IC instead of interface party). The wording used is a personal preference; the main point is to identify who is the *lead* in the interface group relationship.

The *interface parties* are listed in the first column on the left, starting with *Jacket EPC,* then *Transport & Install,* etc. Similar to the *LICs*, here the interface party has been designated as an *IC.* Again, this is a personal preference when setting up the project's interface register. We also observe that *Topside EPC* is listed in the first column or the *LIC* column. An interface group is identified wherever a status indicator (in this case *0/0/0/0*) is located in the intersection between the column and the row; for example, Jacket EPC and Transport & Install form an interface group with Jacket EPC as the LIC for the group.

This process is repeated for each interface network shown in Figure 6.3 until all groups have been established within each network's interface register. With the assistance of the vendor representative, establishing these networks as an organizing mechanism through which the people and entities that are members of the network come together and govern (manage) themselves is quite easy and simple. As we will discuss in the following chapters, ensuring these groups function effectively and efficiently is a much more daunting task.

6.3.3.4 Define Interface Network Settings

One can think of these interface network registers as communities even when they occur in a business situation, and thus, they involve a social element. Therefore, a network organizer establishes a governance structure for what members can and cannot do within the network, especially as it relates to information privacy and access control to these networks. A *choreographed mechanism* implies that the choreographer (the network organizer) selects participants, determines the criteria for participation, and organizes and guides the work of the network (Shuman and Twombly, 2010). Similar to the choreographed networks described by Schuman and Twombly, interface networks have formal governance principles that are agreed to by the potential network members (i.e., interface parties) before a member can participate. Governance is the system for managing the individual and joint work of the collaboration, and has both structural and behavioral components. The intention of the governance structure is to ensure effectiveness and efficiency during interface collaboration.

In essence, interface network settings are rules that govern the interface register for each network. This provides flexibility to adapt the governance structure and rules of each interface network based on its members and the objectives of the constituent members. These rules include, among others, such decisions as:

- Access control (which individuals can participate in the network)
- Access level (which members can input data and information versus those who can only view activity in the register)
- Use of priorities (or not) for individual interfaces to identify interface items with greater potential to create negative consequences
- Process for identifying or inputting interfaces into the register
- Conditions necessary to *resolve and close* interfaces

This is why it is important to provide a description of how each network will operate in the IMP because the network settings in the interface register for the network will need to correspond. This will also become important during initiation of the network's activities during the interface management implementation phase, which will be discussed in Chapter 7; the governance structure is explained during implementation (i.e., *start-up*) of the network.

How rules are determined, and the subsequent interface register settings, will differ based on the nature of the network. In some cases, the project client or sponsor will dictate the rules as is the case for the *CPC* network. In this example case, since these companies work directly for the project sponsor through a formal contract arrangement, the client can mandate the rules and governance system between subordinate interface contractors. In other cases, these rules will need to be negotiated as with a *P2P* network involving multiple different project teams.

As illustrated in Figure 6.5, there are four different projects involved in integrating Project Diamond into the overall field architecture. It is unlikely that the Project Diamond client or prime contractors will dictate the terms of how this network is governed since these are independent projects that are sponsored by competing companies. Further, attempting to dictate the terms in such situations may not be the best way to begin a collaborative process and may undermine achieving the goal and objectives of the network later during collaboration activities. As we progress, we will illustrate how these *rules* that govern the interface networks are translated into *interface register settings* in the interface software tool. Regardless, after the procedures for how the network will operate are determined, the software vendor is typically required to translate procedural rules into interface register settings that align with the interface network's agreed upon procedures.

6.3.3.5 Interface Register Setup Summary

Establishing the interface register for each interface network is a key activity in preparing to implement the project's interface management system. As Shuman and Twombly (2010) note, "Myths about collaboration often result in managers and executives failing to understand that the success or failure of many endeavors hinge(s) on the ability of people to collaborate. All too often people are told to go collaborate, but they have little understanding of what that means and what they are supposed to do in a particular instance. Rarely do managers communicate how collaboration differs from one partner to another, one network to another. It is safe to say that most have not even thought about how it should differ based on the purpose and economic opportunity of the underlying network. Most important, managers do not take the time to build new mental models to reflect the nature of the relationships needed among network members and between the network members and the choreographer. As a result, it is hard to get around the ingrained mindsets and behaviors that have traditionally governed relationships between a firm and external entities" (Shuman and Twombly, 2010). Establishing the interface network and aligning the interface parties within those groups with agreed governance helps to unify the members of the network in achieving their intended goals.

6.3.3.6 The Boeing 787 "Collaborative Management" Lesson

In their article titled, "Collaborative Networks Are the Organization: An Emerging Role for Alliance Management," Shuman and Twombly (2010) discuss Boeing's 787 Dreamliner project as an example for collaborative management systems. More important, they describe Boeing's underestimation of the amount of effort required to govern the alliance and *choreograph* alliance activities. This situation can provide a valuable lesson at this point in this book to reinforce the seriousness of planning and preparation activities to implement a project development model and its underlying management functions and systems.

When Boeing decided in 2004 to make a new product for the mid-sized, long-range commercial jet market, it introduced many engineering and production innovations. "In an effort to control costs, reduce time to market, and access specialist expertise, Boeing assembled a global collaborative network of more than 50 partners, operating in over 130 locations around the globe" (Shuman and Twombly, 2010). To lower the $10 billion development cost, Boeing gave responsibility to these partner-suppliers to design and build components of the plane, which were then shipped aboard specially modified

Boeing 747s called *Dreamlifters* to Boeing's facilities in Everett, Washington, for final assembly. Boeing anticipated that this distribution of work to specialist firms would reduce the time to market from six years to four and shorten the time in the final assembly area from 30 days to three.

To reduce its own costs and share risk, Boeing required the partners to invest a cumulative $4 billion. In many instances, the partners agreed to delay receipt of payment for their work until customers took delivery of the planes; Boeing at that time planned first delivery in 2008. In return for accepting this risk and delayed payment, the partners received long-term contracts, some of which are for the 30-year expected life of the program. The Dreamliner design and production network was an important step in achieving Boeing's long-term strategic objective of transforming itself from a manufacturer to an integrator.

The purpose of employing this collaborative or alliance approach is to spread risk by motivating the parties to work together in the best interest of the project. Each party not only is required to deliver high-quality products and services, but is expected to share equally in the rewards or failures resulting from project success or failure.

As the integrator or network choreographer, Shuman and Twombly noted that a number of manufacturing practices were adopted by Boeing that have come to be associated with best practices in strategic alliances. "Boeing used the design architecture to establish a common set of goals that every partner had a part in achieving. Special attention was paid to ensuring that the partners' roles and responsibilities were thoroughly identified, broadly communicated, and understood. Metrics and milestones were defined, aligned, and agreed upon. Boeing established a common electronic communication and data sharing platform, benefiting from the widely accepted business and technology standards that enable globalization. Recognizing that intercompany teams would govern and conduct much of the work, it invested in team-building and relationship-development activities" (Shuman and Twombly, 2010).

Even given all of this innovation to support the approach, Boeing experienced significant problems with its alliance concept for the 787 Dreamliner; resulting in late deliveries, dysfunction between alliance parties, and ultimately affecting financial performance objectives for the project.

Shuman and Twombly, who studied this case extensively, determined the underlying cause of the dysfunction was Boeing's failure to appreciate that implementing Boeing's engineering and production innovations would require significant changes in structure and ways of working on the part of its partners. Boeing failed in certain key aspects of its role as choreographer. It did not understand the complexity of interdependencies within its collaborative network and the amount of direct management the network would need. Specifically, Shuman and Twombly (2010) note, "They did not appreciate the intensity of the collaboration the network required. It underestimated the quality and richness of information needed across the network as well as the depth and breadth of the coordination required. Indeed, the company viewed the network too narrowly, failing to account for its partners' networks. And Boeing overestimated the ability of its own and partner employees to carry out the technical aspects of their jobs in a network environment. It is not possible to say if all the difficulties could have been avoided had Boeing better managed the network."

The purpose of injecting this case study at this point is to highlight the need for new ways to collaborate to support modern project development models and methods, which are required to support the global marketplace and the multiple entities involved in such projects. The concepts of interface management—and specifically here, of interface networks—groups and registers are key elements for the alliance owner (choreographer) and its members to help them effectively perform and govern their collaboration and prevent the types of problems experienced by Boeing in the early years of the 787 Dreamliner. Equally important is ensuring transparency and auditability among collaborating parties.

The notion of *spreading risk* is a myth in the sense that, ultimately, the project sponsor/owner assumes all consequences from risk events, regardless of where they occur. In the Boeing example, the collaboration approach was intended to spread risk and provide incentive to succeed, yet Boeing ultimately subsumed all the consequences from the alliance's failures, resulting in damage to the Boeing brand and failure to achieve financial targets. Interface management is one key function designed to support the growing trend of strategic and business alliances in new product development and complex capital development projects.

6.4 INTERFACE TRAINING

Regardless of project development approach (i.e., agile, traditional, alliance, rapid development, waterfall, etc.), the scale and complexity of the project will influence the extent of project interfaces the degree to which interface management must be applied across the project and with external stakeholders and entities. Exacerbating the situation is the fact that not all entities governed by the project's interface management system will be activated at the same time; rather they will be activated and deactivated at varying times across the project execution timeline. In addition, individuals with interface responsibilities across the project will join and leave the project, sometimes expectedly and other times unexpectedly. When planning for the implementation of interface management, these factors dictate the need for training, and thus the need to develop and deliver an interface training plan.

Establishing the plan for interface management training is paramount to ensuring a smooth implementation of the project's interface management system and ensuring that entities participating in the system are activated at the right time and efficiently integrated into the project interface management system. Certainly, in this environment, training is not just a one-time event; rather it must be tailored for the specific needs of the training recipient across time, and transition into and out of the project. There are many different objectives to be addressed by the training plan including:

- Initiating various interface entities into the project's system
- Providing the framework for sub-entities (such as contractor and subcontractors) to establish their interface management programs
- Preparing interface management personnel who will help govern the management system
- Readying individuals who will participate in the management process, as well as those who are affected by the management function

In general, there are three types of training to be considered as part of the project's IMP: introductory, initial, and maintenance training (see Figure 6.7).

6.4.1 Introductory Training

Introductory training is completed early in project planning after most of the client's project team has been assembled, and provides a general overview of the project's interface management system. This training is intended to orient the client's project team as to how interfaces will be managed across the project, and toward other entities if the project is integrating to existing facilities or other development projects. In essence, it is designed to orient and familiarize disparate groups directly or

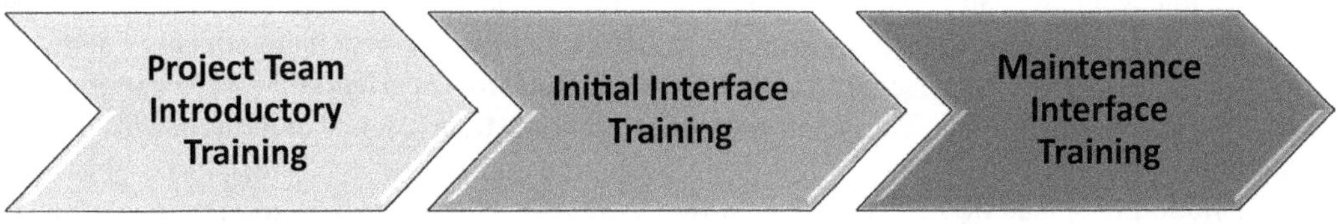

Figure 6.7 Basis for interface training

indirectly affected by the project interface management—such as the client's subproject management teams and organizational departments and units providing support to the project.

Every project uses a variety of processes to manage risk, time, cost, quality, etc. For example, the project's management of change process, also known as change management, is designed to manage changes to baseline scope. Another objective of this training is to ensure that the broader project team understands how interface management is connected to other project processes. The details are not necessary at this stage, but reference to other project procedures should be highlighted in order to identify where additional detailed information is located should the situation arise.

Delivered by the client's project interface manager or designee, this training requires considerable effort and time. However, it is important to do this well—to minimize miscommunication during implementation of the interface management system and prevent problems later during the project's execution phase. Training will also *put a face with a name* for the interface manager. In large-scale complex projects with several hundred people representing the *client*, this training helps to translate a name within a box on an organizational chart into a person. Thus, when questions arise about the managing interface process, project people understand whom to contact.

In some projects, it may also be necessary to provide introductory training sessions for each contractor or contractor team that will provide products or services in development of the project. Typically, after the client awards a contract, the contractor company or team is provided an initial period, for example, 60 days, to prepare initial deliverables consisting of management plans and other administrative documentation. It is during this period that the client's interface manager should consider conducting introductory training with key members of each contractor or contractor team.

In addition, it may be necessary to conduct introductory training with other projects or existing systems. In the Project Diamond example, the system architecture requires the project to integrate into another offshore oil and gas processing facility and two pipeline projects. In our example, the companies associated with these projects agreed to use Project Diamond's interface management process. Thus, it would also be necessary to provide an introductory session for each of these projects for the personnel participating in the applicable interface networks.

Generally, the interface networks derived during interface analysis and the entities listed within those networks serve as a guideline for who should receive this training. The challenge is to plan the training schedule such that each entity has formed its team—or mostly formed its team. As will be observed later in this book, the timing of when the entities will become active in the project creates a challenge in completing the introductory training, which is typically staggered over time as each entity enters the project.

6.4.2 Initial Interface Training

Initial interface training is intended specifically for those personnel who were assigned interface roles and responsibilities—those who have direct involvement in the process. The level of involvement will vary by individual and entity and can range from a full-time position focused solely on interface management to a secondary or tertiary responsibility requiring only minimal or part-time involvement. For example, an interface manager or lead position is typically full time, while for technical engineering disciplines, such as electrical or structural, interface management responsibilities are part time and performed as part of the engineers' overall job responsibilities.

Naturally, this training focuses more on the detailed processes that were designed to comply with the client's IMP and the dynamics of how the rules governing the interface group and its associated network will be practiced. As personnel with interface responsibilities are directly involved in the interface management process, and thus represent various entities across the project, it is important that training be thorough to ensure that all individuals understand how to comply with the rules governing their interface networks.

6.4.3 Maintenance Interface Training

In every management system, there will inevitably be changes, updates, and modifications to account for lessons learned and to adjust the management process to the unique circumstances or phases of the project. Maintenance training includes planned changes to the interface management process to account for unique events occurring during project execution or to specific characteristics as the project moves across different phases. For example, interface management during the detailed engineering phase may be different from the process used during the system level integration process when components and subsystem are being combined to form the final system. Thus, steps in the interface management process may change when moving from one project phase to the other.

Maintenance training in some cases will account for modifications or adjustments due to lessons learned from applying the interface management process. As stated earlier in this chapter, the client makes informed decisions about which aspects of interfaces to manage during project execution and develops the management system accordingly. However, it is natural to find more efficient ways of performing specific steps in the management process or to identify a need for a new step in the process to address a management gap. Maintenance training provides a mechanism to capture these adjustments and ensure they are communicated to appropriate management system participants; ensuring the system continues to operate as effectively and efficiently as possible.

6.5 INTEGRATION WITH OTHER PROJECT PROCESSES

An unfortunate mindset sometimes exists within traditional management that allows *silos* to thrive. That is, a view that specific project management functions are independent of other management functions. In reality, every management function interacts with and exhibits a level of dependency on other management functions. The level of dependency and interaction varies from limited to intense, but planning for integration of interface management with other project processes is essential to effective interface collaboration. The main project management functions with which interface management is inextricably dependent include project change management and risk management so these are addressed in more detail in the following sections. Some other project management functions with which interface management is interdependent include: quality management (verification and validation), schedule and cost management, and document control and information management.

As part of preparation and planning, the relationship between interface management and other project processes needs to be described in the project's IMP after coordination with the owners of these processes.

6.5.1 Project Change Management

Arguably one of the most important project processes is managing change, especially on large-scale complex projects. Change management is focused on managing scope changes; in the case of complex projects, scope is subdivided among many different entities contributing products and services, and scope definitions collide at the interfaces, either gently or otherwise. Ideally, project scope is defined fully and clearly, early in the project. Unfortunately, "practitioners of project management realize that scope change is an inevitable reality for any project. Management of scope change is of vital importance because scope creep can assume horrendous proportions and may even force project cancellation. Scope creep is a term used to describe unauthorized scope changes. Unauthorized changes may creep into project scope as a result of verbal instructions, e-mail instructions, written instructions that have been issued without realizing the magnitude of change, etc." (Khan, 2006). Therefore, each project maintains a formal process to raise, evaluate, and implement approved changes.

Periodically, a change proposal is raised in one part of the project, but also affects a separate part of the project with a different part of the project's scope of work. Such a situation explains why interface management needs to be incorporated into the change management process, which is to ensure each proposed change is evaluated in the context of the entire project to ascertain the extent to which the change will affect other parts of the project. The change management procedure needs to describe how changes affecting multiple scopes of work will be handled and what role the interface management system plays within the process.

Typically, a project's change management process requires initiation of a project change proposal (PCP) within the change management register; the PCP is normally prepared by the change manager or with the assistance of the change manager. It is worth noting that interface activity may be the source or object of a PCP; this will be discussed in more depth later in the book. The PCP includes all the information related to the change to support the change evaluation process. After initiation, the proposed change is placed on *workflow* for relevant project personnel to review and provide recommendations in preparation for the formal change board meeting. Upon completion of the workflow, the project's change board will meet to evaluate the proposed change, review the recommendations and make a decision whether to implement or reject the change. If the change is approved, the results are communicated through a memorandum, which includes the decision and any actions assigned to various individuals as part of implementing the change.

By ensuring that change management includes interface management, changes resulting from interface activity or that result in changes to interfaces will be included in the PCP workflow during evaluations. This inclusion provides an opportunity to assess the impact of each PCP across different parts of the project scope and technical architecture. Interface management must be involved in the process when changes are identified as interface-related—both to communicate the change across the affected entities and to verify that the approved interface changes were implemented by the various parties. This includes adding *interface evaluation* as part of the PCP workflow.

In large-scale complex projects where the project development approach requires contributions from many entities across several scopes of work, changes can be even more difficult to control, implement, and verify. When the approved change affects multiple scopes of work, it is typical for the client's subproject management teams affected by the change to draft a formal communication (e.g., letter) to their contractors directing the change to each relevant scope of work in the contract. In these cases, not only must the change be implemented in each of the scopes, but the change implementation must align between the scopes, which certainly affects interface management.

As is evident in our Project Diamond example, implementing changes can be even further complicated when the project is required to integrate with another project or into an existing system. Thus, an internal change in one project can create a ripple effect on other external projects or existing systems. In these situations, implementing the change requires action by different projects and possibly different project sponsoring organizations. It is normal to think of project change in a generic sense, but the real-world application presents many unique situations and challenges. Understanding how interface management fits within the project's change management system is important to ensure that approved changes are implemented across disparate scopes, and that the implementation actions align between the affected scopes. These are some reasons why there should be alignment between the project's "change management" and "interface management" procedures/plans.

6.5.2 Project Risk Management

Every project is subject to risk and utilizes accepted risk management processes to minimize negative consequences. As noted by Ahmed et al., "In general, unexpected events occur in projects and may result in either positive or negative outcomes that are a deviation from the project plan. Positive outcomes are opportunities while negative outcomes generate a loss" (Ahmed, 2007). On large-scale complex projects, costing billions of dollars and spanning several years, managing risk is a critical aspect of project management. On projects employing complicated contract strategies, or those requiring projects to integrate with other projects or existing systems, managing interfaces is a particularly important risk area.

Several risk register software products are available on the open market that provide the capability to catalog each risk and also typically contains a *workflow* function. Each risk can be *tagged* using several different categories as shown in Figure 6.8. The figure shows an illustration of a notional risk register using the Omega Pims Risk Management module. More information about Omega Pims products can be found at https://www.omega.no/omega-services/software.

Figure 6.8 shows an example format for a risk register for assessing an identified risk. This format is standard, but can be tailored for the specific circumstances of the project. As shown in the *lower-right, boxed* outline area of the illustration, each risk can be *tagged*, or selected, as an *interface* risk. If the risk is particularly critical to the project, additional tags, such as *interface top 10* can be added to ensure management focus. The designation of *interface top 10* is used in this case to indicate that this particular interface risk is of more importance than many of the other interface risks. This designation can represent the severity of the consequences should the risk occur and the probability of the risk occurring. Thus, an interface risk with serious consequences and a high probability of occurring would naturally warrant more management attention. Understanding how to integrate the project's risk management and interface management processes is crucial for minimizing negative consequences resulting from project interfaces and interdependencies.

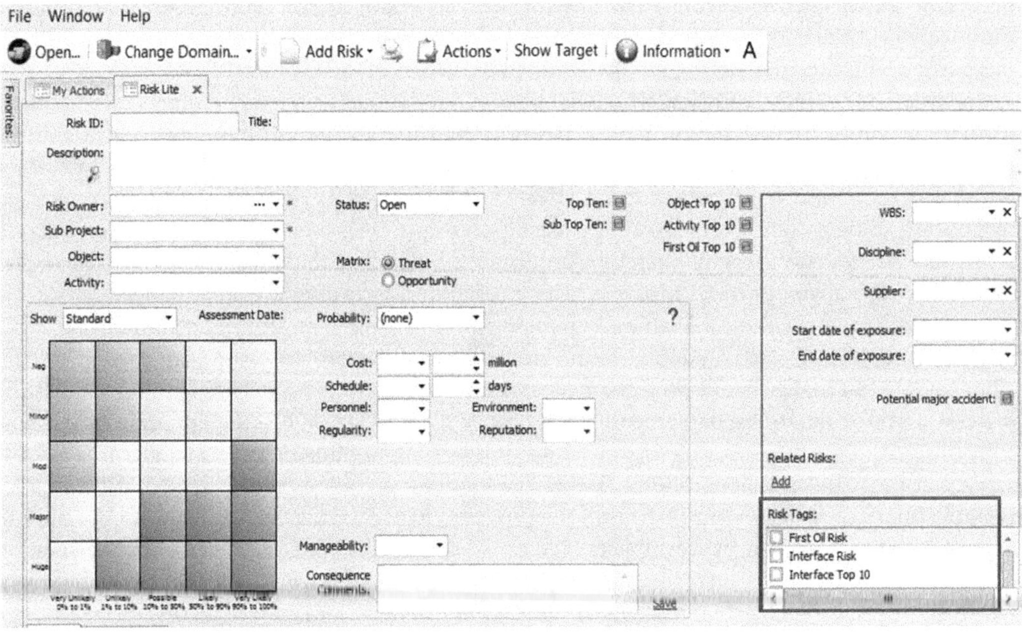

Figure 6.8 Cataloging interface risk—example

6.6 REPORTING REQUIREMENTS AND KEY PERFORMANCE INDICATORS (KPIs)

An important aspect of any management system (or program)—including project interface management—is to ensure it is performing effectively and efficiently for the purpose for which it was created. That is, after implementation, data and information are collected about the management system's performance and if measurements are outside expectations or set tolerances, then corrective actions are implemented to bring performance back within tolerance. This basic construct requires a clear understanding of which management system parameters to measure and what should be the performance targets; these parameters and target ranges allow performance to be measured and determined to be within or outside of acceptable expectations. A common approach is to establish KPIs. While KPIs are not new, they are defined widely and include:

- A business metric used to evaluate factors that are crucial to the success of an organization (http://searchcrm.techtarget.com/definition/key-performance-indicator)
- Key business statistics, such as number of new orders, cash collection efficiency, and return on investment, which measure a firm's performance in critical areas (http://www.businessdictionary.com/definition/key-performance-indicators-KPI.html)
- A set of quantifiable measures that a company or industry uses to gauge or compare performance in terms of meeting their strategic and operational goals (http://www.investopedia.com/terms/k/kpi.asp)
- An actionable scorecard that keeps your strategy on track and enables an organization to manage, control, and achieve desired business results (http://barnraisersllc.com/2012/02/experts-define-key-performance-indicators/)

In essence, KPIs are key measures to monitor the health of a business process, especially aspects of the process that are critical to ensuring the process is performing well. KPIs are used as a proactive management technique to detect problems early so that performance can be maintained within acceptable levels. Accordingly, they are intended to monitor important and meaningful aspects of performance and are metrics directly associated with whether the process is performing well—or not.

In many ways, KPIs are analogous to the *four main vital signs* that are routinely monitored by medical professionals and health care providers when people visit the doctor. Vital signs include the following: body temperature, pulse rate, respiration rate (rate of breathing), and blood pressure (blood pressure is not universally considered a vital sign, but is often measured along with the vital signs). Vital signs can provide an early warning of health problems, which can be verified through additional investigation and diagnostics. That is, they are early warning indicators of potentially more serious problems. KPIs serve a similar purpose for monitoring the health of business processes.

6.6.1 Interface KPIs

In preparing to implement the project's interface management program, KPIs need to be identified to monitor and control performance. As part of the *project control* function, every performance of every management function will be monitored throughout the life of the project. Thus, KPIs serve as an important interface performance communication tool. As a general rule, these metrics should be selected based on the specific circumstances of the project, be easily calculated using relevant data or related statistics, and be consistently and regularly measured against performance expectations. Preferably, data and information needed to support KPI assessment should be kept to a minimum.

In the next section, we suggest some example KPIs. However, when selecting interface KPIs, the following guidelines are recommended:

- Use quantifiable metrics to *measure* interface management performance
- Collect data and report regularly (i.e., weekly, monthly, etc.)
- Assess metric measurements against preset expectations
- Recommendation—use only what you need!

In establishing interface KPIs, there are two basic questions that need to be answered: (1) what is important to the health of our interface management system and (2) how do we know performance is meeting expectations?

What is important to the health of our interface management system? An essential characteristic to monitor is interaction between interface parties; specifically, to monitor their effectiveness in planning interfaces—how well the parties align their interface planning dates to reach agreement on individual interfaces, including implementing the agreements; how well they are identifying and resolving *important* interfaces.

How do we know performance is meeting expectations? Whatever KPIs are selected, the performance expectations need to be realistic and achievable. There has to be some consideration for unique circumstances. An *all-or-nothing* approach is simply not viable nor will it provide true *indications* of how interfaces are being managed. The all-or-nothing mentality leads to negative mindsets, or worse, finding ways of achieving the metrics that run counter to the purpose for which they were instituted. Setting KPIs with some performance tolerances allows for the unexpected circumstances that will inevitably exist in large-scale complex projects with dynamic project environments. Similar to our vital signs analogy earlier, establish a few KPIs to focus on vital signs. Again, these KPIs are indicators or early warning signs of potential problems in the management system. By collecting data and assessing these metrics regularly, the owner can determine whether performance is outside tolerances and investigate further, which is the intent of all KPIs, including interface KPIs.

6.6.2 Interface KPI Examples

While each project will determine the indicators that are essential for measuring their interface performance, most metrics will be based on basic status statistics. As shown earlier, each interface network, shown in Figure 6.4, and interface group within each network, shown in Figure 6.6, will maintain a real-time status summary in the interface register. Meaning, at any time, the process owner will be able to view the current status of all interface items (agreements) between interface groups and within an interface network. The status was shown in Figure 6.6 as *0/0/0/0* which equates to zero *identified/open/closed/overdue* status at this early stage:

- *Identified status*: This status simply means that an interface party has entered an interface in the interface register. This interface remains in this status until both parties have convened an interface meeting and determined the interface to be valid. If it is valid, then the interface is planned and target dates are entered dates in the interface register for the interface item. If it is not a valid interface, then the item will be deleted from the interface register and noted in the meeting minutes.
- *Open status*: An interface item in this status means that the interface group has determined that an *identified* item is valid and thus *opened* in the interface register by determining and entering planning dates to resolve the item.
- *Closed status*: This is the best status for an interface item. This status means that the parties have reached an agreement on how to resolve the interface. Note—each project will need to define the specific conditions under which an item is closed. Some projects will close the

item when the agreement is reached, while other projects require the agreement's implementation to be verified before it is closed.
- *Overdue status*: This status is meant to convey that the planned dates for resolving the interface item and reaching an agreement have passed. This is generally considered to be the least desirable status for an interface item.

From these basic status indicators, summary statistics can be derived to show how many interfaces have been raised within an interface group and network and the distribution of their current status conditions. The primary goal of interface management is to identify and resolve each interface as quickly as possible. Thus, these summary statistics can show warning signs of developing problems within an interface group or network.

Statistics showing high levels of *identified* items early in a project or immediately after forming and activating an interface group may be normal, but high levels *after* the group has been active for a period may indicate lack of activity, group dysfunction, or other problems. Regardless, interfaces in an *identified* status should be temporary and only between meetings. Statistics showing high levels of overdue interfaces can also be an indication of poor collaboration or planning, changing schedules, and delayed work. While it may be normal for *overdue* items to become late as a result of holiday periods, this can typically be addressed through the planning process. Thus, high levels of overdue items or any overdue high-priority or high-risk items should be investigated further to understand why this status condition exists.

6.6.3 Project Diamond KPIs

In our Project Diamond example, it has been decided to use the three interface KPIs noted in Figure 6.9. While these KPIs focus on identified and overdue interfaces, the reader will notice there are two different metrics for *overdue*. In Project Diamond, the client (project sponsor) has included a feature to identify *high-priority* interfaces in the interface register. Given the dynamic environment of the Project Diamond project and the number of different networks and interface groups, the client established this metric to allow the different parties to designate when interfaces, for whatever reason, become time critical. This designation is intended to imply impending negative consequences if the item is not agreed upon and resolved urgently. This metric recognizes, and attempts to account for, the dynamic nature and unpredictability of Project Diamond's environment. Thus, it aids in focusing management attention on urgent priorities.

Figure 6.9 shows the three chosen interface management KPIs, labeled in the # column as *IM1*, *IM2*, and *IM3*, followed by a description of each in the *Indicator* column, the performance target for each in the *KPI* column, and a measurement to be assessed for an example week in the *Week 37* column. The reader will notice that in the *KPI* column, performance targets have been set for each

Interface Key Performance Indicator (KPI)			
#	Indicator	KPI	Week 37
IM1	Overdue "Normal Priority"	<5%	TBD
IM2	Overdue "High Priority"	<2%	TBD
IM3	Identified	<10%	TBD

Figure 6.9 Interface KPIs—example

of the KPIs. For example, for *IM1, Overdue "Normal Priority"*, the performance target is <5%. This metric applies to open interfaces and means that it is expected that no more than 5% of open interfaces will be overdue at any time. For *high-priority* open interfaces, there should never be more than 2% in an *overdue* status. In some sense, the performance targets are arbitrary and their establishment subjective. Ideally, the performance targets are based on prior projects or previous experience in similar projects. The performance targets in Figure 6.9 are only intended as examples. The point is to illustrate the rationale for these metrics and what their performance is being measured against. KPIs can and will vary between projects because of personal preferences and the risk posture of the organization sponsoring the project.

6.7 SUMMARY

The success of implementing project interface management is largely dependent upon translating the output from the interface analysis process into an infrastructure that can support efficient and effective interface management. Taking the time to develop an effective interface management plan that describes how interfaces will be managed over the life of the project, documenting the outputs of the interface analysis process, and performing necessary preparations for implementation will result in a higher probability of successful implementation of the interface management process during project execution.

Equally important is aligning the infrastructure—such as the system supporting the interface register—so that interfaces will be managed effectively and efficiently during the execution phase. In this chapter, the interface register has been initiated with interface networks and groups, but it does not yet include the interface areas and items described in the introductory material. That will come later in Chapter 8.

Similar to all management processes, it is not expected that the perfect process be implemented. Rather, it is likely that adjustments and changes to the process will be required during execution. However, performing the proper planning and preparation can help ensure that the best possible process is established, giving the project a higher probability of success in managing interfaces.

In Chapter 7, we continue a logical progression of the activities needed to implement the project's interface management plan during the early part of the project execution phase. The project execution phase is high tempo and involves a myriad of diverse entities; creating many challenges for the implementation of project interface management. During this period, project teams are being formed, project processes are being implemented, and contract activities are being undertaken, among many other activities. The beginning of the project execution phase can be characterized as chaotic. How well the project's IMP is implemented will affect how well (or not) the interface activity is initiated. The objective of implementation is to initiate the management program, but also to ensure a smooth and fast start to interface activity. Chapter 7 focuses on describing how to accomplish this objective.

6.8 REFERENCES

Ahmed, Ammar, Berman Kayis, and Sataporn Amornsawadwatana. (2007). "A review of techniques for risk management in projects." *Benchmarking: An International Journal* 14, no. 1: 22–36.

Khan, Asadullah. (2006). "Project scope management." *Cost Engineering* 48, no. 6: 12–16.

Shuman, J. and J. Twombly. (2010). "Collaborative networks are the organization: an innovation in organization design and management." *Vikalpa: The Journal for Decision Makers*, 35 (1): 1–13.

7

Interface Management Implementation

"Momentum is a fragile force. Its worst enemy: procrastination. Its best friend: a deadline (think Election Day). Implication #1 (and there is no #2): Get to work! NOW!"

—Tom Peters

In the previous chapters, we have completed the requisite analysis, planning, and preparation to devise and develop an interface management program appropriate for the circumstances of a specific project. That is, the client or its project sponsor team understands how it wants to manage interfaces and interdependencies throughout the project's execution life cycle, but now must decide how to implement the program to ensure a *fast project start*. Completed as part of the larger project planning process group, this implementation planning usually takes place during the very early period of the execution phase as the project transitions from planning to execution. As Tom Peters notes in the opening quote, "momentum is a fragile force. . . ." Thus, the objective is to gain interface momentum as quickly as possible while minimizing confusion and without disrupting other ongoing priorities.

With a goal of transforming the project *idea or concept* into reality, the project execution stage—post-decision gate 3 (DG3)—is where management and technical processes converge to carry out the project plan; it is also the stage which consumes most of the budget and resources. Execution has always been a complex and challenging phase within the project life cycle because it expands the field of participants from the project sponsor team (client) and prime project stakeholders (such as project partners) to those participating in translating the project from an idea or concept into a physical reality. These additional participants include a plethora of contractors, subcontractors, vendors, and suppliers—and potentially other projects, existing systems, and regulatory oversight entities. This project start moment marks an important transition point for the client sponsoring the project as it grapples with competing priorities and a geometrically greater number of resources, both of which push against obtaining momentum.

At this point in the project, the sponsoring organization (client) is likely to have completed the project management plan (or similar document), filled out its own project team, determined project management and control procedures (risk, schedule, quality, cost, scope, etc.), established automated project tools, and begun the commercial activities necessary to acquire the products and services needed during the execution phase. The commercial activities are crucial here since they drive the work needed to realize the system; they include design (engineering), procure, fabricate, construct, transport, install, integrate (e.g., physically *hook-up*), and commission to prepare to hand over the project to the sponsoring organization (or operations). As expected, the start of execution is characterized by a significant increase in project tempo.

In this chapter, we focus on the very early part of the project execution phase, which we will term *initiation*. It is during this initial stage of project execution that management processes specific to executing the project's work are implemented; this is where we begin to use the management system defined earlier. At such a time, project management is faced with an environment of increased chaos and competing demands and priorities constrained against a limited time frame to accomplish implementation. One of the challenges—and a major focus of this book—is to implement the project interface management program. This is a daunting task for the sponsoring organization's interface management team, but it can be achieved through carefully thought out and well-timed techniques. The purpose of this chapter is to discuss techniques to ensure the project interface management program is implemented quickly and infuses the project interface management program into adjacent (related projects and existing systems) and subordinate (main contractors and contractor teams) interface management systems.

7.1 DRIVING INTERFACE MANAGEMENT IMPLEMENTATION

As the quote from Tom Peters at the beginning of this chapter suggests, a sense of urgency is imperative. This is especially true at the beginning of an important project phase, such as execution. Most projects are time constrained and thus it is imperative to obtain a *fast start* that builds momentum quickly. Of course, momentum does not happen by accident. It requires that someone take the initiative to drive the necessary activity. Initially, this responsibility for project interface management falls to the client's project interface manager and interface management team. As the project inducts various contractors and external entities, such as other projects and existing facilities, their interface management teams and personnel will also work to get their respective teams' interface management off to a fast start. However, it is important to understand the particular challenges facing those teams that are implementing project management processes, including interface management. These challenges represent realities that will manifest at some level at the early stage of project execution and can become obstacles to implementation.

7.2 CHALLENGES TO IMPLEMENTATION

It is well-known that projects that fail to get off to a *fast start* tend to perform worse than those that *start fast* and maintain momentum. In many ways, this is comparable to a sporting event. In swimming and track, a fast start—but not a false start—can mean the difference, especially at short distances. In a match between two teams, Team *A* starts fast, builds a sizeable lead early in the game by maintaining momentum, and outperforms Team *B*. Sports enthusiasts know by watching their favorite sport that when this situation arises, it can be difficult for the slow-starting team to recover. While not impossible—as there are cases of teams *coming from behind* to win a game, match, or race—it certainly makes winning a difficult proposition. Project schedules are planned to finish as early as possible and there is a tendency to limit schedule *contingency* in many projects. Slow starts at the beginning of the project, through poor management process implementation, exacerbates the time constraint. The main point here is that implementation sounds easy, and it can be if properly executed; but it is routinely underestimated, which often results in slow implementation of the management process. Some of the key *fast start* challenges that are common to interface management are discussed in the following sub-sections.

7.2.1 Integrating with Other Projects/Existing Systems

The development of systems in modern projects commonly requires integration of the system under development by one project into a separate project (also under development) or into existing systems (which are in operation). Our Project Diamond is an oil and gas industry example. Here, Project Diamond will integrate with (or *tie in* to) Project Sapphire and two pipeline projects in order to transfer its hydrocarbons to oil and gas markets. In this example, the projects are in various stages of development as shown in Figure 7.1. This offset in development between the respective projects creates a host of interface and interdependency challenges.

In a situation such as Project Diamond, it can be quite challenging to introduce new management systems when a project has been in development for some period. To some degree, this represents *change*, which humans typically resist. Specifically, personnel in projects that are in progress are already used to working a certain way with existing processes and tools, etc. It can be difficult to get *buy-in* from those required to participate in the process when introducing new management functions later in project execution.

Another difficulty is overcoming challenges that are presented because the different entities use their own respective management and project development systems, which tend to vary from organization to organization and project to project. In theory, project teams in situations such as Project Diamond will be motivated to cooperate because it is in the best interest of the group. In reality, human personalities and organizational preferences influence process implementation. Some projects are managed in a more formal way, while the informal approach on a related project may be the exact opposite; culture clashes are common in such circumstances. Another common difficulty is determining *when* to implement the management system. We have encountered a case in which two project teams disagreed about the timing for implementing interface management. One project team desired to start interface activity as quickly as possible and another wanted to wait for some (undefined) time. In these situations, the client acts as the arbitrator to make a decision in the best interest of the project. In his particular case, the client intervened to start interface activity earlier.

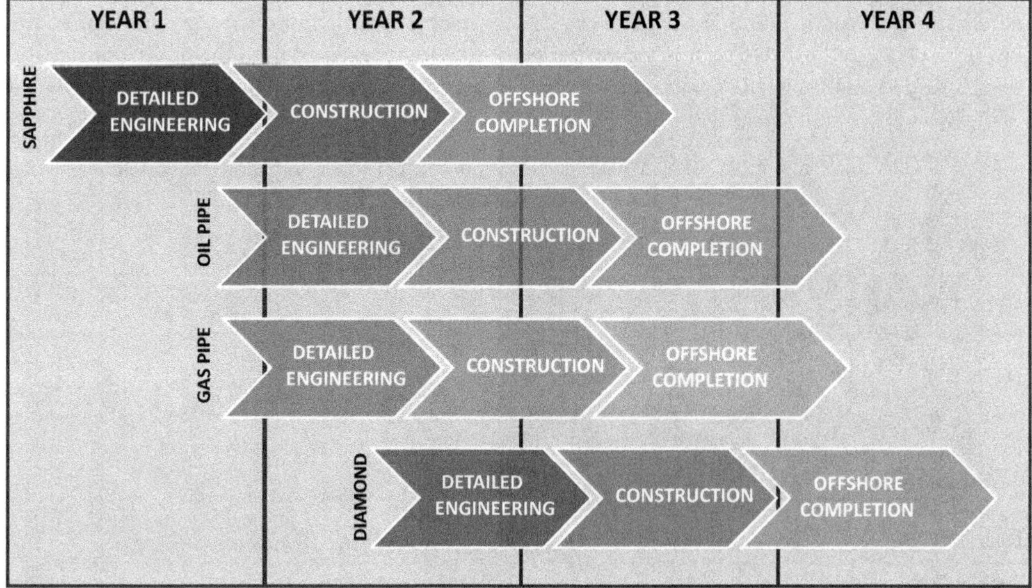

Figure 7.1 Project Diamond integration with other projects

As discussed in Chapter 6 and shown in the Boeing 787 Dreamliner example, it is quite easy to initiate alliance development strategies among companies. However, it requires considerable effort to define and implement the processes and cooperation necessary to ensure that these companies will work together to achieve success. Once again, *the devil is in the details.*

In cases in which one project needs to integrate with another, a formal agreement defines who *owns* the management process between the respective projects; ownership here means who has lead responsibility for its development and implementation. Having such a formal agreement alleviates many of the conflicts and issues that will delay or disrupt implementation because the process of writing it can reveal hidden sources of potential conflict and thus allow them to be addressed before actual conflict arises. In the case of interface management, if a *cooperation* or *commercial* agreement exists between the two projects, then a brief statement should be included to identify ownership responsibility.

7.2.2 Contract Award Timing

Clients who are sponsoring large-scale capital development projects very often use myriad companies to provide the services and products needed to develop and deliver the project result (e.g., military system, new airplane, oil and gas field, etc.). The commercial arrangement can vary from a series of typical client/contractor relationships governed by a formal contract to the now trending strategic alliance relationship in which the affiliation is collaborative and may be governed by agreements—sometimes nonbinding agreements.

It can be challenging to implement an interface management system when contracts have not been awarded to some of the project contractors. Project Diamond's contract award timeline is illustrated in Figure 7.2.

Project Diamond's contract award strategy and timing requires a staggered awarding during the first year, shown as Year 1. For interface implementation, this means that interface groups cannot be initiated until the contracts for the relevant companies have been awarded. For example, we see that the Topside engineering, procurement, and construction (EPC) contract is awarded near the beginning of Year 1 while the subsurface umbilical, risers, and flowlines (SURF) engineering, procurement, construction, and installation (EPCI) contract is awarded midway through Year 1. Any interface between these two contractor parties must wait to be resolved until the SURF contract has been awarded and the SURF contractor has had time to form its team. This creates a *development*

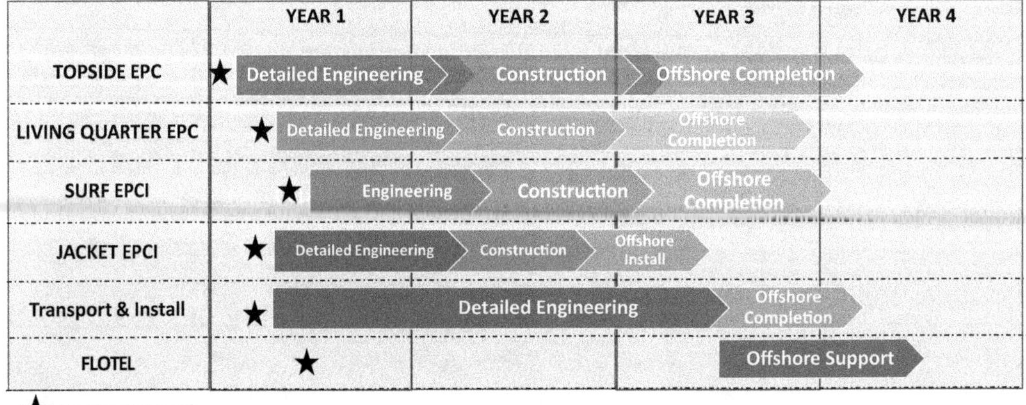

Figure 7.2 Project Diamond contract award timeline

offset that usually affects one or both of the teams. Such a situation can be disruptive to implementing interface management, especially if Topside EPC detailed engineering is reliant upon SURF interface information early in its detailed engineering plan.

When implementing an interface system and launching interface activity, both (or all, if more than two) interface parties are needed. Ideally, interface parties are awarded contracts at about the same time. In reality, there can be and have been significant time lapses between the awarding of a contract to one party and a later award to the other party. In these cases, the client's project team can initiate interface management only for those contractors that were awarded contracts; but the actual interface work between the contractors must wait until the other interface party is under contract. As we will discuss in Chapter 8, this creates significant challenges with establishing momentum. Thus, it is imperative that the client's team collaborate closely with the contracting department to understand the strategy for awarding contracts, coordinate the contracts where possible, and identify any unexpected delays or special circumstances.

7.2.3 Contractor Transition Period After Contract Award

From the perspective of the client's interface manager, the immediate period (45–60 days) after a contract award can be extremely challenging as well because the new awardee ramp-up is considerable. Imagine that your company has just awarded a major contract. The awardee must now begin acquiring additional project personnel, perform project planning, tailor management systems, conduct training, initiate automated tools, etc. During this initial period, the contractor needs time to get organized and to complete initial project planning for its scope of work. Typically, the client will place a milestone in the contract for immediate delivery (30, 45, or 60 days) of management plans. Clearly, these activities have priority and interface activity will not likely start before these initial activities are completed.

Also, the client will typically establish a subproject team to oversee and manage each contract issued for the project; this internal subproject team can range from just a single individual to hundreds of personnel, depending on the scope of the contract. It is important for the client's interface management team to work closely with the appropriate internal subordinate project teams to identify the most appropriate time to conduct initial coordination with the contractor. Regardless, the client's interface manager should make contact with the contractor and the client's subproject team interface manager/lead/coordinator as soon as possible after contract award. These initial discussions should lay the foundation for a formal interface kick-off meeting between the client's interface management team and the contractor's interface management team; the kick-off meeting is discussed in more detail later in this chapter.

7.2.4 Major Changes to Contract Terms, Conditions, or Scopes of Work

The client's team expends considerable effort ensuring that the terms, conditions, and scopes of work are accurate and as complete as possible before beginning the contracting (or procurement) process. However, in large-scale projects characterized by complicated contract strategies, it is common for misalignments or gaps to be identified—either just prior to or immediately after the contracting process. Such gaps and misalignment can be initiated by either the client or the contractor; they are the result of ambiguous contract language, requests for clarification from the contractor team, or misinterpretation of terms, conditions, and statements of work (SOWs) by either the client or contractor during the commercial process or after contract award.

Such situations can delay implementation of interface management (and other project work) as the client and contractor, or prospective contractors, work to resolve the misalignment or gap. This can delay award of the contract, or if already awarded, can delay the contractor's completion of its initial planning activities. When the changes in terms, conditions, and/or scope affect interface boundaries with another scope of work, either circumstance results in delaying or disrupting implementation of interface activity between related interface parties.

7.2.5 Letter of Intent (LOI) in Lieu of Contract

The term *letter of intent* does not have a technical legal meaning; it is used to describe several arrangements in lieu of a formal contract. It is typically used to describe a letter from a client to a contractor (or from a main contractor to a subcontractor) indicating the client's intention to enter into a formal written contract for works described in the letter and asking the contractor (or subcontractor) to begin those works before the formal contract is executed. While an LOI may come in many forms, it is essentially a communication expressing an intention to enter into a contract at a future date. An LOI usually operates in one of three ways:

- As a nonbinding statement of the future intention of both parties, sometimes called a *comfort letter*;
- As an interim contract on its own terms, which will govern the relationship between the parties unless and until a formal written contract is executed; or
- As a final contract which, despite the lack of formal execution, is deemed to have incorporated the terms and conditions of the formal written contract that the parties intended.

In many construction projects, for example, clients, contractors, and subcontractors ideally finalize all aspects of the respective specific agreement and record it in a written, signed contract before any work is performed or expenditure incurred. In reality, however, the parties are often under commercial pressure to commence work, or at least preparatory work, as soon as possible. In such cases, an LOI is used while they continue to negotiate the full contract. In some cases, no formal contract is ever concluded. As expected, this creates a host of unnecessary risks and problems in itself.

Proceeding under an LOI can allow the parties to get a head start on the construction work in a number of useful ways, such as allowing them to begin to instruct subcontractors, begin procurement activities for *long lead items* (i.e., those with long delivery times), or begin the design process. However, LOIs give rise to risks on both sides. Some LOIs create binding obligations on the parties and some do not—depending on the circumstances and the drafting. Parties may not get around to replacing the LOI with a formal contract; in such cases, if disputes arise, the question also arises as to what kind of legal obligation, if any, has been created and what rights such obligation gives each party.

There are also cases in which a contractor has been awarded an LOI with the condition that it meets the initial deliveries. If the contractor has been unable to complete the initial deliverables, the contract may not be subsequently awarded to the initial contractor; this results in starting the commercial process again. Such situations wreak havoc on the management system implementation process. The client's interface team needs to maintain a close watch over the commercial contracting process and be prepared to deal with unexpected situations such as these.

The main point here is to remain alert to the state of the contract and understand whether LOIs will be used in lieu of a contract. If so, then it is important to maintain close coordination with the client's subproject team and contract team to identify and address the impact on any implementation management processes, including interface management. The fact that LOIs are widely used as a mechanism to start activities as soon as possible is an indication of how important it is to "get to work, now!" as Tom Peters says. In recognizing this fact, implementation of interface management needs to be woven into the initial start-up period, but accomplished in a way that does not adversely affect other ongoing activities.

7.3 CLIENT/CONTRACTOR INTERFACE KICK-OFF MEETING

A key activity to establish interface momentum is to conduct a client-sponsored interface management kick-off meeting (KoM) as soon as possible after contract award (e.g., for and with contractors) or project initiation (e.g., for and with other projects and existing systems). A series of client-sponsored KoMs needs to be completed prior to a formal interface KoM. Initiating a project and gaining momentum is comparable to starting to move an enormous but inert supertanker. It requires a great deal of initial effort to get up to cruising speed. These pre-KoMs fall under the purview of the respective project teams. An example KoM sequence is illustrated in Figure 7.3.

Initially, the client's project and or subproject team(s) will complete an internal KoM. Typically, this is conducted after project initiation by the project sponsor (after the team is formed, or mostly formed), but prior to awarding a contract to contractors. After receiving a contract award, the contractor team performs its own internal KoM. Soon after that, the client and contractor project teams conduct a combined client/contractor project team KoM, which focuses on building the foundation for guiding the client/contractor relationship during execution of the scope of work. It is this meeting which sets the stage for further KoMs for relevant project management and technical disciplines such as risk, quality, engineering, and of course, interface management, among others.

For interface management, these pre-KoMs must be completed first. While an interface KoM may be combined with these pre-KoMs in less complicated projects, Figure 7.3 illustrates a scenario in which the scope is extensive and project complexity is high with significant interfaces across many parties. In these cases, the effort to initiate interface activity will be substantially higher than in less complex projects. In such situations, a *client/contractor interface KoM* is an important tool for establishing the foundation for understanding how the contractor or contractor team will manage internal interfaces, and to begin integrating personnel into the client-sponsored external interface management system. Finally, as contracts are awarded that enable the establishment of interface groups, the client sponsors the *interface group KoMs.*

Figure 7.3 Example KoM sequence

7.3.1 Project Sponsor Structure/Organization

It is normal for the client to establish representation to oversee each contract and for the contractor to establish a project management team after contract award as shown in Figure 7.4 for Project Diamond. The unshaded lower boxes represent ABC Corporation's *subproject* teams who have been tasked to oversee and manage contracts associated with various contractors that will be delivering products and services to Project Diamond. These subproject teams are comprised of project management and technical personnel to ensure that the work is progressing according to the contract and according to specifications, requirements, and regulations.

Within each of these teams, personnel will be assigned interface roles of interface lead or interface coordinator based on the level of responsibly and scope of the contract. In essence, an *interface lead* is a primary (full-time) position and tends to be assigned for more complicated scopes, while *interface coordinator* is viewed as a secondary responsibility for smaller, less complicated packages. Contractor teams are shown by the corresponding shaded boxes. While the contractor team will also vary

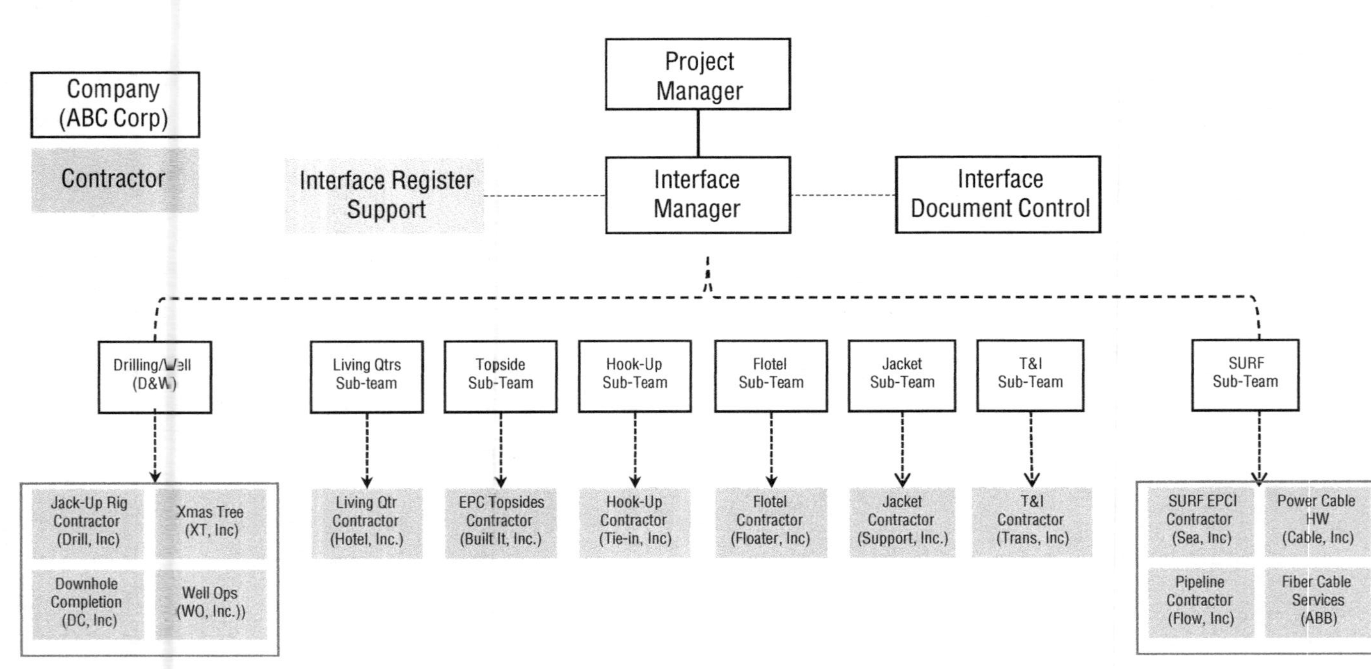

Figure 7.4 Project Diamond interface structure (example)

according to the work to be performed (the scope of work) in the contract, these teams are generally quite large, and are integrated with project management and with specialized technical resources to complete the work required by the contract.

While shown simply in Figure 7.4, a given box in the diagram quite often comprises a team of companies, each providing different expertise. Not shown in Figure 7.4 are the extensive subcontractor, main supplier, and preferred vendor networks supporting each contractor team. This supporting network is also important to understand since it affects interfaces and the contractor's ability to deliver the scope of work. A work delay or delayed component delivery from a supplier or main subcontractor can have a ripple effect throughout other parts of the project. At the client KoM with each respective contractor, understanding this network is important to the client team's oversight responsibility.

Participation in the initial client-sponsored KoMs with contractors varies and, as Pyysiäinen states, "Successful kick-off meetings do not have to include all the members participating in a single event; instead there could be several kick-off meetings at different times associated to, e.g., interdependent subprojects. The important thing was that those individuals, who would be changing information or cooperating with each other, would get to know each other at the beginning of the project" (Pyysiäinen, 2010). While the focus is on initiating the contract and establishing the working relationship between the client and contractor (or contractor and subcontractor), these KoMs do provide a mechanism to begin discussing interface management, including addressing the client requirements in the contract and setting the timeline for conducting a formal interface KoM.

7.3.2 Internal Client and Internal Contractor KoM Meetings

After the contract is awarded or an LOI established, a number of various KoMs will be conducted that involve the client and/or the respective contractor(s). While mainly administrative in nature, these meetings are important for establishing a sound foundation from which project and technical management processes are implemented. For the client, the internal KoM may be conducted prior to awarding the contract, or immediately after, but the contractor's internal KoM will normally be after contract award (or after issuance of the LOI). In essence, these meetings serve as a means for both the client and the contractor to organize themselves in preparation for a client sponsored KoM with the respective contractor (or contractor team). The importance of these meetings tends to be underestimated and their value underappreciated, but they establish an important launch platform for what is to come and what is expected.

As Goffin et al., notes, "The best opportunity for managers to influence the learning that will take place within a team is at the start of a new project, when the team is facing fresh challenges and is keen to try new approaches. Therefore, it makes sense to hold a kick-off meeting to clarify the project goals, to ensure that the process is clear, motivate the team, and share lessons learned from previous projects. At kick-off meetings, knowledge brokers can present key insights from other projects and make the new team aware of the issues that can arise. Examining key lessons from a previous project in the context of a new project can spur new insights, encourage the reuse of effective solutions, and prevent the repetition of mistakes. In addition to the focus on project goals and learning, an effective kick-off meeting can bring a high level of motivation and determination to the team. Managers should not underestimate the long-term value that their involvement in such meetings can contribute" (Goffin, et al., 2010).

This internal KoM meeting represents the first opportunity to start the process of implementing interface management. From the perspective of either the client or the contractor (or contractors) interface team, this internal KoM provides a forum to begin alignment of the project management team and technical staff with the project's interface management requirements; this meeting helps to ensure that interface management is integrated with the team's management oversight process as part of the preparation for the client sponsored KoM with the contractor, which is typically the next KoM to be conducted.

7.3.3 Client Sponsored KoM with Contractor

At some reasonable period (usually 15–30 days) after contract award, the client will sponsor a combined client/contractor project KoM that is focused on establishing a good working relationship. From the client side, this includes all personnel involved in overseeing elements of the contract.

For the contractor, the meeting may not include all personnel, but rather only those corresponding to key management and technical functions. As stated, the main purpose of this meeting is to establish the groundwork for an effective working relationship, which in some cases can last for several years. While there may be some informal introductory conversations between the client and contractor prior to this meeting, it is normal to minimize interaction until the basis for communication is established between the two parties by the respective project management and contract personnel. The client sponsored KoM is the first opportunity for the client and contractor to discuss the broad framework for implementing their management systems.

For the client's and the contractor's interface managers and key interface personnel, it is important to establish a consistent understanding of what is required by the contract and what plans, procedures, and policies the contractor needs to abide by. While the details of the discussion will vary from project to project, those participating within the interface process should strive to clarify any uncertainties prior to planning a formal interface management KoM. From the perspective of interface management, key outputs of the client-sponsored KoM with the contractor are (1) agreement on a date for conducting the interface KoM, (2) a preliminary agenda, (3) a participants list, (4) expectations of the contractor's and client's contributions, and (5) any issues that need to be resolved or clarified prior to the interface KoM.

7.3.4 Client-Sponsored Meeting with Other Projects

Modern projects, especially large-scale complex projects, are increasingly required to integrate with other projects under development or with existing systems, such as the case in the Project Diamond example. Here, Project Diamond is required to integrate with Project Sapphire, and two other pipeline projects (Oil Pipeline and Gas Pipeline). A similar KoM protocol exists as discussed earlier, except that this one is focused on the projects and their interfaces with other projects. The relevant KoMs are shown in order in Figure 7.5. Each of the projects—Diamond and Sapphire, as well as Oil Pipeline and Gas Pipeline—conducts its own internal KoM to initiate personnel who will manage the integration with Project Sapphire. This leads to a combined project-to-project (P2P) KoM to lay the foundation for how the projects will interact during the development process. Typically, the sponsoring organizations have developed a *cooperation agreement* to help guide this process. Finally, this P2P KoM leads to an *interface KoM* between the projects to initiate interface activity.

Figure 7.5 Project Diamond *P2P* KoM sequence

The same KoM sequence may exist when a project that is under development is required to integrate into existing systems or architecture, which is typical with military defense programs and projects. Here, new military projects include interaction with numerous military agencies to ensure the newly developed systems can perform their intended missions alongside other existing military systems. Thus, when performing projects such as these, it is important to sponsor KoMs with all relevant parties.

7.4 INTERFACE PARTY KoM

An *interface KoM* with each interface entity provides the client with a forum to lay the foundation for initiating activity between relevant interface groups. Recall that from an earlier discussion, interface parties will enter and leave the project at different times. For interface parties with extensive scope or scope that is central to system functionality, the interface KoM is normally conducted as a *face-to-face* meeting and includes a diverse set of technical and management personnel who will participate in interface activity with other parties. For interface parties with lesser scope, a video conference meeting may suffice. Ultimately, the preferences of the client and the project circumstances will dictate the forum. Regardless of the forum, this meeting is key to establishing the foundation of interface management for each set of interface parties.

7.4.1 Client's Expectation

Regardless of the interface parties' contractors, internal organization departments, other projects or existing systems, etc., the client (project sponsor) must set expectations for how interfaces are to be managed. The approach for delivering expectations will naturally differ by the *class* of interface stakeholder. For example, the way the client delivers expectations to subordinate contractors is supported by the existence of the contract; a different manner of sharing expectations is needed when addressing external projects or even existing systems or facilities to which the project may *tie in*.

More specifically, with subordinate contractors, vendors, and suppliers, the client has more control because of the contractual relationship and can be more directive in nature; whereas with other projects relying upon cooperation the approach will be more collegial. In fact, the client typically includes interface management requirements in the contracts with subordinate contractors or contractor teams. This interface party KoM is an opportunity to *set the tone* and impress how seriously it expects interfaces to be managed. This may include amplifying text from the contractor's contract regarding interface management and pointing out key aspects of the interface management plan or procedure. To be clear, if interface management is not listed in the contract, the contractor is under no obligation to perform it. Thus, of course, it is paramount that interface management is addressed in the contract, but also to keep in mind that the contract only governs the requirements—it does not build the relationships.

Relationships with other projects, or even existing facilities, are typically governed by an *agreement* between the organizations sponsoring the projects and the organization operating the existing facility or project. Thus, expectations need to be *negotiated* rather than dictated. These *other projects* can be projects by the same project sponsor or projects by other independent entities. In the case of other projects or facilities operated by the same project sponsor, there may be more leverage to *dictate* the terms of managing interfaces than in the case of external projects and systems. In cases in which the project is integrating to or with another project under the same organization, typically one project will be designated the *lead* and will set the terms of interface management. Regarding situations in which the project is integrating with other projects sponsored by different entities, it is important to establish which project is the lead in the agreement. The interface party KoM can be used to set the tone for how interfaces will be managed between the respective projects, or between the project and the existing system.

7.4.2 Overview of Internal Interface Management

The client should understand the contractor's process for managing internal interfaces, or interfaces that are under its contractual control, because the manner in which its contractors manage internal interfaces often has a direct effect on how it manages interfaces with external parties. Many external interface problems and issues between independent parties can be traced to internal issues that ripple outward to other parties or to conflicting internal interface management processes. Thus, it is in the client's best interest to understand each party's process for managing internal interfaces.

Composition of the interface group can dramatically affect the integrity of internal interfaces. For example, it is often more difficult to manage an interface group comprising multiple companies using different management systems to deliver the total scope of work than to manage an interface group in which the parties belong to a single, well-established company with mature internal processes and management systems. Most clients mandate how interfaces are managed when a new project interfaces with an external system emplaced by the client, but many allow the interface parties to use their own interface management systems to manage internal interfaces. However, many management systems are deficient and this is why client understanding of contractor practices becomes necessary.

Seashore's (1954) research concluded that the degree of cohesiveness developed in a group is a function of opportunities for interaction among members of the group and that group cohesiveness is positively related to opportunity for interaction as measured by (a) size of group and (b) duration of shared membership on the job. Thus, small companies with mature processes and employees who have worked together over a long period are more likely to be more cohesive and more productive under certain circumstances than newly formed teams of independent companies for a project task. This is especially true when the team is resourced with new employees and comes from organizations with different management systems.

In terms of managing internal interfaces, the composition and circumstances of the contractor or contractor team must be assessed. In cases where the scope of work involves interfaces that are critical or central to system functionality and where the contractor consists of multiple companies, the client may prescribe how internal interfaces are managed, even if this means a modification to contract terms. Ultimately, the consequences from risks realized by its contractors always affect the client as shown by the Boeing 787 Dreamliner development project. Boeing attempted to *share the risk* but, ultimately, it was the Boeing brand that was most affected by the breakdown of the strategic alliance during the Dreamliner's development. The damage went beyond the brand, involving both cost and schedule, and could be traced to variations in management practices among the parties. It doubtless served as an enlightening strategic lesson to the parties, which have since gone on to produce a successful system.

7.4.3 Review of Interface Areas with Other Interface Parties

Surprisingly, there are cases in which interface parties do not fully comprehend the interfaces they must resolve with other parties. In fact, this is more common than one might think. Even when one party realizes it has an interface with another party, the parties may not fully appreciate the breadth and depth of the interfaces they need to resolve. An interface party KoM helps to ensure that each interface party knows who the other interface parties are and understands the major interfaces to be resolved between the parties. As we will discuss later in this chapter, an interface control document (ICD) is a key tool for documenting and clarifying interfaces among various parties.

It is the client's responsibility to ensure that each party understands the extent of its interface scope with other parties. This is initially, but indirectly, communicated in the contractor's scope of work. However, the scope of work lacks the level of detail necessary for all personnel to understand relationships with other entities, and many project personnel never read the scope of work. The ICD is a tool that proactively identifies the interfaces internal to a project and/or with external projects and existing systems. Without an ICD, the client would need to prepare a responsibility matrix that outlines the areas of interface responsibility for each entity. As will be seen later in this chapter, a properly prepared ICD supplements the SOW and responsibility matrices, and is strongly recommended as a basic tool for effectively managing interfaces.

7.4.4 Identification of Relevant Interface Personnel

The intent of the interface party KoM is to ensure that each interface party has a clear understanding of its boundaries toward other entities and that the right people in each organization have been identified to interact with their counterparts in these areas. For example, if one interface party has an electrical interface area with another interface party, then the contractor or other relevant entity needs to identify which resource will lead this interaction to resolve related interface issues and items.

When an interface party fails to staff properly for interface management, then interface activity tends to be the lowest priority. Sometimes, an interface party has sufficient resources to perform the internal scope of work, but fails to provide adequate resources to effectively perform interface activity with other interface parties. Since the entire purpose of interface management is to ensure proper development and delivery of interfaces and thus reduce a major source of risk on complex projects, preparing for, identifying, and supplying the right resources and holding them accountable is crucial. The client team needs to confirm that appropriate resources are provided by the interface parties and that these resources are available to start interface activity and interact with their counterparts. When an interface party is designated as the lead interface party (LIP), the entity should anticipate significant interface activity with several other parties.

7.4.5 Interface Management Training/Register Setup

In Chapter 6, we discussed setting up the interface register and providing interface training. The interface party KoM provides the first opportunity to conduct initial training on the interface management system and to establish identified interface personnel in the interface register; identifying personnel and entering them into the interface register are prerequisites for initiating interface activity with other active interface parties. Ideally, prior to this meeting, the interface party entity (contractor, other project, existing system, etc.) has acquired and filled out the project team, but often there are gaps in the team which are filled over time. To maximize the effect of training, it is preferable to ensure that interface personnel are on staff and available for this meeting. Training requires education about the client's interface management system and practice using the interface register system.

Naturally, as part of this process all personnel are established in the interface management tool/interface register including specifying who has what type of access (read, write, etc.). Recall from Chapter 6 that the network to which the particular interface party belongs has already been established in the interface register. The casual reader of this book may wonder if all these meetings are necessary. The simple answer is—it depends. A single meeting between the client and contractor or interface party is more than sufficient in many instances. The meetings presented in this chapter represent the organizational complexity that is often present on major projects, and indicates the importance of gaining momentum from a fully informed and engaged set of (often new) players.

Whether interface management training and register setup are part of a single management meeting or conducted during a separate meeting, the main point is to have sufficient time to orient and familiarize interface personnel with the procedures, the processes, and the interface register tool. Regardless of the forum, an interface register representative (e.g., the software vendor or company representative) should provide interface register training, including practical application training. This clears the way to commencing the interface group KoMs with other interface parties.

7.5 INTERFACE GROUP KoM

The most effective means of initiating the interface process between parties and *kick-starting* interface activity is to conduct an *interface group* KoM with each appropriate interface group. This meeting marks a transition point from focus on the management process to beginning the actual work related to solving interfaces. The objective of an interface group KoM is to activate an interface group so that its roles and responsibilities are clear, interface areas are clarified, and plans are established to begin interface activity. This meeting also begins the process of identifying which interface control working groups (ICWGs) may be applicable for the interface group. The ICWGs expands the membership of interface activity to additional interface parties for special situations or overly complicated interface issues and is described later in this chapter.

Sponsored by the client's project team, and usually conducted by the project's interface manager, this meeting acts as a catalyst to *jump start* the interface activity of an individual interface group (normally consisting of two interface parties). In large-scale complex projects, it is possible to establish many (30–50) interface groups across multiple interface networks. Thus, one can imagine the amount of effort required to initiate all interface groups across the entire project. In essence, by sponsoring the meeting(s), the client acts as a *facilitator* to initiate contact between the interface parties in an interface group who do not have a controlling relationship between them. An interface group KoM is conducted for each interface group within each interface network.

This meeting is important to convey the client's expectations and set the *ground rules* for how the group(s) will operate; it begins the process of clarifying the roles and responsibilities of the respective interface parties. Perhaps the most important objective for this meeting is a consistent understanding of the interfaces between the two parties. Interface management is about ensuring good cooperation, collaboration, and communication; this meeting represents the initial opportunity to begin establishing good interface relationships between independent parties. Both parties may be comprised of high-quality competent people, but now they must interact in a professional social setting to solve interface issues; failure to establish this collaborative environment can damage the project. The effectiveness, or quality, of interface interaction between the parties is often established by the effectiveness of this meeting.

The interface group KoM is not only a transition from focus on the process to focus on the interfaces, it is also a transition point from which the client begins to step back into an oversight role and the LIP begins to take proactive ownership for the group and its results.

The client continues to participate in future interface activity, but the role becomes more about oversight and governance. The main purpose of an interface management group is to allow the relevant parties direct access to each other so their respective area experts can discuss and coordinate specific interface items. Ideally, interface activity will be conducted seamlessly between the parties, but the client's presence helps to facilitate resolution when problems occur or require clarification by the client. In reality, client involvement will vary from minimal to quite a lot, depending on the nature of the relationship between the interface parties and the characteristics of the interfaces between their scopes of work.

7.5.1 Client's Expectation of the Interface Group

Just as the client specified its expectations of each individual party, it also clarifies its expectations of each interface group. The primary expectation is that the group will act first and foremost in the best interest of the project, which can be a difficult concept to accept. The natural instinct of any party or entity is to focus on its own priorities and own best interests. For example, a company with a scope of work for just a small part of the project will often focus solely on its scope and meeting its milestones, regardless of any impact on other entities. Many contracts contain *incentives* for meeting specific milestones. Naturally, these incentives are important to this particular contractor to achieve profit. In this circumstance, a party can be reluctant to realize that it is part of a larger effort and may need to compromise on its priorities to achieve the greater good for the project; such reluctance is stronger where there is a potential impact on revenue or profit. Thus, it is important for the client to reinforce the idea that compromise between the interface parties in the group will be necessary to achieve the project's main goals and objectives.

Cooperation, collaboration, and communication are essential for maintaining good interface relationships between parties with no controlling relationship. The client needs to set the ground rules as to how the group will operate and how it will adjudicate situations in which interface agreements cannot be reached. It is naïve of a client to expect that all interfaces will be resolved without conflict. Inevitably, some problems will arise that the parties are simply not able to sort through themselves. Resolving these conflicts is an essential role for the client during the interface process and it should be clear to all parties how these situations will be *arbitrated*. The client should describe how such rules have been established in the interface management procedure, register, and supporting processes.

Another important client expectation is for the group to start interface activity right away. The interface group KoM is useless if it does not lead to immediate follow-up activity. When interface groups have a clear understanding of their interface relationship and the interface areas they share with the other party, it is much easier to move forward in a timely manner into constructive activity—to begin sorting through relevant interfaces and interdependencies. The opposite is certainly true when the parties do not have a clear picture of their interface relationship and are unsure of their interfaces. They tend to delay interaction until the interface *picture* becomes clearer, which does not usually happen by itself. An ICD, discussed in more detail later in this chapter, is a useful tool to ensure that interface activity starts immediately.

7.5.2 Overview of Interface Party Scope

As part of the interface group KoM, each interface party should be given an opportunity to present its scope, with emphasis on the interface boundaries between the two parties. Through these descriptions of the SOWs and the ICD, the interface group can quickly identify the interface areas that need to be resolved and the interdependencies between the interface parties. It should be clear what type of information is needed between the two parties to support the group's activity, including the following examples (among many others, and may be specific to industry):

- *Piping and Instrument Diagrams (P&IDs)*: a diagram in the process industry, which shows the piping and vessels in the process flow, together with the instrumentation and control devices. For more information about P&IDs, see http://www.engineeringtoolbox.com/p-id-piping-instrumentation-diagram-d_466.html (Engineering Toolbox, n.d.).
- *Process Flow Diagrams (PFDs)*: a diagram commonly used in chemical and process engineering to indicate the general flow of plant processes and equipment. The PFD displays the relationships between major equipment or processes of a plant facility and does not show minor details such as piping details and designations. For more information see http://www.engineeringtoolbox.com/pfd-process-flow-diagram-d_465.html (Engineering Toolbox, n.d.).

- *General arrangement (also known as layout) drawing (GA)*: these may be referred to as *location drawings* since they show the location of various components and assemblies within the overall design. These drawings are useful in illustrating the location or layout of areas where one entity's scope begins and another entity's scope ends.
- *Utility diagram (UD)*: a typical process uses utilities such as water, air, and electric power. It is always useful to develop diagrams that show the flow and utilization of each utility. For interface purposes, these diagrams show how utilities flow or are utilized across boundaries.
- *Cause and effect diagram (C&E)*: some projects categorize C&Es as part of the process document while other projects consider C&Es as a part of instrument deliverables. Literally, *cause* means something that makes something else happen and *effect* is what happens as a result of the cause. A C&E is often presented in the form of a matrix. The causes are listed in the left section while the effects are listed in the top section. The two main types of C&Es are emergency shutdown and fire and gas. http://instrumentationportal.com/2011/document-drawing-checklist-form/instrument-document/cause-and-effect/.
- *System control diagram (SCD)*: an SCD is a method of specifying and documenting the control applications for control systems. The method consists mainly of two parts—one set of custom function blocks and one defined symbol set that together are used to draw the logic in one process flowchart. The method has been in use, for example, in the Norwegian offshore environment since the mid 1990s and is defined in the NORSOK standard I-005 (Standards Norway, n.d.). https://www.standard.no/en/sectors/energi-og-klima/petroleum/norsok-standard-categories/i-scd-syst-contr-diag/i-0053/.
- *Design philosophies*: are technical documents that outline the design principles for conceptual and detailed design engineering of systems, subsystems, functions, etc. In essence, they act as constraints with which the respective design must comply.
- *Baseline schedules*: show a sequencing and duration of activities that are necessary to complete the scope of work. These schedules are important because they define when the interface information and interdependencies will be transferred to external parties. Baseline schedules have been reviewed and are used as the basis for assessing schedule performance.
- *Plot plan*: is an architecture and engineering and/or landscape architecture plan drawing (diagram) that shows the buildings, utility runs, equipment layout, the position of roads, and other constructions of an existing or proposed project site at a defined scale. Plot plans are also known more commonly as site plans. See https://en.wikipedia.org/wiki/Plot_plan. (Wikipedia is sometimes considered unacceptable for citation, but in this case, we felt it had the best definition.)
- *Logic—digital signal lists, inputs/outputs (I/Os)*: a digital signal is a signal that represents a sequence of discrete values, whereas a logic signal is a digital signal with only two possible values and describes an arbitrary bit stream. Other types of digital signals can represent three-valued logic or higher-valued logics. These signals provide an important function to maintain proper management and operation of complex systems or facilities. Signal exchange is a common interface in modern large-scale complex systems and is applicable for many different applications including electrical power management, process (fluids, gases, etc.) management, safety control, etc.
- *Area safe charts*: method of analyzing and classifying the environment in which explosive gas atmospheres may occur so as to facilitate the proper selection and installation of equipment to be used safely in that environment.

The previous sample list of the kinds of information to be exchanged between the interface parties is in no way complete. Rather, each industry maintains an extensive library of relevant technical documentation that corresponds to the types of systems being developed within the industry. Projects within the oil and gas industry naturally require a different set of technical documentation from that needed for projects within the telecommunications industry. As expected, oil and gas projects, for example, require significantly more technical safety documentation, while telecommunications projects likely have an extensive list of signals, telecommunication equipment terminations, and signal loop documentation.

More important than any sample list, management personnel should become familiar with all types of documentation associated with the project—including any technical documentation that may be required to design and develop the related system(s); and should also pay special attention to obtaining an understanding of the technical and managerial information necessary to support interface alignment between the parties. This understanding needs to include a review of interdependencies between the parties in the group, particularly when they involve third parties. For example, interface party Contractor *A* may need input from non-interface party Contractor *C* before it can deliver an engineering design document to interface party Contractor *B*. These types of complex interdependencies need to be well understood as early as possible because a delay from the source will ripple throughout the entire dependency chain. Typically, such delays end in negative consequences for each party.

7.5.3 Review of Interface Party Development Schedules

Of course, having each party delivering as agreed is crucial to maintaining effective cooperation, collaboration, and communication. In Chapter 9, we will discuss interface activity during the execution phase. As part of this activity, the project schedule for delivering the respective scopes of work becomes an important part of maintaining interface activity between the parties in an interface group. The interface group KoM provides an opportunity for each interface party to present its high-level schedule for delivering its portion of the project. It is quite typical for the development schedules between two different parties to misalign in some areas; this means that delivery of information or material to one of the parties cannot be achieved to meet the other party's development schedule. An overview of the respective development schedules should reveal any preliminary misalignments and identify how they should be handled before they become a problem. These offsets in development schedules can create friction between the parties in the interface group; resolving these misalignments within the group may affect or ripple into other interface groups. Identifying these issues within the KoM provides an opportunity to address schedule misalignment within the group and thence throughout the project as early as possible.

7.5.4 Review of Interface Processes

In some cases, interface groups may need to interact for several years. Thus, it is important to quickly establish internal processes within the groups. These processes, governed by project level processes, determine how the group will interact—such as frequency of meetings and administrative procedures for conducting these meetings, as well as such matters as the formal exchange of interface documentation, receipt of material (interdependencies), and quality procedures.

When information is exchanged between parties, the status of the information needs to be clear—that is, whether the information is final or in some type of preliminary state. For example, detailed engineering is an iterative process during which partial progress is made and reviewed. Then, changes are implemented in later iterations to improve the design to meet specifications and requirements. Often, this process leads to several preliminary revisions such as *issued for review*, *issued for design*, *issued for construction*, etc. For technical documentation, a revision history is maintained for each document; it is not uncommon for a single detailed engineering document to undergo several (possibly, seven or eight) revisions. The interface parties need to agree upon how they will exchange this information both through interface activity and through the formal exchange process between the interface parties.

The desired outcome of the interface group KoM is complete clarity on how the group will interact, agreement on the interface boundaries and areas between the groups, and identification of any initial interface and interdependency conflicts, such as scope of work gaps and schedule or other misalignments. The roles and responsibilities between the interface group and the client need to be perfectly clear to ensure effective follow-on interaction. It should also be clear to all that this KoM serves as a mechanism to transition from the client driving this process to the interface group taking responsibility to move forward. In essence, the client begins to fall back into a governance and oversight role while the interface parties step forward and take over day-to-day responsibility of interface activity.

If performed well, this meeting will serve as a *launch point* for the interface group. Yes, this meeting requires effort, but the long-term benefits outweigh the short-term investment of effort. Setting expectations and defining how a group of independent parties will function is fundamental to ensuring cooperation. While the aim of the group is to solve technical and managerial challenges, it is important to remember that the people involved and their willingness to cooperate, communicate, and interact will determine the success or failure of this process.

7.6 TRANSITION FROM ESTABLISHING THE INTERFACE MANAGEMENT SYSTEM TO IDENTIFYING AND MANAGING INTERFACES

As interface parties become active in the project and are initiated into interface groups, the focus of effort shifts to the work of identifying and controlling interfaces. It is natural then that this section marks a transition point for this book. Thus far, we have focused primarily on the basics of interface management and the management environment necessary to perform interface identification and control; that is, we have described the processes necessary to establish an interface management system from which to manage interfaces. Progressing further into the remainder of this chapter and the book, the focus begins to shift to the work of identifying and controlling interfaces and interdependencies.

As expected, this discussion tends to be more technically oriented and systems engineering (SE) focused. However, we cannot think of interfaces as technical silos. Rather, interfaces are deeply intertwined with other parts of the project and we continue to address the balance between project management processes (to oversee the work to be accomplished) and technical processes (to design and develop the system). That is, we will maintain a holistic view of both the business aspects of the project and the system under development by the project. While the discussion begins to focus more on the technical aspects of the system, it is neither required nor expected that the reader is or needs to be a systems engineer. Actual SE is not the purpose of this book. Rather, the discussion will be maintained at a level that is understandable by non-technical project and management personnel in order to address managing the development and delivery of interfaces.

7.7 INTERFACE CONTROL DOCUMENT

An interface control document (ICD) is an important SE tool, used widely in several industries at different levels of system development and verification (Sergent and Guennec, 2014). In general, an ICD documents the interface(s) between elements of a system or subsystem. In complicated project development strategies in which multiple parties are contributing to the project's development, the ICD can be structured to describe interfaces between scopes of work or areas of responsibility. ICDs provide a means to establish, define, and control interfaces and to document detailed interface design information. All main interfaces for a system may be documented in one ICD or in separate, multiple ICDs.

In SE, ICDs summarize interface definition and act as a mechanism to maintain interface control throughout a system, and thereby bound its requirements. The main benefit of an ICD is to gain visibility to a system's interfaces and the parties involved in aligning them (i.e., interface groups).

The ICD is a scope document for system interfaces. It should be listed as a deliverable on the master document register. Once delivered, it is not changed unless it has gone through the change process. A change would imply a design change, which should only occur at gate decisions or through the change process. So, the ICD is initially delivered at DG2 (concept selection) based on concept study work, then again at DG3 before project execution begins, and then again at later DGs such as before fabrication and construction and before the project transitions to operations/project sponsor. As detailed engineering matures and the system development moves through project execution, the ICD owner will update a draft copy until it is ready for issuance to the client. This document is approved and accepted by the client, which is the reason it is not arbitrarily revised; that is, it is subject to change control and DG review and acceptance.

Appendix F contains the Project Diamond ICD created during conceptual engineering and approved as part of the DG3 process.

7.7.1 Interface Control Document Development

The timeline for development of an ICD is shown in Figure 7.6, which illustrates an example project development approach consisting of *conceptual design* (also known as front-end engineering design or *FEED*), *detailed engineering, fabrication and construction, completion and commissioning* and *handover and start-up*. While the terminology and approach differs from industry to industry, the intent here is to show where in the project development approach the ICD is developed and how it is used during project development.

In the example, a DG2 decision results in the commencement of conceptual engineering to refine feasibility studies and to identify an economically viable solution that meets user requirements. At

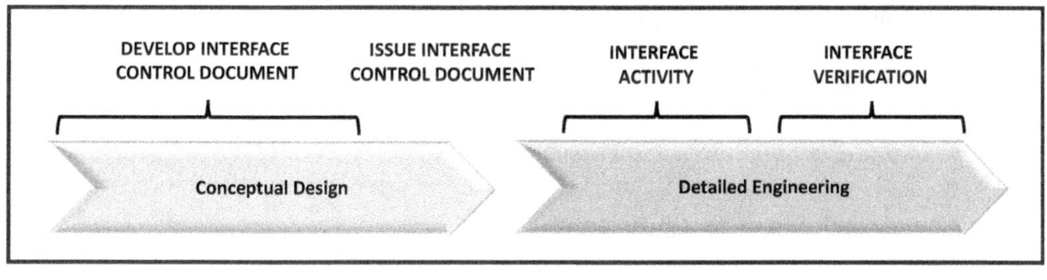

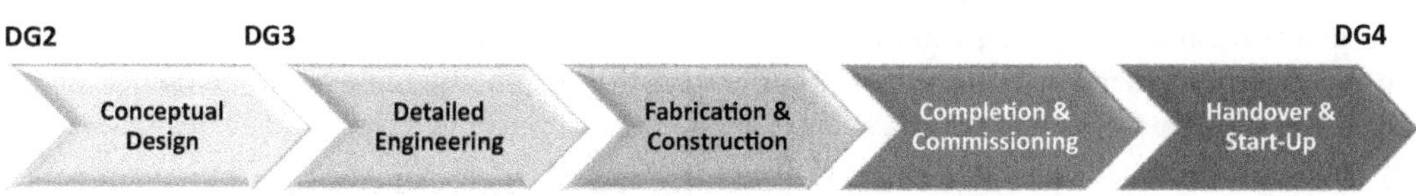

Figure 7.6 ICD application in project development

the conclusion of conceptual design, the basis for the design is established and the overarching architecture of the system is developed, which accounts for known constraints, assumptions, restrictions (e.g., regulations), and operating scenarios. In addition, at the end of conceptual design there is a mature, well-defined understanding of how the project will be developed, including contract strategy, use of commercial off-the-shelf (COTS) products, government furnished items, company provided items (CPIs, also known as *free issue*), and any proprietary technology, processes, or materials that will be used during project execution (i.e., post-DG3).

As shown in Figure 7.6, the development of the ICD needs to occur early in the project development process. To develop the ICD, the client interface management personnel must work closely and concurrently with the engineering design team to understand the concept for design and with the project management team to understand how the project will be developed over time. The results of the conceptual design help to define the interfaces between systems, subsystems, packages, etc., while the project development approach helps to define who is responsible for the delivery of various parts of the overall system during project execution. The ICD can be prepared by the contractor, the client, or as a joint effort; the architecture and particular project circumstance will dictate who will prepare the ICD(s).

The conjoined output of conceptual engineering and project planning results in an ICD at the end of conceptual design that serves as the basis for kick-starting interface parties during project execution. As was shown in Figure 7.6, the ICD is normally developed during conceptual design. This initial ICD version outlines the interfaces between systems, subsystems, components, configuration items, and assemblies. In addition, the ICD structures this information to align with complicated project development contract strategies in which many parties are contributing to project development. This is especially important when various parties will enter and exit the project development process at different points along the project development timeline.

It is important to understand that there are many different project development approaches and philosophies. Some approaches are more simplistic, while others are highly complex. In one example, the U.S. Department of Defense (DoD) often uses highly complex acquisition (contracting) approaches to develop military equipment programs and projects. The DoD acquisition framework provides guidance for such a complicated acquisition process; in this context, ICD development is well defined.

7.7.2 U.S. Department of Defense ICDs

The DoD maintains a well-documented approach to the development and use of ICDs to develop and/or acquire military systems, where interface management is aligned under the configuration management process. In terms of controlling components, that makes sense; but in speaking of the DoD processes, we are addressing an important engineering taxonomy that details the interface elements in the configuration. Interface management in the context of this book is considerably more than a subset of configuration management. However, the defense acquisition process specifies the role of the ICD and where it is required within the SE process.

In accordance with the defense acquisition process, as system interface control requirements are developed, they are documented in an ICD, placed under configuration control, and made available to the appropriate stakeholders. ICDs include interface control drawings, interface requirements specifications, and other documentation that depicts physical and functional interfaces of related or co-functioning systems or components. Interface control documentation should be owned by the project sponsor and developed by the ICWGs or comparable integrated teams. The DoD relies heavily on various schematic block diagrams (SBDs) to develop the ICD.

SBDs depict hardware and software components and their interrelationships. They are developed at successively lower levels since design analysis proceeds to define lower-level functions within higher-level requirements. SBDs provide visibility of related system elements and traceability to other SE documentation. In addition, they describe a solution to the functional and performance requirements established by the functional architecture. As such, the SBDs:

- Show interfaces between the system components,
- Show interfaces between the system components and other systems or subsystems, and
- Support traceability between components and their functional origins.

ICDs are a valuable tool to enhance configuration control, which is used during verification activities conducted during system integration. *The Defense Acquisition Guidebook*, Chapter 3: Systems Engineering, provides more details regarding interface management within the defense acquisition process and development of the ICD (U.S. Department of Defense, 2017).

7.7.3 ICD Format, Style, and Content

The format, style, and detail of an ICD can vary and is sensitive to the project and its circumstances. The document can be very detailed or quite high level, but its purpose is to describe interfaces to the level appropriate for the project circumstances. A software intensive project will likely have a different kind of ICD that is significantly more detailed than a wind energy or offshore oil and gas facility project. Several styles and approaches to creating and managing the ICD are readily available on the internet, but a combination of text and illustrations are commonly useful to a broad audience. If the audience for the ICD is primarily technical experts, then the ICD is often more technology based with specific technical jargon not easily understood by the general project team.

In preparing an ICD, it is important to think critically about how best to control interfaces in accordance with the project's unique circumstances and situation. It is beneficial when the sponsoring organization specifies a required format or template. Even when specified, the format or template should be tailored to the specific requirements of each project.

Some SE purists hold a traditional view of an ICD and believe it is only applicable to software development projects. In some cases, the purist's view may be constrained by an unsubstantiated rationale that *interfaces* only exist within the logical domain (e.g., software, logic, I/O signals). We strongly believe that an ICD can and should include hardware interfaces in addition to software interfaces when the situation warrants; such is the case when the physical interfaces represent technical complexity that increases risk. The ICD can and should, in certain circumstances, include additional items; a few examples are placement of safety equipment, alignment of penetrations through blast walls and steel support structures, intersects of structural or mechanical equipment, coordination of pipe routing, routing of HVAC ducting, etc.

Modern projects in the information age require tools that are adaptable to system complexity and complicated architectures. Limiting the scope of an ICD to software is arbitrary and unnecessary. Readers should feel free to adjust the ICD content, structure, and format to their particular needs. In essence, there is no right or wrong answer in terms of ICD content and it is the concept or idea of what the document is accomplishing, not the format, that matters.

7.7.4 Applying the ICD

ICDs allow systems to be developed in smaller, well-understood components, which must then interface with other components. ICDs are often used where subsystems are developed by distributed teams (perhaps offshore) as a way to communicate information about subsystems interfaces between different subsystem design teams. As the system design and development matures during project execution, the ICD is updated with increasing detail as more information becomes known.

As an interface control tool, this document is fundamental to initiating interface activity between interface parties, especially during the start of the project's execution phase (post-DG3). In large-scale complex projects using complicated project development approaches with many parties contributing to development, the ICD provides a basis upon which interface groups (and ICWGs—described in the next section of this chapter) can begin immediately to address difficult interface issues. Equally important, the ICD helps to clarify and reinforce scopes of work and areas of responsibility for different parties. That is, it should align with the respective scopes of work and, at the same time, amplify interface areas between the respective parties responsible for different parts of the project. Sometimes, rather than clarifying scopes of work and amplifying specific interface areas between the respective parties, the ICD is somewhat messily misappropriated to cover system interfaces without respect to who is delivering various subparts of the project and without considering the relationships among the respective parties, which themselves provide the foundation for effectively managing interfaces.

During project execution, the ICD also acts as a guide against which to verify implementation of interfaces (i.e., to enable interface control) during both design and construction as the project progresses through execution. By presenting an ICD during the start of project execution, the interface parties have a starting point for interaction. Thus, the ICD or similar document is the basis for interaction within the project's interface management system.

7.8 INTERFACE CONTROL WORKING GROUPS

In this book, a typical interface is described as existing between two parties (who thus form an interface group). However, there are occasions when the composition of the interface group must be expanded beyond two parties to accommodate full resolution and follow-through for an interface. This situation can arise when an interface issue is characterized by technical or managerial complexity that directly or indirectly affects several parts of the project. In these situations, the formation of a working group may be necessary to ensure that all dimensions of the interface are resolved to the satisfaction of the extended group and to ensure proper implementation after agreement is reached.

The ICWG is a specialized working group composed of appropriate technical and nontechnical representatives from the interfacing entities and activities and from other interested participating personnel and organizations. The ICWG serves as a forum to develop and provide interface requirements, as well as to focus on detailed interface definition and timely resolution of complex interface issues. These issues may arise at any point in project development and involve a variety of circumstances.

Early in project development, during conceptual or detailed engineering, a technical challenge may arise that directly affects multiple parts of the project(s). Complex issues can also arise during construction—as when design errors are identified after fabrication. Such errors result in construction rework. Typically, these sorts of situations affect multiple parties across several scopes of work, especially when system functionality is affected.

Preferably, issues requiring ICWGs are identified as early as possible in project development—ideally during project planning and early in the SE process. This allows time to identify relevant members and form the ICWG soon enough to positively influence design. Inevitably, some issues will arise during project development, which require new ICWGs to be formed. When ICWGs are identified and formed during the interface management implementation process, special ICWG KoMs may be required to initiate the working groups. Regardless, an *owner* should be assigned to each ICWG to lead the effort under the scope of the working group.

7.8.1 Establishing ICWGs

Establishing an ICWG is intended to enable focus on high-risk interface areas because the issues addressed by the ICWG typically impact several parts of the project or program. Regardless, it is important to identify interfaces that require collaboration with external program offices and contractors in a system or system-of-systems environment. Within the U.S. DoD's Integrated Product and Process Development Framework, ICWGs may be integrated teams that establish linkage between interfacing design Integrated Product Teams (IPTs), or the ICWGs may be integrated into a system-level engineering working group. Membership of each ICWG or comparable integrated team should include appropriate representation from each relevant contractor, significant vendors, and participating government agencies. The procuring program office (for external and selected top-level interfaces) or prime contractor (for internal interfaces) generally designates the chair of the group.

7.8.2 ICWGs versus Interface Groups

It is reasonable to ask why it is necessary to describe both interface groups and ICWGs—an interface is typically a one-to-one relationship. The interaction between the two parties is streamlined in the interface group settings. This allows the efficient resolution of interface issues that only affect the two parties and their relevant interface areas. The vast majority of interfaces require only two parties to resolve. Reaching agreements, especially when only a few people are involved, can be accomplished relatively quickly in most cases.

As the name and description imply, the membership of the ICWG includes considerably more parties (and people) than the membership of an interface group. As expected, an ICWG is created in a situation, and results in a situation, in which significant time and effort are required to ensure *consensus* agreement is achieved across all the relevant interface parties. What may work for some of the parties in the ICWG can be vetoed if the agreement does not account for all parties and their needs. Considerable discussion is needed to fully understand each party's needs, to evaluate alternatives, and to identify the solution that best fits all involved. It is for this reason that we suggest using an ICWG only when the situation dictates. The application and use of ICWGs varies from industry to industry and project to project.

Within the U.S. DoD, the ICWG is the *go-to* method within the department's acquisition framework since most DoD projects occur within programs; the projects in these programs generally require extensive integration with other existing military architectures. ICWGs are extensively used in what are called Major Defense Acquisition Programs. However, it has been our experience while participating in many ICWGs that this forum can be overly bureaucratic and unnecessarily wasteful. An unfortunate byproduct of the ICWG discussions involving relatively simple issues is that they may quickly turn complex with the unnecessary involvement of ICWG members that are not directly involved in the specific issue. While a valuable tool, the ICWG needs to be disciplined and focused on specific interface issues and areas to the fullest extent possible.

7.9 PROJECT DIAMOND ICD AND ICWG

We have routinely referred to our Project Diamond example to illustrate the basic concepts described in this book. Given the importance of the ICD in initiating interaction between related interface parties, we provide a simplified example of an ICD using Project Diamond. The simplified Project Diamond ICD is provided in this book as Appendix F. This sample ICD combines graphical illustrations and text to describe at a high level the main P2P interfaces between Project Diamond and Project Sapphire, as well as Project Diamond internal interfaces among the client (ABC Corp.) and Project

Diamond's contractors and contractor teams. To illustrate situations in which an ICWG is needed, we identify complex interface issues in Project Diamond that require the establishment of an ICWG.

In an actual project, this ICD example would contain much more detail and would be described at a level consistent with the conceptual design that was completed during early engineering, also known as FEED. However, here the sample Project Diamond ICD is intended merely to show a means of communicating systems interfaces aligned with the system architecture and the main entities participating in developing the system. In Project Diamond's case, as the system design matures through the detailed engineering phase, the ICD is updated to reflect gaps or misalignments. Nevertheless, the ICD version following conceptual engineering should provide sufficient information for relevant interface parties to understand their main interfaces at the start of detailed engineering.

In addition to initiating interaction between related interface parties, the ICD becomes important because it is quite possible that different entities perform conceptual and detailed design. Often, both the conceptual design and the detailed engineering are performed by a single entity. However, it is also possible that one entity performs conceptual design while another performs detailed engineering (i.e., different design firms, companies, organizations, and so on). It is common for the organization sponsoring the project to perform conceptual design and then contract out detailed design to specialized engineering firms. In other cases, conceptual design is contracted to specialized engineering companies, but fails to meet the client's expectations and thus detailed engineering design work is awarded to a different engineering firm. When transitioning between conceptual design and detailed engineering, the ICD can play an important role in shaping scopes of work for the detailed engineering phase. In cases in which new entities will participate in detailed engineering, the ICD helps to orient the new entrants to their interfaces and aids in identifying any obvious gaps or errors.

7.10 SUMMARY

The importance of achieving a *fast project start* at the beginning of execution (after DG3) and gaining momentum quickly is imperative to achieving the project's schedule (and cost) constraints. The effort required to implement management systems, including interface management, is typically underestimated and sometimes drastically ill-planned and prepared, resulting in slow or delayed interaction between interface parties. Implementing any project management system requires significant effort initially; in many ways, doing so can be compared to overcoming the inertia needed to begin to move a supertanker from its stationary position. To move a 520,000-ton, full supertanker from a static position to cruising speed requires an incredible amount of effort (engine power and time). Project execution start-ups are comparable, especially in large-scale complex projects with numerous contributing entities. If done well, starting implementation with momentum can provide significant long-term benefits. The opposite is also true; a slow start can have long-term implications. KoMs, ICDs, and ICWGs are key tools and techniques for ensuring a successful start to implementation, especially when planned and sequenced properly.

In this chapter, we have described the tools and techniques required to *kick start* implementation of the interface management system and begin the effective management of interfaces. With the interface management system implemented, we now move forward into Chapter 8 to discuss interface management and control during the project execution phase. This next chapter focuses on interaction within relevant interface groups and ICWGs to align interfaces and interdependencies. While we would like to believe that interface interaction is straightforward, the complexities associated with the dynamics of human interaction coupled with the various organizational needs, priorities, and perspectives of the stakeholders, make this process a challenge. This is especially true when unexpected changes occur or problems within one entity begin to create problems for another entity. The numerous independent factors involved in the process of managing interfaces cannot always be easily controlled; each of the factors is dynamic and tends to create a ripple effect through the entire system. Chapter 8 discusses how to manage the process, offers methods to deal with common challenges, and addresses common situations that occur in many interface management processes.

7.11 REFERENCES

Engineering Toolbox (n.d.). "In the Engineering Toolbox." Retrieved from http://www.engineeringtoolbox.com/p-id-piping-instrumentation-diagram-d_466.html.

Engineering Toolbox (n.d.). "In the Engineering Toolbox." Retrieved from http://www.engineeringtoolbox.com/pfd-process-flow-diagram-d_465.html.

Goffin, K., U. Koners, D. Baxter, and C. Van der Hoven. (2010). "Managing Lessons Learned and Tacit Knowledge in New Product Development." *Research-Technology Management*, 53(4): 39–51.

Instrumental Portal Cause and Effect Diagram (n.d.). From Instrumental Portal. Retrieved from http://instrumentationportal.com/2011/document-drawing-checklist-form/instrument-document/cause-and-effect/.

Pyysiäinen, J. (May 2003). Building trust in global inter-organizational software development projects: problems and practices. In International Workshop on Global Software Development, pp. 69–74.

Seashore, S. E. and University of Michigan. Survey Research Center. (1954). Group cohesiveness in the industrial work group. Ann Arbor: University of Michigan.

Sergent, T. L. and A. L. Guennec. (2014). Data-Based System Engineering: ICDs management with SysML, Esterel Technologies. Retrieved September 10, 2018 from https://www.ansys.com/-/media/ansys/corporate/resourcelibrary/whitepaper/erts+2014+databased+system+engineering+icds+management+with+sysml.pdf.

System Control Diagram. (Rev. 3, February 2013). From Standards Norway (n.d.). Retrieved from https://www.standard.no/en/sectors/energi-og-klima/petroleum/norsok-standard-categories/i-scd-syst-contr-diag/i-0053/.

United States Department of Defense. (2017). *Defense Acquisition Guidebook*. Chapter 3, "Systems Engineering." Washington, D.C.: U.S. Department of Defense. Retrieved from https://www.dau.mil/tools/dag.

This book has free material available for download from the Web Added Value™ resource center at *www.jrosspub.com*

8

Managing Interface Activity During Execution

"Equip them to understand each other's behaviors, and they will be better able to work effectively together, creating a high-performance workplace—and successful projects."
—Unknown

Successfully managing system interfaces and interdependencies during project execution brings many obstacles and challenges that extend beyond the technical domain. As we have seen, project success is influenced by industry, organizational, social, political, geographic, managerial, and a host of other factors that create a highly dynamic project environment. Some project environmental factors are so dynamic and unpredictable that their effects and influences on projects are sometimes beyond the control of the project team or the sponsoring organization.

However, this is not to suggest that members of the project team cross their fingers, hope for luck, and accept their fate at the hands of the forces of nature—not at all. Rather, collectively, we have gained tremendous experience from previous complex projects that gives us valuable insight into the root causes of problems that have contributed to the demise of many complex projects; we can use this insight to proactively prevent, or at least minimize, the impact of these root causes of failure. One root cause of failure that is well within the purview of the project team is insufficient cooperation, communication, and collaboration among those contributing to the project or between the project team and other entities that may have direct influence over the project. It's about people! We can influence the behaviors of people within the project by implementing systems that allow for constructive interaction among the independent parties contributing to or influencing the project.

Ultimately, project execution is about a collection of people from different organizations with varying perspectives and priorities that need somehow to align precisely at specific times in order to contribute their parts of the project exactly when needed—and to quality expectations. In an ideal world, as these various parts of the project are delivered, naturally on time and within budget, they are combined seamlessly with other parts to deliver a single system that fully meets the project sponsor's needs. Theoretically, a fully integrated system delivered on time and within budget leads to project success, but this overly simplistic description of project success rarely happens. Based on historical project performance, success eludes the majority of large-scale complex projects for myriad reasons—some of which are beyond the scope of this book. However, it is reasonable to suggest that some root causes of project failure are preventable; notably, the environment in which the project team and relevant stakeholders cooperate, communicate, and collaborate to deliver their respective scopes of work. It's about people working together!

8.1 BASIS FOR INTERACTION

When we speak about interfaces, our minds naturally focus on the *system* or the result of the project. Whether a new airplane, train, or military system, we try to envision the system in its final physical form and see those system interfaces at work to make the system function as expected. Many humans operate an automobile (system) as a means of transportation, but think little about the interfaces, interdependencies, and interactions needed to operate the vehicle—except when it fails, of course (i.e., *breaks down*). Normally, we just know the car works or fails to work. As users of automobiles, we think little about those people, groups, and organizations who designed and built the new automobile or their efforts to realize the automobile before it was brought to market. Rather, as consumers, our focus is on the final product. How the car looks, operates, performs, etc., is the responsibility of the project team who designed the new product. Even in auto industry projects, each person, organization, vendor, regulator, and supplier has their own role in bringing the new automobile *system* to life, but even though each entity has its own responsibility, all involved entities must work together to achieve the end result successfully.

In the project environment, especially early in project development, the system is just an idea on paper. It does not exist in physical form. Rather, the project environment requires many people with different management and technical specialties who are often from different companies, organizations, cultures, and even time zones—each with their own priorities, perspectives, management systems, development approaches, and project plans. These people work together to translate the idea on paper into the physical form, which may require several years. Interwoven within this complexity are countless system interfaces and project interdependencies that require constructive interaction by those associated with the system's development.

Interaction among those contributing to the project takes the form of cooperation, communication, and collaboration. Preferably, the communication is face-to-face since that represents the richest form of communication, but often face-to-face is not possible and less rich forms of communication are necessary. Regardless, given the number of entities involved and the volume of individual interactions, which can exceed tens of thousands, the laws of probability suggest something will go wrong—personalities will clash, organizational priorities will differ, project plans will not align, deliverables will be delayed, technical challenges will arise, etc. The challenge, then, is to minimize the number of *things that will go wrong* between entities contributing to project development. Theoretically, the probability of project success increases as the number of negative consequences decreases. Essentially, preventing or minimizing bad things from happening will contribute to the increased likelihood of project success.

This chapter builds on the information provided in Chapter 7—in which we implemented interface management—and focuses on actually managing interfaces during project execution. More specifically, it is about exploiting the environment that is created for various people to cooperate, communicate, and collaborate in order to solve difficult technical system interfaces and complicated project interdependency issues.

During this chapter, we provide screenshots or diagrams from the sample Project Diamond interface register. The screenshots in this chapter are taken from the Seaflex Web Interface Register (WIR) tool provided by Kongsberg Maritime (Seaflex WIR, 2017). Kongsberg is headquartered in Kongsberg, Norway, and provides solutions for on- and offshore merchant marine, subsea, navy, coastal marine, aquaculture, and related training services. The KONGSBERG WIR is a specialized interface management tool that is used to keep track of, monitor, and document interface information exchanged among different parties in a project.

In Appendix B, we provide a similar narrative using information about and screenshots from the Coreworx Interface Manager (CIM) provided by Coreworx, a Canada-based software and services company headquartered in Kitchener, Ontario (Coreworx, 2017). Coreworx offers integrated project information management software and solutions for engineering and construction projects in several industries. Several other interface management tools are available as well.

As we have discussed, a reality of large-scale complex projects is that problems will arise with entities and people interacting across the project as they attempt to identify, align, and control interfaces and interdependencies, especially when there are conflicting views on how to solve these challenges given each entity's own priorities. These problems represent not just technical and management issues, but also social interaction issues attributed to the people charged with solving those problems, including clashing personalities and cultural differences. However, there are simple techniques to prevent or minimize many of these problems from occurring.

This chapter emphasizes managing interfaces during the execution phase in a manner that (1) supports sincere cooperation, open communication, and continuous collaboration and (2) provides a way to develop solutions and resolve conflicts before they impact scope delivery. Managing interfaces during execution includes not just system interfaces in the *inanimate object* form, but also the interactions between entities that are responsible for or associated with system interfaces and project interdependencies. Certainly, interfaces do not resolve themselves. Rather, in the project environment, it is people who must work together to find the best solutions to interfaces and interdependencies while balancing their own organizational and individual priorities and preferences. So, the process of interface management is as much about the people (organizations, companies, etc.) as it is about the inanimate objects associated with the system developed by the project.

8.2 INTERFACE GROUP INTERACTION

In the previous chapter, interface groups were initiated using kick-off meetings (KoMs). The interface group KoM served as the transition point for initiating interface activity among various interface parties, but its primary value was to bring interface parties (i.e., people) together. A primary interface challenge during project execution is to maintain productive relationships among all of the interface parties that will potentially last for many years. Often, senior company executives and senior project management personnel direct cooperation between various groups and espouse placing the priorities of the project above their own interests, but fail to implement a project environment that truly facilitates and sustains the necessary collaboration between entities. Unfortunately, these same executives often sit above the day-to-day action and thus fail to contribute to resolving the obstacles to actual collaboration. Many of these executives perceive or assume that cooperation is something that comes naturally to every person or is a gift given to humans at birth. Thus, many believe interaction is so simple we do not need to spend even a moment considering it. This is not the case.

There are many examples of collaborative dysfunctionality in society, especially in politics. We observe vast divides in societies as a result of the unwillingness or inability to cooperate in a civil manner to solve difficult problems in the best interest of the population. Rather, too often modern political mindsets and mentalities focus less on the art of negotiation (win-win) and more toward all-or-nothing solutions (win-lose)—fomenting distrust while creating an adversarial environment. Individual political parties often fail to compromise on their individual positions to achieve a solution for the greater population. We would be naïve to think such mindsets do not exist in organizations contributing to project development where individual interests can and do take priority over the larger interests of the project. This is the first challenge to overcome in order to achieve civil and cooperative relationships among parties contributing to the project's development.

8.2.1 Interface *Rules of the Road*

Before substantive discussion over complex system technical interface issues can occur, rules must be established as to how the interface group will function. These rules, established during the KoM, are put to the test during project execution. These *rules* govern how the group will conduct its business and interaction; they are intended to ensure that the members of the group conduct themselves in accordance with generally accepted professional norms. The main purpose of the rules is to prevent any unwanted behaviors that might adversely affect the dynamics of group interaction or create interpersonal problems between members of the interface group. These rules apply specifically to the conduct of interface meetings where there are generally two parts—administrative and technical. Of course, we know that human interaction can be affected by irrational emotions that introduce unpredictable variables into what might otherwise be rational progress. Establishing governance rules—and more important, *enforcing* those rules—encourages the probability of maintaining an environment in which professional conduct reduces or eliminates unwanted interpersonal conflicts.

Initial interface meetings after the KoM will play a big role in determining how successful the group will be over time. Those groups that enforce the agreed-upon rules have a much higher probability of maintaining control over the environment in which they interact and are less likely to experience social or personal interaction problems. Given the number of entities, people, and personalities involved in interface activity, someone will likely challenge or break the rules. The client, or project sponsor's organization, needs to ensure that the designated lead interface parties (LIPs) are managing interface meetings according to the established governance rules. Often, this requires intervention by the client during the initial few interface meetings until the group develops good interaction habits. This is a simple suggestion, but client involvement is critical to ensuring the group *starts off on the right foot* and does not derail at the crucial beginning.

8.2.2 Meeting Administration

While it may sound insignificant, managing meeting administration is one key to effectively maintaining control of the interaction environment between interface parties. The administrative part of the meeting establishes the dates, times, format (in-person, video, etc.) and agenda, along with designating the meeting chair, recording of minutes, and meeting actions, etc. While this may sound rather easy and straightforward, planning and scheduling of interface meetings can quickly turn into a source of conflict if the dates and times constantly change, the method for participating differs, or the format or how the meeting will be conducted routinely changes. Even the technology to virtually connect to meetings for offsite personnel can become a source of conflict when different companies use incompatible video and teleconference tools and systems, resulting in bad connectivity or continuous interruption. If not managed effectively, a simple aspect such as meeting administration can easily and quickly create relationship tension where people begin to feel their time is being wasted.

This is especially true when many participants are required across many locations and time zones by organizations that use various telecommunication systems, which sometimes are not compatible. It can even be difficult to assemble two organizations that are located in the same city or even the same building. Meeting logistics and infrastructure should be tested ahead of time to ensure productive participation by group members.

Standardizing meeting dates, times, and formats can alleviate a great deal of stress on participants with many competing priorities. With a *recurring* meeting, participants understand when, where, and how they are to participate. While it may not be possible to attend every meeting, a regular recurring meeting creates a routine to which participants will naturally adapt. Of course, circumstances may dictate the need for a meeting outside the regular schedule. Minutes of meetings should be documented using a standard format and be signed by both parties. Most interface register database tools also include a minutes of meeting (MoM) function as shown in the box around "MoM and Action List" on the left side of Figure 8.1 for the SeaFlex WIR.

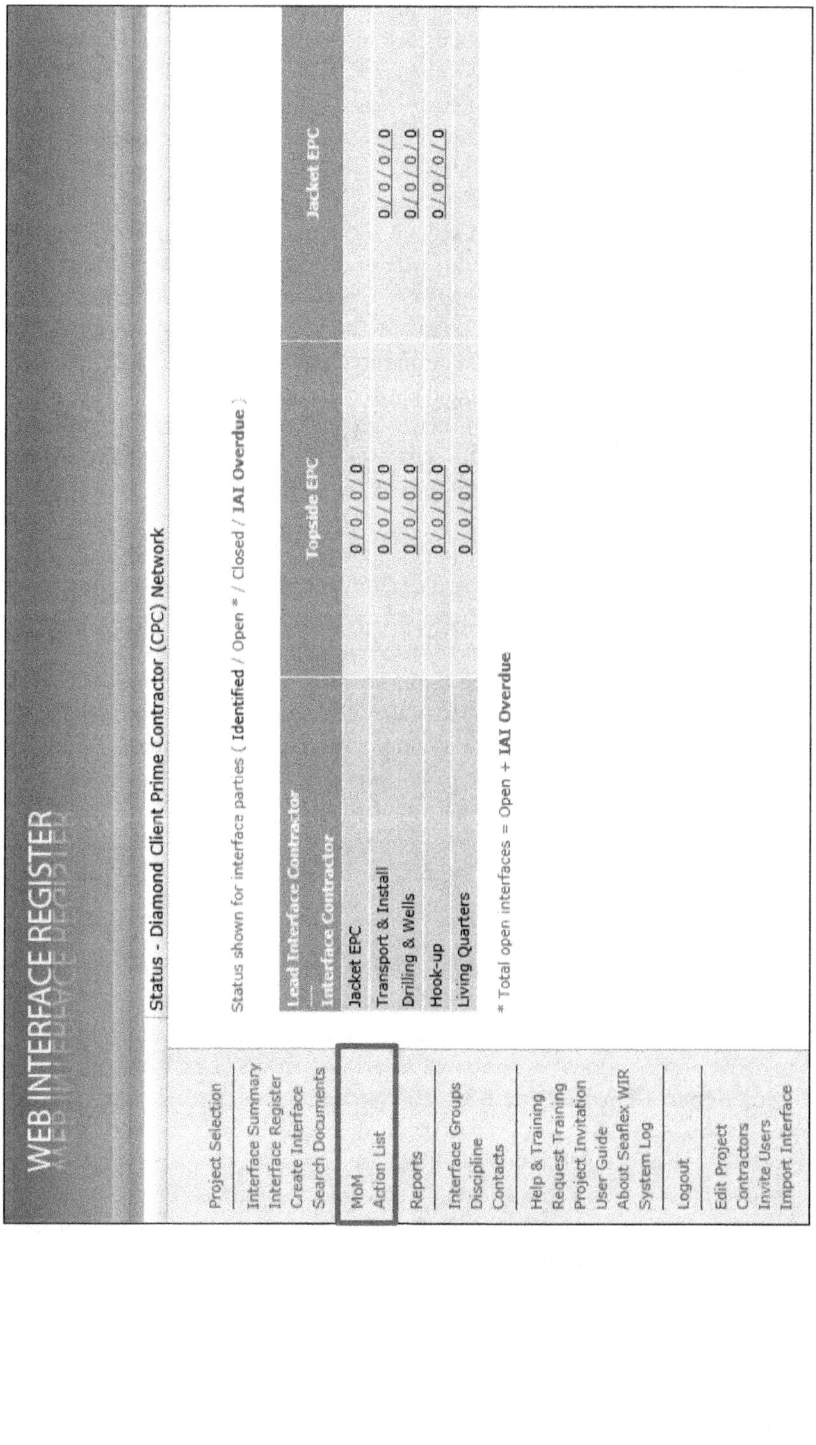

WEB INTERFACE REGISTER

Status - Diamond Client Prime Contractor (CPC) Network

Project Selection

Interface Summary
Interface Register
Create Interface
Search Documents

MoM
Action List

Reports

Interface Groups
Discipline
Contacts

Help & Training
Request Training
Project Invitation
User Guide
About Seaflex WIR
System Log

Logout

Edit Project
Contractors
Invite Users
Import Interface

Status shown for interface parties (**Identified** / Open * / Closed / **IAI Overdue**)

Lead Interface Contractor / Interface Contractor	Topside EPC	Jacket EPC
Jacket EPC	0 / 0 / 0 / 0	
Transport & Install	0 / 0 / 0 / 0	0 / 0 / 0 / 0
Drilling & Wells	0 / 0 / 0 / 0	0 / 0 / 0 / 0
Hook-up	0 / 0 / 0 / 0	0 / 0 / 0 / 0
Living Quarters	0 / 0 / 0 / 0	

* Total open interfaces = Open + **IAI Overdue**

Figure 8.1 Interface group MoM function (SeaFlex WIR)

The MoM function is important because it provides a consistent way of administering interface meetings and uses a standard format that is accessible by any individual with access to the web-based interface register. As part of interface register functionality, most tools also contain some type of *action* tracking function that consolidates the actions recorded during meetings. While simple, these features help to maintain accountability for relevant group members and provide a structured way to document and track interface agreements, the actions that need to be resolved, and by whom. In essence, this simple tool provides a method to document interaction in a transparent way and prevents unwanted misunderstanding later in project development, especially when interface group membership or personnel change. As mentioned earlier in the book, individuals tend to come and go from projects at both expected and unexpected times, especially when the project duration spans many years. The MoMs serve as a formal record of interactions between entities. This means that previous agreements remain in effect should individual members leave or be replaced by other personnel.

In interface groups where relationships last several years, resulting in hundreds of interface meetings, maintaining historical records provides a way to easily confirm previous agreements. A list of all interface MoMs, such as those shown in Figure 8.2, is contained within the web-based register and accessible to all authorized interface personnel. With commercial implications, these historical documents provide a way to resolve contractual disagreements when one party fails to adhere to previous interface agreements. Often, contractors will submit *variation order requests* (VORs) in cases in which interface agreements were not met or project interdependencies were not provided as planned by an interface party. These VOR claims can result in significant strain not only on relationships between interfacing parties, since they affect progress on the scopes of work, but also between the interface parties and the client.

Often, negative financial consequences arise from these unexpected variations and resolution can be difficult, especially if there is no historical documentation to support a claim. As we will address in the next section, the most important content of interface meetings revolves around reaching agreement on various aspects of system interfaces. Ongoing activities leading to these interface agreements are often documented in the minutes or MoMs from such meetings. The MoMs are the source for tracking ongoing activities and actions that each party needs to accomplish to further progress on resolving interfaces. This could be as simple as adding a new interface item to the register or agreeing to send additional information to the other party.

Typically, the interface register will also capture actions taken by each party to resolve an interface item (i.e., reach agreement), which is housed in an *interface record* or *interface sheet*. Interface register tools typically contain the functionality to recall all actions by both parties for each interface item, which is useful in commercial disputes. These historical documents and interface agreement records in the interface register allow the client to validate VOR claims that are related to interface activity. Maintaining an archive that is easily accessible, by both interface parties in an interface group helps to supply historical information when commercial disputes are raised.

Equally important, if not more so, is documenting the content of interface meetings and the result of coordination between the various parties to align various aspects of each system interface. While controlling the environment in which interaction between interface parties occurs is crucial to protecting relationships long term, it is just as important to ensure that the content and conclusions of each meeting are made absolutely clear and recorded accordingly. The simplest method to ensure a common understanding of results is to mandate that the meeting minutes be reviewed and approved by the relevant parties. This is often a built-in feature in the interface register tool. Formally approving the minutes prevents parties from later stating that they did not understand or from claiming the documented minutes were incorrect. By signing the minutes, each party is acknowledging agreement with the content and confirming its commitment to the documented actions.

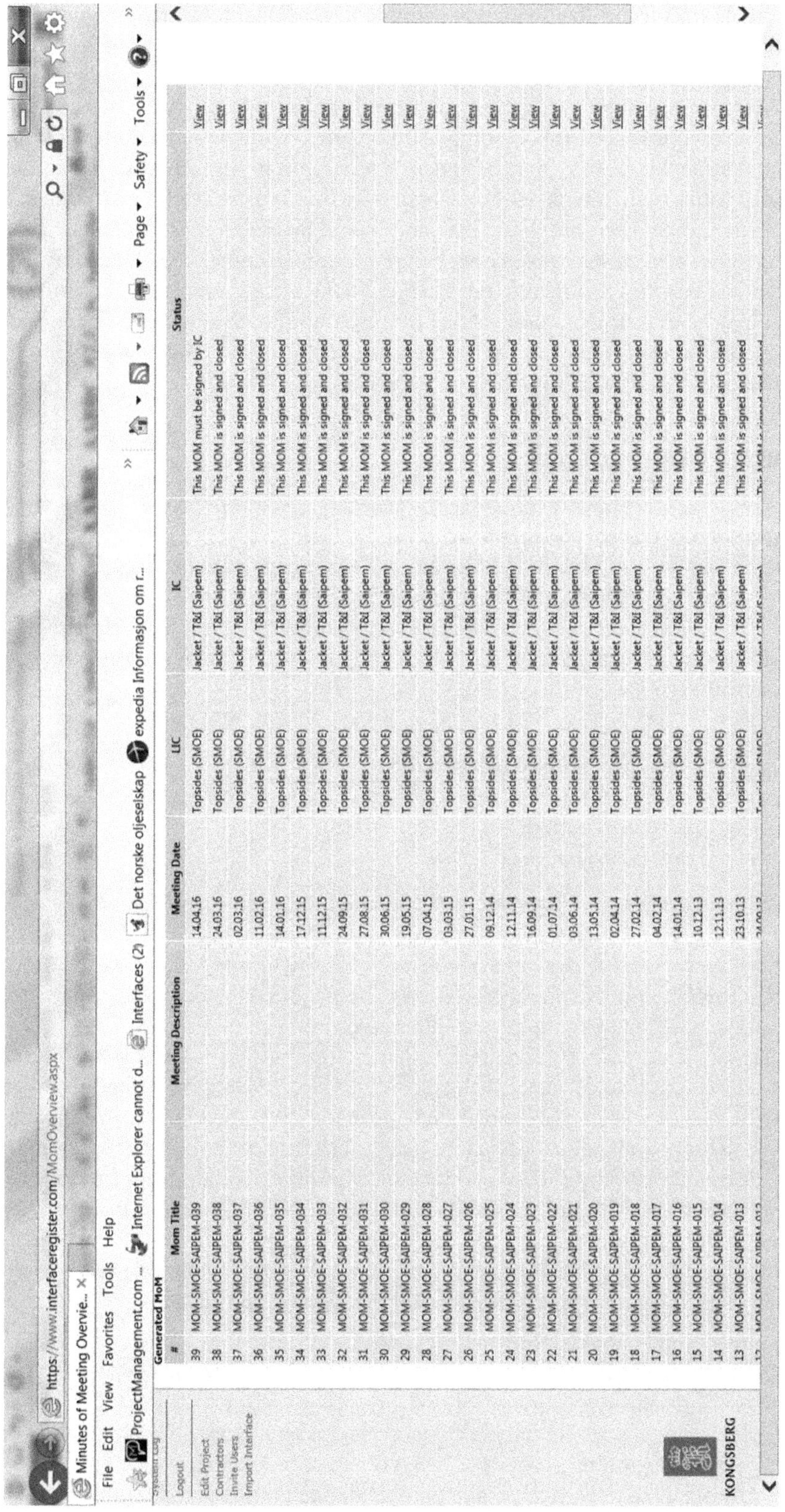

https://www.interfaceregister.com/MomOverview.aspx

Minutes of Meeting Overvie...

File Edit View Favorites Tools Help

ProjectManagement.com ... Internet Explorer cannot d... Interfaces (2) Det norske oljeselskap expedia Informasjon om r...

Page ▾ Safety ▾ Tools ▾

Logout

Edit Project
Contractors
Invite Users
Import Interface

KONGSBERG

Generated MoM

#	Mom Title	Meeting Description	Meeting Date	LIC	IC	Status	
39	MOM-SMOE-SAIPEM-039		14.04.16	Topsides (SMOE)	Jacket / T&I (Saipem)	This MOM must be signed by IC	View
38	MOM-SMOE-SAIPEM-038		24.03.16	Topsides (SMOE)	Jacket / T&I (Saipem)	This MOM is signed and closed	View
37	MOM-SMOE-SAIPEM-037		02.03.16	Topsides (SMOE)	Jacket / T&I (Saipem)	This MOM is signed and closed	View
36	MOM-SMOE-SAIPEM-036		11.02.16	Topsides (SMOE)	Jacket / T&I (Saipem)	This MOM is signed and closed	View
35	MOM-SMOE-SAIPEM-035		14.01.16	Topsides (SMOE)	Jacket / T&I (Saipem)	This MOM is signed and closed	View
34	MOM-SMOE-SAIPEM-034		17.12.15	Topsides (SMOE)	Jacket / T&I (Saipem)	This MOM is signed and closed	View
33	MOM-SMOE-SAIPEM-033		11.12.15	Topsides (SMOE)	Jacket / T&I (Saipem)	This MOM is signed and closed	View
32	MOM-SMOE-SAIPEM-032		24.09.15	Topsides (SMOE)	Jacket / T&I (Saipem)	This MOM is signed and closed	View
31	MOM-SMOE-SAIPEM-031		27.08.15	Topsides (SMOE)	Jacket / T&I (Saipem)	This MOM is signed and closed	View
30	MOM-SMOE-SAIPEM-030		30.06.15	Topsides (SMOE)	Jacket / T&I (Saipem)	This MOM is signed and closed	View
29	MOM-SMOE-SAIPEM-029		19.05.15	Topsides (SMOE)	Jacket / T&I (Saipem)	This MOM is signed and closed	View
28	MOM-SMOE-SAIPEM-028		07.04.15	Topsides (SMOE)	Jacket / T&I (Saipem)	This MOM is signed and closed	View
27	MOM-SMOE-SAIPEM-027		03.03.15	Topsides (SMOE)	Jacket / T&I (Saipem)	This MOM is signed and closed	View
26	MOM-SMOE-SAIPEM-026		27.01.15	Topsides (SMOE)	Jacket / T&I (Saipem)	This MOM is signed and closed	View
25	MOM-SMOE-SAIPEM-025		09.12.14	Topsides (SMOE)	Jacket / T&I (Saipem)	This MOM is signed and closed	View
24	MOM-SMOE-SAIPEM-024		12.11.14	Topsides (SMOE)	Jacket / T&I (Saipem)	This MOM is signed and closed	View
23	MOM-SMOE-SAIPEM-023		16.09.14	Topsides (SMOE)	Jacket / T&I (Saipem)	This MOM is signed and closed	View
22	MOM-SMOE-SAIPEM-022		01.07.14	Topsides (SMOE)	Jacket / T&I (Saipem)	This MOM is signed and closed	View
21	MOM-SMOE-SAIPEM-021		03.06.14	Topsides (SMOE)	Jacket / T&I (Saipem)	This MOM is signed and closed	View
20	MOM-SMOE-SAIPEM-020		13.05.14	Topsides (SMOE)	Jacket / T&I (Saipem)	This MOM is signed and closed	View
19	MOM-SMOE-SAIPEM-019		02.04.14	Topsides (SMOE)	Jacket / T&I (Saipem)	This MOM is signed and closed	View
18	MOM-SMOE-SAIPEM-018		27.02.14	Topsides (SMOE)	Jacket / T&I (Saipem)	This MOM is signed and closed	View
17	MOM-SMOE-SAIPEM-017		04.02.14	Topsides (SMOE)	Jacket / T&I (Saipem)	This MOM is signed and closed	View
16	MOM-SMOE-SAIPEM-016		14.01.14	Topsides (SMOE)	Jacket / T&I (Saipem)	This MOM is signed and closed	View
15	MOM-SMOE-SAIPEM-015		10.12.13	Topsides (SMOE)	Jacket / T&I (Saipem)	This MOM is signed and closed	View
14	MOM-SMOE-SAIPEM-014		12.11.13	Topsides (SMOE)	Jacket / T&I (Saipem)	This MOM is signed and closed	View
13	MOM-SMOE-SAIPEM-013		23.10.13	Topsides (SMOE)	Jacket / T&I (Saipem)	This MOM is signed and closed	View

Figure 8.2 MoM archive in interface register (Seaflex WIR)

The suggestions thus far in this section are simple to implement, but require a disciplined approach including employment of basic techniques covering human interaction, good alignment between processes, governing rules, and the tool selected to house the interface register. Far too often, management systems overlook or underestimate the value of ensuring that the *basics* are performed extremely well. As mentioned at the beginning of the chapter, resolving system interfaces is as much, or more, about the people involved in those system interfaces than the technical or managerial challenges associated with system interfaces themselves. If we cannot establish an environment by which difficult problems can be discussed, evaluated, and solved by the requisite technical and management representatives, then we have failed even before beginning. Quite often, interface management problems occur as a result of diving into technical problems without any form of environment control; the result may be technical discussions that devolve into shouting matches or personal attacks. Once the relationship between parties has been damaged, it is difficult or impossible to recover as long as those same individuals are involved in the process.

8.2.3 Interface Meeting Content

The content of interface meetings revolves around reaching agreement on various aspects of system interfaces. Traditionally, this is viewed as a technical discussion only. In reality, this is only partially true—interface meetings also include discussion and agreement on other factors stemming from technical discussions. For example, parties within an interface group may agree on technical details associated with an electrical connection. While this satisfies the pure technical elements of the interface, technical agreements nearly always result in follow-on action in management and commercial domains. For example:

- When does the connection need to be made?
- Who pays for what part of the connection?
- Are there any procurement activities as a result of the technical agreement?
- Are any certifications required?
- Who will provide the documentation?

These, along with others, are questions that probably need to be answered beyond the technical domain. This is perhaps the most confusing part of interface management. System interfaces act as the driving force behind project interface management, but it is not a *one-to-one* interaction. While the system interface itself is objective, the level of interaction required by the interface parties is subjective and can vary depending upon the personalities involved.

Many project personnel do not readily realize that interface management involves more than just an agreement on the technical details of each system interface. Making the technical agreement real requires a holistic view of what it takes to make it happen to deliver the solution. With many different entities involved in the process, aligning all facets, technical and nontechnical, of each system interface can present an incredible challenge. This is one reason why it is extremely important to (1) emplace a disciplined interface management process to maintain control of the environment in which different entities interact, and (2) capture technical and nontechnical content clearly and precisely. System interfaces need to be aligned between relevant parties as early as possible, but during project execution this is only possible where the project environment facilitates effective and efficient interaction.

8.3 MANAGING INTERFACE CONTROL WORKING GROUPS

With cases in which complex system interface issues affect several scopes of work or areas of responsibility, interface control working groups (ICWGs) are used to facilitate coordination. ICWGs can be initiated by any organization, but normally they are defined by the project sponsor's organization early in the project life cycle. Group membership should be limited to only those organizations and requisite personnel needed to resolve the specific *complex* interface issue. Keeping the group as small as possible increases the likelihood of achieving results more rapidly. These groups are intended to be temporary forums to assemble the right people so that quick decisions can be agreed upon for complex issues. Any situation requiring an ICWG that is not already established should be brought to the attention of the client as soon as possible.

The organization forming the ICWG is responsible for coordinating with requisite personnel, scheduling ICWG meetings, preparing meetings, and leading the ICWG meetings. All actions and decisions should be documented and distributed to each member organization. The main challenge associated with ICWGs is obtaining consensus approval from ICWG membership on relevant interface agreements. Given that ICWGs typically contain several member groups, each with its own priorities and responsibilities, it can be quite difficult to find a single solution that is satisfactory to all members of the group. Typically, any solution requires considerable investment in time and effort and still may fall short of meeting the expectations of all group members. Even when a technical solution is identified that satisfies all participants, follow-on managerial (i.e., schedules, plans, etc.) and commercial (i.e., procurement) activities can create additional challenges, which then require further collaboration and agreement.

As ICWGs are formed to address complex interface issues across several scopes of work and areas of responsibility, the solution is not often as straightforward as that within interface groups of two parties. An agreement may solve the problem in one area of the complex interface issue but may create problems for other members in other aspects of the interface. Typically, the vast majority of interfaces between two parties are resolved fairly quickly. Thus, it is logical to minimize the number of parties to only those required to be as efficient as possible.

ICWGs, while necessary, are not efficient by virtue of the sheer number of entities involved, which probably increases the number of people involved and requires satisfying their respective needs without creating additional problems. The challenges associated with problem solving and reaching consensus in groups of people is well-documented. In fact, many readers of this book have likely experienced difficulty in reaching consensus on a decision or agreeing on a solution while working in a large group. Each individual represents different points of view derived from life experiences, backgrounds, and many other social, psychological, professional, organizational, and economic factors. A potential solution may satisfy a portion of the group, but may create additional problems for others in the group. Problems associated with ICWGs can often be minimized by effectively managing the ICWG to overcome challenges common to this kind of complex group.

Any situation involving large numbers of people representing multiple organizations has the potential to spin out of control without proper management. Even in controlled environments, such as political *town hall* meetings, the situation can quickly become unmanageable as people let their emotions take over the situation. ICWGs are no different. Each member represents an organization that has specific interests, goals, and priorities. Every ICWG meeting needs to be governed by a strict set of rules that allows for participation by each representative, while maintaining focus on the issue at hand and ensuring that the discussion does not devolve into a *battle of wills* between various strong personalities. Even though the rules are set during the ICWG KoM, enforcing these rules consistently during the execution phase must be a priority. At this point the reader may have noticed a *theme*—establishing and enforcing rules. As with interface meetings involving two parties, ICWG meetings need to be conducted consistently and in accordance with the governing rule set. Nothing irritates participants more than believing one representative is receiving preferential treatment or proposing solutions that routinely benefit a single party over others. A key aspect of managing an ICWG function properly is active participation by the project sponsor's team.

ICWGs, by definition, represent risk for the project sponsor, as well as a means of reducing that risk; after all, they are formed to address significant or complex system interface issues that span several parts of the project's system architecture. It is common for the sponsoring organization to delegate management of ICWGs to a prime contractor. This is not the best, or even a good strategy since it can lead to mistrust by other contractors and potential solutions that are one-sided. Rather, while a specific main contractor or organization may have a central role in the ICWG, the project sponsor should maintain control of the ICWG to the highest extent possible. This is not to suggest that the client take a dictatorial role, but rather more of an arbiter role to maintain an environment such that each party is equally represented without concern for organizational or representative hierarchy outside the ICWG, which can intimidate or influence representatives within the ICWG. The client takes a central role in the ICWG, which aides in focusing participants on the goal of acting in the best interest of the project, which helps to achieve consensus.

Every representative participating within the ICWG must understand that concessions sometimes must be made in the best interest of the project and at the expense of some members of the ICWG. While the goal is to find a solution that satisfies all representatives of the group, rarely does this happen; more times than not, members are required to sacrifice their own interests in favor of the project's interests and priorities. This sacrifice can be extremely difficult when some members of the ICWG represent organizations that are higher in the command or management structure, while others are on lower *rungs*. Sometimes, a proposed solution from a senior organization that is participating in the ICWG can be seen as a directive that others must follow. Such a solution may be a legitimate directive as it may be based on a valid legal, regulatory, or even technical consideration; if so, this should be made clear to ICWG members. If not, a higher authority may need to tactfully intervene (the project sponsor). The ICWG chair needs to be cognizant of these factors and manage the ICWG in a way that is fair for all representatives, yet reminds all representatives to stay focused on the best interest of the project.

Each issue being addressed by the ICWG must be precisely defined both in terms of what is part of the problem and what is not part of the problem. Each solution to the interface issue must be evaluated within the context of each representative of the ICWG so that they can assess the impact of a particular solution on their own interests. What appears to be an optimal solution for most representatives may be a *showstopper* for one or a few of the other members. All solutions need to be carefully analyzed to determine whether a suboptimal solution satisfies the majority of the concerns of the total membership. Forcing solutions on various members may work for a particular issue, but is typically not a successful strategy, especially when the ICWG will exist for a substantial duration or when its member entities must collaborate on multiple projects.

It should be expected that some situations will require senior project management or management personnel from the sponsoring organization to adjudicate a final solution to a particular problem, such as when ICWG members are not able to reach a satisfactory conclusion. This is especially true for unique situations not governed by existing laws, governing regulations, organizational policies, etc. Typically, these situations are taken through the project's change management process by preparing and submitting a project change proposal (PCP) to the project change board. The reason for using this process is that these situations typically will result in some commercial impact for some of the representatives of the ICWG. The change process allows these situations to be assessed fully and the financial consequences evaluated by project management.

8.4 INTERFACE CONTROL DOCUMENT (ICD) AND INTERFACE REGISTER

Every project is undertaken to deliver a result. This result takes the form of a system that is designed, developed, and delivered to provide the expected value by the sponsoring organization. The *system* could be a new airplane sponsored by a large aircraft manufacturer, new equipment sponsored by the military, etc. Each system is based on a selected *architecture*, physical and functional, to achieve the intended result. The system architecture may undergo several revisions during the early stages of the project, or even pre-project initiation, to identify an optimal concept that is economically feasible and mission capable. Regardless, each system concept is associated with an architecture, which results in a number (n) of system interfaces to connect the various components, parts, subsystems, packages, etc., of the particular concept. These system interfaces can be physical, logical (e.g., signal exchange), or mass (e.g., fluids, gas)—see Chapter 3, Section 3.3 for a more detailed description of interface types and categories. As discussed earlier but iterated here, as we prepare to focus on the ICD and interface register, system interfaces can be internal (those existing within a defined boundary of the system's architecture, such as scope of work, project, area of responsibility, etc.) or external (those interfaces that extend beyond the system boundary to other systems; that is, project to existing facility, project integrating into another project, etc.).

With each iteration of the system architecture, the system concept becomes more defined until the optimal architecture is identified and agreed upon. The ICD is used to document system interfaces. In early concept architectures, interfaces may be defined at a high level (e.g., main electrical connections, primary steel intersect locations, types of signals to be exchanged such as emergency shutdown, process shutdown, elevations and grid coordinates, etc.). As the optimal architecture is selected and undergoes more thorough development, the interfaces listed in the ICD become more detailed. For example, high-level *emergency shutdown signals* include a list of individual signals and their exchange protocol information. These individual signals are then added to the ICD.

Adjustments to the chosen system architecture can continue well into project execution. Thus, the ICD is a living document throughout project development and is updated as the system architecture evolves. However, as the project matures in the execution phase, the ICD stabilizes substantially as the project moves closer to transition to operations. In essence, the ICD acts to document the interface baseline.

ICDs are used widely in systems engineering and software development across many industries. In U.S. defense industry programs and projects, interface management documentation is contained with the configuration management domain; in other departments of the U.S. government, ICDs are *de riguer* to document interfaces. In some industries, such as the oil and gas industry, the use of ICDs is rare. As we have discussed from the beginning of the book, as many industries evolve and become more complex, they also become more capable with the advancement of technology. However, some industries and some organizations within them continue to conduct projects using outdated and inefficient methods that negatively impact project success. In other words, even where technology and interface complexity has increased, the techniques needed to manage this complexity have not caught up. Failure to use tools such as an ICD is but one example. The ICD, or some form of it, can significantly boost success and reduce risk resulting from interfaces.

8.4.1 ICD Use During Project Execution

Since system interfaces are the main focus of an ICD, it is most often prepared by technical personnel—such as those in engineering disciplines (electrical, mechanical, piping, avionics, etc.)—and contains system interfaces based on the chosen system architecture. As mentioned in Chapter 7, the ICD can take many forms and the content can vary greatly from project to project, since the system concepts and supporting architectures differ. Regardless, this document forms the basis for documenting system interfaces and identifies the parties responsible for each system interface after the project development concept is selected. As expected, the ICD is an important resource that guides interface interaction by various entities during project execution. These entities maintain the interfaces within their scopes of work or across their areas of responsibility; the areas of responsibility are defined by the project development approach. As the system architecture is broken down into logical objects (subsystems, modules, areas, etc.) and contracted out to different entities, the ICD becomes critical to understanding where the interfaces lie between the various entities. While the interfaces themselves are documented in the ICD, the interactions to resolve system interfaces between entities are documented in an interface register tool. Thus, there is a symbiotic relationship between the ICD and the interface register. While the ICD is updated as a result of interactions, the interface register is updated to reflect the interactions and decisions that resulted in updates to the ICD.

Where the ICD may describe a single electrical connection between Entity *A* and Entity *B* at a general location in the system architecture, the interface register will list the *agreements* between the two parties to ensure that both are aligning various aspects of this single interface and designing their scopes of work to align the electrical connection. This is especially important to achieve early in the project to prevent unwanted and more costly integration misalignments later in the project, during the fabrication, construction, and installation phases. The interface register may list several interface items that need agreement between the parties to resolve a single system interface.

In our electrical connection system interface described previously, the interface register may have several interface items requiring agreement to resolve various facets of this one *electrical connection* system interface—including the type of cable to be used, connection or termination details, location (elevation and grid coordinates) of the electrical connection, type of junction box where the connection will be made, and so on. Even when agreement on these technical facets are achieved, then further agreement is commonly required to define follow-on management and commercial facets of the system interface. In a project where there are thousands of system interfaces, the process repeats itself for each interface; this results in a complex web of interactions between different organizations that are contributing to the project—all of which are documented in the interface register.

Aligning system interfaces that occur within an entity's scope of work is traditionally seen as easier than aligning those involving multiple entities, since internal technical and management processes—such as the detailed engineering process—are normally mature or at least commonly understood. In the case of an interface within a single entity's scope, individual technical disciplines have a structured method to ensure that any interfaces affecting their technical discipline are resolved. This is normally part of the engineering, procurement, and construction (EPC) processes and the company's overall governing management systems. However, using this common process mindset to circumvent the use of an interface register can lead to problems. Sometimes a company's own view that its internal processes can handle interfaces within their scope may be exaggerated and result in internal misalignments that can extend outward to other interface parties. For interfaces within an entity's own scope, we recommend using an internal interface register.

8.4.2 Using an Internal Interface Register

Within interface management, the perception that internal interfaces are adequately addressed by a company's internal processes is often flawed and may provide a false sense of security. Even though clients include market research and thoroughly evaluate potential contractors as part of the commercial contracting prescreening process, they cannot assume that a selected company will automatically be able to handle and adequately process interfaces across a highly complex scope of work using their own internal processes. One of the influencing factors is how well a company maintains highly qualified personnel.

Modern business environments are hampered by employee retention. Clients who are considering various companies during the contracting process may assume that a particular candidate company maintains fully staffed teams that have operated together for a long time. This assumption can be very misleading. Even when a client awards a contract to a particular firm, the staffing of the project frequently comes afterward. At best, only *key personnel* are identified and there is no assurance that highly qualified personnel are available within other parts of the organization or can be sourced from outside the company. It is quite common for companies to bring in a significant portion of the project team as *consultants* to work on a project. These personnel are often unfamiliar with the contractor company's internal processes and procedures; this creates problems, especially when a disciplined internal interface management system is not employed.

Another influencing factor relates to the composition of the contractor's team. In many industries, several companies may team up together to deliver a single scope of work. Each company has agreed to perform a specific portion of the work. Often, these companies have not worked together before. In practice, this means that each company has a different business model, unique internal processes, different ways of progressing through their scope, etc. As shown in our Project Diamond case, the *topside EPC* contractor consists of three different companies, each specialized in its own area; when these three specialties are combined, they are, together, able to deliver the entire scope of work. However, these companies do not have a history of working together, do not have the same management systems, and have not developed integrated work processes. This is the reason for the Diamond Prime Contractor Internal (PCI) interface network described in earlier chapters and shown in Figure 8.3.

As is shown in the interface register screenshot in Figure 8.3, Project Diamond established an internal interface network for the Topside EPC team and called it the Diamond PCI network. This network allows each of the companies a formal communication channel with the other companies without disrupting their individual established internal management procedures and processes. The boundary of this network is the main contractors' scope of work or statement of work (SoW). The SoW defines what can be interfaced between the team entities. In addition to using an interface register, we suggest using an ICD as a tool to document even internal interfaces across a complex scope of work such as the Topside EPC contract, regardless of the perceived maturity of internal management processes. Developing an ICD, in this case specific to the Topside EPC SoW, and aligning it with the project ICD minimizes the possibility of late stage interface misalignments.

Far too often, in situations in which internal interfaces are not managed properly, internal problems develop yet go undetected until they reach criticality—resulting in unexpected delays, rework, and additional costs, and sometimes impacting other interface parties and groups. In this instance, the Topside EPC ICD is a more detailed ICD, covering the Topside EPC SoW. Using such an ICD in conjunction with the internal interface network during project execution allows the client greater visibility into potential internal problem areas before they become severe and begin to create problems for other external interface parties and groups.

8.4.3 Interface Register as a Tool

The interface register is a critical tool for structuring and simplifying interface entities across a large complex project development. As we can see from our previous discussion of internal interfaces, the interface register is scalable. That is, the register can be established to manage internal interfaces within a single scope of work, to manage contractors within a single project, or even to manage interfaces between projects—as shown by our Project Diamond example. The key to managing interfaces during execution is to break down and structure the interface register to ensure that the right parties are able to interface with other parties, at the right level, and about the right interface topics. Whether between contractors within a single project or between projects within a single development area or family of programs or projects, use of an interface register is always recommended between interfacing scopes of work that are being performed by different entities; without such registers, unresolved interface problems manifest as *integration issues* that result in rework, extra time, and added cost.

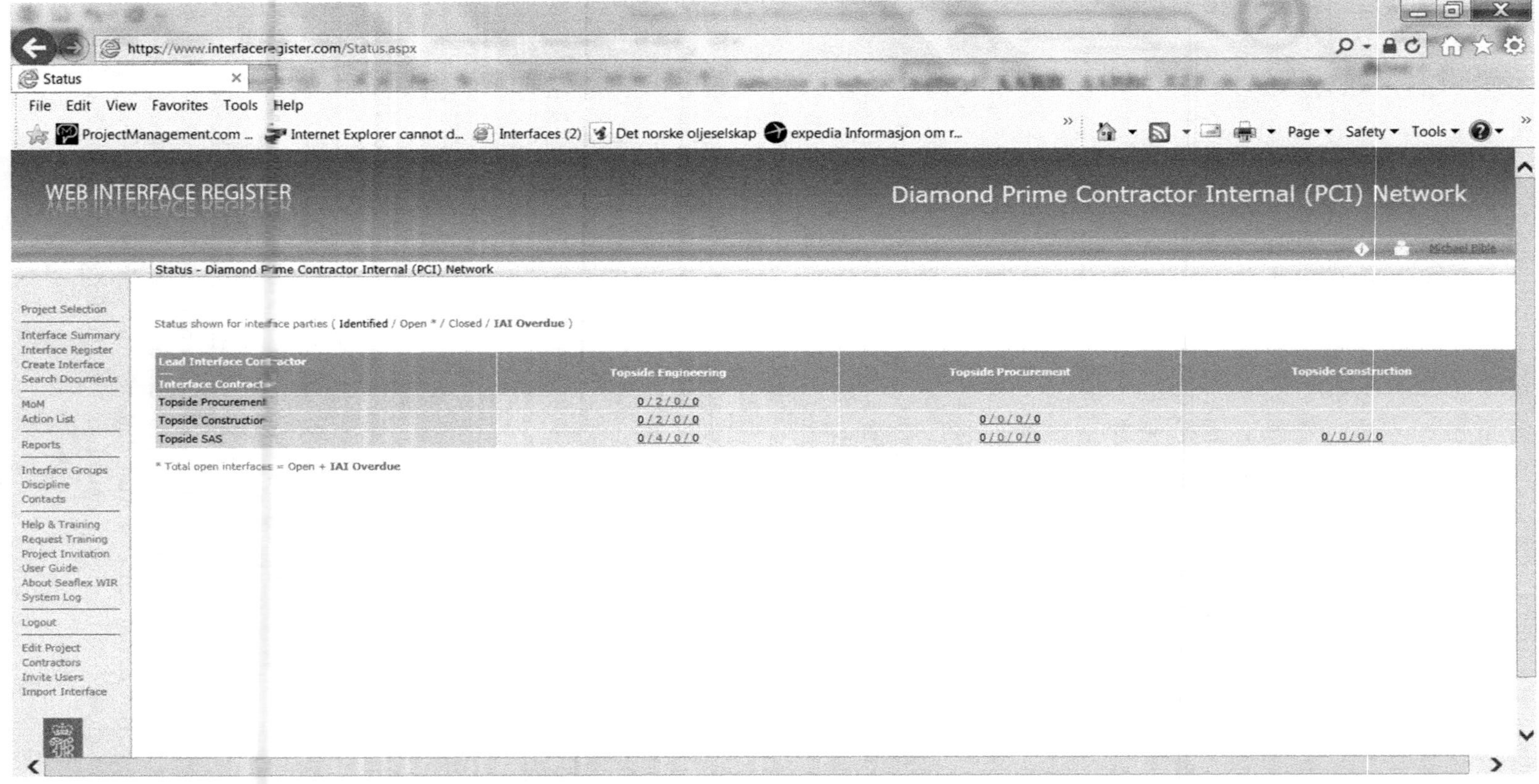

Figure 8.3 Project Diamond—Topside EPC *internal* interface network (SeaFlex WIR)

8.5 INTERFACE PERFORMANCE OVERVIEW

As the project moves deeper into the execution phase, interface activity will intensify across the various interface networks. For a client and its project team, maintaining an overview of interfaces is crucial to identifying issues early. Figure 8.4 provides an interface register screenshot showing an overview of all the interface networks within Project Diamond.

In Figure 8.4, we see a total of six networks being managed by the project. For the sake of simplicity, all the networks fall within the ABC Corporation's Project Diamond interface management system, as shown by the column titled *Company*. In many circumstances, it is common for a project that is integrating into other projects or existing facilities to have its own interface management system while at the same time being an active participant in the interface management systems of the other projects. The owner of this view on a day-to-day basis is the project's interface manager and the client's interface personnel.

All networks are *open* and active as shown under the *Status* column. Once all interface activity has been completed by the interface groups within an interface network, the network can be closed. Typically, this will occur close to the end of the project, as part of the closeout process, which will be covered in Chapter 9. Finally, under the *Interface status* column, we observe a number of interfaces in various states or conditions as noted by the *0/0/0/0* sequence. Recall from earlier chapters that the numbers in these four positions indicate the number of interfaces in each of four states: identified, open, closed, and overdue. Specific interface management software may call these by slightly different names, but all should provide a high-level view at any given time of the status of interfaces in the register.

Although typically the register will be populated with hundreds or even thousands of interface items, the register shown here is only intended to illustrate the concepts described and is thus only sparsely populated.

In this case, the first digit indicates the number of interfaces in the *identified* status. The identified status means the interface item has been raised and entered into the register, but the parties have not yet agreed that it is a valid interface item. Sometimes, one party will raise a potential item that can be easily solved through quick discussion or that really is not related to a system interface. Essentially, these identified interface items are *possible* interface items and will be opened or deleted at the next interface meeting, after the interface parties have reviewed and evaluated their validity. Remember, interface items represent the lowest-level element to be coordinated to resolve related system interfaces, interface issues, and areas (if used). As mentioned previously, some interface management approaches do not use *interface areas or issues*, but rather focus solely on interface item agreements in the interface register in order to resolve system level interfaces between parties.

In total, four interfaces are in the *identified* status, two in the Diamond Sapphire *organization-to-organization* (O2O) network, and two in the *Client's Prime Contractor* (CPC) network. Early in project execution, it is perfectly reasonable to observe a large number of interfaces in this status. This is due to activation of the interface groups. As each group is activated, they begin to enter interface items based on the system interfaces within their scope that are affected by the scope of one or more other interface parties. Interface management needs to monitor items in the identified status to ensure they do not become stagnant; these items should be processed fairly quickly during the next series of interface meetings. Thus, management should observe a rotation of items out of the identified status and their numbers should decrease steadily as interface groups move beyond initial interface activity.

The digit in the second position shows how many interfaces are *open*. This status means that interface items have been reviewed by the interface parties and they have determined the items are valid and are being actively worked by the relevant interface parties within the network. Here we observe a total of 37 interfaces in the open status; 11 in the O2O network, 8 in the PCI network, and finally, 18 in the CPC network.

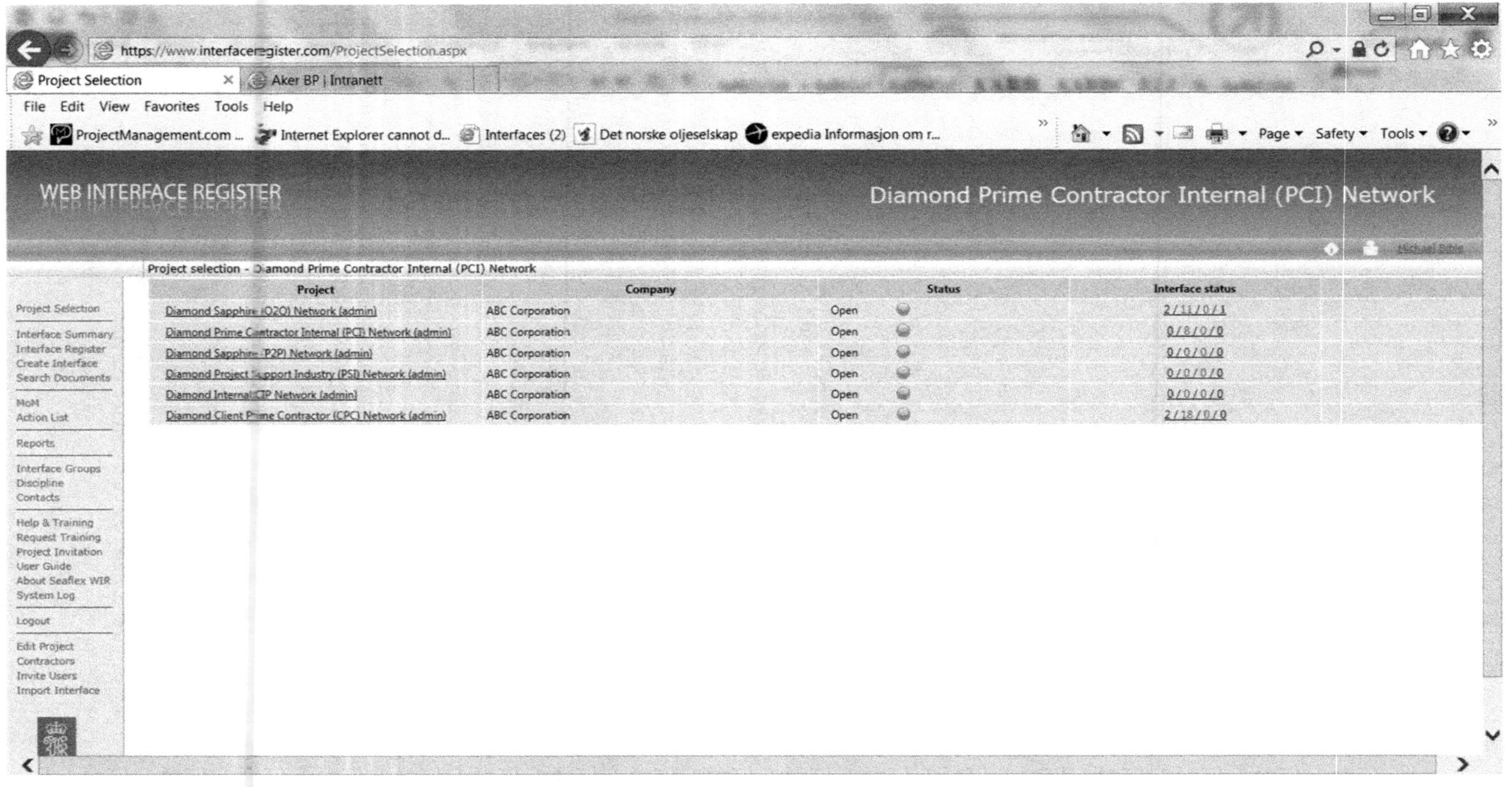

Figure 8.4 Project Diamond—interface network overall status

The third digit shows the number of items closed, which is "0" in our Figure 8.4 example. Finally, the fourth and last digit shows the number of items that are in overdue status. Remember, this status means the interface remains open and is past its planned resolution date. Regardless of the number of interfaces or their distribution across interface networks, this simplistic overview of all networks is an important performance view for the client's project team and helps to identify developing problems early. These kinds of views are essential during project execution to provide an understanding of how well interface parties are planning or even whether they're interacting at all. Key performance indicators are derived from these statistics and can be used to report the performance health of the project's interface management system to adjacent and higher management.

8.5.1 Subordinate (Drill-Down) Management Overviews

Within the project, it is also possible to monitor the interface performance of subordinate groups as shown in Figure 8.5. Recall from earlier discussion that this network supports the interfaces of the client's contractor network. Remember, the Project Diamond development concept called for the project to be segmented into several scopes of work and contracted out to several different specialty companies. Thus, this network allows these independent entities to coordinate, communicate, and collaborate in a common forum that is governed by the client's project team.

During project execution, it is common for one contractor to be named as a *lead interface contractor* (LIC) due to the criticality of the contractor's scope of work; meaning that one contractor may be responsible for a part of the project scope that is crucial to many, or all other, parts of the project. The LIC takes a central role during project execution because this company's scope will be most affected if interfaces are not aligned. Thus, they potentially have the most to lose if things go wrong. The box in Figure 8.5 shows Jacket EPC as the LIC in the interface group that contains Jacket EPC and Topside EOC. For an LIC, maintaining an overview of interface progress in the contractor network is very important.

The LIC has the ability to track and analyze the status of each interface within each group as shown in Figure 8.6. Within the box in Figure 8.5, we see there are five *open* interfaces—0/5/0/0 (identified/open/closed/overdue)—within this group. Selecting or *clicking on* this group in the tool brings up the interface group's detailed interface register. Figure 8.6 shows the interface register for the Topside EPC & Jacket EPC interface group, one of the interface groups within the CPC network.

The interface register contains a detailed listing of all interface items between the parties in an interface group. A similar interface register exists for each interface group within each of the other interface networks. As shown in the interface register, there are a total of five interfaces. Again, only a few interfaces are populated to illustrate the concept, but, in reality, there may be several hundred interface items within a group's register in various status conditions (i.e., identified, open, closed, and overdue).

The statistics provided by these performance views are fairly basic and simplistic, but give a quick indication of how the groups within the network are performing. Naturally, the client will also maintain an overview of this network as with all networks, but it is the LIC contractor who needs to be vigilant particularly if they have a contractual obligation (usually to the client).

This is why a mature automated tool should be used to manage high volumes of interface items and their associated information. Several project teams have attempted to use Microsoft Excel or other spreadsheet software, which may be fine for small, straightforward project developments, but for large-scale complex projects, managing the amount of interaction and number of interrelated agreements is nearly impossible to achieve effectively or efficiently through simple spreadsheets.

Ultimately, failure to maintain oversight of interface performance may result in financial consequences—direct and indirect. Contractual obligations may require performance levels to be

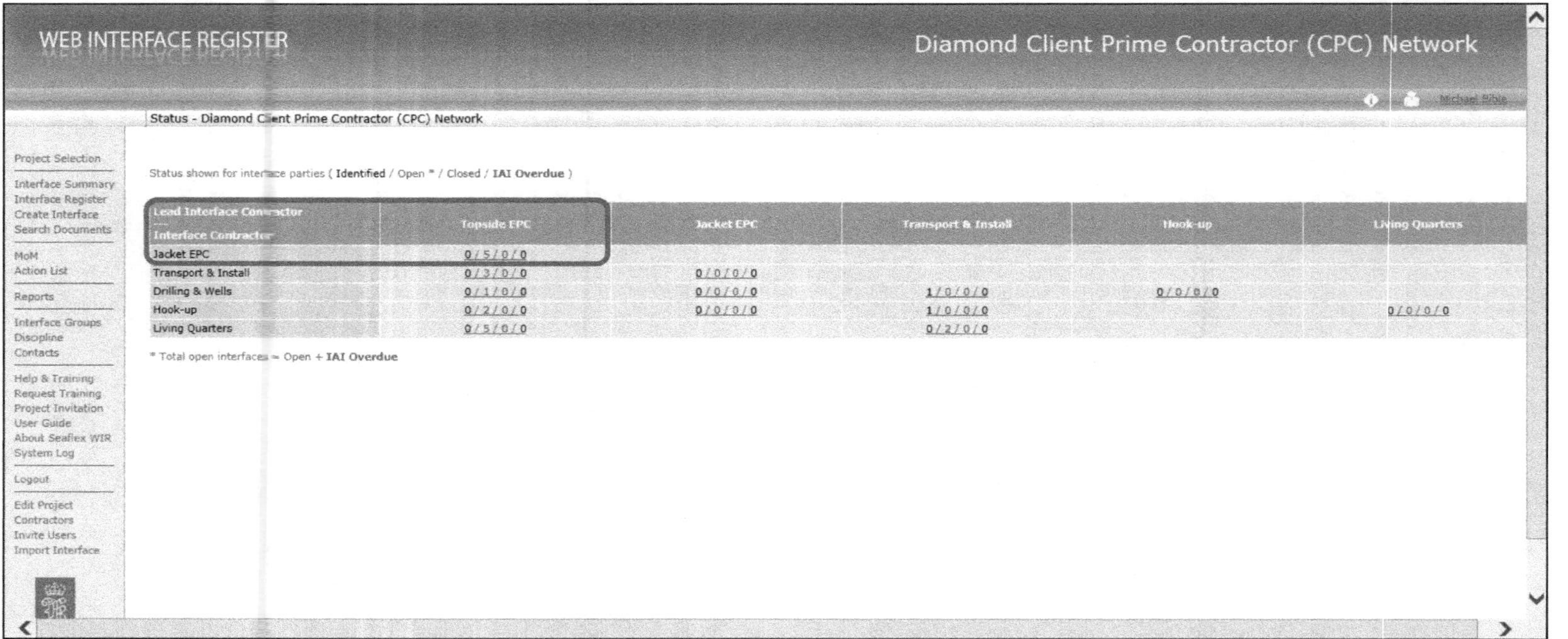

Figure 8.5 Project Diamond—CPC network—interface status

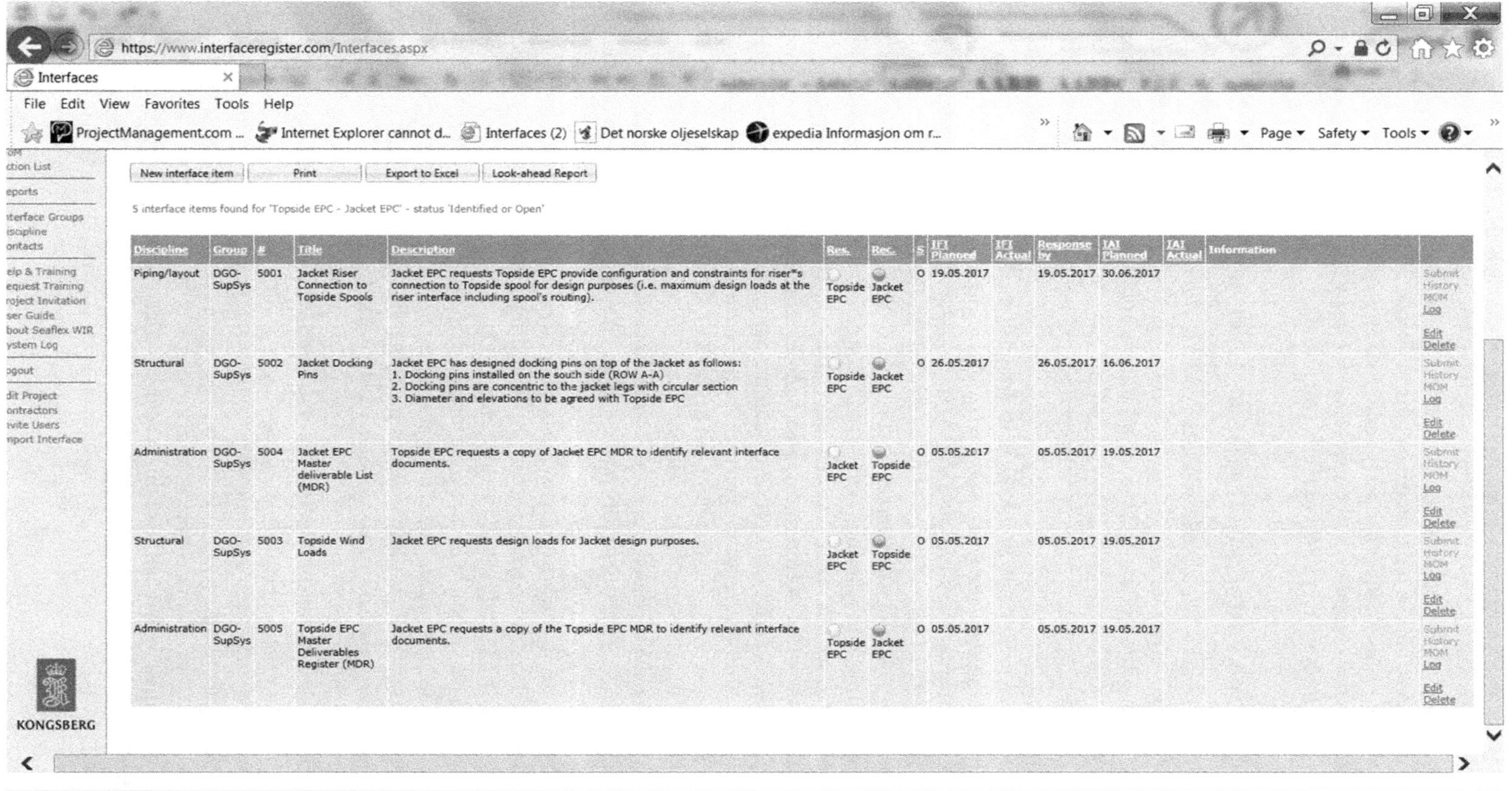

Discipline	Group	#	Title	Description	Res.	Rec.	S	IFI Planned	IFI Actual	Response by	IAI Planned	IAI Actual	Information	
Piping/layout	DGO-SupSys	5001	Jacket Riser Connection to Topside Spools	Jacket EPC requests Topside EPC provide configuration and constraints for riser"s connection to Topside spool for design purposes (i.e. maximum design loads at the riser interface including spool's routing).	Topside EPC	Jacket EPC	O	19.05.2017		19.05.2017	30.06.2017			Submit History MOM Log Edit Delete
Structural	DGO-SupSys	5002	Jacket Docking Pins	Jacket EPC has designed docking pins on top of the Jacket as follows: 1. Docking pins installed on the south side (ROW A-A) 2. Docking pins are concentric to the jacket legs with circular section 3. Diameter and elevations to be agreed with Topside EPC	Topside EPC	Jacket EPC	O	26.05.2017		26.05.2017	16.06.2017			Submit History MOM Log Edit Delete
Administration	DGO-SupSys	5004	Jacket EPC Master deliverable List (MDR)	Topside EPC requests a copy of Jacket EPC MDR to identify relevant interface documents.	Jacket EPC	Topside EPC	O	05.05.2017		05.05.2017	19.05.2017			Submit History MOM Log Edit Delete
Structural	DGO-SupSys	5003	Topside Wind Loads	Jacket EPC requests design loads for Jacket design purposes.	Jacket EPC	Topside EPC	O	05.05.2017		05.05.2017	19.05.2017			Submit History MOM Log Edit Delete
Administration	DGO-SupSys	5005	Topside EPC Master Deliverables Register (MDR)	Jacket EPC requests a copy of the Topside EPC MDR to identify relevant interface documents.	Topside EPC	Jacket EPC	O	05.05.2017		05.05.2017	19.05.2017			Submit History MOM Log Edit Delete

Figure 8.6 CPC network—Topside/Jacket interface register

maintained by a specific contractor. When those levels are breached, penalties could be triggered in the corresponding contract (direct consequences). Interface parties may also be negatively affected by poor interface performance by another interface party. For example, continued delay in resolving interface items can result in the resequencing of planned work, which ultimately results in additional work or rework, thus causing the other party additional time and cost (indirect consequences). Unfortunately, this is often a situation that contributes to the nasty business of claims between client and contractors—often long after a project has been completed.

8.5.2 Cooperation Partners Management Overview

As noted previously in this book, projects are less often stand-alone, and rather, more often require integration with larger ecosystems of enterprise technology systems, existing facilities, and/or other ongoing projects. In some cases, such as in the oil and gas industry, cooperation between competing companies is necessary; for example, competing oil and gas companies may join together to develop a particular offshore area that extends across several exploration and production licenses owned by different companies.

One way to avoid or mitigate problems is to establish a cooperative agreement of some type, which specifies key aspects of the relationship between the parties. Often, however, these agreements are made at a high management level and may be quite vague. Normally, the details specifying how the agreement will be carried out are more precisely defined at a lower level by the project teams assisted by various organizational departments.

Identifying, aligning, and agreeing on the details describing how the organizations will function together is vital to the success of the project(s) affected by the cooperation. Figure 8.7 illustrates the status of Project Diamond's O2O interface network. As a reminder, this is the network for the various companies sponsoring interfacing projects (Diamond, Sapphire, Oil Pipeline, and Gas Pipeline) to agree on the details of the cooperation agreement between the companies. It shows, for example, one overdue interface between Project Sapphire, led by the XYZ Corporation, and Project Diamond, led by the ABC Corporation.

Cooperation agreement-related interfaces can include when two companies need to agree on methods to commercially measure hydrocarbons in an oil and gas project or to ensure commercial boundaries align with system boundaries. Sometimes, integrating one project to another requires some work to be done on the host system. Interfaces related to cooperation agreements can be associated with who will perform what work, and establishing discrete and specific scope boundaries.

Although it is possible to place all the interface groups into a single project network, breaking the interface groups into multiple networks by interface type (e.g., CPC, project-to-existing-system, O2O, etc.) as described in Chapter 5 can enable managing and reporting interfaces in a simpler manner. The screenshots here show a way to decompose interface complexity in a practical manner by segmenting related types of interfaces into interface networks tailored to the specific interface needs of the organization and project.

Analysis of the simple statistics depicted on the interface network status can provide potential warning signs of brewing problems that might otherwise lurk below the surface. A quick look at trends such as a growing number of interfaces in the *identified* status or an increasing number of *overdue* interfaces can be early signs of technical challenges, social interaction problems, poor planning, and the like. Closer inspection is required to uncover the root cause. The aim is to identify and mitigate any situation that can arise that negatively affects an interface partner or group, and of course, to prevent any interface issue from affecting the overall project. In essence, these basic statistics in the interface register are the first line of defense to uncover interface management problems and rectify them before they become serious. As mentioned earlier in the book, the LIP is always

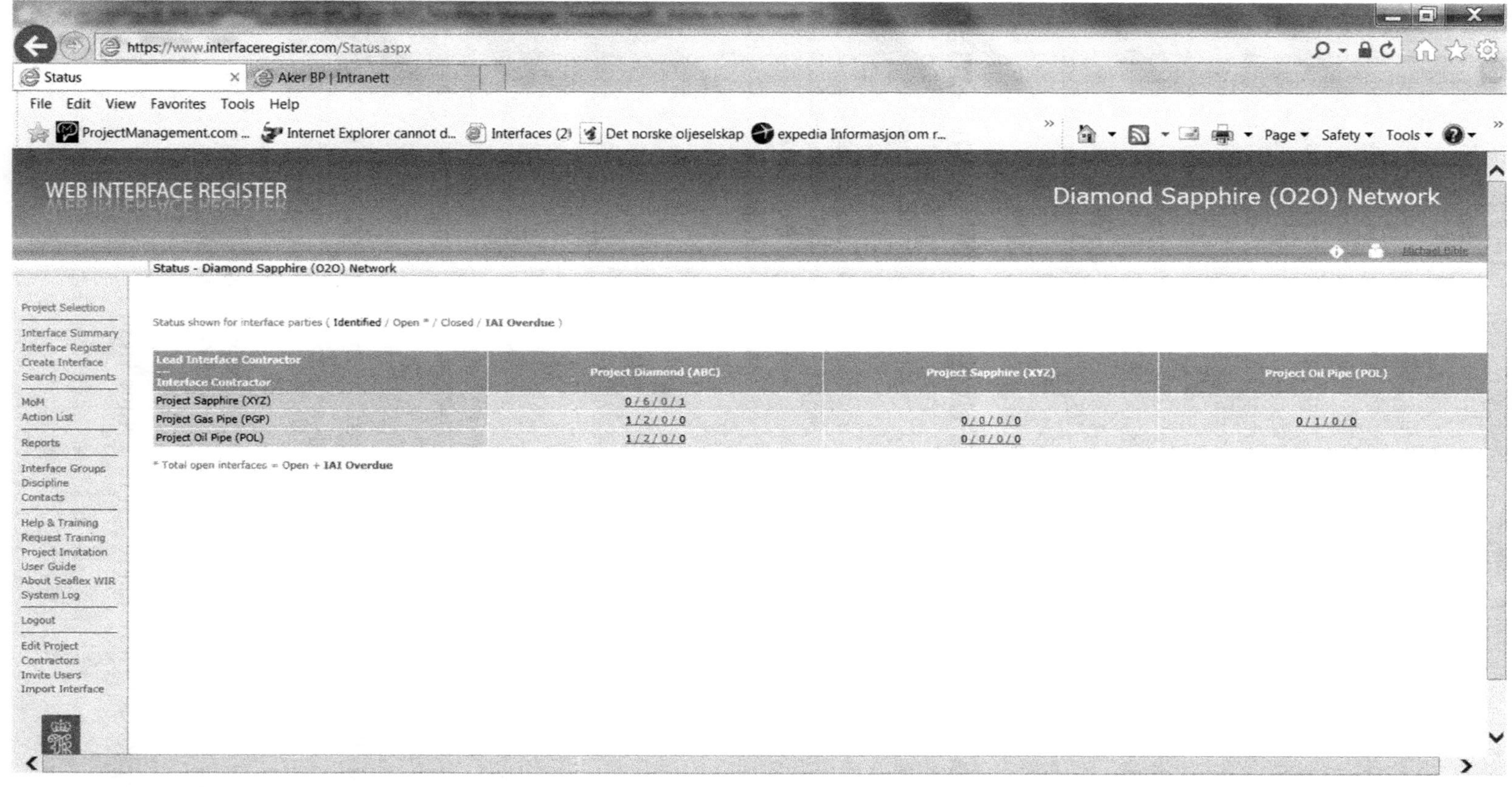

Figure 8.7 Project Diamond—organization-to-organization interface status

responsible for ensuring that the interface register for their respective interface group is updated and maintained accurately; the client's project interface manager verifies that the LIPs (and LICs) are updating and maintaining the interface registers for their respective interface groups.

The ICD, the interface register, and the functionality provided by the register's automated tool exist to help manage high volumes of interface activity. These tools are aids; they do not make decisions and they cannot take automatic corrective action. As mentioned previously, interface management is about people—first and foremost. These tools help people manage by structuring, visualizing, illustrating, etc. But the people are ultimately responsible for managing the interfaces; and they are the ones who must utilize these tools to support investigation and the critical thinking necessary to ensure effective progress in developing the interfaces. As stated, the number of interfaces depicted in the illustrations provided has been kept to a minimum for clarity and the quantity is certainly not representative of the thousands that will exist in the register for a typical large-scale complex project. In the natural course of interacting between a large number of entities and a large quantity of people over hundreds of complicated issues, there will undoubtedly be numerous obstacles along the way that can more easily be identified and addressed by using effective interface management documentation and tools.

8.6 MANAGING INTERFACE DESIGN AND AGREEMENT

In Chapter 9, we will cover interface verification and ways to ensure that agreements that are recorded in the interface register are implemented in the respective scopes of work by each interface party. However, in this current chapter, we want to highlight the connections between the ICD and the interface register and between the ICD and the interface verification traceability matrix (IVTM). The IVTM provides a management tool to assess and record that the solutions agreed upon in the interface register and documented in the ICD have actually been implemented by the interface parties for each interface item.

8.6.1 Interface Verification Traceability Matrix

Whereas the ICD has a direct relationship with interface items recorded in the interface register, it is also directly connected to the IVTM. The ICD, or similar document, is the source for all system interfaces. In essence, it acts as the *scope* baseline document for system interfaces. The project's interface management process, including the interface register, acts as the mechanism to align these system interfaces across the project's disparate parties. The IVTM provides a means to trace that each agreement on each interface item in the interface register has been completed to corresponding specifications documented in the ICD; it is a means of verifying that all agreements have been completed and delivered by the respective parties.

In essence, the IVTM provides the mechanism to apply quality control techniques, such as inspection, test, demonstration, and analysis, in order to confirm that all facets of each system interface have been agreed upon and incorporated in the corresponding scope of work deliverables; in other words, to ensure that the interface agreement associated with an individual system interface has been incorporated in the relevant designs and deliveries. Activities associated with confirming and verifying interface agreements commence early in the project execution phase.

8.6.2 Approaches to Closing an Interface Item

Regardless of when and how an interface item in the interface register is closed, it must always be verified. By *verified*, we mean that an independent party outside of the interface group has conducted a review of the interface item to ensure that it has been implemented into the scope of deliveries of the relevant parties. Once an agreement is made, it cannot be assumed that the agreement will automatically be implemented in the respective designs, procurement activities, or construction; rather, some form of physical verification must be performed. We will talk more specifically about how this is accomplished in Chapter 9, but the main focus now is to understand the basis for closing an interface item in the register since that will impact how verification activities are performed. For the sake of simplicity, this responsibility belongs to the client's project interface manager or titled person with interface responsibility.

We describe two basic approaches that can be used to determine when to *close* individual interface items in the group's interface register. In the first approach, an interface item is closed as soon as both parties reach an agreement on the principles of the item under consideration. For example, an agreement is reached on the location of a junction box for the two parties to make electrical connections. As soon as the parties agree on the location, the interface item is closed. Once the item is closed, it moves to the archive section of the interface register.

Using this first approach, we have no proof that the agreed upon location was ever actually implemented into the design or physically placed in the right location. In this approach, interface verification requires both (1) a review of detailed engineering drawings to confirm the location was added to the relevant documents and (2) a physical check of its placement during installation to confirm that it is indeed placed in the right location. Although this approach minimizes the number of interfaces that are *open* in the interface register, it can also give management a false sense of security that interface issues have been resolved if they base their assessment on what they see in the register. Be careful not to assume that interface agreements will be implemented as agreed. This approach is certainly fine if it is accompanied by a commensurate verification process; one that verifies both the correctness of engineering documentation and the physical compliance in delivered scope. A major cause of late-stage interface integration issues is a failure to ensure that the specifications upon which agreement is reached are integrated into the design and that everything works properly when the items are delivered and installed.

The second approach is to close the interface items in the register only after the agreements have been verified through receipt of final documentation. In this approach, the parties agree to a solution to the item, but wait to close the item until the final documentation (such as detailed engineering drawings) has been updated and reviewed by the other interface party. If accepted, then the interface item is closed. This approach leads to interface items remaining in the *open* status for longer periods, which also means a larger total of interface items remain in the open status. This can become concerning for management that are unfamiliar with the details of the project's interface management system. However, this approach requires less intensive independent interface verification after it is closed. Typically, a third party can independently verify closed interfaces under this approach much more quickly than with the first approach since the archived record normally includes all of the final documentation. It is important to clarify which approach is being used and to ensure that it is followed and understood by management.

8.7 PROJECT PLAN OFFSETS

In large-scale complex projects that are characterized by complicated project development strategies (i.e., using many different entities to contribute to project development), it is normal to experience *offsets* in project plans. Offsets are misalignments between project plans that are dependent upon each other. They are caused by combining project plans from multiple entities or variances in actual accomplishment by one or more of the contributing entities. For example, each entity that is contributing to the project may have developed the *optimal* project plan to deliver its respective scope to the project; however, when the individual project plans are assembled as a cohesive overall project plan, the plans from these multiple entities may no longer align. The challenge of dealing with these offsets can vary depending on the severity of the misalignment and the amount of control a party has over the misalignment. Sometimes, the offsets only create minor schedule clashes that can be easily adjusted in coordination with other dependent (interface) parties.

8.7.1 Project Plan *Offsets*—Minor Impact

Project plan *offsets* are a common challenge in managing interfaces during project execution where planning dates in the interface register can be updated based on changes to the schedule. At a high level, the project plan may contain major activities, critical events, and milestones. However, it is common to shift around individual activities within a work package to accommodate the real-time situations. For example, an unexpected illness of a key specialized resource results in a delay of a specific detailed engineering drawing. In this situation, work does not stop. Rather, the engineering drawing is rescheduled and the engineering department adjusts the work schedule. At the detailed day-to-day or week-to-week planning level, there are always situations that arise that have to be dealt with in real time. These situations are a common theme in interface meetings and typically result in adjustment to the planned dates for individual interfaces.

First, it is important to understand the basic concept of an interface need between the two parties and how it is accounted for within the interface register. Project plan *offsets* by either party influence activity between the parties in the interface register. Figure 8.8 contains a box encompassing the planned and actual date columns for the Jacket EPC/Topside EPC interface group.

8.7.1.1 Interface Item—Receiving & Responsible

The interface register shown in Figure 8.8 houses interface items between the parties of an interface group, which normally consists of two interface parties. Each of these interface parties has the capability to initiate an interface item with the other. The initiator of an interface in the Seaflex WIR system is termed the *receiving* party. This simply means the party that initiated the interface item is receiving something from the other party. The party providing something to the initiator is called the *responsible* party since they are responsible for providing the information. It is typical for each party to assume both roles as shown in Figure 8.8.

In Figure 8.8, we see *Topside EPC* as both the responsible (column heading: *Res.*) for three interface items and the receiving (column heading: *Rec.*) party for two interface items; this designation is solely dependent upon which party raised the interface item. This is natural since both parties have needs and can initiate an interface item toward the other party. Regardless of the interface register tool, this basic relationship exists, although the naming convention may be different. It could be that other tools use words such as *initiator* and *provider* or *requestor* and *submitter*. The naming convention is not important—rather, the main concept to understand is that one party has an interface need and the other party must respond.

A change in either interface party's project plan can create a ripple effect in the interface register. When dates are set in the interface register, the parties are expected to adhere to these dates. In fact, work flow and processes are planned based on these dates. When a party fails to meet these dates, it can create additional work flow problems for the other interface party. Thus, small project plan adjustments can have significant impact on interface parties if they are not addressed as early as possible by the parties.

8.7.1.2 Interface Item Planning Dates

It is common for interface management tools to contain some method for planning interface items. As shown in the Seaflex WIR tool, these are characterized by dates under the headings of:

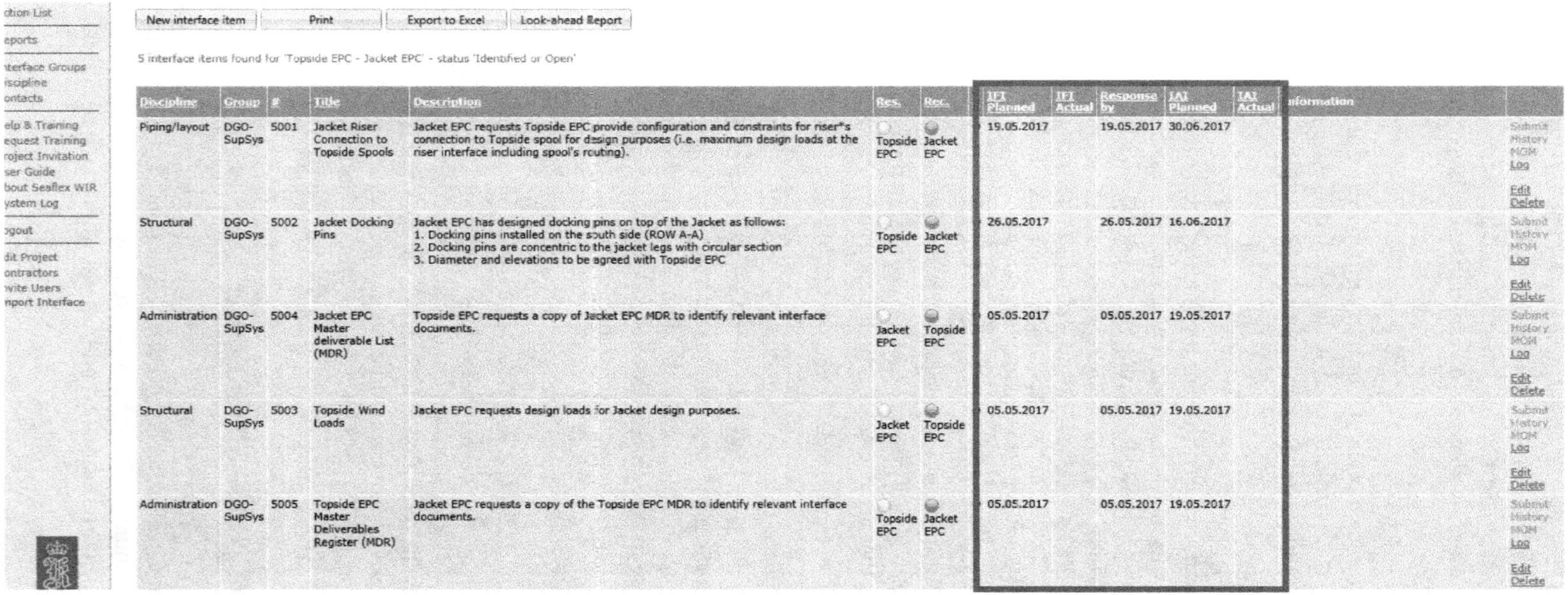

ction List
eports
nterface Groups
iscipline
ontacts
elp & Training
equest Training
roject Invitation
ser Guide
bout Seaflex WIR
ystem Log
ogout
dit Project
ontractors
vite Users
nport Interface

New interface item | Print | Export to Excel | Look-ahead Report

5 interface items found for 'Topside EPC - Jacket EPC' - status 'Identified or Open'

Discipline	Group	#	Title	Description	Res.	Rec.	IFI Planned	IFI Actual	Response by	IAI Planned	IAI Actual	Information	
Piping/layout	DGO-SupSys	5001	Jacket Riser Connection to Topside Spools	Jacket EPC requests Topside EPC provide configuration and constraints for riser*s connection to Topside spool for design purposes (i.e. maximum design loads at the riser interface including spool's routing).	Topside EPC	Jacket EPC	19.05.2017		19.05.2017	30.06.2017			Submit History MOM Log Edit Delete
Structural	DGO-SupSys	5002	Jacket Docking Pins	Jacket EPC has designed docking pins on top of the Jacket as follows: 1. Docking pins installed on the south side (ROW A-A) 2. Docking pins are concentric to the jacket legs with circular section 3. Diameter and elevations to be agreed with Topside EPC	Topside EPC	Jacket EPC	26.05.2017		26.05.2017	16.06.2017			Submit History MOM Log Edit Delete
Administration	DGO-SupSys	5004	Jacket EPC Master deliverable List (MDR)	Topside EPC requests a copy of Jacket EPC MDR to identify relevant interface documents.	Jacket EPC	Topside EPC	05.05.2017		05.05.2017	19.05.2017			Submit History MOM Log Edit Delete
Structural	DGO-SupSys	5003	Topside Wind Loads	Jacket EPC requests design loads for Jacket design purposes.	Jacket EPC	Topside EPC	05.05.2017		05.05.2017	19.05.2017			Submit History MOM Log Edit Delete
Administration	DGO-SupSys	5005	Topside EPC Master Deliverables Register (MDR)	Jacket EPC requests a copy of the Topside EPC MDR to identify relevant interface documents.	Topside EPC	Jacket EPC	05.05.2017		05.05.2017	19.05.2017			Submit History MOM Log Edit Delete

Figure 8.8 Topside EPC/Jacket EPC interface register—planning dates

IFI (interface first issue) Planned, IFI Actual, Response by, IAI (interface approved issue) Planned, and *IAI Actual.* In other interface registers, these dates may be called something else or have a slightly different visual appearance. Regardless, the interface tool should have some capability for planning interface items and for recording planned and actual dates for issue and response.

8.7.1.2.1 IFI Planned

This is the planned date agreed on by the interface group as to when the interface item will be responded to by the *responsible* party. In essence, the two parties have set this date as part of an interface meeting discussion and agreed after reviewing the project plan and work package dates.

8.7.1.2.2 IFI Actual

This is the date the responsible party actually responded to the interface item. Although this field is left blank in Figure 8.8, this metric is a good way to track the *responsiveness* of an interface party. If a particular interface party is routinely missing the planned date, and the *IFI actual* is later than the *IFI planned*, this is a warning sign of developing problems. These situations need to be investigated to ascertain why this is the case. Specifically, the client should take a special interest in these situations as the client can exert a degree of influence that may not be possible by the other interface party.

8.7.1.2.3 Response by Date

The *Response by* date simply means the date by which the current action is due. This metric helps to quickly sort the register to identify actions that are pending in the near future and aids in monitoring near-term activities that are due. This is especially important for any interfaces that have been identified as *high priority.*

8.7.1.2.4 IAI Planned Date

The *IAI planned* date in the Seaflex WIR simply means the targeted date by which the interface parties have agreed to close the interface item. This is an important date because, in theory, this date is tied to the work schedule; this means that the interface party providing the response has planned to complete the response in accordance with its work schedule, and that the work activities of the receiving party are based on receiving the response (information) by the agreed upon date.

8.7.1.2.5 IAI Actual

As with the IFI actual, the *IAI actual* date is the date the interface parties actually closed the item. If this date is routinely past the planned date, then that is also a warning sign of problems or interface planning dysfunction within the interface group. These situations should be identified and investigated to understand why the resolution of interfaces is slipping past the planned dates. As mentioned previously, it is common for a contractor to claim a *variation* as a result of dysfunctional interface activity. This indicator provides insight into how the group is performing and provides a stimulus to correct situations before they become severe either for the client or other interface parties.

8.7.2 Project Plan *Offsets*—Major Impact

Sometimes, even when the project plan or schedule misalignments appear simple, offsets can pose serious problems. In large-scale complex projects, it is normal to re-baseline the project periodically (e.g., annually or semiannually). By *re-baseline,* we mean to analyze and update the project plan or schedule based on the current situation and henceforth to track performance against the newly baselined plan. In an ideal world, once the project plan is established at the beginning of the project, it remains in effect throughout the project's duration. However, this is rarely the case in large-scale projects spanning many years. While the re-baseline process may not result in many, if any, changes to the high-level plan (i.e., level 1 schedule or project milestones), it can wreak havoc on lower-level activities (i.e., work package activities).

When a project is re-baselined, it is normal to experience significant changes in planned completion dates for work package activities. As interface item plans in the interface register are based on work package activities in the project plan, re-baselining can result in a situation that creates major upheaval in the interface management system. Interface items which were previously progressing normally can suddenly become critical if the new re-baseline adjustments result in the inability of an interface party to provide responses as originally planned in the interface register. This is why having a high priority feature in the interface register tool is important. It provides a means to highlight items that can create negative consequences if not resolved as intended.

8.8 INTERFACE PRIORITY PROCESS

During the project execution phase, several hundred/thousand interfaces can be open at any given time. When combined with the project plan offsets and the disruptions created due to re-baselining, it is useful to have some method for highlighting interface items in the interface register that become unexpectedly critical. As shown in the box highlighting the status column in Figure 8.9, the interface register contains a column marked S, which simply means *interface status*. In the illustration, we see the letter O, which means the item is open.

In the first two interface items listed in the register, notice a triangle under the letter O. This triangle denotes that the interface item is high priority. This simple descriptor aids in visually identifying items that require immediate attention. Although the specific implications of failure to resolve a high priority interface may not be known, the purpose of the indicator is to inform management that an interface item is high priority. It is not necessary to know the exact implications should the interface not be resolved; rather, the importance of this indicator is to inform management to focus attention on specific items in the short term to prevent unintended consequences.

In practice, the interface party who initiated the interface item can assign this as a *high priority* designator simply by editing the item in the register. The logical question is: what prevents an interface party from assigning this designation to all of its interface items? The interface register is transparent to the client's interface management team. The validity of each high-priority interface is verified by the client to ensure that the system is not being manipulated, which can be a valid concern.

This feature can be very important after any re-baseline process when activities affecting interfaces are shifted. Using this feature after the re-baseline process helps to highlight these misalignments; it is recommended when an interface item is first identified or when changes external to the interface group (such as re-baselining) affect the criticality of an interface. It can and should be used to allow the parties to align their efforts to the most urgent interface issues.

Of course, the interface management system is much more than an interface register tool. But the interface register and its supporting tool are part of the larger system and provide important support for information exchange and management activities. Certainly, interfaces can be managed using spreadsheet tools such as Microsoft Excel, or even by using a legal notepad—but readily available automated tools make the process much more efficient and effective given the large volume of interface data, information exchange, and the complex relationships that are associated with interfaces.

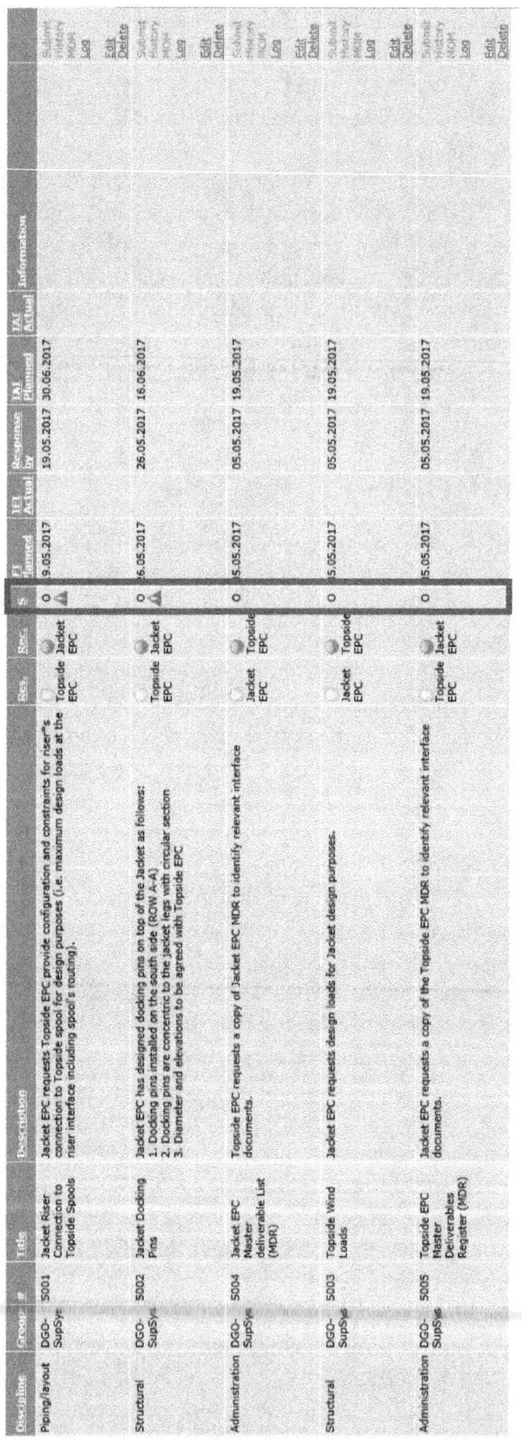

Discipline
Contacts
Help & Training
Request Training
Project Invitation
User Guide
About Seaflex WIR
System Log
Logout
Edit Project
Contractors
Invite Users
Import Interface

Discipline	Group	#	Title	Description	Res.	Rec.	S	FI Planned	IFI Actual	Response by	IAI Planned	IAI Actual	Information		
Piping/layout	DGO-SupSys	5001	Jacket Riser Connection to Topside Spools	Jacket EPC requests Topside EPC provide configuration and constraints for riser"s connection to Topside spool for design purposes (i.e. maximum design loads at the riser interface including spool's routing).	Topside EPC	Jacket EPC	O ⚠	9.05.2017		19.05.2017	30.06.2017				Submit History MOM Log Edit Delete
Structural	DGO-SupSys	5002	Jacket Docking Pins	Jacket EPC has designed docking pins on top of the Jacket as follows: 1. Docking pins installed on the south side (ROW A-A) 2. Docking pins are concentric to the jacket legs with circular section 3. Diameter and elevations to be agreed with Topside EPC	Topside EPC	Jacket EPC	O ⚠	6.05.2017		26.05.2017	16.06.2017				Submit History MOM Log Edit Delete
Administration	DGO-SupSys	5004	Jacket EPC Master deliverable List (MDR)	Topside EPC requests a copy of Jacket EPC MDR to identify relevant interface documents.	Jacket EPC	Topside EPC	O	5.05.2017		05.05.2017	19.05.2017				Submit History MOM Log Edit Delete
Structural	DGO-SupSys	5003	Topside Wind Loads	Jacket EPC requests design loads for Jacket design purposes.	Jacket EPC	Topside EPC	O	5.05.2017		05.05.2017	19.05.2017				Submit History MOM Log Edit Delete
Administration	DGO-SupSys	5005	Topside EPC Master Deliverables Register (MDR)	Jacket EPC requests a copy of the Topside EPC MDR to identify relevant interface documents.	Topside EPC	Jacket EPC	O	5.05.2017		05.05.2017	19.05.2017				Submit History MOM Log Edit Delete

Figure 8.9 Interface register—high-priority feature

8.9 INTERFACE MANAGEMENT FORUMS

So far in this chapter our intent was, in part, to clarify some of the factors that can create misalignment, to evaluate their cumulative effect on the project environment, and to decide how to discover and address those factors that are affecting interfaces in order to restore alignment. Another way to maintain alignment, or in some cases re-establish alignment, is to conduct an *interface management forum*. The name of the event is not as important as the function it serves. So the reader should feel free to title the event as they wish. Whatever it is called, an interface management forum is a periodic gathering of key interface, technical, and managerial personnel across the project to review, discuss, analyze, and align interface plans and activities.

Sponsored by the client, interface management forums provide the mechanism to meet face-to-face with key personnel to re-establish interface alignment. This event is especially important when considering the effects of approved PCP, project plan changes due to re-baselining, etc. In large-scale complex projects that are characterized by highly dynamic project environments, it can be quite difficult to maintain alignment among the various entities simply because of the number of adjustments across the various project plans and changes in key project personnel (i.e., some key people leaving and being replaced by new personnel).

In one real-world project with which we are familiar, these forums were held on a scheduled basis (in addition to those that might be needed to address a major change). These interface management forums focused on the upcoming six-month time frame and served as a convenient and efficient way to re-establish interface alignment among the various entities. As client-sponsored events, interface forums are the responsibility of the sponsoring organization's interface manager with assistance from the client's interface management organization.

Conducted as *face-to-face* meetings where possible, these forums focus on specific causative issues or, periodically, highlight significant issues between interface entities resulting from a re-baseline or other change process. As an integrated event, the forum should be attended by the client's interface organization and key interface, technical, and managerial personnel from across the project—especially those with critical activities in the next period or those particularly affected by changes. Based on our real-life experiences, these forums provide a valuable tool for maintaining or regaining interface alignment among company representatives and for refocusing the project's interface management on achievement of the project's near-term goals. Again, the challenge—and thus the purpose of these forums—is to address the disruption caused by the project's dynamic environment and to *get everyone back on the same page*.

By assembling relevant personnel and highlighting what is happening in the project, it becomes much clearer for individual entities to: (1) see the bigger picture and (2) understand how delays in interface activity can adversely affect other parts of the project. Periodically (e.g., annually or semi-annually) bringing all entities together helps to refocus the interface organization, but it also helps in reminding the various entities of the larger goal of project success. Project interface forums can take many forms and be conducted in myriad ways. Figure 8.10 shows a real-life example from a large-scale complex offshore oil and gas project similar to the Project Diamond example reference in this book.

From the agenda in Figure 8.10, the reader can see that all the *objects* (i.e., major project entities such as Living Quarters, Topside, etc.) are represented. This forum provides an opportunity not just to understand the big picture, but also a chance for each interface entity to highlight areas of importance to their respective scopes. In essence, this forum is a working meeting to ensure that all parties have a good understanding of their interface roles going forward. In projects that last several years, these interface forums are quite useful in ensuring that the project's interface management function continues to perform well, but they also provide a proactive way to stay ahead of technical and managerial issues.

- **07:30 –08:00 Reception**
- **08:00 –08:30 Introduction (Project Interface Manager)**
- **08:30 –09:15 Critical Interface Schedule Review (Project Planner)**
- **09:15 –10:00 SURF & Power Cable Update (SURF Interface Lead)**
- **10:00 –10:15 BREAK**
- **10:15 –10:45 Jacket EPC Update (Jacket Interface Lead)**
- **10:45 –11:15 Topside EPC Update (Topside Interface Lead)**
- **11:15 –11:45 Living Quarters (LQ Interface Lead)**
- **11:45 –12:00 Open Discussion**
- **12:00 –13:00 LUNCH**
- **13:00 –13:30 Transportation & Installation Update (T&I Interface Lead)**
- **13:30 –14:00 Flotel/Hook-up (Mechanical Completion Lead)**
- **14:00 –14:30 Commissioning/RFO (Commissioning Lead)**
- **14:30 –15:00 Interface Risk Review (Project Risk Manager)**
- **15:00 –15:15 BREAK**
- **15:15 –16:00 Interface Register Tool, Procedure, Processes, Lessons Learned (All)**
- **16:00 –16:30 Open Discussion**
- **16:30 –17:00 Summary/Action Item Review (Project Interface Manager)**

Figure 8.10 Project interface management forum—agenda (real project)

8.10 INTERFACE DESIGN REVIEWS

Interface design reviews (IDRs) are verification events conducted to ensure interface technical compliance and system integrity. As verification and quality control events, IDRs serve the important function of ensuring that interface technical designs align across different scopes of work and/or areas of responsibility. We mention IDRs in this chapter because—along with ICDs, the interface register, IVTMs, and interface forums—IDRs are a key element in ensuring effective interface management across the project, and also because they are conducted during project execution and thus bear a relationship with other key activities occurring during project execution. In Chapter 9, we discuss interface management in the context of verification of technical compliance and integrity and closeout; in that chapter, we will discuss the content of IDRs in more detail as part of this discussion.

IDRs are formal reviews of technical design artifacts (e.g., drawings, studies, models, simulations, etc.) to verify system design consistency and compliance. In large-scale projects where the project's scope of work is subdivided into several sub-scopes and contracted to different entities, technical compliance and integrity is a significant challenge. IDRs aid in the process of ensuring technical compliance (with regulations, governing documents, and international standards) and integrity (i.e., all scopes of work are designed consistently to applicable compliance requirements). We'll discuss technical compliance and integrity in more detail in Chapter 9, but in essence the goal is to ensure that every entity contributing to the project delivers its respective scope of work in accordance with industry regulations, the client's governing documents, and international standards.

8.11 RELATIONSHIP BETWEEN INTERFACE FORUMS AND DESIGN REVIEWS

Figure 8.11 shows a sample timeline with key activities that are associated with the project's interface management. On the top side of the timeline, we observe events such as *30%, 60%,* and *90% Model Reviews.* These reviews are design reviews of detailed engineering artifacts and typically are focused within a single scope of work. The objective of these reviews is to ensure that technical personnel (for example, the engineering department) design the system according to system requirements and in accordance with design constraints (e.g., regulatory requirements).

Located below the model reviews are events entitled *Interface Forum.* These are the same interface forum events discussed previously in Section 8.9. Here you can see that the interface forums were planned to be conducted following the model reviews. This is intentional. Model reviews typically result in the identification of numerous changes. This is normal since the detailed engineering process is iterative. The intent is to mature the detailed design as engineering progresses from 30% to 90%. These model reviews and the changes they often generate are factors contributing to the dynamic environment that we have been discussing throughout this chapter.

From an interface perspective, changes resulting from these design reviews can drive significant activity between interface parties. In some cases, this may mean revisiting previous interface agreements. As one may expect, this can be quite surprising, controversial, and alarming to interface parties if they are not made aware of when these model reviews will occur. Planning interface forums after results from the model reviews have been generated can greatly assist in ensuring that significant changes affecting interface partners are identified, discussed, and their impact vetted and resolved, all in a timely manner.

Further to the right side of Figure 8.11, we see interface design review events titled *IDR, E-IDR,* and *D&W IDR.* These represent, respectively, the IDR for the project, an extended IDR to further evaluate a certain type of functional interface, and an IDR that focused specifically on the Drilling & Wells (D&W) technical design.

As we see in the timeline in Figure 8.11, these events are planned after the model reviews. In essence, these IDRs are final quality control events to ensure that technical compliance and integrity is maintained across the various system *objects* (e.g., Living Quarters, Topside, etc.). As shown in the figure, IDRs are flexible and can be customized to a variety of situations. For example, the *IDR* event in Figure 8.11 is focused on system functionality (i.e., export hydrocarbons, process hydrocarbons, etc.) and can examine interfaces across major subsystems, packages, areas, and so on, to ensure interface integrity. In this case, during the IDR event, it was decided that signal interfaces would require an extended interface design review (E-IDR). In the *E-IDR* event, we perform verification of interfaces across various *signal nodes.* This type of IDR ensures the integrity of interface signals across systems, subsystems, components, areas, and so on. Finally, the *D&W IDR* shows that IDRs can be focused on specific operational activities. In this case, D&W operational activities were the focus. For offshore oil and gas projects, D&W activities are critical, especially in the well start-up and handover phase. Other industries, of course, have their own specific kinds of critical activities.

The main point in this discussion is to think critically about how to structure interface management activities beyond the day-to-day interaction between interface parties. As we have stated repeatedly, project interface management is as much about people as it is the system interfaces themselves. These IDRs served as integrated interface verification events covering the entire operating environment. Through the IDR process, as well as maintaining focus on the safety and effectiveness of system functionality, these design reviews provide a logical and thorough assessment of the overall design and interfaces across combinations of scopes of work, systems, subsystems, and areas of responsibility. The desired outcome of the IDR process is the identification of gaps and deficiencies

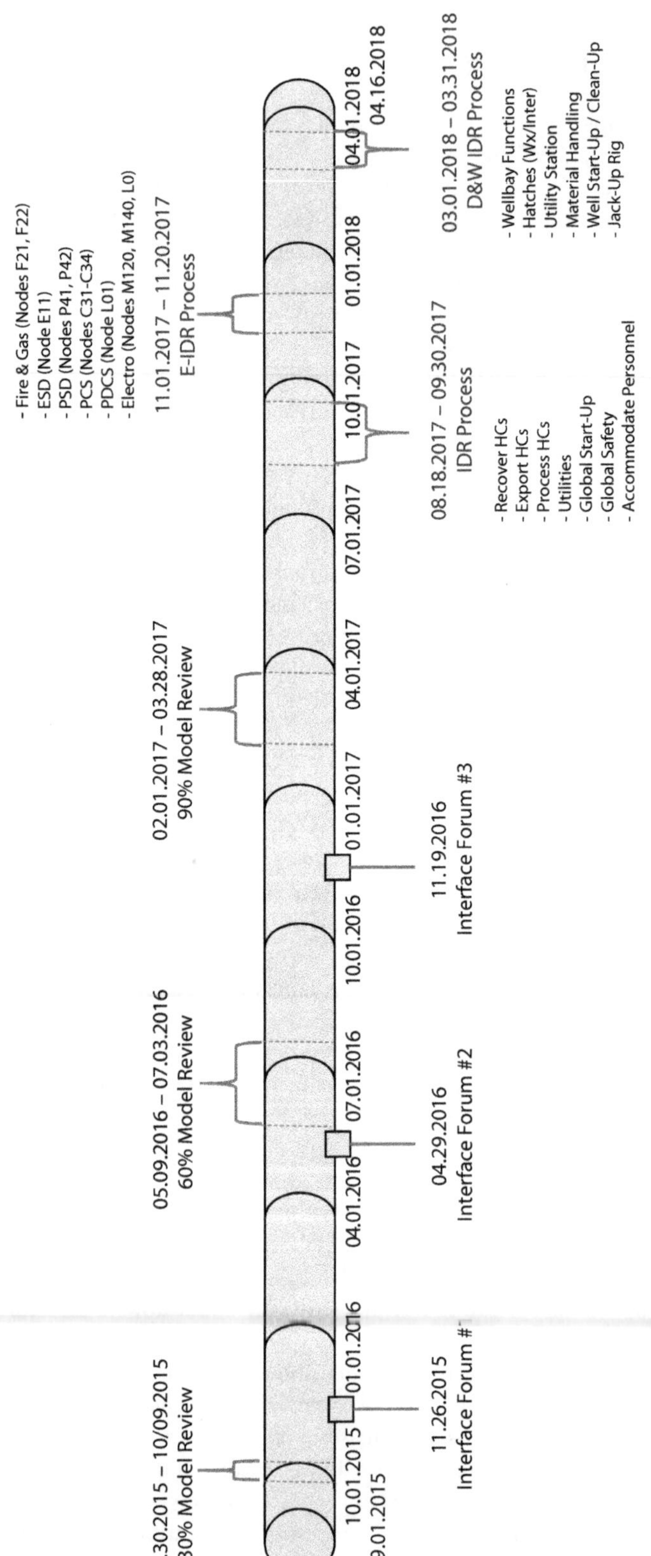

Figure 8.11 Timeline showing relationship between interface forums and design (model) reviews

affecting system functionality so they can be addressed or the confirmation of complete technical integrity across the system architecture.

8.12 SUMMARY

Managing system interfaces during the project execution phase is a difficult challenge that is exacerbated by several uncontrollable factors that influence the project environment. The undeniable truth is that these challenges will exist on every large-scale complex project. In this chapter, we discussed some practical ways of using tools (interface register, ICDs, IVTMs) and techniques (interface forums, IDR, etc.) to minimize these challenges and prevent issues from becoming major problems. Successful interface management during project execution starts with people, and with providing an environment that facilitates and supports professional collaboration; the people-side means establishing an environment in which independent parties can build trust and cooperation while providing a mechanism to arbitrate among the parties in order to overcome perceived impasses.

Against the backdrop of the system architecture, the project's development concept plays a significant role in how to structure and manage interfaces during execution. The system architecture and the contract strategy help to drive both the interface register that contains management information (status, agreements, etc.) about the interfaces, and the one or more corresponding ICDs that contain details about the interfaces. The IVTM provides the means to map the items and agreements in the interface register to their traceability in the technical documentation provided in the ICDs.

Using interface forums as a means to maintain alignment of the disparate interface entities helps to identify and solve potential issues before they become problems. Finally, conducting interface verification and design reviews confirms that what has been agreed to by the parties has been incorporated into their respective scopes of work. All of the tools, techniques, processes, etc., when used together, help to establish an environment by which people representing various organizations can collaborate to deliver their respective scopes of work all in the best interests of the project.

In Chapter 9, we focus on interface management and its connection to technical compliance and integrity, verification activities, and closeout activities. Interface management, like projects, has a life cycle. As the project progresses through the execution phase, system interfaces become agreed upon, verified, and closed. As the project or a major component approaches its end, closeout activities are necessary to archive required data and information, which may be needed to support follow-on operations, contract claims, or legal disputes.

8.13 REFERENCES

Coreworx Interface Manager. Coreworx. (2017). Retrieved from http://www.coreworx.com/coreworx-products/interface-management/.

Seaflex WIR. Kongsberg. (2017). Retrieved from https://www.km.kongsberg.com/ks/web/nokbg0240.nsf/AllWeb/2F6A830C73FEAC55C1257F72004EC275?OpenDocument.

9

Interface Management Verification and Closeout

"Begin at the beginning . . . and go till you come to the end, then stop."
—Lewis Carroll

As mentioned in the previous chapter, the main objective of interface activity during the project execution phase is to align system interfaces across different scope and responsibility boundaries as early as possible in project development. Ideally, interface groups are formed immediately after contract award (i.e., among contractors) or establishment of the project team (i.e., with other projects or existing systems), and interface activity to align common system interfaces commences early in the project execution phase. Although in a less than complex situation, all interface activity might commence early in project execution, in most large-scale complex projects, activities to align system interfaces will usually continue throughout project execution as the project progresses through detailed engineering design, procurement, construction, and installation—and commissioning or validation. In such projects—often lasting several years—it is quite normal to experience project changes and system development updates as new information is developed or discovered throughout the engineering, procurement, and construction (EPC) phases. Regardless of when the interface agreements are reached, there is nearly always a time gap between reaching agreement on interfaces and actually implementing those agreements as deliverables.

In this chapter, we discuss the role of interface verification and how it contributes to technical compliance and technical system and asset integrity. We also address the activity associated with closing down the project's interface management system. In essence, this chapter focuses on activities that occur after interface agreements are reached by the interface parties. Ultimately, at the end of the project, the aim is to assemble and integrate deliverables from various entities to constitute a fully operational system. However, how can the client know agreements between the interface parties are incorporated into their respective scopes of work? Is it presumptuous to say that all agreements will automatically be implemented? Who ensures this is the case? These are logical questions—and the answer is dependent upon the client's risk attitude, resources, and organizational preferences, among other factors.

As we have stated throughout this book, interface management is a risk reduction activity. In essence, by implementing interface management, project teams are contributing to preventing unexpected development and integration problems among various entities that are contributing to the project. Simply put, the objective is to ensure that all parts and pieces of the project—segmented or parceled out to various entities—are brought together and assembled (i.e., integrated) without any misalignments or problems. Specifically, this means that the various parts and pieces not only align when assembled, but also comply with regulatory requirements and deliver the required user functionality.

Closing out the project's interface management system is certainly not a complicated process, but doing it properly matters because the project has accumulated valuable interface interaction information that may or will be useful both in follow-on projects and maturing existing interface management processes. This is the real value in the closeout process—understanding what to do with the information, experiences, and lessons learned from the just completed project. In some situations, this closeout information may be needed to support later-stage commercial disputes that linger past project delivery. As Will Rogers said—and others have paraphrased—"Good judgment comes from experience, and a lot of that comes from bad judgment."

9.1 PROJECT ASSURANCE

Throughout this book, we have described difficulties and challenges in successfully delivering large-scale complex projects. The sheer scale and scope of these projects create unique complications and complexities that typically exist over the life of project development, which often spans several years. Yet empirical and anecdotal evidence continues to show a high rate of poor project performance in the sense of cost and schedule overruns and conflicts among shareholders (Flyvbjerg et al., 2003; Merrow, 2011; Priemus et al., 2008). Typically, these issues arise in the form of late-stage problems, which seem to *suddenly* appear. Then, abruptly, toward the end of the project, problems are identified unexpectedly that result in quality or safety problems, requiring rework, schedule delays, and/or cost overruns. These problems include not only issues with the systems to be delivered, but also a lack of preparedness by those who were expected to take custody of the system produced by the project and who put the system into operation (client, project sponsor, operations, etc.). This may be due to incomplete operational procedures, lack of training, delays in receiving requisite government approvals, and the like.

The problem is that project performance metrics are only useful if they report accurate information. The information that is feeding these performance reports too often is misleading, inaccurate, or misinterpreted. Unfortunately, it is too common in the interface domain to observe one interface party sending (or transferring) substandard interface artifacts, material, or information to another interface party for the sole purpose of showing *progress*. Substandard interface artifacts only transfer the problem to another party or to discovery later in the project. The interface information may be incomplete or inaccurate, may not comply with regulations, etc. There are many reasons why the interface information may not be satisfactory. The quality control and assurance program may not extend to the interface domain; obviously this can create quality gaps, misalignments, and deficiencies that go undetected until later in the project.

Regardless of the reasons, one party inappropriately claims progress for delivering the (substandard) interface artifacts, but has actually only shifted a quality or safety problem onto another interface party. By the same token, the party transferring the interface artifacts is allowed to take *credit* for the purposes of performance reporting and thus shows progress (that hasn't really been achieved). In cases in which another party is dependent upon interface artifacts to further their work, the party inadvertently receiving substandard interface as inputs to their work process is the victim of a *kick the can down the road* situation that is ultimately identified unexpectedly at a later time. Yet, project performance at the time of submittal shows favorable progress in comparison to work that is scheduled and completed. This situation most often happens when performance metrics take precedence over reality or when the metrics are used punitively rather than as a tool for positive discovery; and it can happen frequently when the project team or senior management is dysfunctional in this and other regards. It also happens in situations in which assurance and verification methods may be inadequate. Performance reporting without proper project assurance is meaningless.

Project assurance is a discipline that independently determines the degree to which a project's assets and organization are progressing as planned toward a state of operational readiness. Certainly, traditional project performance measurements and metrics (cost performance index, schedule performance index, etc.) are applicable and should be used together with project assurance to verify that the progress reported has actually been achieved by the artifacts produced. A project assurance program is a system approach that provides a *measure of confidence* that the project will be ready by the time it is required. It is inclusive of traditional project performance measurements and metrics, but also works to ensure compliance to governing regulations and user requirements (i.e., quality and safety in the products created by the projects) and preparedness of those responsible for putting the project result (i.e., the system) into operation. Interface management and interface verification are essential parts of project assurance.

Project assurance requires a holistic view of project performance, including the traditional project performance metrics, but it also requires a systematic perspective on how to view progress in terms of quality, safety, and preparedness to transition the project into operation. In addition to interface management, the project's quality program is also an essential component of project assurance; the project's quality program must also be inclusive of interfaces (technical, system, and asset integrity), safety (technical compliance), and the assessment of progress toward preparing the project for transition into operation (operational readiness and assurance). The project assurance mindset focuses not only on producing deliverables right, but on producing the right deliverables—not just within a single scope of work, but also across all scopes of work and project phases.

Remember, the project scope can be, and often is, divided into scope-of-work parcels that are assigned to different organizations (e.g., contractors, specialty suppliers, or even the client's organization). The scope-of-work parcels are further defined through a *responsibility matrix*. The responsibility matrix serves to further clarify roles and responsibilities and is typically included in contracts. For example, the responsibility matrix may list a project-level activity such as EPC, and then assign responsibility to one of the scopes of work. In these project-level responsibilities, the responsibility assigned spans all the project phases: engineering, procurement, construction, transportation, installation, mechanical completion, and commissioning (these phases may vary by industry and organization). By default, the responsibility matrix begins the process of identifying interdependencies between different scopes of work across project phases. This helps the respective scope owners understand specifically what their responsibility is, and as important, what it is not and what they will require from other parties. In some cases, the *responsibility matrix* may also be called a *RACI (responsible, accountable, consult, inform) matrix*. Regardless of the name, the function remains the same. The scopes of work and the RACI matrix aid in developing an interface control document (ICD).

As the project progresses across its development phase, which in some cases can last several years, organizations contributing scope to the project deliver products and services at different times. In addition, organizations contributing to project development are reliant upon other scopes of work—and the organizations who own those scopes—to deliver inputs to support each of the other's work processes; resulting in a complicated web of interdependencies. Further complicating this situation are the system interfaces which are shared along the scopes of work boundaries, which in the course of interface interaction and achieving agreements, can result in even more interdependencies between organizations contributing to project development. The project assurance mindset captures interfaces and interdependencies and institutes processes to ensure they are integrated as part of the project management system. This helps to increase confidence that as the project progresses through the execution phase, the project does not have any gaps (i.e., missing scope), misalignments (i.e., scope overlap), or *black holes* (i.e., no one is assigned responsibility for scope). The project assurance mindset begins with an understanding of interface verification and how it relates to technical compliance and integrity.

9.2 INTERFACE VERIFICATION AND TECHNICAL COMPLIANCE/INTEGRITY RELATIONSHIP

If we can expand our view from focusing on individual system interfaces, and the interface interactions that must be accomplished between the various interface parties to reach agreement on how to align system interfaces across their respective boundaries, then we can understand the bigger picture of why interface management is important to project success. Interface management is critical to project success by reducing the inherent project and system risk that otherwise would loom large with respect to interfaces; in addition, verifying interfaces plays a larger role within the system design and development process by contributing to technical compliance and integrity assurance.

Systems created by large-scale complex projects are governed by and subject to industry regulation, international standards and best practices, and organizational requirements. While we tend to believe these regulatory requirements are specific and consistently understood, often they are not and are subject to interpretation. It is typical for industry and international agencies and organizations to provide broad guidance in the regulatory requirements, which is then applied to the specific circumstances of the project and the system concept and architecture to be realized by the project. However, typically the project organization is then left to interpret such regulation with respect to the project or projects it undertakes. A design solution for one project may or may not be compliant when applied to another, slightly different system architecture.

In any case, the regulatory and industry requirements provide the first set of constraints in developing and delivering the project result (i.e., the system). If these requirements are not correctly interpreted and incorporated early in the design and then realized in the delivered system, the project's ability to transition the system to operations toward the end of project development may be jeopardized. This is especially the case in industries and countries or locales in which government approval is required to transition the system into operation. Such is the case in the oil and gas and defense industries, among others. In essence, these regulatory requirements represent the initial set of hurdles that must be overcome in terms of ensuring that the system developed by the project complies with these requirements. The intention of regulations is to ensure that the system will function or operate in a manner that is safe for humans and the environment.

In addition, systems that are developed by projects must also meet user requirements and functionality. Every system is designed to create value whether monetary or nonmonetary for the sponsoring organization. This means that once the system is placed into operation, it will provide the necessary functionality to create the value expected by the sponsoring organization. However, to deliver the functionality, the system needs to meet specific system safety and performance requirements. For example, a military system may have lethality requirements, oil and gas facilities have production requirements, and an airplane may have specific engine thrust-lift capacity requirements, among many other potential examples. In large-scale complex projects, the number of user requirements can be several hundred or even thousands. The combined regulatory and system (user) requirements (1) act as constraints to limit design and development possibilities and (2) form the basis for determining technical compliance and integrity during project development.

As the system progresses through the development process, the project team not only desires to design and develop a system that meets regulatory requirements (regulatory compliance), but also to ensure that the system produced by the project maintains the technical integrity of the various project objects or deliverables (technical compliance) as they are received and assembled into or with other objects (integration) into an overall system. This is the challenge! When projects are subdivided into various scope-of-work parcels and contracted out to multiple independent entities, interface verification plays an important role in ensuring that the various system interfaces associated with those scope-of-work parcels are compliant with both regulatory and user requirements as the deliverables from these entities are designed, developed, received, and assembled together into a fully functioning system. That is, interface agreements—and verification of those agreements—ensure that the *gaps* between developer entities are aligned. It is for this reason that we cannot think of interface management as a separate or siloed management function. It is not! Rather, interface management is highly intertwined with the project's other technical and project management functions throughout the development process, including the project's quality management system.

As a key component of the project technical compliance and integrity program, interface verification needs to be planned from the *top down* and conducted to *build up* from the lower-level interface item agreements to confirming compliance of the system interfaces with both regulatory and user requirements. This is the *systems approach* that we have continued to discuss throughout this book because it performs both analysis and synthesis (Chen, 1975) on identifying or creating the interfaces in the system and then verifying that they are technically and regulatorily compliant.

Although we are describing it near the end of this book, the interface verification process does not start at the end of project execution, but rather runs in parallel with interface activity from the start of the execution phase while aligning with more formal project verification activities throughout the execution phase, such as detailed engineering design reviews, factory acceptance tests, software tests, system functionality tests, etc. As we progress through this chapter, we discuss interface verification in the context of its role within the project's technical compliance and integrity program—a component of project assurance, which was described earlier. Interface verification is key to ensuring that the final system is integrated into a whole while preventing late stage development and integration problems that result in quality issues and rework, inevitably resulting in cost overruns and schedule delays.

9.3 WHY THE NEED FOR INTERFACE VERIFICATION

In Chapter 8, we began the discussion of how interface verification plays an important role in ensuring implementation of agreements. Again, the terminology used from industry-to-industry and project to project may vary, but this underlying principle remains the same. There are several methods and techniques to verify implementation of agreements, some of which, like the interface verification traceability matrix and its relationship to the ICD, were briefly discussed in Chapter 8. Verification is about confirmation and transitioning from uncertainty to certainty. Making an agreement on an interface item is a step in the right direction, but the actions by the individual parties to implement that agreement are of the most importance. Further, the completeness and correctness of agreements between parties is equally vital. This is not to suggest that interface parties should not be trusted, but the sponsor and affected interface parties are reliant upon actions taken by the interface parties to ensure those agreements are executed.

The environment in large-scale projects can be intense with high-tempo activity. It is common for individual team leads, technical disciplines, and various project management personnel to be overtaxed and constantly adjusting priorities. In the midst of this intensity, it is not uncommon to see the activities necessary to implement an interface agreement slide down the priority list after the agreement is made. Over time, the actions to implement the interface agreement may get lost among other activities and are sometimes unintentionally forgotten altogether. These situations result in the often-mentioned *late-stage integration problems*, frequently the costliest to fix. It is common to experience a late-stage construction, installation, hook-up (i.e., physical connection), and commissioning (i.e., validation) problem as a result of an agreement that was not implemented or implemented incorrectly. These situations are also the most difficult to explain to management since they demonstrate a substandard interface verification process. The follow through on interface agreements is as important as, if not more so, than making the agreement itself. Interface verification is important not only for assessing workability, but because its specter helps to drive interface parties to execute on the agreements.

The situation surrounding each interface agreement is different. Some agreements are fairly straightforward and easy to implement, such as a minor change to a draft engineering drawing. Typically, such changes can be incorporated quickly and verified through the engineering documentation review and approval process. Other interface agreements can be quite complex to implement and require many major actions to implement the agreement. Further, dependencies among many actions for an individual agreement, or complexities in the resulting interface, may drive the need for multiple verification iterations.

In some cases, both interface parties will be required to take action to implement a specific interface agreement. For example, interface party *A* may need to complete an update to a design *philosophy* document before detailed engineering changes can be made to interface party *B*'s technical drawings. Such situations in which both parties must act to meet the content of the interface item agreement are quite common. In this particular situation, interface verification stretches across both parties and the actions they were required to implement. In the example, what happens if the changes implemented in interface party *A*'s *philosophy* document were not correct and yet this document was issued to interface party *B* to use as a guide to update its technical documentation? Is it reasonable to expect errors in the philosophy document to carry through to more detailed engineering documentation? Certainly! This simple example illustrates the need for interface verification to make sure that actions are implemented completely and correctly.

9.4 INTERFACE VERIFICATION AND QUALITY

A theme repeated throughout this book is the interdependency between interface management and other project and technical management processes. Interface verification is closely linked to the project's quality management system, which specifies how quality will be ensured throughout project development. Naturally, interface verification needs to be conducted in alignment with the project quality system, and arguably as a subset of the quality management program, and coordinated accordingly with relevant quality control and assurance personnel. Unfortunately, it is common for quality control of interface activity to be overlooked in most large-scale projects where the scope of work has been parceled out to several entities. Rather, it is typical to observe a project quality management system with a focus solely on deliverables from each scope of work while omitting quality assurance between scopes of work. As expected, this often leads to the dreaded *late-stage integration problem* that often plagues unsuccessful projects as mentioned several times in this book. The terms *quality assurance* and *quality control* are briefly explained in more detail in the following section since they are fundamental to any project's quality management system.

9.4.1 Quality Control versus Quality Assurance

The terms quality control (QC) and quality assurance (QA) are often misunderstood and confused, but there is a significant difference between the two. In simple terms, QA is process-oriented and focuses on defect prevention, while QC is product-oriented and focuses on defect identification. Together, QA and QC work in unison throughout project development to ensure deliverables meet quality expectations.

QA is defined as a set of activities for ensuring quality in the processes by which products are developed. The focus on QA aims to prevent defects or deficiencies with a focus on the process used to make the product. Specifically, QA is a proactive quality process; for example, using formal design reviews to check the quality of technical engineering design documentation. The goal of QA is to improve development processes so that defects and deficiencies do not arise when the product is developed. Verification is an example of a QA process and a QA management tool. Interface verification is a QA activity. Interface management, including the interface verification process, is intended to be used proactively as early as possible in the development approach. The interface verification process minimizes the number of defects or errors actually implemented into physical or logical (e.g., signals) deliverables; thereby, it also minimizes and prevents rework caused by quality problems. The aim of the process is to *get it right the first time.*

QC is defined as a set of activities for ensuring quality in the products themselves. QC activities focus on identifying defects in the actual products produced. QC aims to identify (and correct) defects and deficiencies after a product is developed, but before it is released or delivered; its goal is to find and eliminate sources of quality problems so that a client's requirements are met. A factory acceptance test is a form of QC. As mentioned earlier, the product (i.e., deliverable) is produced and then subjected to testing at the vendor or supplier's factory before being accepted by the client. The intention is to validate that the client's requirements have been met. Validation/software testing is another example. Software testing intends to validate inputs, processes, and outputs of specific software nodes, such as an *emergency shutdown* (ESD) software node. In this example, software testing validates the ESD software node will perform its intended function correctly and safely when put into operation.

In relation to interface management, QA and QC activities are the cornerstone of interface verification and validation. Verification means testing against requirement specifications (does it do what we said it would do), while validation means testing that what has been built is fit for its intended purpose (is what we said it would do still meeting its intended purpose). In this book, we focus on interface verification because it is a QA activity and is a *proactive* measure. More specifically, interface verification provides the earliest possible opportunity to influence quality in interfaces between independent parties, but there are a number of ways to perform verifications.

9.4.2 Defining Verification

According to the International Council on Systems Engineering (INCOSE), "The purpose of the verification process is to provide objective evidence that a system or system element fulfills its specified requirements and characteristics. The verification process can be applied to any engineering element that has contributed to the definition and realization of the system itself (e.g., verification of a system requirement, a function, an input/output flow, a system element, an interface, a design property, a verification procedure). The purpose of the verification process is to provide evidence that no error/defect/fault has been introduced at the time of any transformation of inputs into outputs; it is used to confirm that this transformation has been made *right* according to the requirements and selected methods, techniques, standards, or rules. As is often stated, verification is intended to ensure that the *product is built right,* while validation is intended to ensure that the *right product is built.* Verification is a transverse activity to every life cycle stage of the system. In particular during the development of the system, verification applies to any activity and product resulting from the activity" (INCOSE, 2012).

9.4.3 Verification Techniques

Verification is performed using a variety of techniques; the techniques are tailored for the element under consideration. Often, several techniques may be applied in sequence to verify the design and development of a particular object. Interface verification uses the same basic verification techniques and they are important to understand when developing an interface verification program or system. Basic verification techniques are as follows (and as described in IEEE 1012, 2012; ISO/IEC/IEEE 29119, 2013; ISO/IEC/IEEE 29148, 2011):

- *Inspection*: This technique relies on visual examination of an element. That is, this technique relies on the human senses (i.e., sight, touch, smell, etc.) or a simple method of measurement and handling. Inspection is generally nondestructive and typically includes the use of simple physical manipulation; mechanical and electrical gauging; and measurement. No tests are necessary. The technique is used to check properties that are best determined by observation (e.g., paint color, obvious physical defects, confirmation of weight, related certificate documentation, etc.). Peer reviews of process artifacts (i.e., material, documents, etc.) are also considered a type of inspection.
- *Analysis*: This technique is based on analytical evidence obtained without any impact on the element under verification and uses mathematical or probabilistic calculation, logical reasoning (including the theory of predicates), modeling, and/or simulation to show theoretical compliance. This technique is often used where testing with realistic conditions cannot be achieved or is not cost effective.
- *Demonstration*: This technique is used to show the correct operation of the submitted element against operational and observable characteristics without using physical measurements (no or minimal instrumentation or test equipment). It generally uses a set of actions selected to show that the element response to stimuli is suitable or to show that operators can perform their assigned tasks when using the element. Observations are made and compared with predetermined/expected responses.
- *Test*: This technique is performed on the submitted element by which functional, measurable characteristics, operability, supportability, or performance capability is quantitatively verified when subjected to controlled conditions that are real or simulated. Testing often uses special test equipment or instrumentation to obtain accurate quantitative data to be analyzed. An example is a factory acceptance test of a deliverable. The vendor may be required to perform a factory acceptance test to show that the deliverable (i.e., equipment, package, etc.) can perform to contract or technical specifications.
- *Analogy or similarity*: This technique is often considered as a type of analysis technique and is based on evidence of similar elements or on experience feedback. It is absolutely necessary to show by prediction that the context is invariant and that the outcomes are transposable (e.g., models, investigations, experience feedback). Analogy or similarity can only be used if the element is similar in design, manufacture, and use; equivalent or more stringent verification actions were used for the similar element; and the intended operational environment is identical to or less rigorous than the similar element.
- *Simulation*: This technique (often considered as a type of analysis technique) is performed on models or mock-ups (not on the actual/physical elements) for verifying features and performance as designed. For example, command control military systems may use mock-ups to assess the layout of equipment and the impact to personnel. Similarly, a cabin for an offshore oil and gas facility living quarter mock-up may be used to assess habitability.
- *Sampling*: This technique is based on verification of characteristics using samples. The number, tolerance, and other characteristics must be specified and be in agreement with the experience feedback.

9.4.4 Verification Independence Levels

Project verification activities, including interface verifications, will be project-phase dependent (e.g., engineering, fabrication, construction, etc.) and performed by a relevant *level* of independence. The level of technical competence required by those conducting verification activities is important. Verification *independence* is an important aspect of increasing confidence in project assurance as the system progresses through design and development. There are three commonly used independence levels; first-party, second-party, and third-party:

- *First-party verification*: A first-party verification is performed by the entity creating the product or providing the service. This is essentially the organization that is required to perform the scope of work. For example, the client hires a contractor to perform the electrical scope of work. The contract will utilize internal quality processes to ensure that the electrical scope is fulfilled to quality and safety expectations. For example, the contractor may have dedicated QC and assurance personnel to oversee and perform verification activities. Naturally, the level of independence is minimal since the control of the verification activity is under the same organization. Naturally, this level is not independent as it is typically performed by someone close to those who created the product.
- *Second-party verification*: A second-party verification is the next layer of independence. This layer extends beyond the boundaries of the organization that is creating the deliverables of their scope of work and is thereby more independent than a first-party verification. For instance, this may be a QA or QC event sponsored by the client. A contractor with a significant engineering scope of work may be required to participate in a client-sponsored engineering design review to allow the client's technical representatives an opportunity to assess the correctness, completeness, and compliance of the engineering design work.
- *Third-party verification*: A third-party verification extends the level of independence even further from the project organization and is typically performed by an entity outside the project scope. For example, industry regulatory requirements may require projects within the industry to perform third-party verification by a specific government-sponsored agency. In other cases, critical elements of the project may require specialized services to evaluate quality. This is especially the case in highly specialized technological areas where only a few firms are designated with the requisite expertise.

The project's interface verification program may require a combination of types and independence levels to verify system interfaces in combination with an understanding of how each scope of work is to be realized over time. This requires considerable coordination between interface personnel and project planning, quality management, and personnel responsible for managing the technical work. The purpose is to ensure that interfaces are agreed upon, verified, and implemented in the respective scopes of work according to the respective project plans and the project's overall development plan, including the interface management plan.

For more information about both verification and validation, please see *The Guide to the Systems Engineering Body of Knowledge (SEBoK)* (BKCASE, 2015) and *Systems Engineering Handbook: A Guide for System Life Cycle Processes and Activities* (INCOSE, 2012), in addition to the standards described earlier in this section.

9.5 TECHNICAL COMPLIANCE AND INTEGRITY

In designing, developing, and delivering the project *result*—which is often a *system*—those who are responsible for interface management act to prevent *gaps* or *misalignments* between independent entities that are contributing to project development, but they also bind technical compliance and integrity (technical, system, and asset integrity) as the system to be produced by the project works through the project development process (i.e., engineering, procurement, construction, integration/installation, hook-up/tie-in, and commissioning (also known as validation) and ultimately, transition and handover to the sponsor or operation/users).

In Figure 9.1, interfaces are conceptually illustrated as an element between technical compliance and integrity (technical, system, and asset). In the following sections of this chapter, we will describe the terms *technical compliance* and *integrity* in more detail. However, in simple terms, interfaces play a role in ensuring alignment between technical compliance and technical, system, and asset integrity. Whereas technical compliance is concerned with regulatory requirements, technical integrity is associated with ensuring that technical specifications are aligned across the system under development. More important, integrity means that the project maintains system integrity as the various deliverables are integrated into building the total and final system. *Technical specifications* in this sense mean the specifications of lower-level elements, such as parts, components, subassemblies, subsystems, and packages (i.e., hydraulic system package or an air compressor package). The aim is to make sure that organizations across the project are designing and procuring elements that conform to regulatory requirements while still being able to meet technical specification requirements and work within the system and its environment. Let's take a look at a simple example.

9.5.1 Interface Role Between Technical Compliance and Technical Integrity

Let us assume that the project has a system requirement to provide *pressured air stations* at two different locations on a natural gas processing plant that is being developed by the project. More specifically, one of the technical requirements is related to *pressured air stations* and that is to provide four hose connection points at each of two pressured air stations and provide a minimum pressure of 80 pounds per square inch (psi). Further, the two station locations shall be divided with one on the east side and one on the west side of the gas processing facility. These air stations are to be used by plant operators and maintainers to perform a variety of important and regular work tasks on plant equipment; and the technical requirements explain why they need them at the different locations. These technical requirements also specify the users desire for what, where, and how much air is to be provided. However, let's also assume that industry regulatory requirements exist for air stations within gas processing plants, and that these regulatory requirements require air stations to be marked with safety signs and protected by a physical safety barrier to prevent damage to the stations (for example, protection against a forklift accident).

During design of the gas processing plant, the designer(s) must consider both the technical requirements from the user and the regulatory requirements governing air stations within the industry. But what if these two air stations fall into two different scopes of work being performed by two different entities?

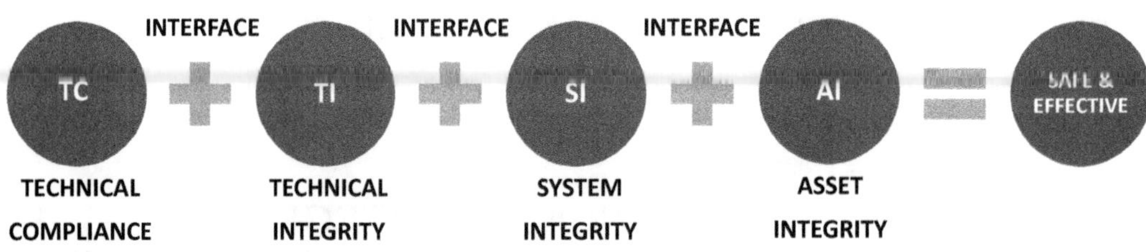

Figure 9.1 Interface technical compliance and integrity

If the two pressured air stations are located in the scopes of work of two different contractors, then this now becomes (and must be recognized as) an interface issue because we need to ensure both stations are standardized and meet all the requirements (both user and regulatory). What would happen if the two different contractors did not coordinate? Would the designs be the same or is it possible the pressured air stations could be installed with different material, connections, and equipment and safety barriers? What if each contractor used different types of air equipment, hoses, nozzles, etc. Lack of commonality and standardization creates problems for the operator and maintainers of the system during operation. Different equipment at the two air stations could mean more training, additional spare parts, different reliability and maintenance inspection routines, etc. Thus, to the extent possible, it is best to have high levels of commonality and standardization in order to make operation and maintenance as easy as possible. Commonality and standardization also saves money as the owner of the system does not need to logistically support as many different subsystems, components, and elements. This is a simple example of the reason interface management becomes critical.

In our aforementioned example, when the two scopes of work are integrated, then we have two air stations that can provide the user's requirements, yet still meet the regulatory requirements while maintaining commonality and standardization. This requires a great deal of cross coordination between the two entities that are responsible for providing the two pressured air stations. It is during interface coordination that specific details of the design are agreed upon between the two entities so that both pressured air stations are designed exactly the same. After the agreements are implemented into the respective designs, then interface verification can be conducted to ensure that the designs reflect the agreements and to make certain the agreements are compliant with both user and regulatory requirements.

In our example, an interface verification could be conducted by reviewing engineering documentation from vendors to ensure the layout of the pressured air stations is the same for both or, if different, there is ample justification. In addition, verification activities need to confirm that the designs comply with regulatory requirements (e.g., safety barriers and safety signage). Later, during procurement activities, purchase orders for equipment can be checked to ensure the same material and equipment is being ordered for both stations. In fact, the interface parties may agree to let the other interface party order all the equipment for both pressured air stations, which helps to ensure commonality. This is certainly not unusual. However, this situation then creates an *interdependency*, discussed in Chapter 2, as a result of interface activity.

By allowing one vendor to order the material and equipment for both pressured air stations, one contractor is now dependent upon the other to deliver the equipment and material by a required on-site date. While such an arrangement ensures commonality of material and equipment, and perhaps efficiency during the procurement process, interface activity is now focused on ensuring delivery of the pressured air equipment and material to meet the construction schedule; creating an interdependency between the two parties. This is just one simple example that repeats itself thousands of times in large-scale complex projects where many parties are contributing to design and development. It may then be easier for the reader to understand the value of interface verification activities at the component level to ensure proactive management and prevention of late-stage problems.

9.5.2 Interface Role in Creating Value

The goal of any large-scale complex project is to create value for the project sponsor. This value does not necessarily mean monetary value, although this is the most typical metric. Before undertaking any project, project sponsors consider the cost of undertaking the project against the expected benefits to be provided by the project. If the project sponsors determine the value to be created by the project exceeds its life-cycle costs (e.g., capital expenditure, operating expenditures, decommissioning expenditures, etc.), then the project likely is undertaken or at least it passes a crucial test for consideration for the sponsoring organization's portfolio. Thus, at the start of the project, there is an *expected benefit*. In large-scale projects that span many years, there are many risks that can adversely affect the expected benefit. Some of these risks are within the project's control, while others are at the mercy of fate or whatever is deemed beyond the control of the sponsoring organization. For example, a well-managed project that delivers high quality scope on time and within budget will contribute to protecting the expected benefit. Of course, a poorly managed project that delivers poor quality scope, late and over budget, naturally puts expected benefit in jeopardy. Although many factors can influence expected benefit, a critically important factor on large capital-intensive projects is interface management. Interface management can overcome a common contributor to what Flyvbjerg and others call the *megaproject paradox*: that while more and bigger major projects are proposed around the globe, ". . . many such projects have strikingly poor performance records in terms of economy, environment, and public support" (Flyvbjerg et al., 2003). Interface management is one element of a well-managed project and provides assurance in a positive way that there are no gaps, misalignments, or overlap between entities contributing to project development. It is a discipline that has been under-serviced in the past, but is now emerging front and center.

As shown in Figure 9.2, the system developed by the project is a bottom-up process during project execution. At the lowest level, entities contributing scope to the project are concerned with adhering to regulations as they design, develop, and deliver their respective scopes. The earlier *pressured air station* requirement is an example. As the system development project progresses, *technical integrity* builds on technical compliance and is concerned with the delivery and integration of designs and individual physical components that are intended to meet requirements. Technical integrity is confirmed as system design and development matures and deliverables begin the process of integration with one another. *System integrity* emphasizes delivering system functionality. Functions are the capabilities in the system that create value for the project sponsor. Finally, *asset integrity* is concerned

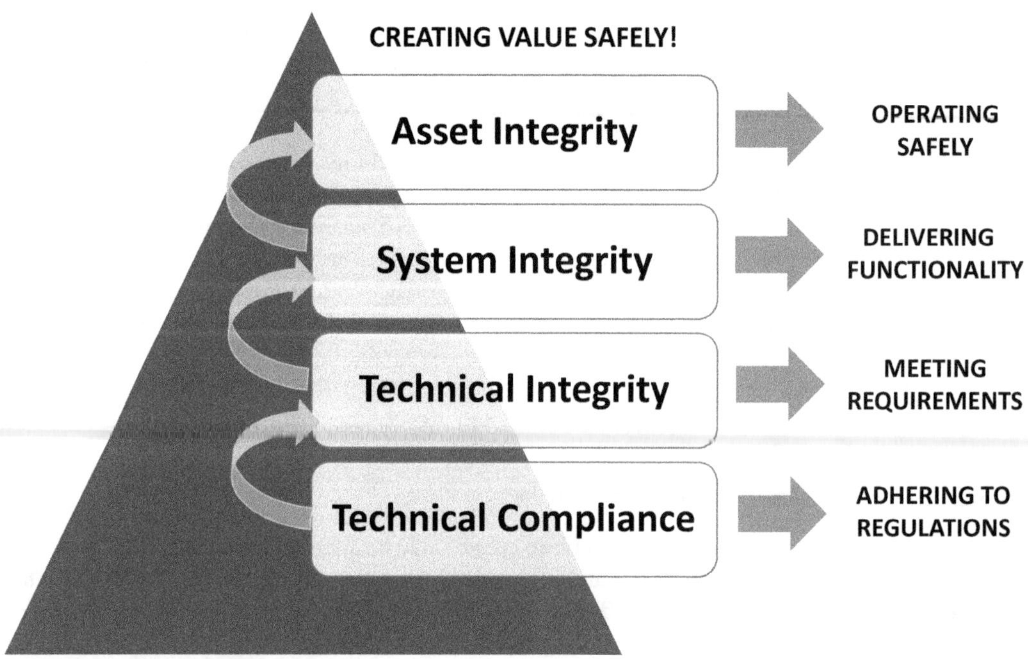

Figure 9.2 Interface role in creating value

with transitioning the system into operation and sustaining its integrity through the operational phase, including during periods of modification and upgrade.

As system design and development progress across the project development timeline, interface management fills the elements between technical compliance and integrity, thus preventing late-stage integration problems that would otherwise (and often do) result in schedule delays and cost overruns. Projects plagued by late-stage integration problems typically have poor interface management regimes, which leads to integrity problems. According to Merrow, "Interface management is one of the most critical jobs on any complex megaproject" (Merrow, 2011), and he goes on to call interface management central to the success of any endeavor and not a job for junior personnel.

It is quite common for senior project management to blame some *unknown-unknown* causal factor, rather than recognizing the impact of poor interface management. Understanding the basic concept of interface management and its role in and impact on technical compliance and integrity is important in terms of assessing the verifying effectiveness of interface management during project execution.

9.6 UNDERSTANDING TECHNICAL COMPLIANCE AND INTEGRITY

In most industries, the terms *technical compliance* and *integrity* tend to be among the least understood. In fact, these terms are not the same and they do not carry the same meaning. Moreover, the role of interface management is also misunderstood or not understood at all, further obscuring the concepts. Given the need to simplify complexity on large-scale complex projects, this lack of understanding is inexplicable, or at least unacceptable. According to Merrow, "Interface management is an issue even for small projects, but it is a major issue for megaprojects. By the time a typical megaproject is completed, there will have been hundreds of organizations involved in varying degrees. In many respects, the task of megaproject management is a task centered around the effective management of the interfaces, the interfaces are opportunities for conflicts and misunderstandings to occur. They are the places where things tend to 'fall between the cracks'" (Merrow, 2011). Too often, project managers fail to fully grasp the very elements of the project that are creating complexity and risk. By not understanding factors that create complexity and risk, they are ill-prepared to implement management systems, especially interface management, in order to adequately monitor and control the project.

The terms *technical compliance* and *integrity* refer to activities that occur within a scope of work to ensure the work is delivered and integrated with other scopes of work according to desired quality standards. But in large-scale complex projects, the project scope of work can be subdivided into many smaller elements or parcels and contracted to many different firms, companies, or teams consisting of many companies. The challenge of maintaining technical compliance and integrity becomes greater as the number of independent parties contributing to the project increases. The reasoning is simple. In addition to the very real issues with respect to the interfaces where their work intersects, the firms, companies, and organizations conducting business within any given industry have different ways of performing work. Yes, there may be similarities, but it is quite normal for different organizations to use different processes, software tools (sometimes incompatible with each other), different approaches to technology, etc. From the perspective of the project sponsor, this makes maintaining technical compliance and integrity a challenge.

Technical compliance and integrity are also challenging where industry regulations vary by country. For example, oil and gas regulations in Norway are much different from those in the United States, which in turn differ from regulations in countries in Asia and Africa. For a project sponsor who is contracting services and products from international sources, the familiarity of the vendors and suppliers with various country regulations will differ; this can be especially challenging if the sources are not experienced with performing projects in intensely regulated countries—such as is

Norway in the oil and gas industry, for example. Interface management serves an important role in bridging the gaps among the different entities delivering their scopes of work. It helps to ensure that scopes are interpreted consistently across all parts of the project and that the scopes of work align when delivered—things that are critical to ensuring technical compliance and integrity.

9.6.1 Technical Compliance

Technical compliance relates specifically to being in accord with specifications issued by a standards body, industry regulations, or even organizational governance that affect the system design and development process. These regulations are constraints that must be considered by detailed engineering disciplines and designers during system concept development, system engineering design, and on through to system transition into operation. A constraint is simply a boundary that limits, restricts, or constricts the options of the concept developers and engineering design. More specifically, these regulations act to prescribe *what you must do* and *what you cannot do*; they are intended as safety barriers or desired/required practices based on previous findings by such regulatory bodies or standards organizations. By limiting or constricting design options, these regulations often add difficulty in concept development and system design, but these difficulties are offset by the prevention of deadly accidents or incidents (from operation of the system) after transitioning the system into operation.

In this book, we define *technical compliance* as: *the degree to which the design, development, delivery, and use of an individual design, part, component, package, deliverable, subsystem, etc., complies to technical and safety specification.* A *specification* implies very specific technical aspects such as the type of material from which the component is made, temperature resistance, thickness, etc. The specification frequently goes beyond just the hardware or software, it often includes how these items are placed in the design of the system; for example, it is common for specifications to stipulate how items are placed, or laid out, in system design.

In simple terms, a *system* is built-up by integrating many individual parts, components, packages, etc., into an overall system design. An airplane is comprised of thousands of individual parts and items, which are assembled into components and subsystems, which are then integrated together to make a complete airplane system. Each part, component, package, deliverable, subsystem, etc., must comply with specific industry regulations, international standards (e.g., ISO, ANSI, IEC, ASTM), and organizational governance requirements (e.g., project design basis requirements, functional requirements, user requirements). In some cases, the standards and regulations include limitations on design—for example, where certain items must be placed and required enhancements to design, such as a need for redundancy.

Determining technical compliance is not an activity reserved for later in the project development process. Rather, it begins during early concept development with the selection of system architectures by ensuring that selected concepts comply with industry regulations, international standards, or other specifying entities. During detailed engineering, the system concept is elaborated down to individual elements, such as power outlets, connection points, types of materials to be used, even types of screws, and the like. Within this detailed engineering process, design reviews ensure that lower-level design elements are compliant with industry regulations, international standards, and organizational governance documents.

As elements of the system complete sufficient detailed engineering, they are then procured through a commercial process that relies on technical information that is produced by the engineering process to make sure that the right item, part, component, or whatever, is procured. Each item procured is then checked at delivery through an examination of the item and its condition, review of documentation (i.e., certification documents), or through some type of demonstration or test event that establishes the item's ability to perform its intended purpose. Given the global nature of vendors and suppliers, it is common for items to then be shipped to a location for assembly with other deliverables, such as may occur during various stages of construction.

As items are received at the construction site, once again they are checked for condition to be sure that the items are correct and have not been damaged during transit. Each item then enters a construction process and is installed with other items according to the construction schedule. Once installed, a physical check is conducted to ensure the work is complete; the assembly or subassembly later undergoes checks, demonstration, and testing to make sure that it operates as part of a larger subsystem or system during commissioning and/or validation testing. This is an overly simplistic description of the process, but it is sufficient to give the reader a general idea of the overall process of EPC.

The point of this description is to articulate that there are several mechanisms along the EPC process to ensure that individual items are compliant, but compliance means more than just compliance of the lowest level item. Compliance also means how the item is being used, that is, considering design. From our *pressured air station* example earlier, we noted a physical safety barrier around the air station to prevent unintended damage. The station itself may contain verified compliant hardware, but if the design does not allow adequate physical protection, then the installed air station is not compliant. Having to consider the design context is part of what makes technical compliance so challenging.

Some elements can be verified for compliance early in the EPCs and never need to be reverified. Other elements require checks only later in the EPC process. Still, other elements require many checks along the EPC process. When combined with the fact that thousands of elements are being delivered by several different project entities (sometimes hundreds), then it is clear why interface management is a critical management function. Again, since it is common for scopes of work to be subdivided and contracted out to several different parties, interface management is one mechanism to ensure these parties interpret regulatory and standards-based requirements correctly and consistently across the project.

9.6.2 Technical Integrity

Technical compliance forms the basis for *technical integrity*, which is defined as: *the degree to which the design, development, delivery, and use of multiple compliant integrated designs, parts, components, packages, deliverables, subsystems, etc., meet a system requirement safely and effectively*. As mentioned previously, a system is built-up from lower-level individual elements to components, then subsystems or packages are integrated in turn up to the overall final system. At different points along the project development process, elements that have been verified as *compliant* can now be integrated with other compliant elements to confirm the ability to meet a system requirement.

These individual elements may be within the same scope of work or integrated from several scopes of work. Regardless, the intent is to ensure that specific system requirements are being met as the system matures through the project development process. The system concept and physical and logical architecture will dictate when the system can be checked for technical integrity, but conceptually, technical integrity can begin only after a certain level of compliance (of the elements) has been completed. This is not to suggest that *system-level* technical compliance and technical integrity are activities in a series (i.e., that one follows the other). Rather, there is considerable overlap between technical compliance and technical integrity activities as the system progresses through the project development process.

During design, as a number (n) of design elements mature, they can then be examined as a whole to ascertain if the sum of the elements meets system requirements. Naturally, this occurs over time since not all design elements will be completed simultaneously. During engineering, this normally happens as part of detailed design reviews, meaning that the design progresses to a point where an *area*, *package*, or *subsystem* of the system can be verified as part of a design review. During procurement activities, vendors and suppliers may be contracted to perform a test event, such as a factory acceptance test, to verify to the client that the item being purchased meets specifications and requirements. During the construction phase, as elements are integrated and installed, physical checks are made to assess technical integrity. For example, a gas processing plant may be designed with many areas. An *area* is defined as a section of the plant that is designed to perform a specific function. Each area may be required to meet numerous system requirements that enable it to satisfactorily perform the main function, such as to process natural gas. As an area is built-up by physically installing elements within the area, checks can be made to verify that the installed elements can perform system requirements.

The main intent of technical integrity is to ensure that different *technically compliant* elements are properly integrated to meet the system requirements and to identify problems as early as possible in the project development process. Identifying technical integrity problems, misalignments, or gaps early allows the issue to be corrected at minimal cost and time. For example, identifying technical integrity problems during engineering reviews allows engineers to revise their technical documentation before the items are procured and certainly before they are delivered to construction and integrated with other elements. Catching the problem or mistake early allows for a problem to be addressed before it becomes an even larger problem later in development. Similarly, during procurement, items undergo verification checks (such as the factory acceptance test mentioned earlier) to make sure that they meet requirements. It is common during factory acceptance tests, for example, for items to be documented as punch items. A *punch item* is a discrepancy that the vendor must fix before the client will take receipt of the item. Although identifying problems, errors, or defects with an item after it has been produced is not ideal, it is still better than not realizing the problem until after it has been integrated into the system during the construction process. The latter, of course, creates even more work and expense to undo the problem.

9.6.3 System Integrity

The term *system integrity* is defined as: *the degree to which the design, development, delivery, and use of a system (typically at the project level) performs system-level functions effectively and safely.* Every system, such as an airplane or military equipment, requires the final product to perform functions. In this context, a *function* is a noun and designates some type of action or capability. An airplane requires functionality to take off, navigate, land, etc. These are the actions the system must perform to deliver the value for which it was created. This is the focus of *system integrity*. To perform a *function*, each system relies upon different combinations of subsystems, components, signal inputs and outputs, and the like. Think for a moment about an aircraft taking flight. The plane needs to have the capability to taxi to the launch area, increase speed, maintain control, lift the aircraft at desired speed, control direction of flight, and so on. To perform these *functions*, the aircraft relies on combinations of related subsystems, controls, etc.

As technically compliant elements (e.g., components, subsystems, packages) are integrated into a whole, they produce a system. This system must be capable of performing specific functionality expected by the project sponsor, which is verified and validated before the project sponsor takes custody of the system. During the engineering phase of the project, once the system design has matured, an integrated, detailed design review may be conducted to focus on evaluating the entire system design against the required functionality. While the entire system design may not be complete, performing such a verification event provides a valuable opportunity to evaluate continuity of the entire system design, especially when the project has been segmented into many different scopes of work. Checking *system integrity* during the engineering design phase provides one of earliest points in project development to not only assess progress toward achieving functionality, but also to identify areas that may not be technically compliant or may not have technical integrity.

Interface verification as part of verifying system integrity provides critical input to integrated design reviews and analysis of system integrity. In Chapter 7, we discussed developing an ICD. The ICD forms the basis for interface verification activities between interface parties. In the ICD, main system interfaces between different scopes are listed, described, and/or illustrated. During execution, interface activity is conducted between the interface parties who own different scopes of work.

Interface activities between these parties is focused on the specific system interfaces that span their respective scopes, resulting in agreements on individual items associated with their shared system interfaces. Interface verification first confirms that the interface agreements between the parties have been implemented into their respective scopes. In essence, this represents the lowest interface verification level. Verification of the agreements then feeds into verification of the ICD.

Verifying system integrity is about understanding whether and to what degree the system can perform its intended functionality and about examining the system architecture across the value chain. In an offshore oil and gas facility, the value chain starts in the hydrocarbon reservoir and ends at the market or the operational boundary of the market, such as another project, processing facility, etc. Assessing functionality begins at the start of the value chain and examines the functions along the chain. In our oil and gas example, system functionality is examined by first analyzing the architecture (physical and logical) to recover hydrocarbons from the reservoir. To perform the assessment of this function, the examination requires a holistic review of the physical and logical design from the wells into the reservoir to a logical end point of the offshore processing facility. This multifaceted review integrates different scopes of work, subfunctions, technical disciplines, components, and subsystems to ascertain the system architecture (1) is in compliance with regulatory requirements (e.g., safety), (2) ensures that the design meets user requirements, and (3) assures there are no gaps, misalignments, or black holes.

System integrity is confirmed throughout the project development process from engineering, through construction, and prior to hand off to the project sponsor or operations. As mentioned previously, a series of detailed design reviews may be used to verify functionality of integrated designs; quality checks such as factory acceptance tests may be used to ensure that critical subsystems and components are checked for compliance to specifications; and construction inspections are used, among other techniques, to verify that the system is developed according to regulations and specifications. As systems are integrated into the final product, they are tested or checked as part of a robust mechanical completion and commissioning process before hand over. Finally, at hand over to the project sponsor or operations, a formal process is established to transfer custody of an operationally ready system to the group that will operate the system, which ultimately leads to initiating operation of the system. As a system is transferred from the project to the system owner, asset integrity begins and continues until the asset is decommissioned and disposed.

9.6.4 Asset Integrity

Asset integrity is the responsibility of the system owner (often referred to as *asset owner*) and commences when the system, or part of the system, is put into operation; and it remains in effect until the asset is decommissioned (i.e., until operations have ceased and the asset is disabled and disposed). For the purposes of this book, asset integrity is defined as: *the degree to which design, development, delivery, and use of an integrated system in operation remains compliant* (*e.g., remains compliant with safety regulations*) *and meets value expectations* (*that is, the asset is effective*). A system in operation needs to continue to perform the value-creating functions safely during all operational modes, including any periods during system upgrade or modifications. This includes normal operations mode when the system is operating at predetermined levels, and also includes planned shutdowns (also known as *process shutdowns*) and emergency shutdown operating modes. These shutdowns are abnormal states that require the system to operate in a controlled state since it is either expectedly or unexpectedly shut down. In addition, every system requires some form of maintenance to ensure safe operation and maximum availability such as might occur for a system upgrade or modifications.

From an interface verification perspective, activities to prepare to hand over the system to operations commence early in the project execution phase and include developing system start-up procedures, operating procedures, training, simulations, and carryover work from project execution among many other activities. The challenge from the perspective of interface management is to ensure alignment between how the system is designed and how it is to be operated—more precisely, to assist in aligning operational preparedness efforts with the ongoing efforts to design and develop the system.

Asset integrity is highly affected by the maintenance applied to the system during its operational life. Many factors affect the maintenance program for a particular system. In principle, preplanned maintenance programs are intended to be proactive and are expected to replace, rotate, or check specific system items before they are expected to fail. External factors, such as the environment in which the system operates, can have a significant impact on maintenance and inspection routines. While these external factors are outside the scope of this book, the main point is that a system in operation needs to remain safe and operate at performance levels expected by the asset owner, thus, such external factors need to be considered in developing maintenance and inspection routines.

In some cases, a complicated maintenance routine can be viewed as a separate (but related) project in itself. In processing facilities, for example, planned shutdowns are scheduled periodically to complete a series of expected maintenance actions to ensure the future operation of the facility. The activities sometimes can be so expansive and time sensitive that they are managed as a project. Whether for a military system, airplane, IT system, or other kind of system, major maintenance efforts are usually designed to minimize, or if possible avoid, downtime.

The challenge for the project, and those designated to take charge of the system when it is completed, is to implement a transition program which ensures that (1) the project will be prepared and ready to transition to operations as planned and (2) those taking custody are able to put the system into immediate operation. There is considerable debate in various industries, organizations, and projects about the right time to begin such a program. Certainly personnel, organizational, and project circumstances will largely dictate timing, but the fact remains that such a program is essential and is an element of the project. Operational readiness and assurance programs are deeply coupled with the project and thus are part of the *project assurance* and verification mindset. For interface personnel, there are numerous interface areas between the project team and those eventually taking custody of the system. This should be considered as part of the overall project assurance program.

9.7 TECHNICAL COMPLIANCE AND INTEGRITY MODEL—PROJECT DIAMOND

Visualizing the relationship between interfaces, technical compliance, and the various levels of integrity can be a challenge. Figure 9.3 has been provided as a technical, compliance, and integrity (TCI) model for Project Diamond. This illustration is intended to show (1) how interface management affects and supports technical compliance and integrity, (2) how the various elements (i.e., interface management, technical compliance, and integrity) reinforce each other, and (3) at a high level the responsibility relationship among the numerous actors contributing to the project. Every project, organization, and industry is different, and the approach to ensuring interface alignment and technical compliance and integrity varies. However, the point of this illustration is to demonstrate an approach

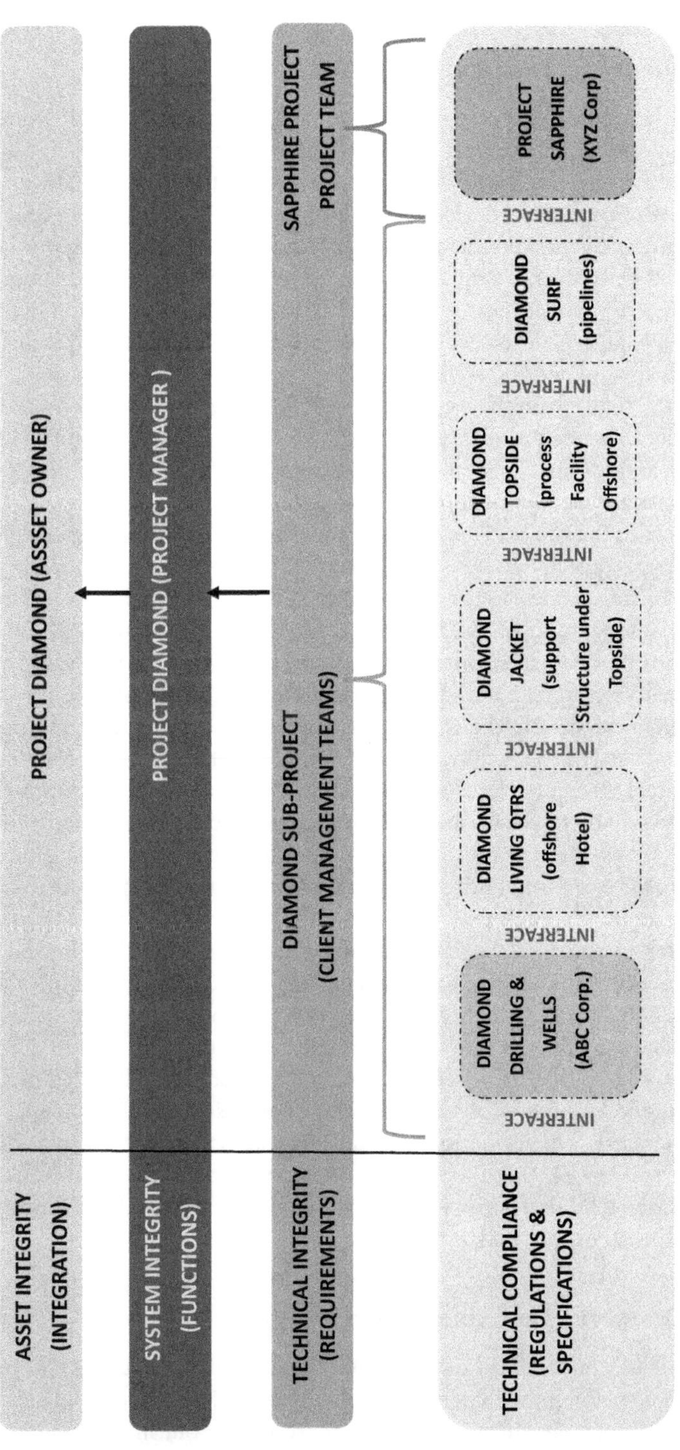

Figure 9.3 Project Diamond—example TCI model

for managing interfaces and technical compliance and integrity on the sample project—from the lowest level to the finished result—and to show how they support each other.

9.7.1 Project Diamond Technical Compliance

At the lowest level of Figure 9.3, boxes are shown to represent the scope of work of each of the individual organizations contributing to Project Diamond's development. These organizations are each responsible for a discrete scope of work with deliverables to be integrated with the project at a specific point in Project Diamond's development. Each of these scopes of work follows its own subproject plan for engineering, procurement, construction, etc. As expected, the word *interface* shown vertically in *gray* text between the various boxes is intended to provide a communication channel for individual owners of these scopes of work to interact for the purpose of aligning their system interfaces. Each deliverable for each scope of work must be compliant with industry regulations, international standards, and existing technical codes.

As indicated in the figure with the words *Technical Compliance* (*Regulations and Specifications*), each organization contributing products and services to Project Diamond has a responsibility to ensure those products and services are compliant with regulatory requirements and are procured and constructed to specifications. The quality management system of each company that is delivering products and services to the project is responsible for ensuring that these deliverables meet specifications and regulatory requirements. However, individual deliverables must then be combined with other deliverables (i.e., integrated) to begin producing subsystems, packages, system areas, etc.

In our Project Diamond example, the *Living Quarters* (*LQ*) scope requires the EPC of an offshore hotel to accommodate personnel for long stays offshore. The LQ will be physically connected to the Topside process facility offshore. Naturally, the contractor that is responsible for this scope uses a management system to ensure that the scope is engineered and that all items are procured and then assembled at its own construction facility. As the LQ progresses through its project execution, checks are made of individual elements' detailed engineering documentation to ensure requisite regulations, applicable codes and standards, and user requirements have been designed into the system. This detailed engineering information then feeds specifications for procuring the individual elements. The word *specification* is intended to mean the detailed data that is sufficient to order items from catalogs (such as pumps, compressors, and so on) or to fabricate an item to be produced (such as weight, size, material type, etc.). Specification information requires that the vendor, supplier, or fabricator be given specific guidance as to what is to be provided to the ordering organization.

Interface verification activity that is related to technical compliance ensures that common items across scope boundaries are designed to the same codes and standards, procured from similar vendors and suppliers, and that they are assembled and verified using standardized methods. Earlier in the book, the role of the *lead interface contractor* (*LIC*) was discussed. The LIC plays an important role in ensuring technical compliance in common items across different scopes of work, but it is through interface management that they communicate and reach agreement on these items. Ultimately, the organization that is responsible for providing deliverables is also responsible for ensuring that each deliverable is compliant with regulations, codes, and standards.

9.7.2 Project Diamond Technical Integrity

At the next higher level, the *technical integrity* level, focus shifts to assuring that requirements are met and requires the assembly or integration of multiple individual components, subsystems, or elements. More specifically, these elements are arranged or laid out in an area or in a way that allows verification of the element's ability to perform specific requirements. In our previous *pressured air* example, this element of the design is first engineered, and then the components are procured and assembled into a cohesive element to provide pressured air. In addition, this element is physically located (east and west side of the processing facility) to best support maintenance functions. Finally, technical integrity checks are performed to confirm that the safety requirements (technical compliance) are incorporated into the design. Throughout this process, interface verification plays an important role.

During engineering, interface activity provides a forum to ensure consistency in interpretation of user and regulatory requirements. Typically, interface verification is initially performed by reviewing interface agreements and comparing the agreements to engineering artifacts, ensuring that the agreements are implemented into the respective design scopes of work. In our *pressured air* example, this may also include a multidisciplined (e.g., engineering disciplines such as mechanical, electrical, piping), detailed design review of the pressured air design documentation. During procurement, interface management helps to coordinate agreement between interface parties and groups on procurement of common hardware and aligning technical specifications. This may include agreeing to assign procurement responsibility of all material and hardware to one interface party, such as our *pressured air* example. Finally, during construction, technical integrity is determined by physically demonstrating that the system meets user requirements and complies with regulatory requirements. Again, referring to our *pressured air* example, an inspection of the layout is performed and may include a physical demonstration or test to confirm that the supplied pressured air conforms to requirements.

In our Project Diamond example, responsibility for technical integrity has been placed on the subproject teams. Remember, the project's scope was subdivided into several scope-of-work parcels and contracted to different organizations. Here, the client (ABC Corp.) has established a subproject management team to oversee each contractor's performance. The responsibility of the subproject team is to ensure the technical integrity of the scope of work they are managing and for ensuring this scope meets regulatory and user requirements. In this responsibility, interface management and verification are important to ensure alignment of one scope of work with other (interfacing) scopes of work.

9.7.3 Project Diamond System Integrity

The delivery and integration of several scopes of work results in a final system, which has been designed, developed, and delivered to meet the user requirements. That is, the system must be compliant to safety while still meeting user requirements, allowing for safe and effective operation of the system. In our Project Diamond example, this means delivery of an offshore oil and gas processing facility that is integrated with Project Sapphire. Here, all scopes of work have been delivered and are physically and logically connected together to perform a value-creating and supporting function. For Project Diamond, value-creating functions include *recovering hydrocarbons, processing hydrocarbons, and transporting processed hydrocarbons to Project Sapphire.* These are *value-creating* functions because these functions allow for the generation of revenue to the sponsoring organization (ABC Corp.). However, to perform these functions, Project Diamond also must be able to perform *supporting* functions, such as *providing accommodation for personnel, providing utility services (water, air, power, etc.), and providing an emergency escape.* These supporting functions allow those operating the system to perform the value-creating function safely and effectively.

The responsibility for system integrity has been placed on the Project Diamond project manager and the focus is on delivering a system to the project sponsor that will perform its functions safely and effectively. This requires a holistic view of the system and a management system to ensure consistency, compliance, commonality, and standardization as the system progresses across its development life cycle. For interface verification and management, this means not just aligning system interfaces early in the project, but also across the project phases as the project progresses from engineering, to procurement, and through construction and turnover to the sponsoring organization.

Early in project development, the Project Diamond project manager may require an *integrated detailed design review* to evaluate system functionality across all scopes of work including interfaces. Such an early view allows an opportunity to identify gaps, misalignment, nonconformities (e.g., a failure to comply with a requirement of a company's quality system standard), or deviations (e.g., noncompliance with contract, regulatory codes, and standards, etc.) to be identified. System integrity begins the moment the project is initiated and encompasses technical compliance and technical integrity. This is the *systems view* often expressed in this book. The systems view or systems approach means thinking about the end result from the initial moments and understanding how the system evolves from details on paper to its final physical form. System integrity ends only when the system has been handed over to the project sponsor or representatives and the system is put into operation. In complex systems, this happens in stages, such as hand over of individual systems as they complete their verification and validation process.

Interface management acts as the *glue* to bind the disparate system elements and scope-of-work parcels as the project moves through design, development (fabrication, assembly, and construction), and ultimately into operation. Interface verification is an important means of providing confidence against unexpected late-stage problems, which, as we have seen, result in added cost, time, and rework. At the system-integrity level, the interface verification process is part of functionality confirmation that culminates in the system hand off to operation. It is at this stage that the project has completed its job and asset integrity becomes the focus.

9.7.4 Project Diamond Asset Integrity

Once a system is developed and delivered by a project, it is handed over to the project sponsor's organization (i.e., operations) and put into operation for the purpose for which it was created. Systems are typically intended for use for extended periods of time over several years or even decades. Every system has an owner. In this book, the owner is referred to as the asset owner who is responsible for the day-to-day operation of the system or an entity that operates the system on behalf of the system owner (ABC Corp. for Project Diamond). The asset owner's responsibilities include asset integrity, which is focused on maintaining safety and effectiveness over the life of the system with effectiveness equating to providing the value for which the system was created. As expected, every system will undergo a number of upgrades and modifications to retain or improve system performance and safety. This may be due to regular maintenance intervals, the incorporation of new technologies, replacing aging subsystems with more efficient subsystems, integrating with additional external projects, etc.

Regardless of the reason, asset integrity ensures the continued safe and effective operation of the system. In our Project Diamond example, asset integrity is complicated by the integration of the project to Project Sapphire. In these types of system architectures, Project Diamond is affected by Project Sapphire's asset integrity. A problem requiring shutdown on Project Sapphire also results in a shutdown on Project Diamond because of the interdependent system architectures. This includes planned periods where operation is halted, such as planned maintenance activities. Occasionally, the system may be under modification or upgrade without taking the system out of operation, such as an upgrade to nonessential equipment. In other cases, the environment may require immediate shutdown of the system. For example, extreme weather conditions may require the unexpected shutdown of power generation facilities due to storm damage—or to prevent damage to the facility. Interface management and verification continue to play a role as part of asset integrity.

When an existing system undergoes an upgrade or modification, the existing physical and logical system architecture is changed to include the new components, software, signals, etc. Those performing the modification may or may not be familiar with the original system design or have been involved in its creation. Here, interface management assumes the role of ensuring alignment between the existing architecture and those new system elements to be integrated. This situation persists for as long as the system remains in operation. Asset integrity only ends after a system is decommissioned and disposed of.

9.7.5 Interface, Technical Compliance, and Integrity Summary

Maintaining a system view of the project from the beginning and understanding how the system is to be designed and developed is crucial to performing interface management and verification activities. Many gray areas exist between interface management and technical compliance and integrity, but understanding the synergies among interface management, compliance, and integrity helps to see the *bigger picture* and the role that interface management plays in the process of designing and delivering a system that is safe and effective.

9.8 INTERFACE CLOSEOUT

As mentioned in earlier chapters, interface groups will initiate and end at different times during the project. That is, it can be expected that some groups will complete their interface work earlier than others due to the timing of their contracts and the necessary duration of work. Still other groups will carry on throughout the project execution phase and finish as the project finishes. Interface closeout begins as individual interface groups complete their interface work and all verification activity has concluded. Once the related contractors or responsible organizations complete their scopes of work, the process of closing out the interface group can commence. After all interface groups have concluded, then a formal project interface closeout process can be completed.

9.8.1 Interface Group Closeout

Each interface group maintains an interface register as discussed in Chapter 8. This register captures all of the results of interface activity within the group, including the interface agreements, the summary of interaction between the parties on individual interface discussions, minutes of meetings including decisions and actions, and relevant supporting documentation. In essence, the register provides a formal trail of relevant interface information for historical purposes.

This information has two basic uses. First, historical interface information may be used by the client or contractor to support commercial actions, such as variation order requests, which are common when one contractor fails to receive promised interface artifacts from another party and may impact delivery of their scope of work. Analysis of the group's interface register information can yield evidence supporting a claim or provide the basis for denying a claim. The second reason interface register information is important is for use by the organization on future similar projects. In projects of a similar nature within a specific industry, one can expect to observe similar interface activity. This is especially so if the project development approach and system architecture are similar. Looking back at interface activity on previous similar projects can provide a basis for what to expect in future similar projects. Aside from assisting with specific interface issues, this information also helps to improve the interface management process and to reduce required resources; it can also increase the effectiveness of the process.

When the client mandates the use of an automated tool to house the interface register, then closeout of an interface group's register is quite easy. As is the case with the tool used in this book and other interface management products, the vendor can provide a data download with all the historical information. Thus, a historical file can be included in the project's closeout interface folder. This file can include all supporting documentation, interface sheets describing a summary of requests and responses, and all minutes of meetings between the group. It should be noted that each party that is participating in the group already has a record of this register by virtue of being a participant in the group. By actively participating in the interface management process, each group is obviously provided access to the information. Thus, they can also maintain copies of the information within their respective management systems. The project sponsor, or client, may decide to also provide a copy of the interface register to each party within an interface group, but this varies from project to project. In the case that one project must be integrated with another (external) project, transfer of the interface register is normally a condition that was specified in the cooperation agreement between the two sponsoring organizations.

9.8.2 Project Interface Closeout

The requirements for project closeout will vary from organization to organization. In mature project organizations, the requirements for closeout are usually well established. For interface management closeout, it is not uncommon for a formal report to be required that documents key aspects of the interface management system used, key lessons learned, challenges or issues faced during the planning or execution, and lessons learned and recommendations. In organizations that have been established for a specific project and do not expect follow-on projects, the closeout process may be abbreviated or not performed at all.

More likely, the closeout process will include many different activities. A separate lessons-learned register may exist and the owners of the project development process may request a formal review to understand how to incorporate improvements to the interface management process in the future. In some situations, interface management and other individual management function owners, such as change and quality management, may seek to debrief one another to discuss the challenges with interdependencies among various management systems.

9.8.3 Project Interface Management Closeout Report

A formal project closeout report is always beneficial for future use. A concise, well-written report can be a useful aid to other projects that are setting up their management systems, and in fact, help to institute the right (efficient and effective) interface management system (and other project management systems). Unfortunately, those closing down the project are often focused on other matters at hand and less concerned about how they can help others on different or future projects. Although we recommend a comprehensive, detailed, closeout report that describes key aspects of the interface management system; as an alternative, describing its challenges and how it functioned and changed over the life of the project are worth considering given other rising demands. An example project interface closeout report is provided in Appendix G and is based on a real-world project.

9.8.4 Interface Register Closeout

After confirming that interface activity has concluded by all interface groups and networks, and when relevant interface parties have disbanded or demobilized, then the project's interface register is formally shut down after the historical information is transferred to the client. By shutting down the register, all access is removed and the information that is stored at the vendor's web-based location, if such is the case, is deleted.

9.8.5 Lessons Learned

Lessons learned is one of the most important aspects of closing out any management system, including the interface management system. Unfortunately, these lessons are not applied often enough to revise the conduct on future projects, causing history to repeat itself in sometimes unflattering ways. Most project organizations maintain a *lessons-learned register* where all project lessons are catalogued. The value in these lessons is not just what happened, but also what actions were taken to correct the issue or make the situation better. These lessons may or may not be applicable to future projects; nevertheless, understanding the problem and how it was corrected is important—and we recommend that it can and should be used to prevent future mistakes and improve future outcomes.

9.8.6 Information Archive

The interface information archive consists of all information within the interface register, interface verification results, interface design reviews, interface control documentation, and information from any other events that aid future projects. In similar projects within the same industry, archived interface information can be useful in developing future interface management systems and aid in preparing future interface control documents, economizing verification programs, and helping to resolve similar interface challenges earlier.

9.9 SUMMARY

Throughout this book, we have attempted to provide a systems view while describing interface management and its role within modern large-scale complex projects. Over the last few decades, project complexity has increased as a result of many factors: technological advances, demands of the global marketplace, and accelerating societal change, among many others. Looking forward into the future, current trends suggest project complexity will only increase as technology continues to rapidly evolve and penetrate every facet of society, world populations continue to grow and shift, natural resources become scarcer, and governments and corporations look to develop more projects through global suppliers and vendors.

Interface management is not a *magic pill* to guarantee project success. Rather, interface management is a rising risk reduction function that can dramatically contribute to project success rates by managing what has heretofore been largely unrecognized and unaddressed. Interface management, properly implemented, can help minimize or prevent late-stage development problems and challenges that seem to routinely plague large-scale complex projects. The essence of interface management is not only to address the technical issues associated with system interfaces, but also to effectively manage the interface relationships among the entities responsible for the interfaces.

In the modern world, connectivity is essential for development and prosperity. The ability to share information, coordinate, and communicate is essential for progress in society as a whole and in projects specifically. Interface management is one mechanism to cope with difficult challenges in modern and future projects and is expected to surge in both relevance and capability as more and more organizations recognize its potential for reducing complexity on large-scale capital projects with many participating entities.

9.10 REFERENCES

BKCASE Editorial Board. (2015). *The Guide to the Systems Engineering Body of Knowledge (SEBoK)*. v. 1.4. R.D. Adcock (EIC). Hoboken, NJ: The Trustees of the Stevens Institute of Technology. Accessed November 5, 2015, from http://www.sebokwiki.org.

Chen, G. (1975). What Is the Systems Approach? *Interfaces*, 6(1): 32–37. Retrieved from http://www.jstor.org/stable/25059250.

Flyvbjerg, B., N. Bruzelius, and W. Rothengatter. (2003). *Megaprojects and Risk—An Anatomy of Ambition*. Cambridge University Press, New York, NY.

IEEE 1012. (2012). *IEEE Standard for System and Software Verification and Validation*. Institute of Electrical and Electronics Engineers. New York, NY.

INCOSE. (2012). *Systems Engineering Handbook: A Guide for System Life Cycle Processes and Activities*, version 3.2.2. San Diego, CA: International Council on Systems Engineering (INCOSE), INCOSE-TP-2003-002-03.2.2.

Merrow, E. W. (2011). *Industrial Megaprojects—Concepts, Strategies, and Practices for Success*. John Wiley & Sons, Inc., Hoboken, NJ.

Priemus H., B. Flyvbjerg, and B. van Wee, editors. (2008). *Decision-Making on Mega-Projects: Cost-Benefit Analysis, Planning and Innovation*. Edward Elgar Publishing, Ltd., Cheltenham, UK.

SO/IEC/IEEE 29119 (2013). *Software Testing Standard*. International Organization for Standardization. Geneva, Switzerland.

SO/IEC/IEEE 29148. (2011). *Systems and Software Engineering—Life Cycle Processes: Requirements Engineering*. International Organization for Standardization, Geneva, Switzerland.

Appendix A

Interface Management Definitions and Terminology

Approved for construction (AFC): Data that has been developed sufficiently to allow related interface fabrication/construction works to progress without holds.

Approved for design (AFD): Data that has been developed sufficiently to allow related interface design to progress without holds.

Client (company): The organization or corporation contracting products or services in support of one or more of their projects.

Common boundary: A common boundary (also known as *battery limit*) with shared contractual, functional, organizational, or project area between two (or more) interface parties. Common boundary are the identified interface points between two or more interface parties as defined by each party's respective contract scope of work.

Contractor (supplier): The supplier, or contractor, is the organization contracted by the client to provide products and services.

External interface: An external interface is outside the boundaries of a project or it can be between two different projects sponsored by two different sponsors.

Interface: An interface is a common boundary between two (or more) independent projects, systems/subsystems, contract scopes of work, organizations, or project phases that requires an exchange of data or information to obtain agreement between entities to prevent interface problems when the common boundaries are developed and integrated.

Interface agreement: An interface agreement is an interface item between two interface parties. The interface agreement recognizes an acknowledgment by two or more interface parties for an interface item. Interface agreements form the foundation for effective interface management since they represent progress toward resolving interface issues along interface points. For example: Interface Party *A* submits an interface item to Interface Party *B* to confirm pipe sizing at an interface point.

Interface coordinator: The representative of a client or contractor who is responsible for coordinating and responding to interface requests from contractors and subcontractors. The interface coordinator is most closely associated with work related to project interfaces and use of the interface management database.

Interface group: A group consisting of two (or more) independent parties who share a common boundary but have limited or no direct control over each other's activities.

Interface issue: An interface issue is a statement identifying areas (such as physical or functional) of the interface point requiring interface activity with another interface party.

Interface item: An interface item is a specific interface data or information request(s) resulting from an interface issue from one interface party to the other interface party. The interface items are typically coordinated through the use of an interface management database tool and use of interface management meetings. The items are coordinated and closed when an interface agreement has been reached.

Interface lead: The client or contractor representative responsible for interface management within a subproject. The interface lead is responsible for managing interface at the major subproject level (such as Topside facility for an offshore facility). At the contractor, the interface lead may be assigned to engineering and construction discipline leads.

Interface management system: The people, process, procedures, structure, tool, techniques, and training that is necessary to effectively and efficiently manage technical, project, organizational, and stakeholder interfaces.

Interface management: Interface management is the formal management process used to identify, document, communicate, coordinate, monitor, control, and resolve issues occurring across common boundaries by independent projects, project phases, systems, contracts, scopes of work, or organizations.

Interface manager: The client or contractor representative responsible for interface management for the project. The interface manager is responsible for the interface management program that is utilized on the project and for ensuring effectiveness during planning and execution of the project.

Interface management program: The project interface management program is a *system* that is comprised of people, processes, procedures, organization and structure, tools, techniques, and training to identify and resolve interface issues between various entities or parties associated with the project.

Interface party: A single entity, such as a contractor or client, with the responsibility to interface with other entities on a common interface boundary.

Interface point: A defined or precise area on the common boundary between two or more interface parties. An interface point is characterized by one or more interface issues that require the interface parties to agree and resolve.

Internal interface: An interface occurring within an interface party's scope of work or area of responsibility within the same project for the same client contract; including any derived subcontracts.

Preliminary: Best available interface data provided by company personnel or relevant contractors at a given point in time.

Shall: The word *shall* is used when a provision is mandatory.

Should: The word *should* is used when a provision is advisory or recommended only.

Will: The word *will* is used to predict or indicate a future action, event, or consequence.

Work: Scope of work specified in *agreements* that contractually obligate the contractor to adhere to the company's specified requirements.

Appendix B

Coreworx, Inc.

COREWORX INTERFACE MANAGEMENT OVERVIEW

Coreworx Inc. is a software solution company whose technology traces its roots to the North Sea oil and gas explorations of the 1980s. Our solutions are purpose-built to provide robust project information control and project execution for major capital projects.

The Coreworx Interface Management (CIM) solution is a leading web-based software solution used to manage project interfaces on large capital projects since 2005.

When implementing CIM, major interfaces are identified in the project as early as possible through a structured process and then managed effectively to prevent adverse impacts to the project. Coreworx replaces the traditional informal methods of managing interfaces with an online system that can manage thousands of interfaces, provide visibility and transparency, and allow for automated notifications and alerts.

The Coreworx solution increases transparency of interface activity and assists in scope delineation by proactively assisting in the identification of interface issues before they become critical. It does this by providing a central repository of all interface agreements that can be sorted and monitored by a planned completion date. Additionally, high-risk interfaces can be integrated with the overall master schedule through identification and monitoring of key interface milestones that are related to interface activity.

The solution also provides *management by exception* capability through the provision of drill-down dashboards that alert interface managers proactively of impending problems that need to be addressed before they impact the project critical path.

Coreworx provides a simple, easy-to-use user interface, which was developed in partnership with some of the world's leading oil and gas companies. Perspectives from both owner/operators and engineering, procurement, and construction (EPC) personnel have helped to build a high quality, intuitive system for managing both internal and external interfaces. Contractors can easily manage deliverables and keep track of due dates using web-based forms, reports, and dashboards. All communication is tracked providing a history and complete audit trail of each interface.

Business rules are enforced through the use of automated workflow templates that help to ensure compliance and consistency in execution. Alerts, notifications, and task-based actions are embedded in each work process to ensure that users are aware of task assignments and any modifications or additions made to the online interface register. Direct interfacing parties are kept informed as well as other interested parties using the Coreworx Distribution Matrix.

A robust roles-based security model ensures appropriate visibility levels and confidentiality requirements of interface activity.

Key components of the solution include:

- *Packages*: organize and manage work using packages; supports pre-award and post-award processes—interfaces are identified and documented referencing the responsible packages
- *Interface point*: used to document and describe an interface; manage and define scope split—supports ability to transition to different project phases and/or contracting parties
- *Interface agreements/action items*: used to facilitate the exchange of information and deliverables related to project interfaces
- *Automated work process*: enforce business rules, manage reviews and approvals; automated notifications ensure all interface stakeholders are kept informed and aware of decisions made
- *Reporting*: measure and monitor progress via reporting and graphical dashboards
- *Web-based interface register*: single central register accessible to all authorized users

B.1 INTERFACE DATA STRUCTURE

Coreworx supports a data structure that creates relationships between scopes of work, interfaces, and the interface agreements that have been raised for each interface. Figure B.1 below displays the relations between the various components:

- *Scope package*: typically represents a project work package or contract. Scope packages are awarded to contracting parties during the contract award process.
- *Interface points*: identify and describe project interfaces. An interface is a common boundary or connection between two interdependent stakeholders. The interface point form is used to define the scope split between two parties, outlining the roles and responsibilities of each.
- *Interface agreements*: support the exchange of information and deliverables between two contracting/interfacing parties. The interface agreement form is used to request information as well as the date the information is required.
- *Action items*: are requests to complete a task. Action items can be linked to interface agreements in order to capture additional actions taken by each party or required deliverables to resolve the interface.

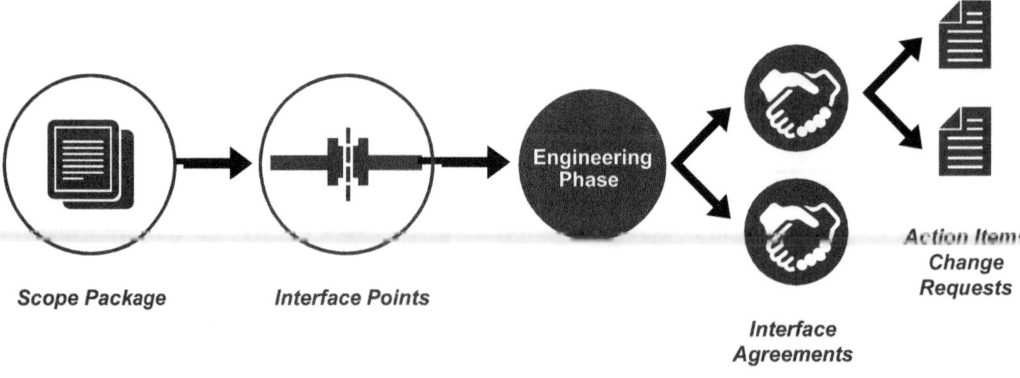

Figure B.1 Interface data structure

B.2 KEY ROLES AND RESPONSIBILITIES

The key to successful interface management is clearly defining roles and responsibilities. In building the interface register, Coreworx identifies the contracting or interfacing parties that are responsible for an interface.

As part of the onboarding process, user accounts are created and membership to a contracting party is identified. Coreworx supports the use of a global contractor register, which can be used to track prequalifications and previous work history. All interfacing parties, including contractors, subcontractors, suppliers, internal business units, and external third parties are identified for the project. With the interfacing parties identified, users are created and assigned to one of four primary roles:

- *Interface Manager*: each interface party must identify at least one interface manager. It is not uncommon on large-scale projects for the project team to not only identify an interface manager, but also to identify one or more interface coordinators. The interface team works with both internal and external interfacing parties to ensure successful delivery of the project.
- *Technical Contact*: is responsible for providing technical information for the contracting party to which he or she is assigned. The technical contact can also create and modify interface points and agreements.
- *Support*: is responsible for providing support to the interface manager or technical contact. This can include reviewing and gathering information and preparing action items for interface managers or technical contacts. The support role is not able to create or modify interface points and agreements.
- *Observer*: has read-only access to all interface-related information.

Users can belong to multiple roles. The documents and features available to a user in the system are determined by their role membership and the contracting party to which they are assigned. Figure B.2 shows example contracting parties and their roles.

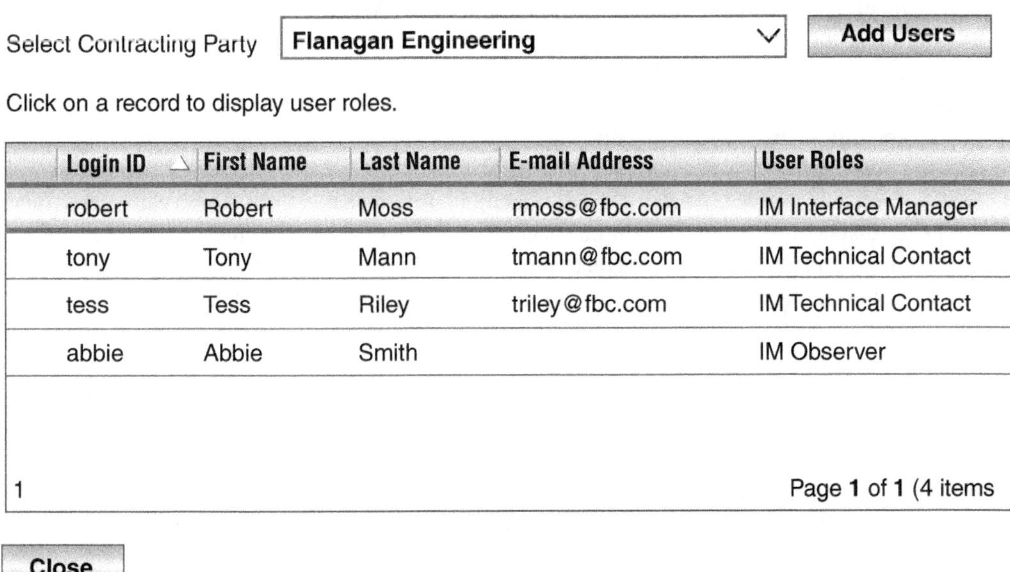

Figure B.2 Contracting party and role membership

B.3 MANAGING INTERFACING GROUPS

All interfaces involve at least two parties—some involve multiple parties. Users belonging to the interfacing parties (contractors, vendors, suppliers, etc.) have full access to all interface points that have been identified for their scope of work and can easily identify the party they are required to interface with. Users have the ability to search the online web-based interface register. Multiparty interfaces—referred to as the interface control working group (ICWG) in this book—are possible using various approaches. Each project team may choose what works best for them. The options include:

- Add additional parties directly to the interface point
- Configure distribution matrix to keep the other parties informed
- Grant selected interface parties additional access rights to selected interface points

Coreworx uses the term *contracting party* to represent interfacing parties. Contracting parties may include:

- Prime contractors
- Internal business units/disciplines/departments
- Project sponsors
- Third-party suppliers/subcontractors

Contracting parties are assigned to a project and awarded a package(s). A package represents a scope of work. The members or users of a contracting party can access interface information, raise and participate in interface agreements, and execute reports.

Contracting parties and scope packages can be created manually within the system or can be bulk loaded by using the Coreworx import process.

B.4 MANAGING INTERFACE MEETINGS

Regular interface meetings are required to ensure continued collaboration. Many projects will schedule regular meetings between the interfacing parties, along with the regularly scheduled global meetings that include all parties. Various methods are used to execute meetings; a common approach is to use the online conference to support interfacing parties that are located in various cities and countries around the world.

Meeting minutes are captured and stored within the system. Authorized users have the ability to view current and archived meeting minutes. Figure B.3 shows the location of the meeting minutes on the projects menu.

The web-based interface register is used to facilitate interface meetings. Users can query the online register, displaying a list of all open interfaces to be discussed. As each interface is reviewed, real-time comments and updates can be made that reflect discussions during the meeting. Comments are captured including the date and the individual who added the comment. It is important to keep all parties informed, even those who may not have participated in the meeting. Coreworx supports the ability to send a notification to all interested stakeholders when comments are added and the interface documents are updated. Figure B.4 shows an example of a new comment notification.

Meeting minutes are an important tool to all project teams. Keeping people informed and aware of decisions that have been made is critical. Using the interface register with the ability to update real-time data is a huge step forward in tracking decisions that were made during meetings, while at the same time ensuring that a log/audit is captured on the interface document itself.

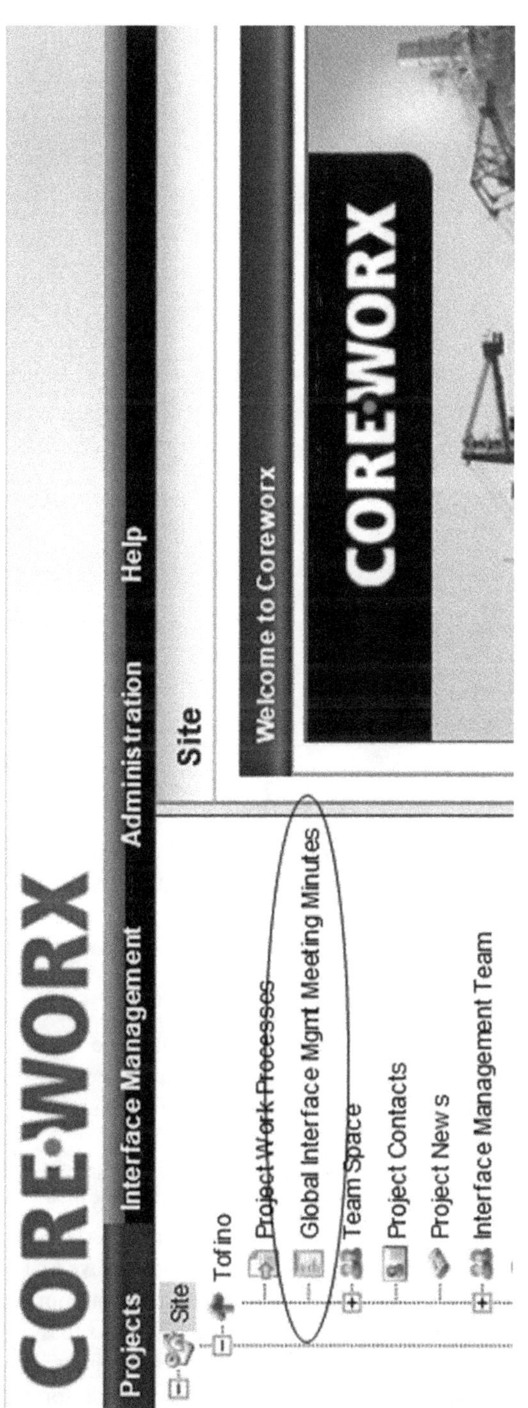

Figure B.3 Interface meeting minutes

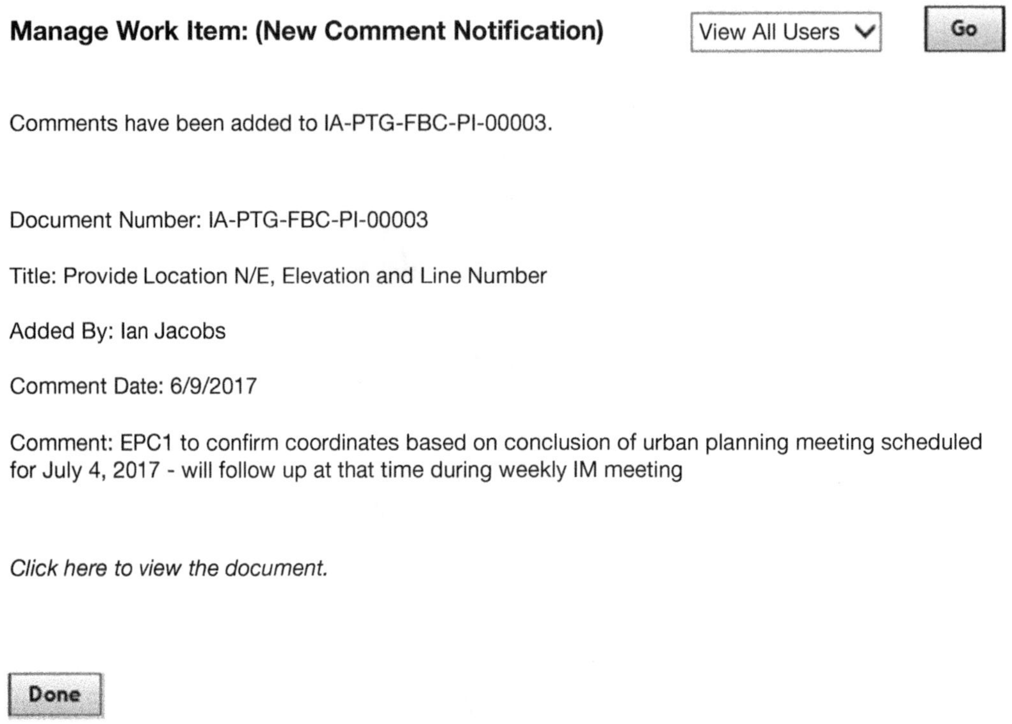

Manage Work Item: (New Comment Notification) View All Users Go

Comments have been added to IA-PTG-FBC-PI-00003.

Document Number: IA-PTG-FBC-PI-00003

Title: Provide Location N/E, Elevation and Line Number

Added By: Ian Jacobs

Comment Date: 6/9/2017

Comment: EPC1 to confirm coordinates based on conclusion of urban planning meeting scheduled for July 4, 2017 - will follow up at that time during weekly IM meeting

Click here to view the document.

Done

Figure B.4 Comments notification

B.5 WEB-BASED INTERFACE REGISTER

The online interface register provides the ability to successfully manage interfaces in a single central location, often replacing multiple spreadsheets that are frequently distributed by multiple parties. Day-to-day management of interfaces and ongoing updates are done using the online register. With all of the information tracked and stored in a single central location, new project participants can get up to speed quickly, thus handling user turnover is more easily done. Interface parties have the ability to search the interface register, create interface points, and raise interface agreements. A robust security model ensures that users have access only to interface documents to which they are a party, or to which they have been granted special viewing authorization. *Note*: this is referred to as the *Need to Know* security model. Coreworx also supports an *open* security model that provides full transparency for all parties.

Additional access rights can be granted to expand access to the interface points and grant the ability to create/respond to interface agreements if required (referred to as ICWG in Chapter 7).

Users have the ability to filter search results using various criteria. When a search is executed, the actions relevant to the selected document are dynamically displayed—guiding users through the process and life cycle of managing interfaces. The online register supports the ability to export the entire register or a subset; possible export formats include Excel and PDF Booklet.

Figure B.5 shows a screenshot of part of the online interface register. The search results display a list of interface points that match the search criteria entered. Key information is provided such as title, status, and significant dates. Users also have the ability to click on the interface point ID (document number) to open and view the details. The *actions* column provides a list of actions that are available to the user.

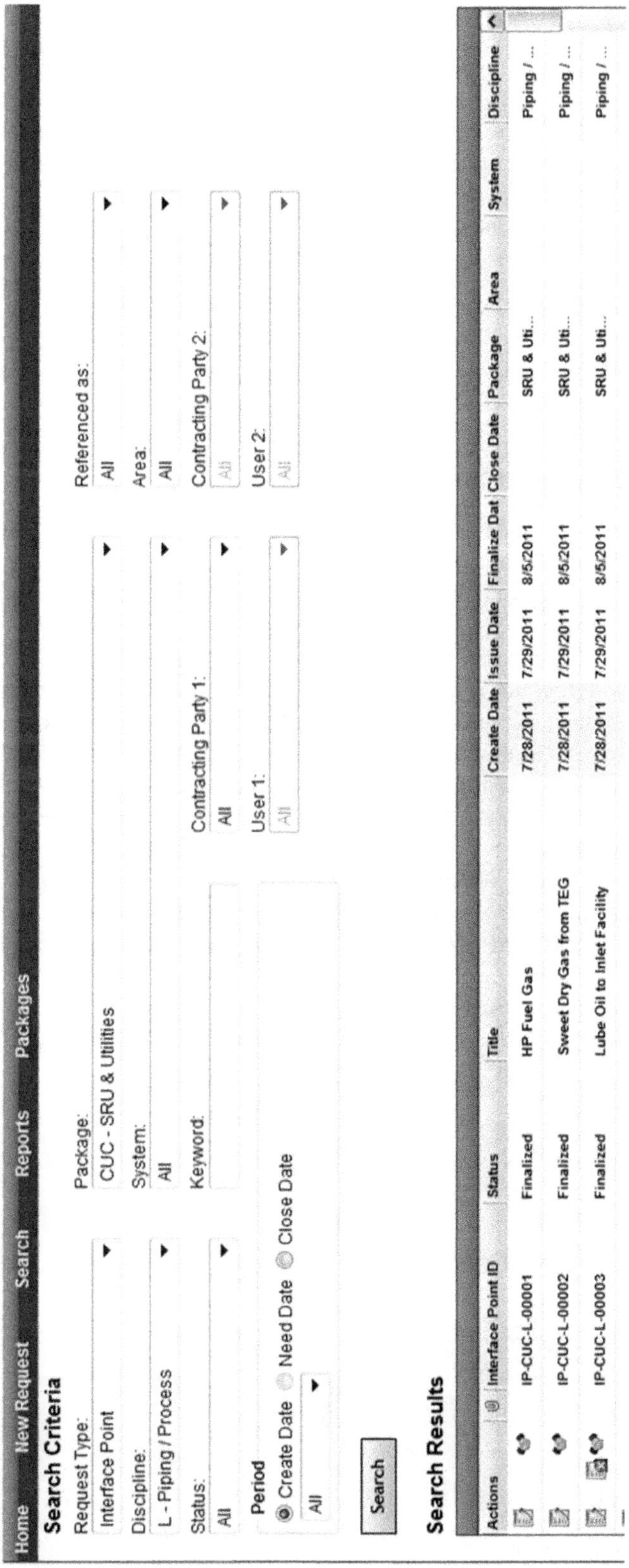

Actions	Interface Point ID	Status	Title	Create Date	Issue Date	Finalize Dat	Close Date	Package	Area	System	Discipline
	IP-CUC-L-00001	Finalized	HP Fuel Gas	7/28/2011	7/29/2011	8/5/2011		SRU & Uti...			Piping / ...
	IP-CUC-L-00002	Finalized	Sweet Dry Gas from TEG	7/28/2011	7/29/2011	8/5/2011		SRU & Uti...			Piping / ...
	IP-CUC-L-00003	Finalized	Lube Oil to Inlet Facility	7/28/2011	7/29/2011	8/5/2011		SRU & Uti...			Piping / ...

Figure B.5 Online interface register

B.5.1 Preliminary Interface Register

The development of the interface register is typically done during the front-end engineering design (FEED) stage of the project. Coreworx supports the ability to identify interfaces pre-award with an automated process to update the interfaces post-award. As contractors come onboard, they must *accept* the interfaces that fall under their scope of work and responsibility. Once accepted, the contractors can begin creating interface agreements.

The overall Coreworx approach includes:

- Identify and document interfaces using the interface point form
- Ongoing management of interfaces using the web-based online register
- Exchange of technical details and queries specific to interfaces via interface agreements
- Ongoing management and oversight using reporting and graphical dashboards
- Interface completion and closure

B.5.2 Identify and Record Interface Points

Interface points are used to document project interfaces. Interface areas, as described in the book, are presented as interface points in Coreworx. Interface points are assigned a document number, identify the scope packages/contracting parties responsible for the interface, capture key dates and attributes, and provide a detailed description.

It is common practice to identify a preliminary interface register during the FEED phase of a project. The preliminary interface register can be bulk loaded into Coreworx to generate the online register to be available during execution phases. The project team can also choose to develop the preliminary register directly in Coreworx. During delivery phases, the authorized users have the ability to identify additional interface points as required.

An interface point is defined as the position within a system at which responsibility passes from one EPC contractor to a third party or another EPC contractor. Interface points are commonly located at or near a geographic or functional contract boundary, but may also be located anywhere inside a plant area. Figure B.6 illustrates an example interface point.

Every interface point is identified by a unique number. The document number is determined by the project. A sample document number may appear as IP-XXX-Y-ZZZZ with the document number being derived from the fields shown in Figure B.7.

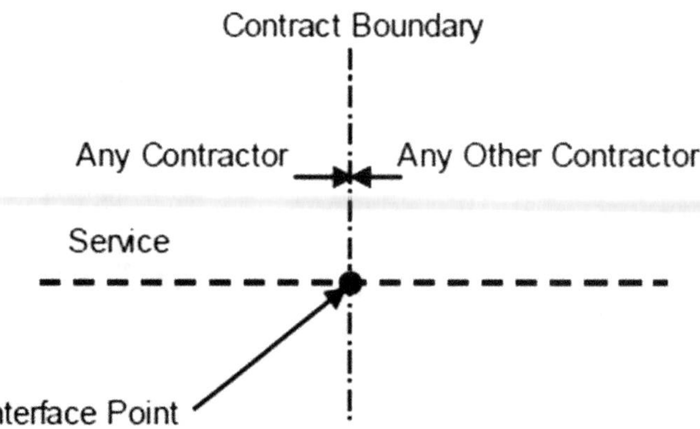

Figure B.6 Sample interface point

IP	Interface point
XXX	Scope package
Y	Discipline
ZZZZ	Sequential number

Figure B.7 Sample showing how document number is derived

As interface points are created and/or updated in the system, an automated review-and-approve work process is initiated. All parties to the interface must agree to the updates; and if configured, the project team must also approve. The work process records a complete audit trail tracking individual responses, actions, and timing of those actions.

B.6 INTERFACE AGREEMENTS

Interface issues and items are captured as interface agreements. Interface agreements support the exchange of information and deliverables between two parties, such as contracting parties and delivery teams. They track the information that one party generates and another party needs so that the party can continue with its scheduled project tasks. Interface agreements identify the document number, parent interface point, key dates (start date, need date, and closing date), attributes, and key stakeholders, as well as a detailed description of the request and the subsequent response.

Interface agreements can be created during any phase of the project and are *tied to* or *related to* an interface point. All interface communication is done using the interface agreement form. A sample interface agreement is shown in Figure B.8.

Every interface agreement is also assigned a unique document number, which is often configured to identify the requesting and responding parties. A sample document number may appear as IA-XXX-YYY-EL-ZZZZ with the document number being derived from the fields shown in Figure B.9.

A typical interface agreement request would follow the following process:

1. New interface agreement:
   a. Interface managers and technical contacts can raise a new interface agreement. The contracting party initiating the interface agreement is considered the *requesting party* and the contracting party responding is considered the *responding party*.
   b. The requesting party completes the online form by providing a detailed description of the information or deliverable required and providing the date the information is needed.
2. If owner endorsement is configured (see upcoming section), the interface agreement is reviewed and approved by the project team and/or client:
   a. This endorsement task provides the ability to accept the request or return the request to the requesting party for clarification.
   b. If the request is accepted, the interface agreement is submitted to the responding party.
3. The interface manager or the responding party receives the request and either confirms acceptance or returns the interface agreement to the requesting party for clarification (for instance, if the need date is not acceptable).
   a. If the terms and conditions described in the agreement are acceptable to both parties, the status of the request is updated from *submitted* to *accepted.*
4. On or before the agreed need date, the responding party issues the response.
5. The response is received by the requesting party. The interface manager of the requesting party can either confirm receipt of response and close the interface agreement or request

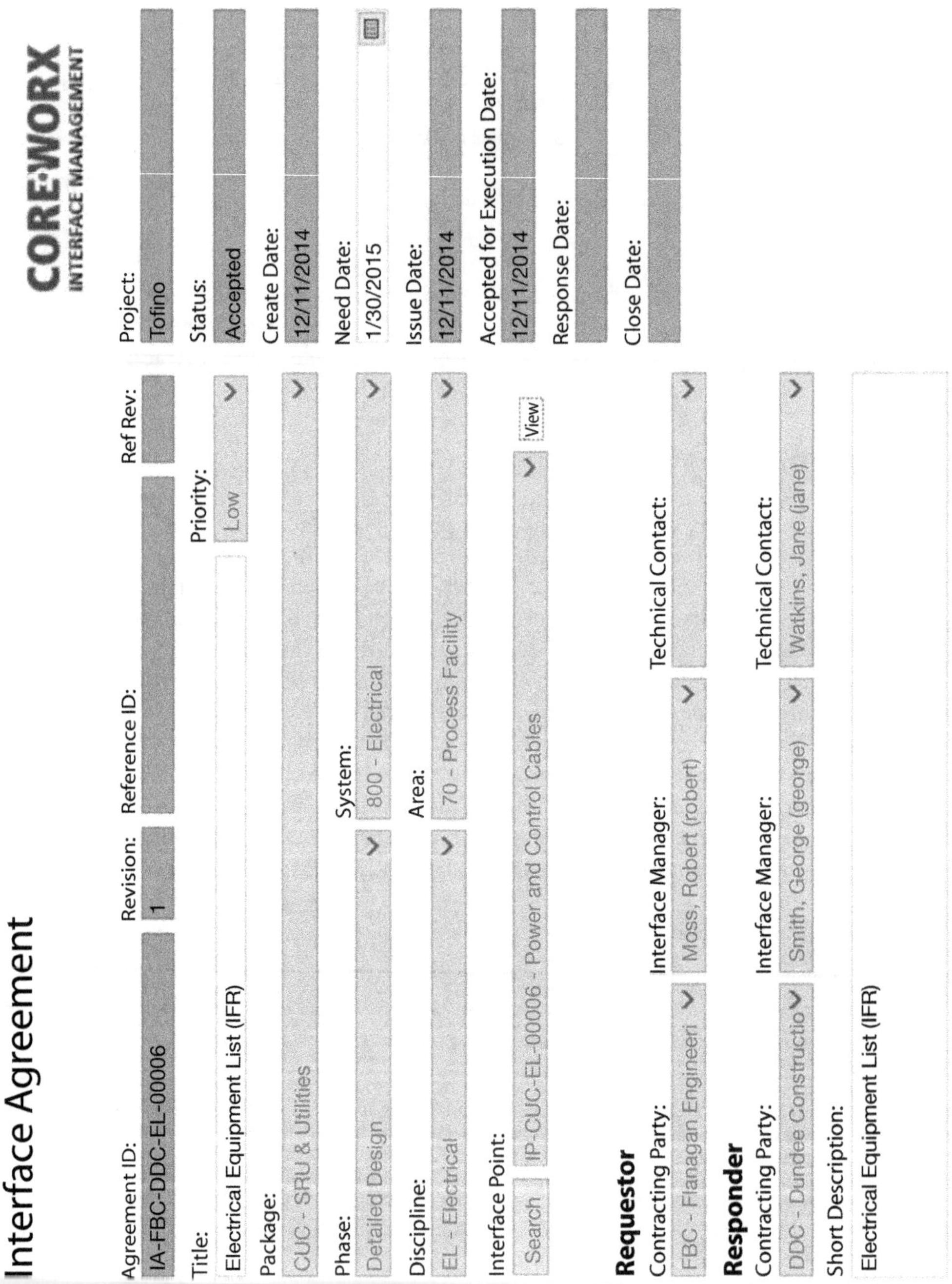

Interface Agreement

CORE·WORX
INTERFACE MANAGEMENT

Agreement ID: IA-FBC-DDC-EL-00006

Revision: 1

Reference ID:

Ref Rev:

Project: Tofino

Title: Electrical Equipment List (IFR)

Priority: Low

Status: Accepted

Package: CUC - SRU & Utilities

Create Date: 12/11/2014

Phase: Detailed Design

System: 800 - Electrical

Need Date: 1/30/2015

Discipline: EL - Electrical

Area: 70 - Process Facility

Issue Date: 12/11/2014

Interface Point: Search IP-CUC-EL-00006 - Power and Control Cables View

Accepted for Execution Date: 12/11/2014

Response Date:

Close Date:

Requestor

Contracting Party: FBC - Flanagan Engineeri

Interface Manager: Moss, Robert (robert)

Technical Contact:

Responder

Contracting Party: DDC - Dundee Constructio

Interface Manager: Smith, George (george)

Technical Contact: Watkins, Jane (jane)

Short Description:

Electrical Equipment List (IFR)

Figure B.8 Sample interface agreement

IA	Interface agreement
XXX	Requesting party
YYY	Responding party
EL	Discipline
ZZZZ	Sequential number

Figure B.9 Sample document number derived from an interface agreement

clarification of the response, at which point the agreement would be sent back to the responding party.

It is important that the project interface team manages and monitors the interface agreements being raised to ensure that timely responses are issued. Coreworx supports the ability to keep all parties informed and aware of interface agreement progress through notifications and alerts. For example, project teams can monitor upcoming workload using look ahead at reports and the online register can be used to facilitate online interface meetings. Overdue notifications and late acceptance notifications can also be configured.

B.7 OWNER (PROJECT MANAGEMENT TEAM) INVOLVEMENT

In the majority of cases, projects will encourage open and direct lines of communication between the parties involved in the EPC stages of a project. The more these parties share information and collaborate efficiently and effectively, the greater the chance of a successful project. Interface agreements can involve requests which may take significant time and cost; therefore, there may be instances in which the owner/operator wants to be involved in the direct dealings between these parties. For example, when dealing with cost reimbursable contracts, it is often desirable to have the option to review and approve a request from one party before the request is submitted to the responding party. In addition, when dealing with developing technology or potentially proprietary information, it may be desirable to broker these requests in an effort to ensure sufficient and detailed information is exchanged. The granularity and clarity of the information exchanged becomes increasingly important in these scenarios. Coreworx has termed this capability *owner endorsement.*

Owner endorsement is optional on a project-by-project basis. If configured, the interface agreement work process automatically includes an endorsement step to be completed by representatives of the client (e.g., owner/operator, EPC management, project management team). The endorsement step lets the owner review each request, discuss it with the parties involved if needed, and work with the contractor to prioritize.

B.8 INTERFACE AGREEMENT CLOSEOUT

The interface agreement is considered closed when the requesting party is satisfied with the content and timing of the provided deliverables by the responding party. Interface agreements could be closed at different phases of the project. Since an interface point includes multiple interface agreements, an interface point is considered closed once all of the associated interface agreements are closed.

B.9 ACTION ITEMS

Action items provide another channel for communication between or within interface parties. Action items are less formal than interface agreements and, as such, do not require the direct involvement of interface managers. Unlike interface agreements, action items can exist between two users in the same contracting party.

As with interface agreements and interface points, the action item form is completed and routed via an automated work process that supports the business rules defined by the project. The CIM system fully supports searching the online register for action items and provides a full set of tabular reports and graphical reports.

B.10 RESPONSIBILITY MATRIX

CIM uses a responsibility matrix to identify who is notified when an interface point, an interface agreement, or an action item is created/updated.

B.11 MONITORING AND CONTROL

Coreworx provides dashboards and reports to assist with the monitoring and control of interfaces to help ensure that progress and quality are visible and can be managed in the project and that the risk of potential delays is reduced.

Powerful reporting ensures that the owner and project team have the visibility needed to spot problems and control risks that can lead to delays and cost overruns. Coreworx graphical dashboards and robust reporting provides accurate, up-to-date information in real time. Project teams have the

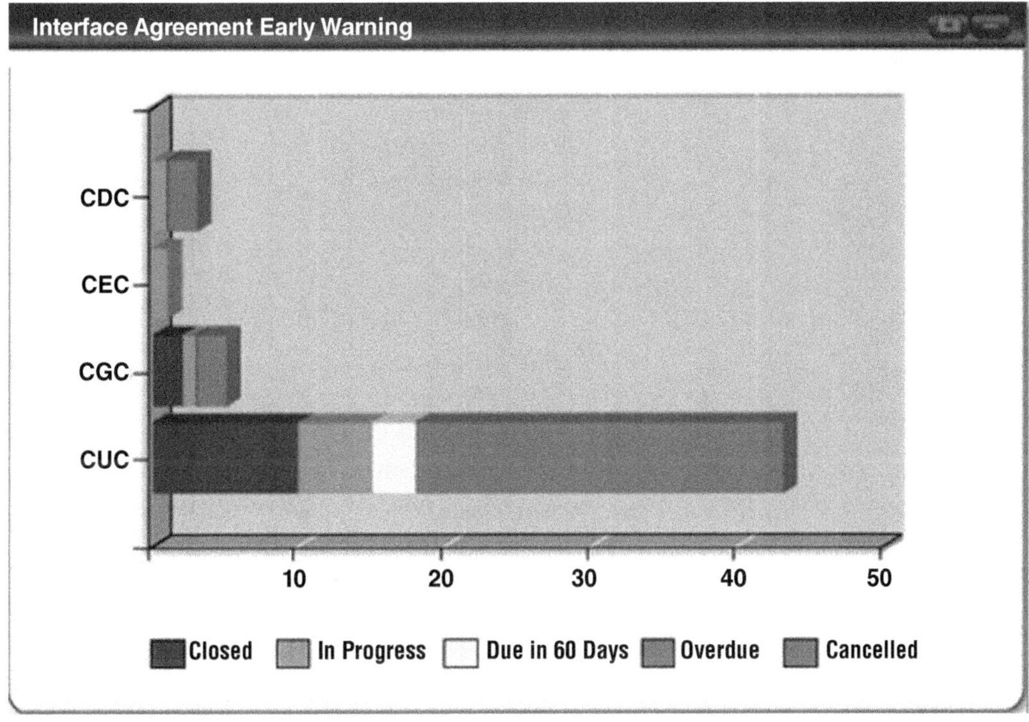

Figure B.10 Interface agreement early warning

information they need to make better decisions, manage change, and ensure continued progress. Figure B.10 shows an interface agreement early warning report.

The interface trends report provides an overall view of the project's interface management program. The report provides a graphical view of the register, identifying on a month-by-month basis the planned progress compared to actual progress. The monthly view allows interface managers to track progress visually and see a historical record of progress to date for each scope package. Potential problems can be identified: for example, a growth in the difference between planned versus actual is an indicator of a potential problem—shown in the interface trends report in Figure B.11.

For more information on Coreworx Interface Management, please visit http://www.coreworx.com/coreworx-products/interface-management/.

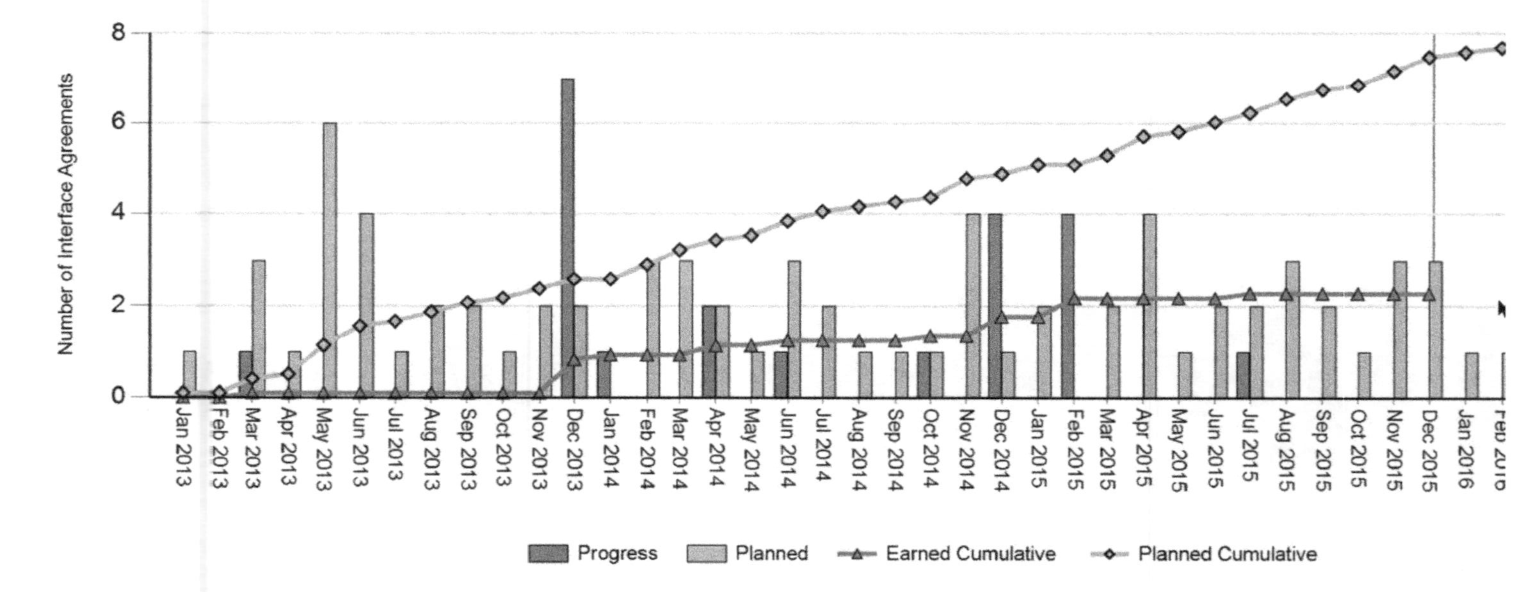

Interface Agreements

	CCC	CDC	CEC	CFC	CGC	CIC	COC	CPC	CSC	CUC	CXC
Total	0	4	4	2	15	0	0	0	0	52	0
Open	0	1	4	2	12	0	0	0	0	36	0
Overdue (Requestor)	0	0	1	0	5	0	0	0	0	2	0
Overdue (Responder)	0	0	2	2	4	0	0	0	0	31	0

Figure B.11 Interface trends report

Appendix C

ABC Management of Project Development

PREFACE

This document prescribes ABC Corporation's general approach to managing project development. This document serves as a guiding document for the development of project mandates and project execution plans (PEPs) for ABC development projects.

C.1 OBJECTIVE, APPLICATION, AND PROVISION

C.1.1 Objective

This document states ABC Corporation's requirements for evaluating, planning, maturing, and executing field development projects—divided into decision gates (DGs)—from the decision to initiate a commercialization project of petroleum resources (DG0) up to the hand over to the operating organization (DG4). The key objective is to ensure an orderly planning and execution of a development project and to ensure a consistent evaluation and decision process within ABC and toward partners and other stakeholders.

While each of the project development DGs are described in this document, Project Diamond has successfully achieved DG3 and is now preparing for the project execution phase. This document shall serve as ABC's guidance for further development of the Project Diamond project execution and operation plan (PEOP).

C.1.2 Application

This document applies to all field development projects being planned and executed by ABC Corporation. Relevant parts of this document, in particular, the requirements for documentation at DGs, shall be used as a guideline when following up field development projects operated by other companies (partner operated licenses).

C.2 PROJECT DEVELOPMENT

C.2.1 Project Development Phases and DGs

Project development includes planning and execution of an investment project. The project development period is defined as the period from confirmation of a discovery or acquisition of reserves to DG3 (see Figure C.1 for a diagram of the project development phases and DGs). The project execution phase typically starts after DG3 and is concluded with the decision to start operation and production (DG4).

C.2.2 Decision Gates

The major DGs in the project development process are defined to ensure a stepwise maturing and firming up of the development project. The established DGs are:

- DG0: Decision of initiating a commercialization project (start feasibility study)
- DG1: Decision of feasibility, technically and economically confirmed for at least one development solution
- DG2: Decision on concept selection and start preparation of a plan for development and operation (PDO)
- DG3: Decision on adopting a PDO and submitting a development application
- DG4: Decision to start operation of the field installations and production of the hydrocarbons

C.2.3 Project Development Principles

The following principles shall be governing for planning of field development projects:

- Health, safety, environmental, and quality (HSEQ)
  - ▸ Prioritization of health, safety, and environment
  - ▸ Risk management as a management tool to enhance project robustness and contingency alertness
  - ▸ Quality and consistency in early phases
- Planning and development
  - ▸ Short lead time to commercialization of the resources
  - ▸ Project activities in parallel when this may significantly reduce the lead time toward PDO
  - ▸ Integrated technical and commercial project development teams
  - ▸ Establish specific performance targets on selected key performance indicators (KPIs) for project execution
  - ▸ Experience transfer from one DG to the next

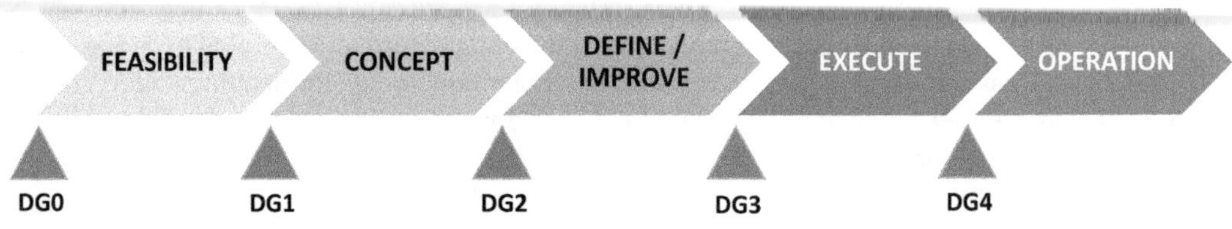

Figure C.1 Project development phases and decision gates

- Technology
  - Use of field-proven equipment when new technology does not provide clear, compensating, commercial benefits for extra risks, costs, and a longer lead time to PDO
  - Use of industry competence in project maturation, execution, and operation
- Business development/economics
  - Total value chain and business orientation with focus on project robustness and life-cycle economics
  - Early focus on needs for commercial agreements (key commercial terms concluded at DG2 for tie-in solutions)
- Execution
  - Safe—safe execution of projects; no-incident philosophy
  - Aligned—aligned with market capabilities; build on contractors' competence
  - Predictable—maximize front-end loading to support predictable outcome
  - Cost effective—capture market opportunities

C.3 PROJECT ORGANIZATION AND MANAGEMENT

C.3.1 Project Initiation

The project is normally initiated by ABC executive management and defined in a project mandate accepted by the project owner. The project mandate shall be updated at each DG. The project mandate shall normally include:

- A brief description of the business case and commercialization strategy
- Objectives, main value drivers, and critical success factors
- Scope and deliverables
- KPIs, main milestones, project specific quality, HSE, and technical requirements
- Time, schedule, and budget for the next phase

C.3.2 Project Organization

The asset owner manages ABC's ownership interest in the project/license. A license is defined as the right of the holder of the license to a predefined onshore/offshore area for the purpose of exploring and developing hydrocarbons. The asset owner appoints the chairperson for the license management committee. ABC's executive management appoints the project owner. The project owner is responsible for bringing the project to the next DG. The project owner appoints the project manager and the chairperson of the Technical/Field Development Committee.

The asset owner and project owner roles are both held by the COO up to project sanction (DG3). During the project execution phase, Senior VP–Projects, who shall assign the project manager, holds the project owner role. The project manager shall mobilize a cross-functional integrated project team in cooperation with ABC functional department managers:

- All relevant disciplines/functions shall be represented in the team, which shall collectively hold the necessary competence, skills, and experience covering all functions relevant to the project
- The team (size, competence, etc.) shall be adapted to the project characteristics and phase
- Roles and responsibilities shall be clearly defined
- A plan for the organization and manning of the project shall be established

- A project start-up meeting shall be arranged for internal stakeholders; the main purpose of the start-up meeting is to align the team

From project sanction (DG3), a steering committee is established. The steering committee shall support the project manager and contribute such that the project objectives are achieved.

C.3.3 Project Management and Project Customization

As part of the project development process, certain activities shall be performed and deliverables established for management of the project. Projects have different magnitude, complexity, and commercial consequences. The detailed work process and accompanying documentation therefore has to be decided for each project. This process is called project customization. A project customization shall be performed at the beginning of each project phase and the results from the project customization shall be documented and approved by the project owner. From DG2, activities and deliverables related to cost estimates and planning requirements for facilities shall be approved by Senior VP–Projects. Some of the most important documents in the project development process are described here:

- Project execution and overall procurement strategy (PEOPS)
  - The PEOPS is the main governing document for the project. The PEOPS shall describe the main challenges and risk profile for the project, align the project team, and describe strategies/plans for procurement activities and project planning/execution.
- Design basis
  - Reservoir pressure and temperature, fluid composition and chemistry, production profiles
  - Environmental and geotechnical conditions
  - Facilities capacities and regularity requirements
  - Product (oil, gas, condensate, etc.) specification
- Functional requirements
  - Functional requirements shall be developed for relevant installations/systems to be used as a consistent input to the design work
  - Regulations, codes, and standards
  - Requirements for each system
  - Operational and maintenance requirements
  - Drilling and well design
  - Intervention technology

C.3.4 Project Control

C.3.4.1 Time Management

A project master schedule shall be developed in the project initiation phase. The schedule shall be the formal, main project schedule, and present a high level, total overview of the project scope. A project detailed schedule shall be developed in the concept selection phase. The schedule shall be developed as a logical precedence network and present a detailed overview of the project scope. The project master schedule and project detailed schedule shall contain a work program and an execution schedule.

C.3.4.2 Cost Management

C.3.4.2.1 Cost Estimation

Investment cost estimates shall be established and revised according to technical requirements for cost estimate classes. Operating expenditures (OPEX) estimates shall be established based on analysis of the operational philosophy, manning studies, and benchmarking against similar fields/installations. Economic evaluations shall be performed according to ABC's basic assumptions for investment analysis.

C.3.4.2.2 Cost Management

A cost management system that includes the following shall be established: A work breakdown structure (WBS) covering all project deliverables or activities shall be established and maintained. A project control basis for cost and schedule shall be established at DG3, and the baselines updated (re-baselined) twice a year and as otherwise necessary. Cost development shall continuously be monitored.

C.3.5 Interface Management

An interface management system shall be established to ensure consistent and coordinated solutions within the project. The system shall include technical, operational, and organizational interfaces as relevant and shall reflect all involved parties and emphasize task responsibility. The system should account for high-risk areas and factors driving interface and interdependency complexity within the project and toward external entities that can influence project development.

C.3.6 Quality Management

C.3.6.1 Quality Planning

Quality management shall be an integrated part of the management of a project where all project units shall contribute actively in the process. Quality activities shall be planned and documented in order to ensure the quality of the project deliverables. Quality planning and execution shall satisfy the ISO 9000 series of standards.

C.3.6.2 Quality Monitoring

Systematic monitoring of activities shall be carried out according to the project monitoring plan, including:

- Audits, verifications, and reviews
- Monitoring of contractors' work

Third-party verifications—using industry experts and organizations—shall be considered where appropriate. Contractors' monitoring plans and inspection and test plans shall be reviewed and used actively. The reviews shall cover:

- Key assumptions
- Methodology used
- Conclusions and recommendations

The use of partner expertise may be part of such activities. The project shall carry out a self-assessment of its status relative to the requirements described in Appendix A at all DG.

C.3.6.3 Experience Transfer

At project start-up and at the beginning of each phase, the project team shall establish an overview of relevant experience information and lessons learned from other projects, from operations, and from partner-operated licenses. The project quality function is responsible for arranging appropriate experience handover to relevant line and project organizations.

C.3.6.4 Benchmarking

Benchmarking studies, where selected indicators are measured against comparable projects internally and externally, shall be carried out before each decision gate. Project indicators shall be defined and agreed upon with relevant process owners. In addition to the benchmark of selected indicators, benchmark/comparison of relevant key figures for weight, cost, and schedule shall be done.

C.3.7 Value Improvement Process (VIP)

VIPs are used to improve project performance and shall be performed after concept selection and before the start of execution. The project shall:

- Identify relevant VIPs
- Incorporate selected VIPs in the project plan
- Document applied VIPs

C.3.8 Change Management

Change control shall be established from DG2 and managed through a formal project system. The system shall cover changes in:

- Functional requirements and design basis
- Frame conditions (authority requirements and other governing documents)
- Macroeconomic assumptions
- PEOPS
- Approved budget/cost control basis
- Project schedule

C.3.9 Risk Management

Risk management shall be used actively throughout project development. Prior to DG1, a risk management system shall be established and maintained as a continuous management process throughout the project development process.

C.3.10 Technology Qualification

A technology assessment shall be carried out prior to DG1. Possible benefits from standardization and re-use shall be examined. If use of new technology is required, a technology qualification program shall be established and updated at each DG. The technology qualification activities shall be integrated into the project scope and schedule.

C.3.11 Communication, Information, and Document Management

C.3.11.1 Reporting

The project shall establish reporting routines satisfying requirements by ABC, authorities, and license agreements. The reporting shall, as a minimum, include:

- HSE
- Progress, cost development, and forecasts
- Status in relation to project main objective and project targets
- Threats and opportunities (risks)
- Mitigation of top-ranked risks
- Results from audits and project reviews

C.3.11.2 Stakeholder Management

To ensure understanding of internal and external stakeholders, a stakeholder analysis and project communication plan shall be developed. The stakeholder plan shall include a description of authority contact and coordination. Information should be provided to relevant stakeholders at the various DGs, according to the PDO and plan for installation and operation (PIO) guidelines.

C.4 PROJECT PHASES

The activities and deliverables for each project phase are listed in Appendix A of this document. For each phase from DG0 up to DG4, a DG support package shall be prepared consisting of a short DG document and more detailed support documents.

C.4.1 Project Initiation (-> DG0)

This phase covers the work needed to support the idea that there is a sufficient potential resource base and economic incentives to initiate a multidiscipline project in order to document technical and economic feasibility of a discovery. The work shall be based on the license application and the results from the discovery/delineation well(s).

The evaluation may be based on the preliminary in-place resources that were established in the discovery evaluation—a simplified reservoir evaluation using typical recovery factors for the type of reservoir formation(s) and fluid(s)—combined with order-of-magnitude historical cost data for an assumed field development solution.

A preliminary activity program with a project main plan giving the main activities (geological and geophysical analysis, reservoir evaluation, drilling of wells (appraisal and production)) and the major milestones from the start of business planning through the start of operation shall be part of the DG support package. A work program covering the feasibility phase shall be developed.

C.4.2 Confirmation of Feasibility (DG0 -> DG1)

This phase covers the work needed to demonstrate that there exists, at a minimum, one technical and economical field development solution for exploiting the resources. Issues to be considered follow.

C.4.2.1 Field Development Solutions

- It shall be considered to prepare both a *reference* development solution and at least one alternative development solution to promote competition and attract interest from more contenders

C.4.2.2 Facilities

- Screening studies shall be performed to define candidate development concepts and prepare preliminary cost and schedule estimates
- The screening studies shall also include evaluations of tie-in to infrastructure and possible need for and extent of modifications at host platforms—including the modification costs and schedule
- Simplified flow assurance analyses shall be undertaken when the development solution assumes well-stream transfer to a host platform

C.4.2.3 HSE

- Preliminary HSE assessment to identify main challenges, authority requirements, and risk reducing measures

C.4.2.4 Risk Management

- Establish risk register
- Preliminary risk assessment covering all aspects from subsurface to oil and gas export, economy, project execution, and stakeholders

C.4.2.5 Procurement

- Provide input to economic analysis on price ranges; consider carrying out market survey *expression of interest* (EoI)

C.4.2.6 Commercial—Tie-In and Processing Agreements

- Establish overall commercial strategy for the project
- Issue request for capacity overview to third-party host operators when tie-back to infrastructure is a principal part of the development alternative to be evaluated
- In cases when tie-in to infrastructure is the only alternative, a request for use may be considered as part of the DG1 phase in order to shorten the lead time (fast track); a prerequisite then shall be that the resource base has been firmed up and no further appraisal well is justified

C.4.2.7 Commercial—Transportation Agreements

- Define alternatives for transport and processing of oil and gas *unitization*
- Review requirements for unitization and establish plan for unitization

C.4.2.8 Project Control

- Establish the work program and execution schedule based on the project mandate, premises, assumptions, scope of work, and experience
- Establish cost estimates for capital expenditures (CAPEX) and OPEX based on case books

C.4.3 Concept Selection (DG1 -> DG2)

This phase comprises the work needed to mature and evaluate alternative field development solutions to a level where screening can be performed and one concept selected. The selected concept is then matured and preparation for the next phase performed in order to pass DG2. Two alternative solutions may be maintained and matured further after DG2 up to the DG3 decision when this may secure or enhance the competition without impairing the quality of the work. Issues to be considered are:

- Resource base and functional requirements
  - The reservoir development plan shall be firmed up by selecting the primary drainage strategy and performing the in-place, technical reserves and production profile uncertainty assessment (P90 pessimistic assessment case, P50 likely assessment case, and P10 optimistic assessment case)

There is considerable unpredictability in the volume of hydrocarbons within a deep reservoir. These assessment cases are based on well test data, geologic data, etc. P90 is the *worst-case* assessment, meaning that we know with high certainty that there will be that volume of hydrocarbons or greater in the reservoir. The P10 represents the *best-case* assessment, meaning that the probability of achieving that volume or better is only 10 percent.

  - Resource differences attributed to concept dependencies such as platform versus subsea wells, local off-take versus well stream transfer, or intervention frequency shall be accounted for
  - Subsurface related functional requirements for facilities and wells shall be defined for the different development alternatives considered
- Field development strategy
  - A range of development alternatives shall preferably be studied, evaluated, and successively screened out before concept selection
  - Establish a field development strategy including area considerations
  - If area development turns out not to be the selected concept, the basis for this conclusion shall be described and documented
- Evaluate drilling and well alternatives and establish a drilling and well design
  - Establish a plan for how to execute drilling and completion operations
  - Establish a rig strategy
  - Establish an intervention program
- Facilities
  - Concept studies shall be performed as a basis for defining the building blocks with cost and schedule estimates as a basis for comparing and narrowing down the development solutions
  - In some cases, it may be warranted to also start pre-FEED (front-end engineering design) studies in this phase. In such cases the field development strategy should have been concluded
  - Concept selection to be concluded before DG2
  - Flow assurance analysis shall be performed for the recommended solution(s), if relevant
  - Site surveys for field installations
- Preparations for operation
  - Establish concept/model for operation including integrated operations
  - Preliminary requirements regarding operational regularity
  - Participation in project HSE assessments (risk analysis, work environmental assessments, layouts, etc.
  - Provide operational personnel to development project activities (engineering, fabrication, and subcontractor follow-up, precommissioning, and commissioning activities, etc.)
  - Preliminary cost estimate for operations
  - Preliminary plans for onshore/offshore manning

- HSE
    - HSE assessments of the various development alternatives to identify main challenges, authority requirements, and risk-reducing measures
    - Prepare and issue environmental impact assessment plan and program
- Quality
    - Experience transfer
    - Establish quality plans
    - Establish project quality system for FEED as required
    - Prepare decision support package for selected concept
- Risk management
    - Risk assessment of the various development alternatives and identification of risk-reducing measures
- Procurement
    - Establish overall procurement strategy for the project
    - Market surveys shall be performed for procurement planning and to obtain an updated picture of cost level and capacity situation among contractors and suppliers
    - An EoI shall be issued to potential contractors in order to identify and screen any interested contractors. The result of the EoI to be used for DG2 evaluation
    - After EoI, a short list of contractors is established
    - Specific procurement strategies shall be prepared in case firm bids are required
    - Preparation of invitation to tender (ITT) for contracts for the FEED phase
- Commercial—tie-in and processing agreements:
    - Issue request for capacity overview to third-party host operators
    - Short listing of tie-in candidates
    - The tie-in solution to a host platform shortlisted as a candidate for offering processing and other services as a result of the capacity overview in the feasibility phase shall be agreed on with the third-party operator
    - Necessary concept studies of tie-in solution(s) at shortlisted host platforms shall be performed by the third-party operator prior to requesting an offer and to start commercial negotiations
    - Issue request for use to shortlisted tie-in candidates
    - A negotiation team shall be established and given a mandate approved by the management committee prior to the start of commercial negotiations
    - Commercial agreements (including appendices) should be completed for DG2, at least to a *heads of agreement* maturity level, unless several field development alternatives are brought forward to the next DG
- Commercial—transportation agreements
    - Issue request for capacity overview to third-party host operators
    - Short listing of tie-in candidates
    - The tie-in solution to a facility shortlisted as a candidate for offering transportation and processing and other services as a result of the capacity overview in the feasibility phase shall be agreed on with the third-party operator
    - Necessary concept studies of tie-in solution(s) at shortlisted facilities shall be performed by the third-party operator prior to requesting an offer and to start commercial negotiations
    - Issue request for use to shortlisted tie-in candidates

  - A negotiation team shall be established and given a mandate approved by the management committee prior to the start of commercial negotiations
  - Initiate gas flow architect study
- Commercial—unitization
  - Finalize plan for unitization or carve out when the discovery comprises more than one license
  - A negotiation team shall be established and given a mandate approved by the management committee
- Project control
  - Prepare/update execution schedule and master schedules based on project assignment, premises, assumptions, scope of work, and experience
  - Schedules shall be developed for each concept
  - Update cost estimates for CAPEX and OPEX based on case books
  - Establish a WBS

C.4.4 Define and Detail the Project (DG2 -> DG3)

This phase comprises the work needed to define and detail the selected field development solution and to prepare and issue the PDO documentation including the environmental impact assessment. An important part of the work in this phase is preparation for the execution phase. Issues to be considered include:

- Subsurface (from top of well to hydrocarbon reservoir)
  - In this phase, a further improvement of the geological and reservoir simulation model shall take place
  - Detailed drainage strategy shall be described. The following shall be included:
    - Recovery per well
    - Integrated well deliverable study including artificial lift and well chemistry management
    - Water management strategy
    - Allocation and well testing philosophy
    - Scale management philosophy
  - Functional requirements for facilities and wells based on subsurface uncertainty assessment (P90 pessimistic assessment case, P50 likely assessment case, and P10 optimistic assessment case) shall be concluded
  - Possible improved oil recovery (IOR) measures shall be described and the potential evaluated; a description of how this potential could be realized with the chosen concept/strategy shall be included
  - A description on how exploration potential can be implemented in the development plan shall be included
- Field development solutions
  - Normally, one field development solution is brought forward in this phase; however, if there are good commercial reasons for maturing alternative development solutions through the FEED phase, this can be performed after approval by the license management committee
  - The principle shall be to keep competition between alternatives as long as possible without compromising the quality of the work; issues which may be important in this respect are availability and commercial terms for the use of third-party facilities for the processing and transportation of products

- Update and detail an area development strategy, as seen in the DG2 phase
- Drilling and wells
  - Establish a final drilling and well design on an individual well basis, including a plan for execution
  - Establish and dimension a well life-cycle intervention program
  - Update drilling expenditures (DRILLEX) estimates including cost uncertainty analyses
  - Prepare tender for rig and other specified long-lead items
- Facilities
  - Implementation of results from site surveys including geotechnical investigations for the design of field installations, including surveys of pipeline routes
  - FEED studies for field installations shall be performed to define the technical basis for further engineering work, and be the basis for tender packages in order to receive firm tenders
  - Update design basis and functional requirements
  - Perform value improvement process
  - Requirements regarding operational regularity, reliability, and availability of essential equipment and systems to be concluded
- HSE
  - Detailed HSE assessments of the selected development solution including ALARP (as low as reasonably practicable) and BAT (best available technique) evaluations
  - Prepare and issue environmental impact assessment
  - Total risk analysis
  - Authority applications
- Quality
  - Experience transfer
  - Detailed quality planning
  - Independent verification of key project items essential for project execution and project economics
  - Establish project quality system for execution as required
  - Prepare DG3 decision support package
  - Establish project manual with governing documents and system for the execution project
- Risk management
  - Risk assessment of the selected development solution and implementation of risk reducing measures
- Procurement
  - Award of contracts for FEED studies
  - Prequalification of tenderers for the various contract packages shall be performed in this phase if it is decided that prequalification through the Achilles system is not used
  - Tender packages for major contracts and long-lead items (if relevant) shall be prepared in this phase
  - Firm offers (bids) for the main project building blocks shall be secured before submittal of the PDO
  - If relevant, project sponsor and partners agree on and issue contracts or purchase orders for long-lead items and obtain government approval—in the case of Norway, the Ministry of Petroleum and Energy (MPE)—to allocate funds for these items prior to approval of the formal project application; this reduces impact on schedule while awaiting delivery of such items

- Commercial—tie-in and processing agreements
  - Fully-termed agreement
- Commercial—transportation agreements
  - Gassco architecture study completed and presented to approval authority MPE (Gassco is the system operator for transporting gas from the Norwegian continental shelf to other European countries. The government of Norway oversees Gassco operations and its relationship to transport system owners)
  - Fully-termed agreement for transportation and processing of oil and gas
  - Participant agreement for new joint ventures (e.g. new gas/oil pipelines)
- Commercial—unitization
  - Complete unitization agreement
- Project control
  - Update WBS
  - Prepare/update execution schedules and master schedules based on project assignment, premises, assumptions, scope of work, and experience
  - Schedules shall be developed for each concept
  - Schedule risk analyses shall be performed
  - Establish cost estimates for CAPEX and OPEX based on case books
  - Cost and schedule risk analysis shall be performed
  - Establish project reserves
  - Prepare work program and budget for the execution project including three years of investment and operation budgets
  - Preparation for project execution by establishing:
    - Organization charts and manpower plans
    - Procedures for cost control and cost baseline updates
    - Procedures for progress reporting and schedule baseline updates
    - Authority matrix in connection with variation order handling
    - Project reserve handling

C.4.5 Execution Phase (DG3 -> DG4)

The execution phase starts after DG3 when the license has approved the PDO submission. It comprises drilling and completion of production wells and construction, installation, and commissioning of all field installations. Issues to be considered are:

- Subsurface—the main activity in this period is to develop the first long-range reservoir management plan based on the PDO. The main elements to be included are:
  - Field overviews and brief reservoir descriptions with references to detailed descriptions
  - Overview of in-place hydrocarbon volumes and associated recoverable volumes including resource classification and uncertainties
  - Data acquisition and reservoir monitoring strategy including plans for mitigating remaining key uncertainties
  - The strategy shall be cross-disciplinary covering all data types relevant for monitoring and further development of the field, including IOR
  - Plans for geophysical reservoir monitoring
  - Production management strategy
  - Long-term water management strategy (including discharge of produced water)
  - Future reservoir development strategies throughout total field life, including specific strategies for IOR

- Identification of current and future exploration/business opportunities and their impact on reservoir information needs and reservoir development
- Long-term production and injection plan, including forecasts of yearly deliveries of oil, gas, and natural gas liquids with uncertainty ranges and assumptions
- Long-term drilling and well work-over plans
- Pore pressure development and the impact on future drilling
- Late field-life considerations

- Support drilling and wells in detailing the production drilling and completion program
- Drilling and wells
  - Prepare detailed drilling procedures and main completion program and issue to authorities
  - Prepare individual well programs
  - Start predrilling of production/injection wells
- Facilities
  - Detailed design
  - Construction and installation of facilities
  - Mechanical completion
  - Commissioning
  - Handover to operations
- Preparation for operation
  - Establish the organization for operation personnel to project activities as planned; operations personnel shall be involved in precommissioning and commissioning activities
  - Establish document system for life-cycle information (LCI), if required
  - Develop maintenance and inspection programs for equipment, systems, and structures; define and procure all required spare parts and consumables
  - Perform training of operational personnel as required according to authority and internal requirements; participation in project activities is considered an important part of personnel training
  - Execute all other required preparations for facilities start-up (establish agreements/contracts required for operation; establish on-shore base functions/agreements, etc.)
- HSE
  - HSE follow-up on construction sites and installation operations
  - Prepare and issue authority applications
- Quality
  - Experience transfer
  - Review of contractors' quality plans
  - Quality follow-up on construction sites
- Risk management
  - Risk assessments during construction and installation
  - Follow-up implementation of risk-reducing measures
- Procurement
  - Award of major contracts and purchase orders for field development
  - Contracts and purchase order expediting and follow-up
  - Change order management
- Project control
  - Update schedules based on project mandate, premises, assumptions, scope of work, and experience
  - The main schedule and detailed schedule shall be frozen and issued as the master control schedule

- The master control schedule shall be the schedule for project follow-up during execution
  - ▸ Schedule and cost risk analyses shall be performed
  - ▸ Master control estimate to be established based on FEED information—master control schedule and contingency from risk analyses—project reserves to be defined
  - ▸ Project change management process with approved authority matrix for execution shall be established
- Commercial
  - ▸ Operational type of appendices to be finalized (e.g., metering and allocation)

C.4.6 Project Completion and Closing

The project is completed when the project has accomplished delivery of all agreed deliveries; i.e., all facilities, wells, etc., are completed, commissioned, and delivered to operations—including documentation. The project manager is responsible for ensuring that the project closeout is performed according to agreed project procedures. This includes demobilization of project personnel, closeout of contracts and project accounts, filing of project documents, controlled and systematic conveyance of lessons learned, and arranging completion of any remaining work, tasks, and services.

C.5 DEFINITIONS

Definitions can be found in Table C.1.

Table C.1 Definitions for ABC management of project development

Asset owner	The asset owner is the person in ABC executive management responsible for managing ABC's ownership interest in the project/license.
Benchmarking	Comparison of selected indicators for a project against corresponding indicators for compatible facilities, normalized for relevant parameters, e.g., resource basis, capacities, product(s) etc.
Completion	Completion is a generic term covering mechanical completion, installation, and commissioning.
Decision gate (DG)	A predefined point in the project model where ABC and the license partners have to make appropriate decisions whether to move to the next phase, make a temporary hold, or terminate the project.
FEED (Front-end engineering design)	Equivalent to the term "pre-engineering."
Life-cycle information (LCI)	Life-cycle information: Information required by the company for engineering, preparation for operations, start-up, operation, maintenance, repair, modification, and decommissioning of an installation. LCI includes both information submitted to the company and retained by the supplier on behalf of the company. LCI includes what has previously been termed documentation for operations (DFO).
Mechanical completion	Mechanical completion of an installation means that the installation is built in accordance with relevant drawings and specifications. All relevant LCI shall be quality checked. All specified tests and inspections are carried out and documented in a uniform way. The installation is ready for handover to Commissioning.

Project control basis	Plans, estimates, and commercial assumptions that form the basis for control and follow-up of a project in the execution period.
Project manager and project management team	Management group of a project team given the responsibility for planning and realizing an investment project.
Project mandate	Document accepted by the project owner defining the project frame, scope, deliverables, schedule, and budget to the project manager.
Project owner	The project owner is the person in ABC executive management responsible for bringing the project to the next DG.
Project review	A technical and readiness review of the documented decision basis to evaluate whether status/condition in a project is in accordance with ABC requirements at a DG.
Self-assessment	Review performed by the project to confirm that project requirements have been met at defined stages of project planning and execution (DG1, DG2, DG3, DG4).
Stakeholder	Person, group, or authority having an interest in the activities, performance, or success of an organization.
Stakeholder analysis	Method of identifying and evaluating internal and external stakeholders that have an interest in and that can influence the project in a negative or positive direction. Such stakeholders may be owners, authorities, environmental organizations, land-owners, fishermen, internal ABC units, and others. The preparation of strategies with respect to the stakeholders for the different phases of the project is part of the analysis.
Technology qualification program	Document containing activities, acceptance criteria, and DGs needed to qualify new products or new technologies to ensure they are fit for purpose.

Appendix D

Project Diamond Mandate for Execution Phase

This project mandate document covers the responsibilities for the execution of Project Diamond with regard to:

- Objectives
- Governance requirements
- Success factors
- Principal scope of work
- Main deliverables
- Key milestones
- Organization

D.1 PROJECT OWNERS

The Senior VP–Projects is the project owner and has the overall responsibility for Project Diamond. The daily planning and running of the project activities is assigned to the project director in close cooperation with the project management team. This version of the document covers the period between two specific decision gates (DGs): DG3 approval and the DG4 milestone.

D.2 PROJECT OVERVIEW

Project Diamond encompasses a 20 km area within the DL 0072 and DL 0046 development licenses. ABC Corporation (65%) is the operator for the Diamond Project, while TDN, Inc. (25%) and Waverly Exploration (10%) are partners.

This project mandate document covers the development of Project Diamond with a fixed offshore platform, pdQ (partly processing, drilling, and quarters), and with a subsea development to transfer the Project Diamond wells stream to the Project Sapphire platform for final processing and export of stabilized oil and rich gas.

D.3 OBJECTIVES AND SUCCESS FACTORS FOR PROJECT DIAMOND

D.3.1 Business Objectives

- Develop the resources in the Project Diamond field in accordance with the scope and framing defined by the Project Diamond plan for development and operation (PDO)

D.3.2 Project Objectives

- Execute the project in accordance with national laws and regulations
- Execute the project according to health, safety, and environmental (HSE) and quality objectives
- Deliver first oil October 1, 20xx
- Enable a first year Project Diamond injection and production regularity of 96.6%
- Execute the approved project scope within the overall and approved execution budget and schedule
- Plan, develop, manage, and document the project activities according to ABC Corporation's governing documents
- Deliver the facilities at DG4 that can be operated according to design-basis requirements and functional requirements
- Prepare for operation so that the facility may be put straight into operation at DG4 with all personnel and operating procedures in place

D.3.3 Project Success Factors

The following success factors have been identified for the project execution phase:

- Strong HSE commitment within the project management team, zero target
- Utilize best business practice to achieve a safe, aligned, predictable, and cost-effective project delivery; lessons learned; and benchmarking from similar projects
- Experienced, competent, and sufficient internal and external resources
- Motivated team, aligned with common goals
- No change philosophy
- Proactive interface, risk, and contract management
- Integrated team execution model; build team culture

D.3.4 Project Priorities

The project priorities shall be

1. HSE
2. Quality
3. Schedule
4. Cost

These priorities thus support the optimized net present value of the project.

D.4 GOVERNING DOCUMENTS

The main documents governing Project Diamond are listed hierarchically as follows:

1. National laws and regulations
2. Joint operating agreement and PDO
3. ABC management system
4. Project mandate and project execution and overall procurement strategy
5. HSE program, design basis, functional requirements, and project-specific processes and procedures
6. Technical and contractual requirements
7. Standards and guidelines

D.5 PROJECT EXECUTION FRAMING DOCUMENTS

The key documents for execution of the project are:

- Project design basis
- Project functional requirements
- Project concept selection report
- Case books and economy analysis for DG3
- Master control estimate and schedule for the project execution phase
- Project execution work breakdown structure
- Project organization charts for project execution
- HSE strategies and HSE program
- Risk management plan, risk summary, and mitigation plans
- Interface management and control plan
- Quality control plan
- Front-end engineering design reports for Topside, Jacket, and subsurface umbilical, risers, and flowlines (SURF)
- Recommendation on contracts for Topside, Jacket, and SURF
- Recommendation on contract for transport and installation
- Long-lead item list and purchase order status
- Commercial agreements, such as nonbinding Heads of Agreements with potential buyers at DG3 with third party for oil and gas export (commercial)
- Conditions for governmental approval of the PDO

D.6 PROJECT ORGANIZATION

The Project Diamond organization for the execution phase, reflecting the integrated team philosophy, is shown in Figure D.1.

The asset owner for the Project Diamond development is the COO. The asset owner is responsible for planning and stewarding the license activities and for securing the coordination with the Project Diamond partners, the Ministries, and the Petroleum Directorate (PD).

The project owner for the Project Diamond development is the Senior VP–Projects.

The Project Diamond director (project manager) is responsible for delivering Project Diamond from DG3 (sanction) into DG4 (the production phase) and together with the integrated Project Diamond team by:

- Ensuring optimization of Project Diamond value throughout the duration of the development

- Ensuring that the field's development plan is clearly outlined and communicated to all stakeholders
- Making sure all the key objectives and drivers are clearly communicated and understood by the Project Diamond team and other stakeholders
- Ensuring that the Project Diamond team is focused on a timely delivery of the project planned milestones in an effective and efficient manner while adhering to safety and environmental goals of the ABC Corporation

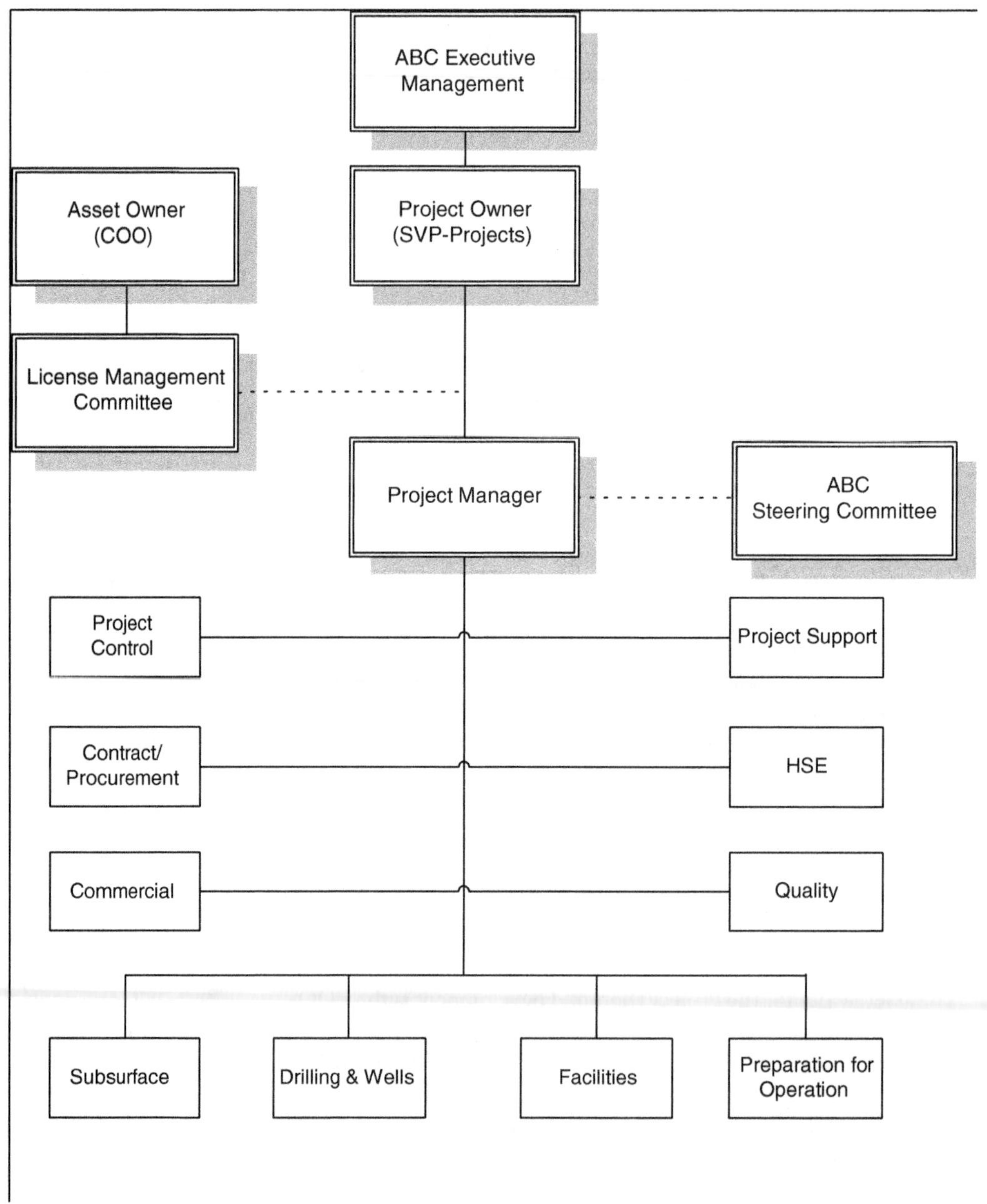

Figure D.1 Project Diamond organization for execution phase

- Making sure that a continuous improvement process is applied using an integrated discipline approach to reduce and manage project uncertainties
- Ensuring that a risk management and contingency planning system is in place and updated on a continuous basis
- Making certain that preparation for operation is conducted such that the facility may be put straight into operation at DG4 with all personnel and operating procedures in place
- Exercising strict project control with respect to actual and planned budgets, schedule planning, and product quality
- Overseeing selection and training of employees to meet project and operations milestones
- Overseeing planning and updating of long-term production capacity, capital investments, and long-term drilling

D.7 STAKEHOLDER MANAGEMENT

A separate stakeholder management plan has been developed. In addition, responsibility for external communication with investors/media and other interested parties rests with the investor relations manager and the communication manager.

D.8 INTERFACES

The Project Diamond operational concept is illustrated in Figure D.2. As an offshore partial-production facility, Project Diamond will recover hydrocarbons, process out bulk water, and export its hydrocarbons to Project Sapphire for further processing through the oil pipeline project and gas pipeline projects to onshore facilities and markets. Project Diamond must coordinate activity to tie-in physically to Project Sapphire and ensure its pipeline and hydrocarbon compositions meet export requirements by the various pipeline projects. In addition, Project Diamond will receive 110 kV power (to power the Project Diamond offshore facility) through a subsea power cable. This power cable also includes two fiber cables so that Project Diamond and Project Sapphire can operate safely and manage combined production, and finally, to help Project Diamond start wells and maintain reservoir pressure and *gas lift* (which is used to aid in Project Diamond's production process).

In addition, Project Diamond has undertaken a complicated contract strategy to deliver its project, which is illustrated in Figure D.3. This contract strategy creates several interfaces between main entities that are delivering products and services to Project Diamond.

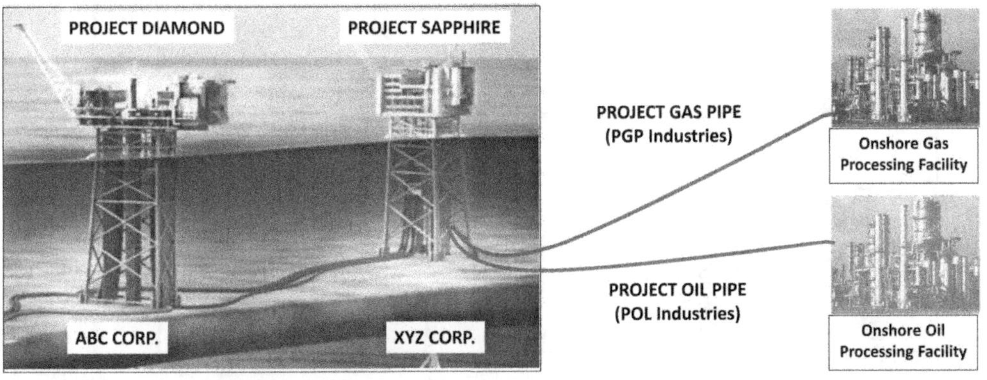

Figure D.2 Project Diamond operational concept

DG2

DG3

DG4

Diamond Project "Phases"	Drilling		Subsea Flowlines and Power Cables	pdQ Topside	Jacket	Transportation and Installation	Flotel
	Rig	Services & equipment					
Project Management	ABC Corporation						
Concept Development	NA	Study contracts as relevant	Concept study contract	Study contract	Study contract		NA
FEED			FEED contract Reimbursable	FEED contract Reimbursable	FEED Contract Reimbursable	Study Contract under Topside FEED	
EPC	Rig Contract Reimbursable	Service and equipment contracts Reimbursable and Lump Sums	EPCI Lump sum and Reimbursable	EPC Norms and rates for construction. Target sum for engineering & procurement Lump Sum for preliminaries and Living Quarter	EPC Lump sum	EPCI Lump sum	Flotel Contract Reimbursable
Transportation and Heavy Lift				EPCI Lump Sum			
Installation and Hook-up			Reimbursable	Reimbursable	NA	NA	
Commissioning	NA	NA	ABC Corporation			NA	NA

Figure D.3 Project Diamond contract strategy

APPENDIX E

Project Diamond Execution Plan

This appendix contains the sample Project Diamond execution plan that governs the project during execution after decision gate (DG) 3 and up to DG4.

E.1 INTRODUCTION TO THE DIAMOND PROJECT EXECUTION PLAN FOR DG3 TO DG4

E.1.1 Purpose

The purpose of this document is to outline how Project Diamond is planned to be executed from DG3 to DG4. This document describes project targets, strategies, and the management and control systems established to meet the project objectives within the given project framework. The project execution plan (PEP) is a part of the project governing documents for Project Diamond. The document outlines the most important elements in the project execution phase, along with how the project intends to handle these in order to achieve a timely, cost effective, and safe development of the project.

E.1.2 Responsibility

In the sample organization, the field director is responsible for the preparation and maintenance of the PEP with support from relevant representatives in the project team. The field director is also in charge of the facility and the 500-meter zone around the facility. This includes operations, resupply, helicopter operations, and transiting in and out of the surrounding safety zone. The PEP is approved by the Project Diamond owner/director. In the sample organization, the project director is also the Senior VP–Projects, to whom the project manager reports.

E.1.3 Governing Documents

The Project Diamond governing documents are listed hierarchically as follows:

- National laws and regulations
- Joint operating agreement and plan for development and operation (PDO)
- ABC Corporation management system
- Project Diamond mandate and PEP

- Project Diamond health, safety, and environmental (HSE) program, design basis, functional requirements, and project specific processes and procedures
- Project technical and contractual requirements
- Project standards and guidelines

E.1.4 Definitions and Abbreviations

CAPEX	capital expenditure
CCE	current control estimate
CCS	current control schedule
CRA	cost risk analysis
DG	decision gate
DRILLEX	drilling expenditure
EIA	environmental impact assessment
EPC	engineering, procurement, and construction
FEED	front-end engineering design
HAZID	hazard identification study
HAZOP	hazard and operability analysis
HSE	health, safety, and environmental
HUC	hook-up and commissioning
KPI	key performance indicator
LCI	life-cycle information
LoI	letter of intent
MC	management committee
MCE	master control estimate
MCS	master control schedule
OPEX	operational expenditure
PDO	plan for development and operation
pdQ	partial processing, drilling, and living quarters [platform]
PEP	project execution plan
PEOPS	project execution and overall procurement strategy
VO	variation order
VOR	variation order request

E.2 PROJECT OVERVIEW

E.2.1 Description of the Project

Project Diamond encompasses a 20 km area within the DL 0072 and DL 0046 development licenses. The development license is an authorization from the government that allows an entity the access rights to a specific and defined area for developing hydrocarbon resources. The percentage of ownership is mandated by the government as part of licensing rounds conducted by the government's petroleum directorate. Development licenses describe, govern, and specify the percentage of interest to each licensed firm. ABC Corporation (65%) is the operator for Project Diamond, while TDN, Inc. (25%) and Waverly Exploration (10%) are partners.

ABC's main business objective for Project Diamond is to develop the resources in the DL 0072 and 0046 license fields in accordance with the scope and framing defined by the Diamond PDO. The reserves are estimated to be 280 million barrels of oil equivalent (BOE). BOE is a measure to quantify crude oil, natural gas liquids, and natural gas amount using the same metric to determine the amount of energy available to a firm. The development is based on a pdQ platform. The wells on Project Diamond will be drilled by a *jackup rig* (self-elevating hull with legs) from the pdQ.

In order to tie-back to future third-party fields, the pdQ will be equipped with spare J-tubes. (Tie-backs are additional risers that are connected to the original platform. They allow drilling of surrounding marginal fields in addition to the main field, without the significant investment required for the main platform. Risers are subsea pipelines used to transport produced hydrocarbons and other materials. J-tubes are conduits for risers.) Diamond is coordinated with the Sapphire development with partial processing on Diamond (first-stage separation and injection of water) and final processing on Sapphire. The wells are drilled by a jack-up rig. Diamond's integration with the Sapphire pdQ is outlined below:

E.2.1.1 Diamond

- A 20-slot wellbay area
- First-stage separation at Diamond
- Boosting of oil and gas streams at Diamond before they are co-mingled and sent to Sapphire
- Treatment of produced water and reinjection of produced water mixed with sea water at Diamond

E.2.1.2 Sapphire

- Pressurized gas for gas lift and electric power from Sapphire to Diamond
- The oil will be exported from Sapphire through the Oil Pipeline Project and further on to the onshore terminal system for processing
- The gas will be exported from Sapphire through the Gas Pipeline Project to onshore terminal facilities for further processing and transport to market

E.2.2 Background

The Diamond and Sapphire license groups signed an agreement for a coordinated development of the field in March 20xx. This implied a pdQ at the Diamond field center with final processing of the dewatered hydrocarbon fluids on Sapphire before exporting the combined hydrocarbon stream (combined oil and gas, minus the water) onshore to processing terminals. In March 20xx, the Diamond license group gave the Diamond operator (ABC Corp.) approval to start FEED studies for pdQ topside, jacket, and pipelines. Further, the management committee approved the Diamond project DG2 work (*define*) leading toward a DG3/PDO decision (*execute*).

Evaluations and FEED studies were performed for nearly one year to ascertain the best option to develop discoveries in the license area. These studies led to the development and submission of the PDO, which was submitted to the government for approval. Based on recent approval of the PDO by the government, the execution phase of Project Diamond will commence with an estimated project development cycle of five years and an operational life of 25 years. A conceptual rendering of the entire field development is provided in Figure E.1.

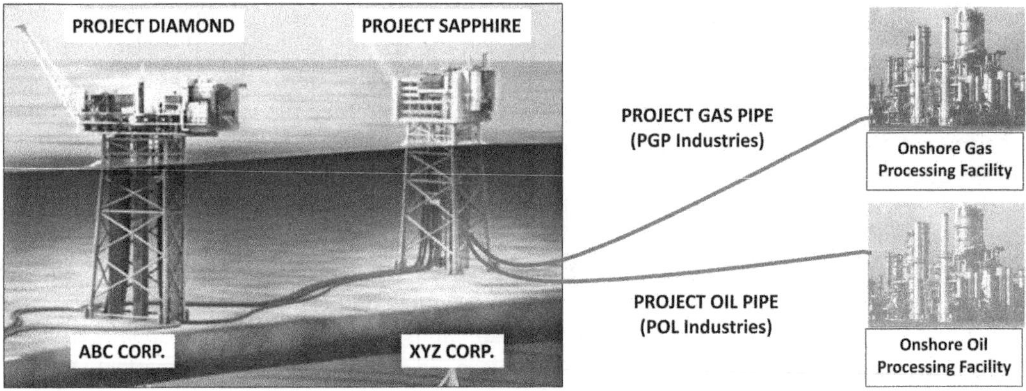

Figure E.1 Conceptual illustration of Project Diamond and Project Sapphire field development

E.3 PROJECT DEVELOPMENT PLAN AND CONTRACT STRATEGY

Project Diamond will utilize a contract strategy that maximizes expertise in the marketplace while providing best value to the sponsoring organization. Accordingly, the project has been segmented to deliver the offshore facilities. Major contract components include: Topside, Living Quarters (LQ), Jacket, Subsea, and Drilling and Wells (D&W). Figure E.2 conceptually illustrates the major systems comprising Project Diamond.

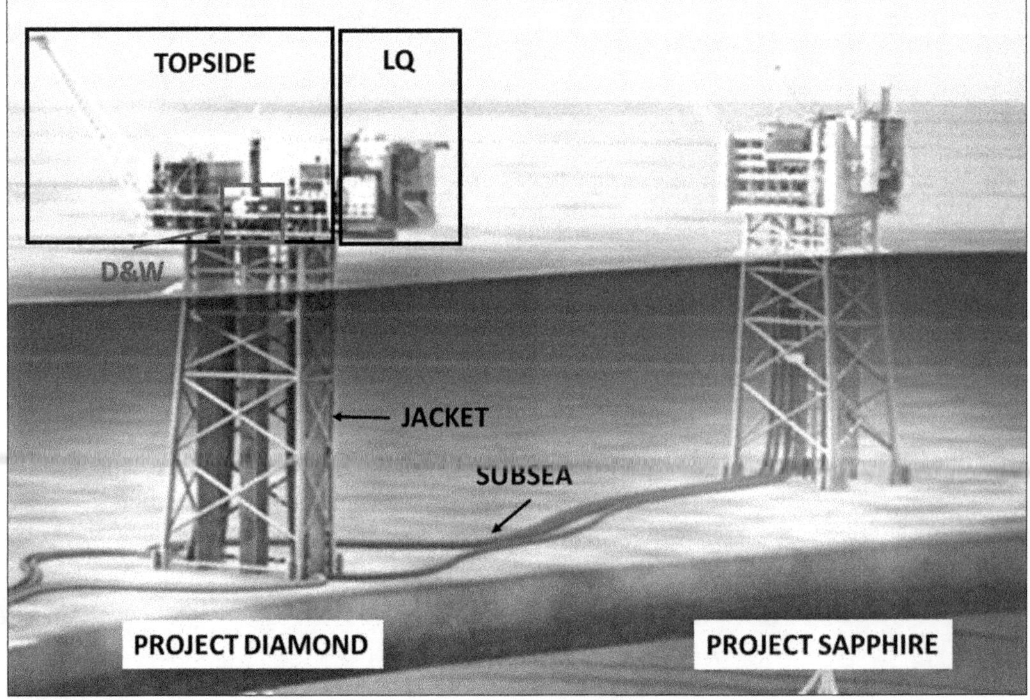

Figure E.2 Conceptual illustration of Project Diamond major subprojects

E.3.1 Topside EPC

The Topside facility provides the main function of recovery of hydrocarbons from the reservoir—partially processing the hydrocarbons to remove water content and transferring the partially processed hydrocarbons to Project Sapphire through pipelines. This contract includes all work necessary to design, procure, and construct the Topside facility, consisting of the utility module, processing module, wellbay module, and flare boom. In addition, the Topside EPC will be responsible for *system technical integrity*—that is, the integrity of the entire system comprising Project Diamond—and will ensure standardization and alignment across the entire project.

E.3.2 LQ EPC

The LQ is the part of the facility that will provide accommodation, food, recreation, and utility services to personnel to support a comfortable habitat for personnel performing work on the facility. The LQ EPC contract will include all work necessary to design, procure, and construct the living quarters to house facility personnel during operations. The LQ EPC contract will also include a helipad to support helicopter operations to and from the LQ.

E.3.3 Jacket EPC

The Project Diamond jacket will be a steel support structure that provides support for the offshore facility. Steel jackets are vertical sections made of tubular steel members that will be piled into the seabed. The Jacket EPC contract will include work necessary to design, procure, and construct the jacket.

E.3.4 Subsea Engineering, Procurement, Construction, and Installation (EPCI)

Project Diamond must send its partially processed hydrocarbons to Project Sapphire for further processing and transport to onshore processing facilities. Transfer of Project Diamond's hydrocarbons will be accomplished through subsea pipelines connected to both projects. The Subsea EPCI will include all work necessary to design, procure, construct, and install the pipeline between the Diamond and Sapphire projects (estimated to be 10.3 kilometers in length).

E.3.5 Transportation and Installation (T&I)

A separate contract will be established for T&I of the Topside modules, LQ, and Jacket from their construction locations to the offshore installation location and include the scope needed to install the Topside, LQ, and Jacket systems and modules offshore. This contract will include all work necessary to design for transportation including all lifting, loading, and securing for transport.

E.3.6 D&W

The D&W department is an ABC Corporation organizational asset and will manage the D&W subproject. As a result, the D&W department will contract for all hardware, services, and support required for drilling and completing wells for the Diamond project. D&W contracts will be managed by the D&W department, but their contractors need to interface with Project Diamond to ensure physical, logical, and functional alignment during project integration.

E.3.7 Project Diamond Completion Team

ABC Corporation takes responsibility for completion of the offshore facility. Completion is defined to mean physical hook-up between various components after installation. After hook-up is completed, the facility will undergo system validation as part of the *commissioning* process. Commissioning ensures that the facility is ready to deliver required system functionality. Upon successful commissioning, the facility will be turned over to the Diamond operations group who will be responsible for starting up and operating the facility.

E.4 PROJECT EXECUTION PLAN

E.4.1 Project Execution Principles

In order to meet the project objectives and secure the project execution phase, ABC Corporation applies the following project execution principles. The project priorities are:

- HSE
- Quality
- Schedule
- Cost

E.4.1.1 HSE Principles

- Clear HSE commitment from project management and throughout the project organization
- Clear HSE commitment from contractors and suppliers
- Adherence to Project Diamond's overall HSE program
- Ensure that HSE issues are addressed both in design and execution

E.4.1.2 Quality Management Principles

- Ensure high-quality performance in the execution phase by following ABC Corporation's project quality management system
- Ensure a well-functioning change control system
- Further develop and follow the risk management system to reduce, mitigate, and eliminate potential project execution risks
- Establish reporting routines satisfying the requirements set down by the authorities, license agreements, and ABC Corporation's internal requirements

E.4.1.3 Schedule Principles

- Early placement of LoI for major contracts
- Identify need and place order(s) for long-lead items (LLI) early in order to secure project execution schedule
- Arrange for float in the execution schedules to secure a robust plan
- Minimize carryover scope from onshore to offshore (Carryover work is work that was planned to be conducted onshore, but was not completed and is thus rescheduled as offshore work. Onshore work is generally faster and less expensive than offshore work—thus the need to minimize carryover work.)

E.4.1.4 Commercial Principles

- A thorough prequalification and tender evaluation process for all major contracts was carried out by ABC Corporation
- International competition for all major contracts
- Balanced compensation strategy; ABC Corporation to take risk on scope and contractors to take risk on productivity
- Apply well-known technology
- Attention to life-cycle costs toward contractors and subcontractors
- Front-end loading of design activities and thereby optimize maturity of design and minimize changes during execution
- Close follow-up with selected vendors to achieve defined quality of the product, documentation, and schedule
- Strict management of change process
- High commercial awareness during project execution including development of commercial follow-up strategies for all subprojects
- Introduce incentives to contractors in order to achieve first oil

E.4.1.5 Organizational Principles

- Employ experienced ABC Corporation project teams for controlling and monitoring the EPC contractors during the execution phase
- ABC Corporation project teams are to be integrated with their respective contractor teams, even collocated, in order to secure alignment and good communication
- Employ highly qualified and motivated project team members in all phases of the project
- Utilize consultants where ABC Corporation needs additional resources
- Key operation personnel to be included in the execution team in order to secure operational requirements into the design/execution
- Ensure cultural understanding as well as experience from multidiscipline projects and operation experienced
- Continuity advantages will be ensured by transferring personnel that have been involved during the DG2/FEED phase into the execution phase, including hook-up and commissioning

E.4.2 Project Success Factors

- Strong HSE commitment within the project management team
- Utilize best industry practice through lessons learned and benchmarking
- Experienced, competent, and sufficient internal and external resources
- No-change philosophy
- Integrated team execution model
- Proactive collaboration with EPC contractors to meet project milestones

E.5 PROJECT ORGANIZATION AND RESOURCES

E.5.1 Project Governance

Project Diamond will closely adhere to ABC's governing documents and the governance system established for the project. The Project Diamond owner/director from DG3 to DG4 is the Senior VP–Projects. The project owner is responsible for contributing to alignment internally and with the Project Diamond partners and key external stakeholders (e.g., the Ministry of Petroleum and

Energy and the Petroleum Directorate). On behalf of the CEO, the project owner is responsible for ensuring that ABC's values are maintained and that the project's business objectives are met. The project director is responsible for completing the project from DG3 to handover to operations at DG4 according to the approved PDO, project mandate, and the Diamond authority procedure. The responsibility is governed by the Project Diamond mandate. Change management is strict to prevent delays in first production. A strict management of change process is applied in the project in order to secure first oil at the earliest possible date.

E.5.2 Project Organization

The project director is responsible for adequate manning of the project organization with competent resources, ensuring that the project can be executed as agreed within the approved baseline cost and schedule.

E.5.3 Key Roles and Responsibilities

The upcoming subsections describe the principal roles in the project management team's organization and their main responsibilities.

E.5.3.1 Project Director

Has overall responsibility for execution of the project according to approved plans and governing documents. This position is also directly responsible for facilities (the entire offshore platform), including Topside, Jacket, Subsea, completion, and T&I.

E.5.3.2 Field Director

Has overall responsibility for the field preparations including the Petroleum Technology (PETEK) department, the D&W department, operations, and coordination with Project Sapphire. The field director and the project director share responsibility for effective project execution.

E.5.3.3 Subproject Teams

Each subproject (Topside, Jacket, LQ, Subsea) will be managed by a subproject team representing the project sponsoring organization, ABC Corporation. Their responsibilities include:

- Delivery of the subproject scope of work within the agreed quality, cost, and time
- HSE for subproject
- Lead and manage the subproject team
- Manage resources allocated to the project
- Report cost, progress, and any areas of concern
- Contribute to good cooperation and communication between project team members

E.5.3.4 PETEK Department

- Prepare and be ready for operational phase
- Document the resource basis (for the project and for the area) including uncertainties
- Develop and update geological model(s) and dynamic reservoir assessments including uncertainties
- Establish reservoir development solutions with production strategy and production/injection forecasts including uncertainties
- Develop and update data acquisition strategy

E.5.3.5 D&W Department

- Prepare and be ready for operational phase
- Develop and update well design for optimum production performance, reflecting reservoir uncertainties
- Develop and update well cost estimates
- Plan and perform safe and efficient D&W operations
- Secure control of the interfaces toward other disciplines
- Develop optimum execution schedules with regard to preparation and actual drilling and completion operations
- Follow-up construction of jack-up rig

E.5.3.6 Facility Operations

- Prepare and be ready for operational phase
- Establish onshore and offshore organization of operation and maintenance
- Establish systems for operations and maintenance
- Support engineering, procurement, and commissioning with operation personnel

E.5.3.7 Project License and Support

- Ensure that all necessary actions with Project Sapphire are handled in a timely manner
- Secure Project Diamond's interests in the coordination, development, and operational agreement with Project Sapphire (XYZ Corporation)
- Contribute to good cooperation and communication with XYZ Corporation (Project Sapphire)
- Handle day-to-day license issues

E.5.3.8 HSE Department

- Identification of applicable legislation, regulations, and codes
- Establishment, implementation, and follow-up of the HSE Management Systems
- Provision of HSE program
- HSE audits and surveillance of the performing organizations
- Identification of nonconformities to HSE and closure of corrective actions

E.5.3.9 Office of Administration/Information Management/Risk

- Establishment, implementation, and follow-up of the project management system
- Project audit and verification plans
- Project risk register
- Project manual (on intranet)
- Information processes
- Procurement of information and communications technology (ICT) systems for operations (those who will take custody of the platform and operate it)

E.5.3.10 Project Control

- Establishment and implementation of best practices, methods, and systems for project control
- Estimating, cost control, and reporting
- Planning and progress reporting
- Budget and schedule updates and forecasting
- Monthly status reporting
- Project change management

E.5.3.11 Procurement, Contracts, and Logistics

- Overall contract strategy
- Specific contract strategies and prequalification of bidders
- Contract and procurement plans
- Competitive tendering
- Issues invitations to tender and performs bid evaluation and negotiations
- Purchase order (PO) preparations
- PO administration
- Review of correspondence with contractors—monitor EPC contractors and follow-up of critical subcontractors
- Implement, as needed, incentive programs on subcontractor level
- Insurance and guarantee handling
- Systems and methods for logistics

E.5.3.12 Human Resources

- Recruitment of permanent staff and the hiring of consultants
- Establishing competency requirements and a training plan for offshore personnel as part of PEOPS
- Ensuring that local administrative standards are in place at each site regulating administrative- and personnel-related issues for expatriate personnel
- Contact person toward suppliers with regards to hiring of consultants
- Relocation of personnel and, if applicable, their families

E.5.3.13 Marine Coordinator

- Acquire and manage all necessary permissions for marine operations
- Coordinate all vessel movements and maintain marine calendar and weekly planning during offshore completion operations toward the end of project execution
- Solve marine operations interface issues, monitor vessel schedules, and act as general advisor in marine operations (such as when multiple ships are operating in the same area at the same time)
- Advise and recommend priorities among different activities offshore

E.5.4 Stakeholders

The project will perform stakeholder analysis to identify relevant stakeholder needs and requirements and develop a communication plan to address stakeholder concerns. The purpose of the stakeholder management plan documents is to contribute to a systematic, effective, and well-coordinated dialogue with Project Diamond stakeholders.

E.6 PROJECT STRATEGY, MANAGEMENT, AND CONTROL

E.6.1 Project Management

ABC Corporation's execution model is based on an integrated team. This will ensure the quality of the overall project and ensure a seamless transition from project to operation. ABC Corporation is managing the project from its headquarters in London, United Kingdom. In addition, ABC will establish local project offices at contractors' offices to manage the work on a daily basis.

ABC will control Project Diamond activities by:

- Ensuring a high standard of quality, health, safety, and environment throughout the project implementation and at all project locations
- Ensuring that the project delivers on budget and schedule and with the right quality
- Ensuring that project deliverables meet the requirements of international laws and regulations as well as ABC's own requirements

ABC Corporation will, in general, seek to reduce risks and in particular interface management risk to reduce/limit the project's exposure. The project has implemented a project information management system (PIMS) for project monitoring and reporting.

E.6.2 Interface Management

Interface management will be performed according to the Project Diamond interface management procedure. ABC Corporation maintains overall responsibility for ensuring that interface management is being performed effectively in Project Diamond while contractors are responsible for managing interfaces within their scope of work and interfaces with other contractors. Unless specified by ABC Corporation, contractors will use their respective interface management systems to manage interfaces within their scope of work to their subcontractors, suppliers, and vendors.

During the project execution phase, the Topside EPC contractor will have the primary lead interface coordination responsibility toward other execution phase contractors. Lead interface coordination responsibility for interface groups not involving the Topside EPC is designated by ABC Corporation in the interface management procedure. ABC Corporation internal interfaces and all formal interface requirements between ABC subproject teams will also be managed through the interface management system; this system will provide a formal communication channel to all other ABC teams to transmit/receive/process internal interface requirements.

Interfaces shall be managed in the interface procedure in accordance with the following principles:

- ABC has the overall project interface responsibility and will be headed by an ABC interface function in the project
- ABC Corporation representatives shall be invited to all interface meetings and receive copies of all interface correspondence
- Topside EPC contractor shall be the lead interface coordinator toward the other main contractors
- Interface issues shall be resolved directly between the interface parties at the relevant level in the organization
- All interface information between contractors shall be documented and continuously updated as a best practice within interface management
- Each interface party is responsible for ensuring that required interface information is made available with sufficient detail and in accordance with an agreed upon schedule
- All interface parties shall establish an interface coordinator position
- All interfaces and agreements shall be documented in the interface register
- Interface responsibilities will be clearly defined in each of the EPC contracts

E.6.3 Information Management

Information management includes all activities and systems related to information transfer, including document control and LCI. The project managers are responsible for supplying information according to project requirements, and the information management team is responsible for establishing systems and procedures and supporting the organization in using them. Interface documentation needed to support scopes of work and areas of responsibility shall be identified as part of the initial interface group kick-off meeting through an exchange of Master Document Registers (MDRs). Each contract contains a list of document deliverables. These are listed in an MDR that is included in the contract. These documents shall be identified and flagged within respective document control and distribution systems to ensure that interface parties receive the latest revision of interface documents.

E.6.4 Document Control

The client and each contractor maintains a document control system at the kick-off meeting, each contractor provides their MDR to each of the interface parties to review and vice versa. Each interface group reviews the other's MDR to identify documents they need to support their scope of work.

For document control, each document on the contractors' MDR is delivered to the client via a document control system to show formal delivery of the document to the client. In addition, because many documents undergo numerous revisions, the contractor sends the document to each of the relevant interface parties.

Appendix F

Project Diamond DG3 Interface Control Document

F.1 INTRODUCTION

This document represents the interface control document (ICD) for Project Diamond.

F.1.1 Purpose

This interface control document describes and tracks the necessary information required to effectively define the Project Diamond system's interfaces as well as any rules for communicating with them in order to give the development team guidance on the architecture of the system to be developed. The purpose of this ICD is to illustrate and describe primary hardware, software/logic, and mass (oil, gas, water, etc.) interfaces between Project Diamond and Project Sapphire and define the high-level internal interfaces between the various project scopes of work.

This ICD was created during the conceptual engineering front-end engineering design (FEED) phase and approved as part of the DG3 process. Its intended audience is Project Sapphire, along with the entire Project Diamond team including the project manager, project team, development team, and stakeholders interested in interfacing with the system. This ICD has been developed by ABC Corporation and devised in alignment with the conceptual design for the Diamond system and the project's approach for development of Project Diamond to ensure the main interfaces. Accordingly, the ICD serves as the documented interface baseline between the two projects and between the various parties contributing to Project Diamond's development.

F.1.2 Responsibility

In the sample organization, the Project Diamond interface manager is responsible for the preparation and maintenance of the ICD with support from relevant technical, commercial, and management representatives in the project organization.

F.1.3 Governing Documents

The Project Diamond governing documents are listed hierarchically as follows:

- National laws and regulations
- Joint operating agreement and plan for development and operation (PDO)
- ABC Corporation management system
- Project Diamond mandate and project execution plan (PEP)
- Project Diamond health, safety, and environmental (HSE) program, design basis, functional requirements, and project specific processes and procedures
- Project technical and contractual requirements
- Project standards and guidelines

F.1.4 Definitions and Abbreviations

CAPEX	capital expenditure
CCE	current control estimate
CCS	current control schedule
CRA	cost risk analysis
DG	decision gate
DRILLEX	drilling expenditure
EIA	environmental impact assessment
EPC	engineering, procurement, and construction
FEED	front-end engineering design
HAZID	hazard identification study
HAZOP	hazard and operability analysis
HSE	health, safety, and environmental
HUC	hook-up and commissioning
KPI	key performance indicator
LCI	life-cycle information
LoI	letter of intent
MC	management committee
MCE	master control estimate
MCS	master control schedule
OPEX	operational expenditure
PDO	plan for development and operation
pdQ	partial processing, drilling, and living quarter [platform]
PEP	project execution plan
PEOPS	project execution and overall procurement strategy
VO	variation order
VOR	variation order request

F.2 PROJECT OVERVIEW

Project Diamond is an offshore oil and gas processing facility, which is to be developed and operated by ABC Corporation. Project Diamond will recover hydrocarbons, process hydrocarbons on the facility by removing water, and then export the hydrocarbons to Project Sapphire for further processing. Project Sapphire is a separate independent offshore oil and gas processing facility project being developed by XYZ Corporation. In addition to recovering, processing, and exporting hydrocarbons

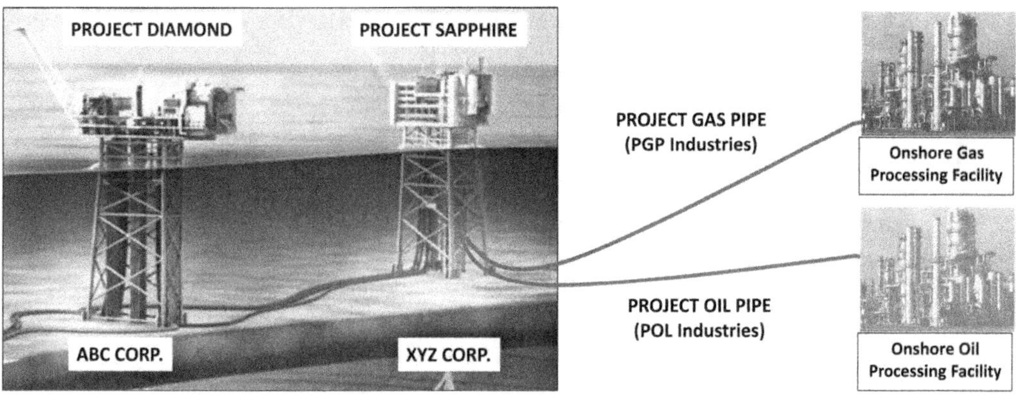

Figure F.1 Conceptual illustration of Project Diamond and Project Sapphire field development

within their licensee area, Project Sapphire will also receive Project Diamond's hydrocarbons, further process the hydrocarbons, combine with the Project Sapphire stream, and export to the market via the Project Gas and Project Oil Pipelines. A conceptual rendering of the entire field development is provided in Figure F.1.

F.2.1 Description of the Project

Project Diamond encompasses a 20 km area within the DL 0072 and DL 0046 development licenses. The development license is an authorization from the government that allows an entity the access rights to a specific and defined area for developing hydrocarbon resources. The percentage of ownership is mandated by the government as part of licensing rounds conducted by the government's petroleum directorate. Development licenses describe, govern, and specify the percentage of interest to each licensed firm. ABC Corporation (65%) is the operator for Project Diamond, while TDN, Inc. (25%) and Waverly Exploration (10%) are partners.

ABC's main business objective for Project Diamond is to develop the resources in the DL 0072 and 0046 license fields in accordance with the scope and framing defined by the Diamond PDO. The reserves are estimated to be 280 million barrels of oil equivalent (BOE). BOE is a measure to quantify crude oil, natural gas liquids, and natural gas amount using the same metric to determine the amount of energy available to a firm. The development is based on a pdQ platform. The wells on Project Diamond will be drilled by a *jackup rig* (self-elevating hull with legs) from the pdQ.

In order to tie-back to future third-party fields, the pdQ will be equipped with spare J-tubes. (Tie-backs are additional risers that are connected to the original platform. They allow drilling of surrounding marginal fields in addition to the main field, without the significant investment required for the main platform. Risers are subsea pipelines used to transport produced hydrocarbons and other materials. J-tubes are conduits for risers.) Diamond is coordinated with the Sapphire development with partial processing on Diamond (first-stage separation and injection of water) and final processing on Sapphire. The wells are drilled by a jack-up rig. Diamond's integration with the Sapphire pdQ is outlined here.

F.2.1.1 Diamond

- A 20-slot wellbay area
- First-stage separation at Diamond
- Boosting of oil and gas streams at Diamond before they are comingled and sent to Sapphire

- Treatment of produced water and reinjection of produced water mixed with sea water at Diamond

F.2.1.2 Sapphire

- Pressurized gas for gas lift and electric power from Sapphire to Diamond
- The oil will be exported from Sapphire through the Oil Pipeline Project and further on to the onshore terminal system for processing
- The gas will be exported from Sapphire through the Gas Pipeline Project to onshore terminal facilities for further processing and transport to market

F.2.2 Background

The Diamond and Sapphire license groups signed an agreement for a coordinated development of the field in March 20xx. This implied a pdQ at the Diamond field center with final processing of the dewatered hydrocarbon fluids on Sapphire before exporting the combined hydrocarbon stream (combined oil and gas, minus the water) onshore to processing terminals. In March 20xx, the Diamond license group gave the Diamond operator (ABC Corp.) approval to start conceptual design FEED studies for pdQ topside, jacket, and pipelines. Further, the management committee approved the Diamond project DG2 work (*define*) leading toward a DG3/PDO decision (*execute*).

Evaluations and concept FEED studies were performed for nearly one year to ascertain the best option to develop discoveries in the license area. These studies led to the development and submission of the PDO, which was submitted to the government for approval. Based on recent approval of the PDO by the government, the execution phase of Project Diamond will commence with an estimated project development cycle of five years and an operational life of 25 years.

F.3 PROJECT DEVELOPMENT PLAN

F.3.1 Contract Strategy

Project Diamond will utilize a contract strategy that maximizes expertise in the marketplace while providing best value to the sponsoring organization. Accordingly, the project has been segmented to deliver the offshore facilities. Major contract components include: Topside, Living Quarters (LQ), Jacket, Subsea, and Drilling and Wells (D&W). Figure F.2 conceptually illustrates the major systems comprising Project Diamond.

F.3.1.1 Topside EPC

The Topside facility provides the main function of recovery of hydrocarbons from the reservoir—partially processing the hydrocarbons to remove water content and transferring the partially processed hydrocarbons to Project Sapphire through pipelines. This contract includes all work necessary to design, procure, and construct the Topside facility, consisting of the utility module, processing module, wellbay module, and flare boom:

- *Utility module*: is designed to provide water (potable), air, and electrical services across the facility (*platform*)
- *Processing module*: contains all equipment necessary to recover, process out water from the hydrocarbons, and export the fluids to Project Sapphire
- *Wellbay module*: contains the central location for drilling production wells
- *Flare boom*: is used to burn off unneeded or small amounts of natural gas

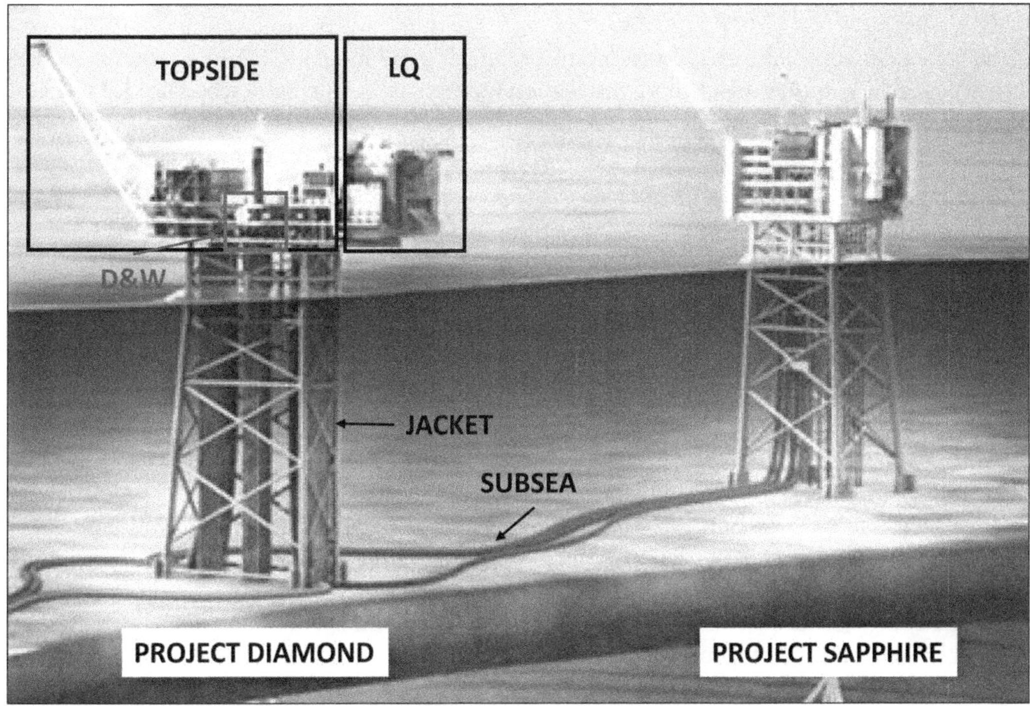

Figure F.2 Conceptual illustration of project Diamond major subprojects

In addition, the Topside EPC will be responsible for *system technical integrity*—that is, the integrity of the entire system comprising Project Diamond—and will ensure standardization and alignment across the entire project.

F.3.1.2 LQ EPC

The LQ is the part of the facility that will provide accommodation, food, recreation, and utility services to personnel to support a comfortable habitat for personnel performing work on the facility. The LQ EPC contract will include all work necessary to design, procure, and construct the living quarters to house facility personnel during operations. The LQ EPC contract will also include a helipad to support helicopter operations to and from the LQ.

F.3.1.3 Jacket EPC

The Project Diamond jacket will be a steel support structure that provides support for the offshore facility. Steel jackets are vertical sections made of tubular steel members that will be piled into the seabed. The Jacket EPC contract will include work necessary to design, procure, and construct the jacket.

F.3.1.4 Subsea Engineering, Procurement, Construction, and Installation (EPCI)

Project Diamond must send its partially processed hydrocarbons to Project Sapphire for further processing and transport to onshore processing facilities. Transfer of Project Diamond's hydrocarbons will be accomplished through subsea pipelines connected to both projects. The Subsea EPCI will include all work necessary to design, procure, construct, and install the pipeline between the Diamond and Sapphire projects (estimated to be 10.3 kilometers in length).

F.3.1.5 Transportation and Installation (T&I)

A separate contract will be established for T&I of the Topside modules, LQ, and Jacket from their construction locations to the offshore installation location and include the scope needed to install the Topside, LQ, and Jacket systems and modules offshore. This contract will include all work necessary to design for transportation including all lifting, loading, and securing for transport.

F.3.1.6 D&W

The D&W department is an ABC Corporation organizational asset and will manage the D&W subproject. As a result, the D&W department will contract for all hardware, services, and support required for drilling and completing wells for the Diamond project. D&W contracts will be managed by the D&W department, but their contractors need to interface with Project Diamond to ensure physical, logical, and functional alignment during project integration.

F.3.1.7 Project Diamond Completion Team

ABC Corporation takes responsibility for completion of the offshore facility. Completion is defined to mean physical hook-up between various components after installation. After hook-up is completed, the facility will undergo system validation as part of the *commissioning* process. Commissioning ensures that the facility is ready to deliver required system functionality. Upon successful commissioning, the facility will be turned over to the Diamond operations group who will be responsible for starting up and operating the facility.

F.3.2 Other Relevant Project Development Plan Information

Insert other relevant information here as needed.

F.4 PROJECT DIAMOND/PROJECT SAPPHIRE INTERFACE OVERVIEW

As required by the field development, Project Diamond will export its partially processed hydrocarbons to Project Sapphire. To support Project Diamond operations, Project Sapphire will provide 110 kV of power to Project Diamond through a subsea power cable and gas lift through an eight inch subsea flowline to support the start up of Project Diamond's production wells. To safely manage the exchange of fluids, power, and gas lift, both projects will exchange a variety of safety and process signals including: emergency shutdown (ESD), process shutdown (PSD), power management system (PMS), power distribution and control system (PDCS), and process control system (PCS). In addition, interface activity includes the work to integrate Project Diamond to Project Sapphire and includes working locally at Project Sapphire to install, physically connect/terminate, and test flowlines and the power cable. This forms the basis for interface activity between the two projects as shown in Figure F.3.

F.4.1 Project Diamond/Sapphire Interface Control Working Groups (ICWGs)

Given the cooperation agreement terms and conditions between the two projects and the technical complexity associated with aligning interfaces between the projects, ICWGs will be established for

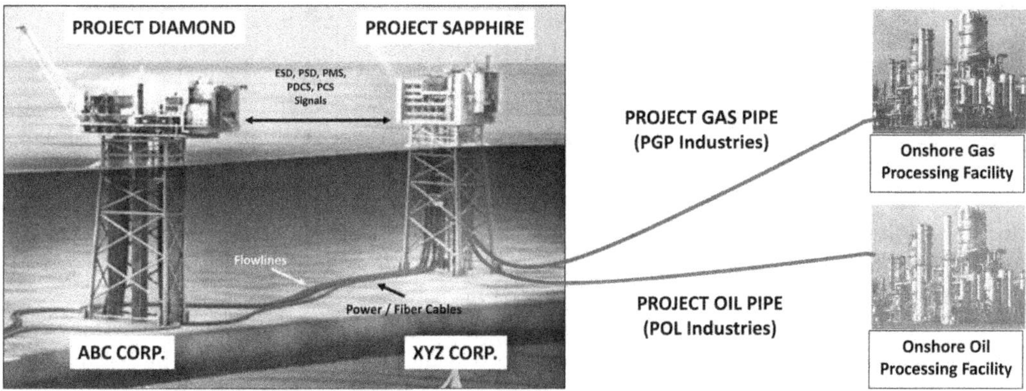

Figure F.3 Main interfaces conceptual illustration of Project Diamond and Project Sapphire field development

the interface areas shown in Figure F.4. These ICWGs provide an integrated forum to discuss the full breadth and depth of issues spanning into other organizational and project domains.

These groups will be comprised of specific technical, management, and commercial personnel to ensure that as technical solutions are agreed upon and are checked for compliance against cooperation agreements and terms. These groups will also work to align deliveries of associated interdependencies such as procedures, tie-in equipment, support requirement, etc.

Figure F.4 Project Diamond/Sapphire ICWGs

F.4.2 Project Diamond Internal Interfaces—Responsible, Accountable, Consulted, and Informed (RACI) Matrices

The scopes of work described previously in Section 4 provided the basis for establishing RACI matrices between scopes that share interface boundaries. The RACI matrix defines which interface party is responsible for what activity across the EPC phases of the project. The RACI provided as part of the contract to each party is intended as a baseline and is subject to interface coordination between the parties after initiating the interface group. Changes to the respective RACI matrices are acceptable to find cost savings and to ensure technical integrity and project efficiencies, but all changes must be handled through the project's management of change processes.

In addition to the scope of work, the RACI matrix shall also act as a key interface driver during project execution between the interface groups. As a result, the RACI matrix will be utilized to assist interface verification activities and to confirm system interface issues have been resolved and incorporated into the respective scopes of work. As shown in Figure F.3, Project Diamond is to be integrated into Project Sapphire including the project's safety automation system (SAS).

F.4.3 Project Diamond/Sapphire SAS RACI Matrix

The Project Diamond/Sapphire SAS RACI matrix has been provided in Figures F.5 through F.8 to illustrate the SAS. This RACI matrix illustrates major interface areas across engineering, procurement, fabrication/construction, and installation and commissioning activities, and serves as the mechanism to establish *battery limits*, or interface responsibility boundaries, between the two projects for design, development, and integration of the two SASs. Figure F.5 shows the major interface areas with respect to engineering.

#	Engineering Activity	Project Diamond	Project Sapphire
1	Update ESD/PSD block line diagram (BLD)	C	R A
2	Update/Develop new Project Sapphire system control diagrams (SCD)	C	R A
3	Update Project Sapphire fire and gas (F&G) cause and effects (C&E)	C	R A
4	Develop Project Diamond SAS philosophy document	R A	C
5	Develop Project Diamond SAS functional design specification (FDS)	R A	C
6	Develop new Project Diamond ESD and PSD BLD	R A	C
7	Develop new Project Diamond SCD	R A	C
8	Develop new Project Diamond F&G C&E	R A	C
9	Test Project Sapphire SAS interface	I	R A
10	Update Project Sapphire safety requirements specification (SRS) document	C	R A
11	Develop Project Diamond SRS (technical safety deliverable)	R A	C
12	Develop Project Diamond network drawings for extension to Project Sapphire	R A	C
13	Develop Project Diamond FDS for remote testing of wells	R A	C
14	Develop Project Diamond FDS for virtual metering software	R A	C

Figure F.5 Diamond/Sapphire SAS RACI matrix—engineering activity

Figure F.6 shows the major interface areas with respect to procurement.

#	Procurement Activity	Diamond Project	Project Sapphire
1	Procurement of Project Diamond SAS equipment (cabinet, controllers, IO)	R A	I
2	Procurement of SAS license extension	R A	I
3	Procurement of virtual metering server and required software/license	R A	C
4	Procurement of temporary test system/simulator to be used for testing	R A	C
5	Procurement of engineering tools and licenses for test system/simulator	R A	C
6	Procurement of simulator services	R A	C

Figure F.6 Diamond/Sapphire SAS RACI matrix—procurement activity

Figure F.7 shows the major interface areas with respect to fabrication and construction.

#	Fabrication and Construction Activity	Project Diamond	Project Sapphire
1	Programming of Project Diamond SAS nodes	R A	C
2	Programming of modification in nodes at Project Sapphire	C	R A
3	Develop new Project Diamond HMI F&G overview display	R A	C
4	Perform initial or internal acceptance test (IAT)/factory acceptance test (FAT) of new Project Diamond logic in SAS supplier location	R A	C
5	Perform IAT/FAT of modified logic for Project Sapphire facility	C	R A
6	Dynamic/interface testing on simulator (remote testing of wells, slug control, well control, gas lift, chemical injection, diesel, fresh water, etc.)	R A	C
7	Perform system site acceptance test of the control system at the Project Diamond construction yard	R A	I
8	Loop testing of instruments and valves at the Project Diamond construction yard	R A	I

Figure F.7 Diamond/Sapphire SAS RACI matrix—fabrication and construction activity

Figure F.8 shows the major interface areas with respect to installation and commissioning.

#	Installation and Commissioning Activity	Diamond Project	Project Sapphire
1	Integrate Project Diamond SAS into Project Sapphire system (post temporary installation system removal)	C	R A
2	Patching of SAS network on Project Sapphire	C	R A
3	Patching of SAS network on Project Diamond	R A	C
4	Commissioning of Project Diamond nodes	R A	C
5	Commissioning of Project Sapphire nodes	C	R A
6	Loop testing of new instruments and valves at Project Sapphire	I	R A
7	Integration testing and dynamic commissioning offshore (systems that not have been tested on simulator)	C	R A

Figure F.8 Diamond/Sapphire RACI matrix—installation and commissioning activity

F.4.4 Project Diamond/Sapphire SAS Signal Interfaces

The main SAS interface between Projects Diamond and Sapphire relate to ESD and PSD scenarios. Figure F.9 identifies the primary ESD signals to be exchanged between the projects. The ESD signals ensure that if an unsafe consideration is identified on either offshore facility, then a corresponding action will be generated with the other facility.

Figure F.10 identifies the PSD signals, which are used to guide an expected shutdown of the facilities.

F.5 SUMMARY

This example ICD illustrates one method to construct an interface control document, but the aim of an *ICD*-like document is to describe the system interfaces between interface parties to a level that is adequate to maintain control of those interfaces during project development. This example serves as a template from which other interface areas between the two projects will be defined, monitored, and controlled.

There is no standard format or template for an ICD. Rather, each project and situation will vary with respect to the kinds and amount of information required. For information technology projects, ICDs may be heavily weighted with signal or data exchange tables. Other projects may use more illustrations and text. Regardless, the main intent is to communicate main interface areas between interface groups.

In addition, development of an ICD will align with the project development phase and the maturity of the system concept. Early in project development, the system concept may only be illustrated as a high-level system architecture. Thus, an ICD will not likely be overly detailed. As the system concept becomes mature and further defined during later project development phases, the ICD likely will be updated to reveal more details about the interfaces that are internal to the project and to external systems.

LINK No.	Area	Tag	System	Frequency	Unit	Source	Description	Platform	Tag no	Cause & Effect
Link 5	NA	79NXO0002A	ESD	1 second	NA	E01	APS SIGNAL TO DIAMOND	SAPPHIRE	ABCO0002A	XYZ-001-I-XR-00004.001
Link 5	NA	79NXO1000A	ESD	1 second	NA	E01	ESD 1 ALARM TO DIAMOND	SAPPHIRE	ABCO1000A	XYZ-001-I-XR-00007.001
Link 5	NA	79NXO2002A	ESD	1 second	NA	E01	ESD 2.2 SIGNAL TO DIAMOND	SAPPHIRE	ABCO2002A	XYZ-001-I-XR-00010.001
Link 5	NA	79NXO4402A	ESD	1 second	NA	E01	EL.TRIP 4 DIAMOND, 80EH0500=E02 CB	SAPPHIRE	ABCO4402A	XYZ-001-I-XR-00006.001
Link 5	NA	79NXI0033	ESD	1 second	NA	E01	ESD 1 SIGNAL FROM DIAMOND	DIAMOND	ABCI0033	XYZ-001-I-XR-00005.001
Link 5	NA	79NXI0034	ESD	1 second	NA	E01	ESD 2 SIGNAL FROM DIAMOND	DIAMOND	ABCI0034	XYZ-001-I-XR-00011.001
Link 5	NA	79NXI0032	ESD	1 second	NA	E01	APS SIGNAL FROM DIAMOND	DIAMOND	ABCI0032	XYZ-001-I-XR-00004.001
Link 5	NA	79NXI4430	ESD	1 second	NA	E01	MEI from DIAMOND trip 80EH300+04 CB	DIAMOND	ABCI4430	XYZ-001-I-XR-00006.001

Figure F.9 Diamond/Sapphire ESD signals

LINK No.	Area	Tag	System	Frequency	Unit	Source	Description	Platform	Tag no	Cause&Effect
Link 6	NA	87NXO0003	PSD	1 second	NA	P03	PSD 5.13.4 DIAMOND IMPORT 1	SAPPHIRE	XYZO0003	XYZ-001-I-XL-87-00002
Link 6	NA	87NXO0004	PSD	1 second	NA	P03	PSD 5.13.5 DIAMOND IMPORT 2	SAPPHIRE	XTZO0004	XYZ-001-I-XL-87-00002
Link 6	NA	87NXO0005	PSD	1 second	NA	P01	PSD 5.13.8 DIAMOND GAS LIFT PIPELINE	SAPPHIRE	XYZO0005	XYZ-001-I-XL-87-00002
Link 6	NA	87NXI0006	PSD	1 second	NA	P01	PSD 3,1 SIGNAL FROM DIAMOND	DIAMOND	XYZI0006	XYZ-001-I-XL-87-00002
Link 6	NA	87NXI0007	PSD	1 second	NA	P0?	PSD 4.27.3 SIGNAL FROM DIAMOND	DIAMOND	XYZI0007	To be determined

Figure F.10 Diamond/Sapphire PSD Signals

Appendix G

Example Interface Management Closeout Report

G.1 INTRODUCTION

G.1.1 Purpose

The purpose of this closeout report is to document key aspects of Project A's interface management system during the project execution phase from the first quarter of 2013 through the fourth quarter of 2016. Primarily, this document provides a record for decisions driving the project's approach to managing interfaces as well as documenting lessons learned to serve as a useful reference for future projects.

G.1.2 Header Information

Often the reports will contain header information that names the document, revision number, and other relevant information as shown in Table G.1.

Table G.1 Header information about report

	Interface Management Closeout Report—Project A	Doc No: Rev: Date: Page:	

G.1.3 Definitions

- *External interface*: an interface requiring coordination along common boundaries between two independent entities or interface parties with no controlling, contractual, or organizational relationship
- *Interface group*: a group consisting of two (or more) independent parties who share a common boundary but have a relationship with limited or no direct control over one another's activities

- *Internal interface*: an interface occurring within an entity (e.g. organization, project, department, etc.) scope of work, or area of responsibility, within the same project for the same client contract, including any derived subcontracts
- *Interface network*: a group of interface parties established to coordinate interface issues associated with specific types of project stakeholders
- *Interface register*: a database where each interface item and its associated information are stored
- *Lead interface contractor*: a contractor assigned with additional interface responsibility (mostly administrative) for an interface group by the owner of the project's interface management system.

G.1.4 Abbreviations

CPI	company provided item
DG	decision gate
D&W	drilling and wells
OP	Project B Oil Pipeline
E-IDR	extended integrated design review
ENS	engineering number system
EPC	engineering, procurement, and construction
ESD	emergency shutdown
FEED	front-end engineering design
IDR	integrated design review
KoM	kick-off meeting
LQ	living quarters
MDR	master document register
MoM	minutes of meeting
PDCS	power distribution and control system
pdQ	production, drilling, and quarters
PFS	power from shore
PMS	power management system
PSD	process shutdown
SAS	safety automation system
SURF	subsea, umbilical, riser(s) and flowline(s)
T&I	transportation and installation
TQ	technical query
UHGP	Utsira High Gas Pipeline
WIR	web interface register

G.1.5 Referenced Project Documents

Often, other project documents are referenced in interface management closeout reports. In this case, we reference the interface management procedure for the project as shown in Table G.2.

Table G.2 Project documents

Document Number	Title	Revision
XXXX-XX-X-XXX	Interface Management Procedure—Project A	02M

G.2 PROJECT A: OVERVIEW

With completion of DG3, Project A formally entered the execution phase in the first quarter of 2013. As a result, the project's FEED interface management procedure (DN02-DN-Z-KA-0011) was updated (02M) to govern management of the project's interface throughout the project execution phase, which remained active through *first oil* (12/24/2016). The foundation for establishing the project's philosophy toward interface management was derived from the assessment of interface and interdependency complexity and risk areas associated with the project's operational concept, project development approach, and contracting strategy.

A key aspect of the project's interface management philosophy mandated that Project A establish a system for managing *external interfaces* between various scopes of work (e.g., between various contractors, between Projects A and B, etc.) and areas of responsibility (e.g., between Project A sub-project teams and organizational departments), through a series of *interface networks*. The interface management procedure allowed *internal interfaces* to be managed using the respective contractor's management system and processes. However, Project A clients reserved the right to prescribe an *internal interface management system* in case the internal systems proved to be ineffective.

G.2.1 Operational Concept

Project A consists of discoveries 13/2-6 and 13/2-7. The field is located in the northern North Sea. Development of Project A included a pdQ platform with a steel jacket and a separate jack-up rig for drilling and completion. The platform has spare slots for possible additional wells. The platform is equipped for tie-in of a subsea template planned for the future development of local areas and for possible development of other nearby discoveries. First-stage processing is performed on Project A—and the partly processed fluids are transported to Project B for final processing and export.

In addition to receiving, processing, and exporting Project A hydrocarbons, this concept requires Project B to provide power and gas lift to Project A. Thus, interface and integration with Project B included physical tie-in of a 110 kV subsea power cable containing two fiber cables (24 fiber pairs in each cable), two 12-inch flowlines, and one 8-inch gas lift flowline. In addition, logical interfaces ESD, PSD, PDCS, and PMS signal exchange formed a significant area of interface between the two projects.

G 2.2 Contract Strategy

A simplified representation of the contract strategy for development of Project A is depicted in Figure G.1 and illustrates the project's use of multiple contract types to support Project A's facilities development from *concept development* through *commissioning*. The EPC, Transportation and Heavy Lift, Installation and Hook-Up, and Commissioning sections represent the project's execution phase and are the subject of this closeout report. Note: Project A's LQ was initially included in the Topside contract. However, the LQ portion of the Topside contract was removed and awarded as a *lump sum* EPC contract. This included a *provisional sum* on critical packages (HVAC and life boats) and areas with too great of uncertainty to include in the lump sum (i.e., commissioning assistance and construction and installation of packages, such as company-provided electrical, instrumentation, control, and telecommunications, etc.).

Not depicted in the contract strategy were significant wellbay (module M20) interfaces toward the client's D&W organization, such as Christmas trees, well operations equipment, etc. The client's D&W department, through a network of specialized companies, managed D&W related products and services to Project A. To facilitate interface activity to Project A, the client D&W provided onsite

DG2

DG3

DG4

Diamond Project "Phases"	Drilling		Subsea Flowlines and Power Cables	pdQ Topside	Jacket	Transportation and Installation	Flotel
	Rig	Services & equipment					
Project Management	ABC Corporation						
Concept Development	NA	Study contracts as relevant	Concept study contract	Study contract	Study contract		NA
FEED			FEED contract Reimbursable	FEED contract Reimbursable	FEED Contract Reimbursable	Study Contract under Topside FEED	
EPC	Rig Contract Reimbursable	Service and equipment contracts Reimbursable and Lump Sums	EPCI Lump sum and Reimbursable	EPC Norms and rates for construction. Target sum for engineering & procurement Lump Sum for preliminaries and Living Quarter	EPC Lump sum	EPCI Lump sum	Flotel Contract Reimbursable
Transportation and Heavy Lift				EPCI Lump Sum			
Installation and Hook-up			Reimbursable	Reimbursable	NA	NA	
Commissioning	NA	NA	ABC Corporation			NA	NA

Figure G.1 Project A development project contract strategy

representation to the Project A Topside EPC team during the engineering phase (FEED and detailed engineering) to assist with D&W related design interfaces.

G.3 PROJECT A: INTERFACE MANAGEMENT ORGANIZATION/STRUCTURE

To support the project development strategy, the client established subproject management teams to oversee work being accomplished by Topside, LQ, SURF, Jacket, T&I, Flotel, and D&W contractors. Within each of the client's subproject teams, personnel were assigned with either primary or secondary interface responsibilities depending on the complexity and intensity of expected interface interaction. This interface structure maintained adequate company oversight of interface activity by the corresponding contractor teams and ensured interface performance in accordance with Project A's interface procedure throughout Project A's execution.

To support interface activity toward Project B, a number of interface working groups were established. These groups consisted of relevant technical personnel from the Project A and Project B engineering and management teams to coordinate and align interfaces for their technical or project management domain. In addition, Project A provided technical representation to the Project B Oil Pipeline and Gas Pipeline projects as needed. However, this interface activity was not part of Project A's interface management system and not a subject of this closeout report.

G.4 INTERFACE MANAGEMENT APPROACH

To manage Project A's interface complexity, six interface networks were established to compartmentalize project interfaces into groups of related parties and the interface interests they commonly share. A brief description of each network is provided in the following sections, but this approach helped to decompose (*break down*) interface complexity into more manageable parts. Over 3,000 interfaces were identified and resolved across the project during Project A's development.

Project A utilized Kongsberg's Seaflex WIR as the web-based automated tool to house all interface information, including supporting documentation, interface sheets describing responses and agreements between interface parties, and MoMs for each interface group. An information archive from each interface network has been downloaded and stored at the project archive.

G.4.1 Project A/B: Network

This network served to conduct interface activity related to tie-in, integration, and commissioning of Project A to Project B (operated by a separate company). While initially activated during Project A FEED in 2012, this network remained active and transitioned into Project A's execution phase in early 2013 and remained active through Project A *first oil*. Interface activity within this network was restricted to company-to-company interaction between the two project sponsoring companies who acted on behalf of their respective contractors.

While interfaces toward Project B were successfully resolved, two major factors detracted from the effectiveness and efficiency in managing interfaces between the two projects: (1) offset in project development timelines and (2) lack of direct involvement by the respective projects' engineering contractors.

G.4.1.1 Project Development Timelines

Project A and B's developments, while having similar durations and development approaches, were offset by approximately one year. Specifically, Project B's development remained one year ahead of

Project A. This resulted in a constant offset in design and development activities, which created difficulty for each project to provide key engineering design interface information when required by the other project. While it is understandably not realistic to mitigate timeline offsets between different project developments, this *offset* issue could have been mitigated through the utilization of a small colocated integrated team.

G.4.1.2 Lack of Involvement by Engineering Contractor

Interface activity between Project A and Project B was performed directly by the project's sponsoring companies as a *company-to-company* interaction. Interaction did not include the direct participation of the respective engineering contractors. Rather, each company coordinated directly with one another, then returned to their respective projects and coordinated separately with their respective contractors and then repeated the cycle. This created an unnecessarily elongated process requiring significant time and effort. For similar future *project-to-project* tie-in developments, it is recommended an agreement be obtained to allow contractors (engineering especially) to be part of the project-to-project interface network. Direct participation by engineering contractors with project sponsor oversight will increase common understanding of interface issues and reduce the time frame to align and resolve interfaces.

G.4.2 Project A: Contractor Network

Comprised of 43 interface groups, this extensive network consisted of all contractors contributing products and/or services to Project A, including D&W contractors. This network provided a transparent communication mechanism to formally coordinate interfaces along Project A contractors' respective scope of work boundaries. As expected, this network accounted for approximately 66% of all interface activity across the project with the Topside EPC contractor assigned as the primary lead interface contractor.

In general, this network performed well. However, misalignments between the various contractor subproject plans created difficulties in aligning dates for resolving interfaces and interdependencies, such as the delivery of CPIs. The semiannual project *re-baseline* process exacerbated this challenge. While the re-baselining process rarely affected project milestones, it did result in numerous schedule adjustments to individual subproject activities.

As expected, schedule adjustments to some of the subproject activities impacted interfaces; requiring replanning and resulting in more interface planning misalignments. Ultimately, the inability to maintain alignment of the respective subproject schedules resulted in several *variation order requests* due to out-of-phase engineering, especially from the LQ subproject, which were attributed to delayed interface resolution and delivery of CPIs.

As the lead interface contractor, Topside EPC represented the central interface party against most other contractors. The Topside engineering subcontractor was assigned interface management responsibility on behalf of the Topside EPC prime contractor. However, while Topside Engineering performed admirably in its interface management role, topside design progress and quality hampered the team's ability to meet time critical interfaces and interdependencies toward key interface parties, including the LQ and SAS contractors.

G.4.3 Project A: Company Internal

This network allowed the client's subproject management teams and various company departments to interface and document agreements-related changes across scope boundaries, functional requirements issues, and to clarify operational requirements and other matters extending across multiple subproject boundaries. While used sparingly through Project A development, the network did provide a useful forum to coordinate and align interface issues between subproject management teams and various organizational departments including operations and D&W before engaging the affected contractors.

G.4.4 Client D&W Network

Established as a means for the client's D&W department to interface on issues related to integrating the jack-up drilling rig (JUR) with the Project A pdQ, this network included interface activity related to installing, hook-up, and commissioning of the primary and secondary bridges to the Project A pdQ. While only utilized for a brief period, this network aided in preparation and work leading to a successful integration of the JUR to Project A's pdQ.

However, this network could have been expanded and used more extensively by D&W with their respective contractor network. Instead, a manual *technical query* system was established between D&W and its contractor network using an Excel spreadsheet on *Projectplace* resulting in overly time-consuming activities that elongated timelines to resolve issues.

G.4.5 Topside EPC Internal (Engineering)

Findings from the E-IDR identified a highly bureaucratic and ineffective TQ process between the Topside Engineering and SAS contractor resulting in excessive administrative work, long process time frames, and delays to critical SAS development scope. Established after the E-IDR, this network facilitated control node interfaces (fire and gas, ESD, PSD, Process Control, and PDCS) between the Topside Engineering subcontractor and the SAS contractor. While only utilized for a short duration (November 2015–July 2016), implementation of this network greatly improved transparency and traceability of the SAS design information requirements between the two parties.

G.4.6 Project A: (Subsea Team)—Project B: (Maintenance Contractor)

To accommodate Project A's power cable pull-in, hang-off, and installation, this interface network served as the forum for direct interface between Project A's subsea team, who were responsible for subsea cable installation, and Project B's maintenance contractor, who was assisting with the activities. While only used for the power cable pull-in, hang-off, and termination period, this network was nevertheless very valuable in resolving related interface issues quickly and with transparency to both project organizations.

G.5 INTERFACE LESSONS LEARNED

Several lessons learned were documented during Project A's execution. These lessons vary from those directly related to interface management to indirect lessons that affected interface management effectiveness. Interface lessons learned have been compiled in the project's "Lessons" module and are identified with the word "Interface" as the first word in the title. Highlights of the lessons learned are provided here for convenience to the reader.

G.5.1 Interface Control Document (ICD)

The lack of a project-level ICD at the beginning of Project A's execution hampered interface management activity between the interface parties. An ICD describes the system interface boundaries that reflect the system's operational scenario and expected system behaviors (e.g., normal and abnormal conditions). At a minimum, the ICD should identify the expected interactions between major systems (or subsystem, package, component) to the control boundaries of external systems and structured to align with the project development's expected work breakdown structure (e.g., scopes of work and contract strategy).

With the absence of an ICD, Project A's interface parties expended unnecessary effort initially attempting to clarify *battery limits* (e.g., discrete control boundaries) instead of focusing on the technical effort to resolve interfaces. An output of the FEED phase should include a document describing, graphically and textually, the interfaces between the various systems and across scope boundaries, and by interface object (e.g., system, subsystem, component, etc.). This ICD should fundamentally align with scopes of work and areas of responsibility (responsibility matrices) and focus especially on high-risk or technically complex aspects of the system. This type of document (e.g., ICD) at the beginning of the project execution phase provides a meaningful starting point and allows interface parties to identify any scope or technical integrity gaps, overlaps, or misalignments.

In addition, the ICD should address interdependencies provided from one entity to another. These interdependencies manifest in many forms, but can include CPIs (e.g., safety automation system material), material to verify procedures (e.g., pipe pieces to validate welding procedures, perform destructive testing, etc.), and others. Interdependencies can delay project work if not delivered by the *required on-site* date. Thus, the ICD should also identify when critical interdependencies are required if known.

G.5.2 Interface Priority Process

During the project, several hundred interfaces were open at any given time, but the interface register lacked a mechanism to identify which interfaces were *priorities* at any given time. Due to varied circumstances, individual interfaces would suddenly become important and need more management attention. For example, after the semiannual re-baseline process, some activities within the subprojects became rescheduled. In turn, some of the rescheduled activities affected interfaces requiring interface-planning dates to be adjusted, which created misalignments. A system to identify critical interfaces helped focus attention and resources on specific interface items that could negatively affect (risk) ongoing work, cost, or schedule.

As a result, a *priority* feature using a *red-light* system implemented in the interface register tool allowed interface parties to highlight critical interfaces. This feature became very important after the *re-baseline* process when activities (affecting interfaces) shifted. Typically, after a re-baseline process, a number of interfaces became misaligned between interface parties. This priority feature helped to highlight these misalignments and allowed the company to align its efforts to the most urgent interface issues.

G.5.3 Interface Documentation Policy

Early in the interface management process, a widespread misunderstanding existed regarding the use of the Seaflex WIR—specifically, how this tool aligned to the document control process. Project A's contractors were using the interface management tool, Seaflex WIR, as a *document control* tool to exchange interface documentation. A significant portion of interface information consisted of contractor design documentation, controlled according to the project's ENS. However, it became impractical to manage control of these documents in Seaflex since the iterative engineering process produced several revisions.

As a result, an interface documentation policy was established and formally communicated to all parties. This policy required the exchange of MDRs between interface parties to identify relevant interface documentation. Agreed-upon MDR documents were added to the distribution matrix within each contractors' document control system; and any future updated revisions would be *pushed* to interface parties through a formal document control transmittal. Implementation of this lesson learned resulted in better monitoring and control of interface documentation exchange.

G.5.4 Interface Management Forums

Given the number of different interface parties, scale and scope of Project A and the changes affecting the project as it progressed through the project life cycle, it became difficult to maintain interface-planning alignment. Further, alignment was complicated by the project's *re-baseline* process, which created numerous *micro* changes that rippled into interfaces. As a result, an *interface forum* was created to plan ahead for the next six months. An example interface forum package is provided in the lesson learned and forum timeline illustrated in Figure G.2.

Project A convened three interface forums over an 18-month period to deconflict schedule misalignment that was associated with interdependencies and interfaces between respective parties. Conducted as a *face-to-face* meeting, these forums focused on the next six-month period and highlighted significant issues resulting from the rebaseline process between interface entities. As an integrated event, the forum was attended by the client's interface personnel across the project. While the event proved a valuable tool in maintaining interface alignment among company representatives, the event should have been expanded to include primary interface representatives from each contractor.

G.5.5 Interface Kick-Off Meetings

During implementation of the interface management system for Project A, interface management KoMs were sponsored and hosted by the client with each Project A contractor and then with each interface group. This was a positive experience and helped to set expectations, align interface management processes, and establish the foundation for quickly starting interface activity. However, the interface group KoM could have been improved by having the interface parties exchange scopes of work (in lieu of an ICD).

To initiate each interface group, the client's interface manager conducted an *interface group* KoM with each interface group within each network. These meetings included the respective contractors and their client representatives. While these KoMs required significant effort, they were extremely important toward establishing interface momentum, especially given the initial uncertainties regarding specific interfaces between parties (e.g., lack of an ICD).

G.5.6 Integrated Design Reviews

A requirement in the Topside EPC contract was responsibility for *technical integrity*, of which interface management served a primary function and was primarily verified through model reviews. However, it became apparent that typical model reviews (e.g., 30%, 60%, and 90%) were not adequate to verify technical integrity and functionality across scope boundaries. To address this deficiency, several IDRs were conducted by the client to evaluate system functionality from reservoir to Project B, inclusive of the JUR. Figure G.3 shows Project A's integrated design review timeline.

In essence, these IDRs served as *integrated interface verification* events covering the entire operating environment. Through the IDR process, and by focusing on the safety and effectiveness of system functionality, these reviews provided a logical and thorough assessment of the overall design across combinations of scopes of work, systems, subsystems, and areas of responsibilities. The outcome of the IDR process was the identification of numerous gaps and deficiencies affecting system functionality that were subsequently addressed through engineering efforts preventing potential late-stage integration, hook-up, commissioning, and start-up problems.

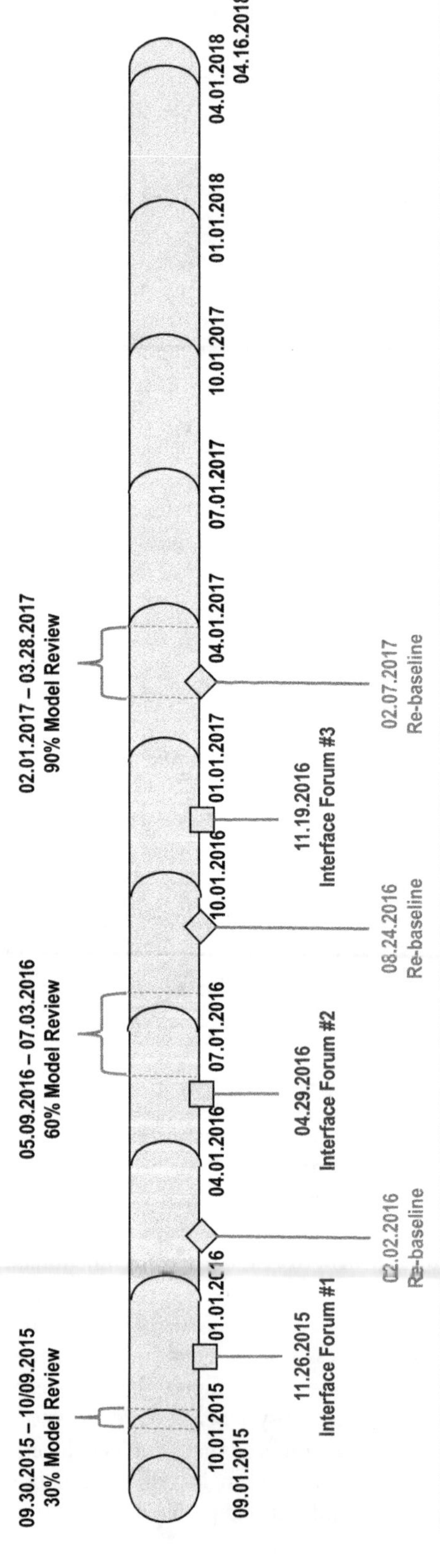

Figure G.2 Project A interface forums

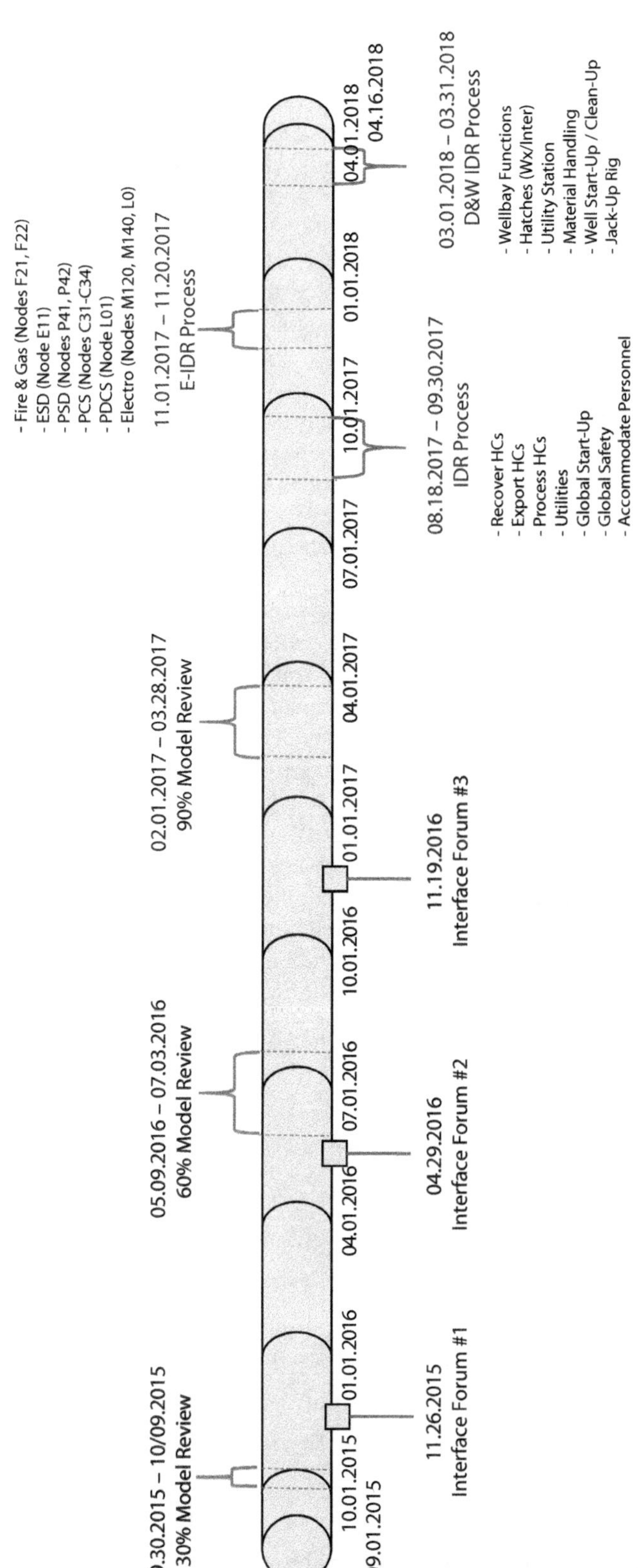

Figure G.3 Project A integrated design reviews

G.6 SUMMARY

While difficult to quantify, anecdotal evidence suggests that the application of interface management as part of Project A's management system contributed to reducing the realization of negative consequences and contributed to the project's *on-time* and *within budget* success. By implementing a lean, yet comprehensive interface management system, the client increased its ability to (1) ensure efficient collaboration, (2) effectively monitor cooperation between key entities contributing to project development, and (3) proactively influence interface activity when required, reducing the number of late-stage integration issues. While comprehensive, the interface management system remained flexible incorporating lessons learned while adapting to specific circumstances of the project and the needs of those participating in the interface process. Yet, notable deficiencies prevented maximum effectiveness of the system.

The lack of an ICD to define interfaces and interdependencies detracted from the effectiveness of the interface management process, especially during project execution start-up. An ICD is key to managing technical integrity, especially in large-scale complex projects with complicated contract strategies and extensive CPIs. An ICD should be developed during FEED and delivered at DG3.

In addition, Topside's scope of work was a central element to delivery of the facilities' value functions (recover, process, and export hydrocarbons) and ensuring technical integrity. Yet, the Topside EPC internal interface management system was nonexistent, particularly between the Topside Engineering and SAS contractors. The lack of an internal Topside EPC interface management system created carryover interface problems with other contractors (e.g., LQ) resulting in numerous variation order requests. The project's interface management system should extend into the contractor's internal team (subcontractors, key suppliers, and vendors, etc.) when their scopes of work are central to system functionality or technical integrity. Doing so provides the client with the transparency needed to intervene when *warning signs* begin to emerge, enabling the client to mitigate problems before they become severe.

As of this report, all interface issues have been resolved and there are no open items in the interface register. Information in the interface register (Seaflex WIR) database has been downloaded by Kongsberg and is archived locally. A copy of the relevant Project A/Project B interfaces archive has been transferred to Project B's organization. In addition, Projects A and B have agreed on *as-built* interface documentation and these documents have already been transferred between the projects.

Index

Note: Page numbers followed by "f" indicate figures.